The Middle East and North Africa

The Middle East and North Africa
A Political Primer

Joseph N. Weatherby
California Polytechnic State University

Longman

New York San Francisco Boston
London Toronto Sydney Tokyo Singapore Madrid
Mexico City Munich Paris Cape Town Hong Kong Montreal

Publisher: Priscilla McGeehon
Senior Acquisitions Editor: Eric Stano
Associate Acquisitions Editor: Anita Castro
Senior Marketing Manager: Megan Galvin-Fak
Production Manager: Mark Naccarelli
Project Coordination, Text Design, and Electronic Page Makeup: Nesbitt Graphics, Inc.
Cover Designer/Manager: John Callahan
Cover Illustration: Courtesy of PhotoDisc, Inc.
Art Studio: Mapping Specialists, Inc.
Senior Manufacturing Buyer: Dennis J. Para
Printer and Binder: R. R. Donnelley & Sons/Harrisonburg
Cover Printer: John P. Pow Co., Inc.

Library of Congress Cataloging-in-Publication Data
Weatherby, Joseph.
   The Middle East and North Africa : a political primer / Joseph N. Weatherby.
     p. cm.
   Includes bibliographical references and index.
   ISBN 0-321-08106-4 (alk. paper)
    1. Middle East—Politics and government—20th century. 2. Africa, North—Politics and government—20th century. 3. Nationalism—Middle East—History—20th century. 4. Nationalism—Africa, North—History—20th century. 5. Islam and politics—Middle East—History—20th century. 6. Islam and politics—Africa, North—History—20th century. I. Title.

DS62.8 .W42 2001
956.04—dc21
                                                                                              2001038235

Copyright © 2002 by Addison Wesley Longman, Inc.

All rights reserved. No part of this publication may be reproduced, stored in a retrieval system, or transmitted, in any form or by any means, electronic, mechanical, photocopying, recording, or otherwise, without the prior written permission of the publisher. Printed in the United States.

Please visit our website at http://www.ablongman.com

ISBN 0-321-08106-4

1 2 3 4 5 6 7 8 9 10—DOH—05 04 03 02

To Jane

There is something in a woman beyond all human delight: a magnetic virtue, a charming quality, an occult and powerful motive.

ROBERT BURTON

Contents

Preface   xi

CHAPTER 1

Middle East Geography   1
Introduction   1
Where Is the Middle East?   2
What Special Names Are Associated with the Middle East and North Africa?   4
What Geographical Features Make Up the Middle East and North Africa?   9
What Are the Important Rivers in the Middle East and North Africa?   19
Where Are Some of the Famous Smaller but Important Cities?   23
Where Are the Famous Dead "Cities of the Sand"?   27
What Additional Terms Are Important to Know?   32
Summary   34

CHAPTER 2

The Geostrategic Middle East and North Africa   37
Introduction   37
Why Are the Middle East and North Africa Geographically Important Areas?   37
What Are the Politics of Geography in the Middle East and North Africa?   39
Who Are the Geographic Theorists Whose Ideas Have Influenced the Politics of the Middle East and North Africa?   39
How Do These Four Theories of Global Strategy Apply to the Study of a Region Such as the Middle East and North Africa?   41
What Events Dragged the Middle East and North Africa into Containment of Russian Communism Strategy?   44
What Are Some of the Most Important Geopolitical Flashpoints in the Middle East and North Africa?   49
Words Commonly Used in Describing the Politics of Geography in the Middle East and North Africa   65
Summary   66

CHAPTER 3

The Politics of Religion in the Middle East and North Africa   69
Introduction   69
Why Is Religion Important in the Middle East and North Africa?   70
What Is the Most Influential Religion in the Politics of the Middle East and North Africa?   71
What Is the History of Christianity in the Middle East and North Africa?   89
What Is the History of the Jews of the Middle East and North Africa?   94
Who Are the Zoroastrians?   98
Summary   98

CHAPTER 4

The Politics of Culture in the Middle East and North Africa   101
Introduction   101
Is There a Single Race of People in the Middle East and North Africa?   103
Summary   119

CHAPTER 5

The Politics of Islamic History, Colonialism, and Nationalism in the Middle East and North Africa   121
Why Study the Political History of Islam?   121
How Did the Three Major Islamic Dynasties Develop?   121
What Is the History of Western Colonialism, Neocolonialism, and Imperialism in the Middle East and North Africa?   131
The Development of Nationalism in the Middle East and North Africa   140
Modern Middle Eastern Nationalism   143
What Are Some Examples of Nationalism in the Middle East and North Africa?   144
What Are Some Other Events, Organizations, and People Important to the History of Islam, Colonialism, and Nationalism?   152
Summary   154

CHAPTER 6

The Politics of Issues   157
Introduction   157
The Dispute Between Arabs, Palestinians, and Israelis   157
The Political Impact of Petroleum on the Middle East and North Africa   169
The Political Conflicts Over Pipelines and Canals in the Middle East and North Africa   173
Religious Fundamentalism in the Middle East and North Africa   177
The Conflict Over Islamic Fundamentalism in Algeria   181

The Changing Role of Women in the Middle East and North Africa   183
The Impact of New Young Leaders on the Policies of the Middle East and North Africa   186
The New "Great Game" in Central Asia   188
The Muslim Rich Get Richer While the Muslim Poor Are Left in the Dust   190
Summary   191

CHAPTER 7

Some Final Thoughts for Americans About the Politics of the Middle East and North Africa   194

Eight Laws Shaping Politics   194
What Are the Future Prospects for the Middle East and North Africa?   203
Summary   203

CHAPTER 8

Country Profiles   205

Algeria   205
Azerbaijan   206
Bahrain   207
Cyprus   208
Egypt   209
Iran   210
Iraq   211
Israel   213
Jordan   214
Kazakhstan   215
Kuwait   216
Kyrgyzstan   218
Lebanon   219
Libya   220
Morocco   221
Oman   222
Qatar   223
Saudi Arabia   224
Syria   225
Tajikistan   226
Tunisia   227
Turkey   228
Turkmenistan   229
United Arab Emirates   230
Uzbekistan   232
Yemen   233

Index   235

Preface

Somewhere between laughter and tears there is Egypt.

JUDITH MILLER[1]

Many years ago I found myself a beginner in a university class on the Middle East. Although listed as an introductory class, the students enrolled were almost exclusively from the Middle East or North Africa. Soon I found that while I was trying to master the basic ideas of Islam, most of the other students wanted to discuss the merits of some obscure Sufi poet. Our textbook was a difficult one that had been written by a famous linguist from Iran! I found myself without a common base of knowledge about this part of the world. My previous studies in history were of no help. They had focused on the glories of Western civilization to the detriment of other regions.

What I needed was a short, jargon-free primer that could provide a background for understanding the basics of geography, history, politics, and religion in the Middle East and North Africa. Luckily I found a little out-of-print book that met most of my needs. To this day I believe that this paperback, *Government and Politics of the Middle East* by Maurice Harari, is one of the best. Unfortunately, it has been out of print for many years.

Beginners today face the same problems that I had. While there are hundreds of books with subjects covering all aspects of the Middle East and North Africa, most are of little use to the generalist who would like to know just enough about the region to become an informed citizen. Almost *every book* written on the area is either too advanced or too focused and narrow, or takes a one-sided view, causing it to be of little use to someone new to the study of the Middle East and North Africa.

The Middle East and North Africa: A Political Primer is offered to provide the reader with a general body of knowledge covering the region. It is intended for the lay audience that has little or no acquaintance with the geography, religion, culture, history and politics of the Middle East and North Africa. It is hoped that with this information the novice can make informed judgments about "news behind the news" as events unfold in this part of the world. For those who wish to learn more, the book can serve as background information to better understand the many excellent advanced works on the Middle East and North Africa.

The Middle East and North Africa: A Political Primer is organized into chapters covering regions, setting, political geography, religion, history, and the emergence from colonialism. Specific studies on the nationalism of Turkey, Iran, Egypt, and Israel are emphasized. When appropriate, the chapters use a question-and-answer format. Two chapters

---

[1] Judith Miller, *God Has Ninety-Nine Names* (New York: Simon and Schuster, 1996), p. 20.

cover current issues. Finally, a country profile chapter appears at the end of the text. Each state in the Middle East and North Africa is represented. The profiles all contain a brief section on current politics.

Because of the breadth of the subjects covered in the *The Middle East and North Africa: A Political Primer*, certain generalizations have been made. Time does not stand still, especially in the Middle East and North Africa. I apologize in advance for any inaccuracies that may appear because of these two problems. It is hoped that, on balance, this book will prove to be useful to those readers wishing to begin a journey of learning about one of the world's most fascinating places.

Acknowledgments

This book has benefited from comments made by the following reviewers: Adam L. Silverman, University of Florida; Stephen Zunes, University of San Francisco; W. Lynn Rigsbee, Marshall University; Ira Reed, Trinity College; Ed Angus, Fort Lewis College; Yury Polsky, West Chester University; Sharon Murphy, Nazareth College of Rochester; Charles H. Winslow, Indiana University-Purdue University Indianapolis. In writing about issues as vast and varied as those covered in this book, I have had to minimize the suggestions of some reviewers in order to accommodate those given by others. However their comments, and sometimes criticisms, have made this effort better. Disagreement among experts only illustrates the difficulty of providing coverage of a complex region such as this. This text is also stronger because of the help from others. Those who offered general comments include Dr. John Dunn, Dr. David George, Dr. Jack Shelton, and John Nickerson. My colleague, Dr. John Culver, was kind enough to read and comment on every page of the draft. My wife, Jane, not only typed the draft but also used her skills as an English teacher to perfect it. Her continued encouragement helped me through some rough periods as the text evolved. I also received a great deal of help from Anita Castro at Longman Publishers, who guided this project through the editorial stages. Others who gave me help and encouragement at Longman include Eric Stano and Mark Naccarelli. Jennifer Harper was indispensable in working to get the text ready for publication. The copy editor was Tina Rebane. Any errors that remain are solely the responsibility of the author.

Joe Weatherby

Chapter 1

Middle East Geography

Introduction

The Middle East, linking Africa with Eurasia, can be called the land bridge of civilization. This region has been the major artery of continental contact for over 3000 years. One hundred years ago, the scholar adventurer John L. Stoddard recognized this fact when he described a small portion of the area, Palestine:

> Palestine has an area only a little larger than the state of Massachusetts, while Russia occupies one seventh of the habitable globe: yet in the scales of intellectual and moral value the little province of Judea outweighs beyond comparison the empire of Czar.[1]

The geographic position of the region has dictated that it would always play a pivotal role in world history. The Middle East has been seen as important both for what it was and for what it was not. It was a leader in the development of civilization, the idea of monotheistic religion, modern science, and mathematics.

For centuries, Middle Eastern leaders gained power and wealth through their conquests in Africa and Europe. Men such as Christopher Columbus and Vasco da Gama did not simply set sail into the unknown Atlantic because they wanted adventure. Their sponsors in Spain and Portugal financed these expeditions because they were not powerful enough to challenge the states of the Middle East for the trade routes to China and India. Those European states that were unable or unwilling to risk the Atlantic, like Venice, quickly went into decline.

The Middle East was also important geographically for what it was not. The Middle East was not a continent. It was a traditional artery for the passage of peoples east and west, north and south, from Africa, Europe, and Asia. This favorable location allowed the inhabitants to absorb and to transmit ideas from other parts of the globe.

By the end of the 18th century, the military power of the Middle East was in decline, producing a vacuum that was quickly filled by the increasingly powerful West. In the 19th century, British, French, German, and Russian competition for control of the region was called "the great game." During World Wars I and II, the Middle East became a zone of actual military conflict. This prompted the cynical comment that, "the Middle East was too important to the West to allow it to be ruled by Middle Easterners."

After World War II, the Middle East witnessed great changes. First came the establishment of the State of Israel. Then, a number of Arab states gained their own independence from previous colonial rulers. Finally, some Arab countries benefited from the development of the world's center for petroleum production. All of these events were complicated by the Cold War competition between the West and Russia. In this struggle, each new incident was a potential flashpoint. Many believed that any conflict in the Middle East had the capacity to explode into World War III.

Today, the Middle East still retains its former importance. Although the traditional trade routes to the East have lost their previous significance, the economic and political issues that spring from the geography of the region are as important as ever. This chapter will focus on two aspects of Middle East geography: physical and human. Using a question-and-answer format, the most fundamental issues raised by the geography of the Middle East will be discussed.

Where Is the Middle East?

At first glance, this should be an easy question to answer. Almost all Americans can point to a map and identify a general area as the Middle East. It may surprise most readers, however, to learn that geographers can identify no single area as the Middle East. The U.S. State Department and the U.S. Department of Defense, through its agency the Central Command (CENTCOM), have identified different areas as the Middle East. The State Department's definition includes North Africa, the Eastern Mediterranean, the Gulf States, and Arabia. They include Turkey in their European grouping. The Department of Defense omits all of North Africa except Egypt in their definition. They include the African states of the Red Sea, the Arabian Peninsula, the Persian Gulf, the Eastern Mediterranean, Iran, Iraq, Afghanistan, and Pakistan. Because of other arrangements, Turkey, Israel, Syria, and India are not included in the CENTCOM list of Middle Eastern responsibilities. Other lists often refer to the Arab Core of the Eastern Mediterranean and the Arabian Peninsula as the true Middle East.

Both history and ideology further complicate this issue. During the 19th-century Age of Imperialism, Western colonialists commonly organized their overseas possessions into geographic categories that were related to the location of their mother country. Europeans referred to the East as anywhere that was east of the Ottoman Empire. Thus, the *Near East* was considered to be the lands of the Eastern Mediterranean. The *Middle East* was defined as being approximately where Iran, Pakistan, and India are located. The *Far East* covered the European colonies and trading areas of Asia. The European possessions in North Africa were considered to be a part of greater colonial Africa. By the end of the 19th century the British colonial administration regularly used these designations. Although the specifics of these definitions changed from time to time, the terms *Near East, Middle East,* and *Far East* remained in use until World War II.

European losses of colonies in the early days of World War II made the traditional colonial definitions irrelevant. The Asian colonies ceased to exist. The greater Indian subcontinent was under the threat of a Japanese invasion. Consequently, the British au-

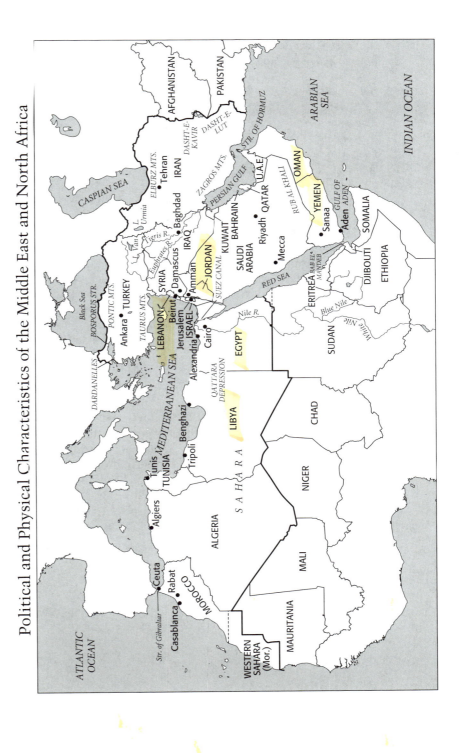

Political and Physical Characteristics of the Middle East and North Africa

thorities relocated their Middle East military command to Egypt. This action superimposed the "new Middle East" on top of the old "Near East," to the confusion of readers since that time. Today the Middle East and the Near East are considered to be essentially the same place.

In the postcolonial world, questions arose about where to place the newly independent states of Morocco, Algeria, Tunisia, and Libya. Middle Easterners themselves further complicated the issue. People from the region were quick to point out that the terms *Near East*, *Middle East*, and *Far East* referred to an ugly colonial period that was best forgotten. Scholars and diplomats are still searching for a geographically neutral but sufficiently descriptive term to describe this region.

Some writers have used the phrases "the Arab world" and "the Islamic world" as descriptive substitutes. These terms are often as misleading and offensive as were the former ones when describing the region as a whole. The term *the Arab world* recognizes the more than one hundred million Arabic speakers of the region. It is fatally flawed, however, because it omits the combined one hundred million Turks, Iranians, Israelis, and other significant minorities who also inhabit the region. Furthermore, it ignores the realities that large numbers of Arabic-speaking people also live in Africa south of the Sahara.

Although the term *Muslim world* may describe the religious identity of approximately 90 percent of the region's population, it, too, makes several false assumptions. As shown in a later chapter, the Muslim world is no more homogeneous than is the Christian world. Furthermore, large numbers of Muslims are living outside of the Middle East in East Africa, Central Asia, Western China, India, Malaysia, and Indonesia. Finally, this designation ignores the Christian, Jewish, and Zoroastrian minorities who, although small in number, exercise a great deal of influence.

Because the term *Middle East* is still widely used, it will be retained in this book. It should be considered to include the Arab states of the Arabian Peninsula and the Eastern Mediterranean, Egypt, Turkey, Israel, and Iran. In addition to this Middle Eastern core, other states should be added because of economic, religious, or other cultural associations. Thus, the states of North Africa should be considered to be a periphery, as depicted on the map on page 3. Simply put, the Middle East consists of an Eastern Mediterranean, Turkish, Iranian, and Arabian core with a North African periphery.

What Special Names Are Associated with the Middle East and North Africa?

THE HOLY LAND

The first mention of the Holy Land appears in the Old Testament in the book of Zechariah.

> And the Lord shall inherit Judah his portion in the Holy Land, and shall choose Jerusalem again.[2]

Today, Jews, Christians, and Muslims venerate the Holy Land because it is associated with their respective religions. Geographically, the Holy Land encompasses almost the same territory as ancient Roman Palestine. It stretches from the Lebanese border down along the Jordan River to Egypt. The western boundary follows the Mediterranean coast.

The Holy Land is centered around the city of Jerusalem. To Jews, the Holy Land also includes the territory that they believe was part of a promise made to them by God. Many events in ancient Jewish history chronicled in the Old Testament are linked to sites in and around Jerusalem. The modern State of Israel is located where it is because of the belief that God's promise to give this land to the ancient Hebrews and their descendants is still in force.

Christians view the Holy Land as the place that witnessed the life of Jesus. To them, this area includes the region around Lake Tiberius (the Sea of Galilee), Nazareth, Bethlehem, and Jerusalem. Jerusalem and the surrounding areas are sacred to Christians as the places where they believe Jesus was born, died, and was resurrected from the dead.

During the Middle Ages, Christians conducted a series of crusades to retake the Holy Land from Muslim control. They hoped to establish a permanent Christian enclave in the heart of the Muslim world. The Christian-held lands would eventually reach from what is now southern Turkey to Gaza. Four major efforts to conquer the territory were mounted between the years 1096 and 1204. By 1291, the Crusades were recognized as failures and were abandoned. Gradually, Christians settled for obtaining pilgrimage rights to those sites in the Holy Land that they associated with Jesus. Christians continue the pilgrimage tradition to the present time.

Muslims consider Jerusalem to be the third most important holy site after Mecca and Medina (Al-Madinah). To them, the Holy Land has both ancient and Muslim associations. According to tradition, Hebron is the burial place of the patriarch Abraham. Abraham is believed to be the father of both the Arabs and the Jews. Jerusalem is associated with the Koran's account of the Ascension of Muhammad to heaven. Muslims believe that Muhammad rose to heaven from the site of one of Islam's most important shrines, the Dome of the Rock. The Golden Dome of the Rock is the most visible symbol in the Old City of Jerusalem.

Today, as in the past, the Holy Land is an area that is contested by Jews, Christians, and Muslims. Each religion asserts that its claim to the Holy Land is superior. This conflict makes the modern Holy Land one of the most contentious places in the world.

THE LEVANT

As surprising as it might seem, the word *Levant* is French. On closer examination, it is perfectly logical, as it reflects a long-standing French relationship with the Eastern Mediterranean coast. The word *Levant* comes from the French "lever," which means to rise. As it is used geographically, Levant is the place where the sun rises in the Eastern Mediterranean. Every 24 hours, it begins a regeneration of the day. As early as 1592, the English used the French term *Levant* in setting up a Turkish company with trading privileges obtained from the Ottoman Sultan. The Levant Company carried on trade with the Ottoman Empire for two hundred years.

The Levant became a popular term in 17th-century France, when Louis XVI established direct trading relations between his country and the lands of the Levant without going through intermediaries, as had previously been the custom. In this way, France claimed a special relationship with the Christian inhabitants of the region. The long French involvement in the Levant evolved into direct control after World War I. It was during this period of direct French rule that the high commissioner, General Henri Goureau, drew the boundaries that shaped the futures of Lebanon, Syria, and southern

Turkey. The French did not abandon their control until World War II. They did not withdraw their military from the Levant until 1946.

French influence is still strong in the region. French is the second language after Arabic in Lebanon, and the French still claim a moral right to protect the safety of the Christians living in Lebanon.

Today the Levant is thought to include the modern states of Syria, Lebanon, and Israel. At various times in history, Greece, Turkey, and Egypt have also been considered Levantine states.

The geography of the Levant has promoted diversity and ethnic tribalism. Its wonderful climate and beautiful scenery mask a terrain that isolates people. The Levantine coast is narrow. The land quickly becomes mountainous only a few miles from the beach. Beyond the mountains lie the fertile valleys of the interior. This region has witnessed countless invasions. Each invasion quickly withered and was soon replaced by another. Those people who survived these conflicts retreated to the isolated mountains and valleys near the coast. In the same way that people living on islands become isolated from their neighbors, the mountains and valleys of the Levant tended to isolate separate ethnic groups.

Geography has encouraged the survival of mutually hostile sectarian "tribes." Like the Balkans, the mountains and valleys of the Levant facilitate this process. Here, Maronite Christians, Greek Orthodox Christians, Armenian Christians, Shiite Muslims, Sunni Muslims, Druze, Kurds, and others live in a presently peaceful but permanently hostile relationship. As the 21st century begins, the Levant is one of the most beautiful but potentially most dangerous places on earth.

THE MAGHREB

The word *Maghreb* is Arabic, meaning "the land where the suns sets." The area known as the Maghreb is located in northwest Africa. During the centuries of Moorish occupation in Spain, the Maghreb was considered to include both Muslim Iberia and the coast of northwestern Africa. In the 18th century, the Maghreb coast became known as the Barbary Coast. Barbary was the center of piracy. The leaders of the region carried out raids and collected tribute from most of the leading European states.

Early in the 19th century, the U.S. Navy mounted a series of expeditions against the Barbary pirates. The British bombardment of Algiers in 1816 finally ended pirate raids and the tradition of Europeans paying tributes to "Barbary." The European subjugation of North Africa began with the defeat of these pirates. By the beginning of World War I, the entire North African coast had fallen under the colonial rule of Spain, France, Italy, and the United Kingdom. The region did not gain independence from Europe until the middle years of the 20th century.

Today the modern states of Morocco, Algeria, and Tunisia are considered to make up the core of the Maghreb. They share a common Berber population that maintains a separate language and culture.

For reasons of politics and trade, Libya and Mauritania also claim to be part of the Maghreb. On occasion Egypt has also attempted to exert influence along the North African coast.

In 1989 five North African countries—Algeria, Libya, Mauritania, Morocco, and Tunisia—formed the Arab Maghreb Union. The chief aim of this union was to develop

The Barbary Coast
Once the abode of pirates and adventurers, this Tunisian fortress now hosts European tourists enjoying the beach.
Source: Joe Weatherby

trade and other forms of cooperation while reducing conflict among its members. At the time, Morocco's King Hussein II predicted that the Union would achieve its stated goals faster than would the European Union.

Unfortunately, King Hussein's prediction has not come to pass. Geographic disputes, such as the one between Morocco and Algeria over the western Sahara, have hindered relations. Internal conflict in Algeria has hurt the Union's development. The aggressive anti-Western actions of Libya's Colonel Qaddafi have frightened the Union's more moderate members. More recently, the moves by Morocco and Tunisia to establish low-level contacts and the recent decision of Mauritania to establish ambassadorial-level relations with Israel have all but shattered Arab Maghreb Union unity.

The positions of Morocco, Tunisia, and Mauritania are in stark contrast with that of Libya, which denies Israel's right to exist. They are also in conflict with the position of the Arab League, which has resolved to refuse to cooperate with Israel until the control over the disputed lands in the occupied West Bank, southern Lebanon, and the Golan Heights is resolved.

In spite of the talk of Maghreb unity, most North African economic contact is with southern Europe, not within the Union. The Maghreb remains a geographic entity, but political, cultural, and economic union is a distant dream.

A Cork Oak Forest in Western Morocco
The outer bark or cork has been removed from the lower part of each tree. Cork is harvested for many purposes, including bottle stoppers.
Source: Joe Weatherby

THE TRUCIAL COAST

Sometimes called *Trucial Oman,* the states of the Trucial Coast are located at the southwestern end of the Persian Gulf. The Coast acquired its name because of a series of truces that were made by the British with local leaders in 1820. At the time, the British objective was to reduce tribal warfare and end piracy in the Gulf. This action was considered essential if Britain was to maintain secure routes to its empire in India. Under these agreements, the local chiefs would conduct their foreign affairs through Britain. In return, the British agreed to defend the places that were parties to the arrangement. These included the Emirates of Abu Dhabi, Ajman, Dubai, Ras al Khama, Sharjah, and Umm al Qaiwain. In 1892, these truces were made into a formal agreement.

This arrangement remained largely unchanged until oil was discovered in the area in the 1960s. The sheiks of the lower Gulf terminated their agreement with Britain and established a federation in 1971. Ras al Khama did not formally join the federation until 1972. The federation of former Trucial states became the United Arab Emirates.

It should be noted that the British established similar arrangements with other neighboring Arab Emirates, including Oman, Qatar, Bahrain, and Kuwait. This association with the British has sometimes caused confusion about who should be included as a Trucial state. The situation has been further complicated because both Qatar and Bahrain were originally considered for membership in the United Arab Emirates but did not join.

The states of the Trucial Coast, along with Oman, Qatar, Bahrain, Kuwait, and Saudi Arabia, are members of a regional organization called the *Gulf Cooperation Council.* Like its counterpart in North Africa, the Arab Maghreb, the Gulf Cooperation Council seeks to reduce conflict among its members, facilitate trade, and present a united policy. To those Arabs outside the Gulf Cooperation Council, this arrangement is looked at with envy as one of the rich versus the poor. While all of the member states are wealthy, United Arab Emirates has the highest per capita income in the world.

THE HEJAZ

The *Hejaz* is the name of the western region of modern Saudi Arabia. It is a desert area that extends along the west coast of the Red Sea from the Gulf of Aqaba to south of the port of Jidda. Sometimes called the *Muslim Holy Land,* the Hejaz is known to all Muslims as the location of Medina and Mecca. A pilgrimage route has existed for centuries to enable Muslims to visit these cities. In addition to the holy cities, the region also contains two great ports: Jidda and Yanbu. These ports give access to the Red Sea from the desert interior. Yanbu is the terminus for a new pipeline that stretches across the desert from the oil fields in eastern Saudi Arabia. This pipeline allows the Saudis to bypass the dangerous Straits of Hormuz when shipping oil from the Persian Gulf to the West.

During World War I, the Hejaz became famous among Westerners because of the exploits of the Englishman Lawrence of Arabia (T. E. Lawrence). As a British agent, Lawrence took part in the famous Arab revolt against Ottoman rule. That revolt began in the Hejaz Desert and focused on the destruction of the Baghdad Mecca Railway. This famous railway, built to carry pilgrims to Mecca, was used by the Ottomans to carry troops and supplies to the Red Sea. It was destroyed by the Arab irregulars and has never been rebuilt.

After World War I, the British recognized the Hashimite Sharif of Mecca as the king of the Hejaz. As king, he controlled the holy sites of Mecca and Medina, plus most of the Red Sea coast and the desert interior. The Sharif was originally appointed as the protector of the holy sites by the Ottomans, but he proclaimed himself the caliph and leader of all Muslims when the Turkish Republic abolished the position of protector in 1924.

The ruler of the Arabian interior, called the Najd, was Abdul Aziz ibn Abdul Rahman ibn Saud. Ibn Saud steadily consolidated his power after returning from exile in Kuwait in 1902. He and the Sharif soon clashed. After being defeated by ibn Saud, the Sharif went into permanent exile in 1926. Ibn Saud created the basis for the modern state of Saudi Arabia by uniting the territories of Hejaz and the Najd. His sons continue to rule the Hejaz to protect the holy cities there as the new century begins.

What Geographical Features Make Up the Middle East and North Africa?

Most Westerners picture the region as one vast sea of unending desert. To be sure, there are great deserts here. In some places the desert defines the existence of human life. For example, the desert of Saudi Arabia occupies about 98 percent of the land. In Egypt, the population has avoided the desert by living along the banks of the Nile for 5000 years. If there were no Nile, there would be no Egypt.

Nevertheless, the Middle East and North Africa contain a great physical variety, ranging from desert to rich farmlands to soaring mountains to mighty rivers and sultry swamps. In its simplest form, the Middle East and North Africa can be divided into three distinct geographic regions: the plains of North Africa and Arabia, the Fertile Crescent, and the Northern Tier. These areas are surrounded by five seas and five straits. They are bisected by two of the world's great river systems: the Nile and the Tigris and Euphrates.

THE PLAINS OF NORTH AFRICA AND ARABIA

The Deserts The deserts of the Sahara in North Africa and the Rub al Khali in Arabia make up most of the land in this region. The Sahara is a land mass of desert, with a sprinkling of oases, that stretches from the Atlantic in the west to the Red Sea in the east. At 3.5 million square miles, the Sahara is easily the largest desert in the world. It should not be surprising that the topography of such a large area is varied. The Sahara's low point is almost 400 feet below sea level, but there are isolated peaks that reach heights of 11,000 feet. The desert itself is also complex, ranging from areas with scrub plants, to rock, to gravel, to sand.

Throughout history, the bleakness of the Sahara has confined human travel to specific recognized trade routes. For Westerners, the interior of the Sahara was almost unknown until modern times. It was not until 1828 that a European successfully reached the fabled city of Timbuktu and lived to tell the story. In the hope of winning a 10,000-franc prize offered by the Geographical Society of Paris to the first traveler to reach Timbuktu, the adventurer René Caillié took up the challenge. Disguised as a Muslim, he entered Africa from the Atlantic, visited Timbuktu, and then crossed the Sahara, exiting through Morocco to win the prize. Only two years earlier, an Englishman, Alexander Gordon Laing, attempted the same trip, only to lose his life to nomadic tribesmen.[3]

Today the Sahara remains a formidable barrier to land travel. Only a few regularly used desert tracks exist. There is little effective political control over the desert. Much of the Sahara still remains an untraveled, dangerous place. In January 2000, some desert portions of the road rally to Dakar had to be canceled because of threats of attack made by nomadic bands of rebels operating from southern Algeria.

One of the Sahara's most interesting land forms, the Qattara Depression, is located in Egypt near the border with Libya. Occupying an area of over 4,000 square miles, the depression drops from the Sahara surface more than 400 feet to the Qattara floor. The depression played a significant role in the British victory over the Germans at the World War II Battle of El Alamein in November 1942. Located only 40 miles from the seacoast, at the El Alamein rail junction, the Qattara formed the southern end of the British line of defense. The Sahara prevented German passage to the south of the depression, forcing them to confront the British forces at their strongest point. The location of this depression meant that the British could place their forces in the narrow strip of land stretching from Qattara to the sea. This narrow strip was the only place that the British could make a stand against the Germans with a good chance of success. That chance turned into a British victory, spelling the eventual end of the German threat in North Africa. In reality, "General Qattara" deserved a great deal of the credit for the British victory at El Alamein.

The Kingdom of Saudi Arabia is almost four times the size of France. Although largely desert, the topography of the Arabian state is varied. A mountain range with heights that reach 9000 feet runs along the coast of the Red Sea. The land then slopes gradually down across the peninsula until it runs into the Persian Gulf in the east. Across this territory are deserts of gravel, lava, rock, and sand. A few mountains and occasional oases break the uniformly flat surface. There are two major sand deserts in the north and

Sacrifice at El Alamein
The remains of a British Crusader tank still stands guard over the El Alamein battlefield site. It was on this spot, in 1942, that the British "desert rats" of the 8th Army stopped the German advance into Egypt.
Source: Joe Weatherby

central parts of Arabia. The Nefud begins in the north and moves down through the center of Arabia to meet another sand region that is called the Dahna. The Nefud then extends southward to the Rub al Khali.

The capital city, Riyadh, is located in the center of Arabia and is the ancestral home of the ruling Al-Sauds. Until recently, Riyadh was the capital only in name while Jidda was the commercial center of the Kingdom. Within the past twenty years, however, Riyadh has become a major city. Today it houses government ministries, a royal palace, museums, hospitals, research centers, and universities. Major businesses operating in the kingdom maintain offices here. During the Gulf War, Iraq successfully targeted Riyadh with missile attacks. Today the king and other dignitaries maintain residencies in both Riyadh and Jidda. They spend part of the year in each city.

The Rub al Khali, sometimes called the "empty quarter," is the greatest sand desert in the world. The Rub al Khali is approximately the size of Texas and extends across southern Arabia to Yemen in the west and to the United Arab Emirates in the east. The Rub al Khali is famous for its sand mountains, which cover large portions of the desert's surface. Reaching heights as high as 600 feet, these sand mountains take many shapes, ranging from sharp long ridges to rounded hills. This is one of the last unoccupied places in Arabia. Bedouins occasionally visit parts of the Rub al Khali during rare periods when moisture allows some plant life suitable for pasture to grow. It is then that animals can exist in this region. The Rub al Khali, however, still remains one of the least visited places on earth.

The deserts of the Arabian Peninsula were largely unknown to the West until recent times. Most maps of the 19th and early 20th centuries showed the interior of Arabia as simply a blank spot. This isolation was due to two factors. First, the region was inaccessible and appeared to have little economic value. Second, the inhabitants opposed the presence of anyone who was not a Muslim. Very few Europeans entered and returned from Arabia before the 20th century. An early visitor was an Islamic convert, Joseph Pitts, who visited Mecca as a pilgrim in 1687. In the 19th century, several Europeans disguised themselves as Muslims and visited Mecca. The famous explorer Richard Burton was able to accomplish this feat in 1853. Almost all of the early European visits to Arabia were limited to the Hejaz, which was easily reached from the Red Sea.

The first known European to actually cross the peninsula was Captain George Sadler, who "accidentally" accomplished this feat in 1819. It was not until 1862, however, that the great explorer William Gifford Palgrave crossed Arabia from what is modern Jordan, exiting near the present city of Dhahran. His account of this journey ensured that features of the peninsula became known to the West.

Europeans did not penetrate the great southern desert, the Rub al Khali, until the 20th century. Bertram Thomas successfully crossed this desert in 1931. In 1932, the advisor to Ibn Saud, Harry St. John Philby, gained permission to visit the Rub al Khali. He made two extensive trips to the desert, one of which covered more than 1,250 miles. His observations were printed in a well-known book on the region. It was not until 1946 that the southern desert was crossed by motor vehicles. With the development of the Saudi oil industry, more interest has been shown in the Rub al Khali. Still, this desert remains one of the last great mysteries of the world.

The Mountains The mountains of North Africa are limited to the states of Morocco, Algeria, and Tunisia. The Atlas Mountains stretch across central Morocco, northern Algeria, and northwestern Tunisia. At various points, this range is called the *High Atlas,* the *Middle Atlas,* the *Tell Atlas,* and the *Sahara Atlas.* Some peaks in Morocco reach heights of 13,000 feet. The highest peak is Jebel Toubkal in western Morocco, which has an altitude of 13,671 feet.

Near the Moroccan coast lie the Riff Mountains. They begin near the sea between the cities of Tangier and Ceuta, running south through Xauen before turning east to follow the coastline to the Algerian border. The Riff is the heartland of the Berber people. It was in the Riff that the Spanish fought a long, bloody, "Vietnam-type" war during the 1920s. The leader of the Riff tribes, Abd el-Krim, defeated the Spanish army in 1921. It was not until 1926 that the combined forces of Spain and France were able to capture el-Krim and pacify the region. In 1958, King Muhammad V of Morocco recognized the Berber fight and awarded Abd el-Krim the title of national hero.

The mountains of Arabia border the western, southern, and southeastern portions of the Arabian Peninsula. As has already been mentioned, the Hejaz chain runs from the Gulf of Aqaba down the east coast of the Red Sea to become the Asir south of Jidda. These mountains continue down the coast through Yemen to the city of Aden.

The mountains are generally lower in the north and gain height in Yemen. Jebel Sharr south of Aqaba has a height of only a little more than 6,000 feet. But the peaks in Yemen can reach 12,000 feet or more.

FEATURES THAT MAKE UP THE MIDDLE EAST AND NORTH AFRICA

North African Mountains
The Atlas Mountains near the Moroccan city of Marrakech.
Source: Joe Weatherby

Lower mountains follow along most of the southern coast of Yemen. East of the Port of Aden is an area of deep canyons and rich valleys called the *Hadhramaut*. The Hadhramaut contains a number of skyscraper cities built of dried mud. One of the better known skyscraper cities is called Yashbum.[4]

The North African Coast Most people in North Africa live along the coast, away from the desert. This coastal belt generally conforms to what is known as the Mediterranean climate. This climate characteristically has cool, wet winters and warm, dry summers. Stretching from Casablanca on the Atlantic to the Nile Valley, the coastal zone ranges in depth from a few miles to almost 50 miles.

For centuries, people have taken advantage of the ideal climate and good prospects for agriculture along the North African coast. This zone is littered with the remains of great cities from the past. The ruins of Carthage lie adjacent to the modern city of Tunis. Carthage once rivaled the Roman Empire in power. Leptis Magna is a ruined city in Libya. It has survived as the most complete artifact from the ancient world. These are only two of the dozens of abandoned cities in coastal North Africa. Most declined and were abandoned as Roman influence in North Africa ended. There was no longer a European market for the products of North Africa, so the people simply left.

Human Geography With the rise of Islam, new cities were built and some of the surviving old cities were expanded. These cities have become the great urban centers of modern North Africa. They include Cairo, Africa's most important city, with a population of 9.5 million. Other important cities are Casablanca (3.1 million) and Rabat (1.2 million) in Morocco, Algiers (3.7 million) in Algeria, Tunis (1.7 million) in Tunisia, Tripoli (1 million) in Libya, and Alexandria (3.5 million) in Egypt. The population of North African cities generally exceeds that of the cities located in Eastern Mediterranean.

Cairo is located astride the Nile at the head of a delta. The city is well positioned to take advantage of the river trade, which is the "life blood" of Egypt. Although new by Egyptian standards, Cairo was founded by the Arabs in 969 of our era. The city was sited near the most spectacular ruins and monuments in Egypt. Just across the Nile are the ruins of the ancient capital of Memphis. Nearby are the great pyramids at Giza.

Cairo is the center of government, religion, education, and commerce in modern Egypt. The famous mosques of Ibn Tulun, Sultan Hassan, and Muhammad Ali are visited by people from all over the world. The Al-Azhar University claims to be the world's oldest. It is recognized as one of the great centers for the study of Islamic law. Cairo also has the famous American University, which compares favorably with the best universities in Europe and the United States.

Cairo has been a seat of government since it was founded as an Arab political center more than a thousand years ago. Today, it is the capital of Egypt. In recent years, Cairo has experienced a population growth that has outstripped the existing city services, causing severe social problems. Unable to find housing, large numbers of the poor have been forced to live in the "city of the dead." Here one can find thousands of poor people living in old tombs.

The most imposing structure in the city is the Citadel. Built as a fort by Saladin in the 12th century, the Citadel was intended to defend the city against a Crusader attack that never came. During the period of British rule, the Citadel, Shepherds Hotel, and the Gezira Club became symbols of imperial domination. Today the Citadel is largely a museum; the original Shepherds was destroyed during anti-British riots, and the Gezira Club is now patronized by Egyptian elites.

One of the most interesting developments of the late 20th century was the rapid evolution of the coastal cities of the Arabian Peninsula. Benefiting from the wealth generated by oil, great cities have grown from almost nothing.

When Lawrence of Arabia first visited the port of Jidda in 1916, he said of the place,

> It was like a dead city, so clean underfoot, and so quiet. Its winding, even streets were floored with damp sand solidified by time and as silent to the tread as any carpet. There were neither carts nor any streets wide enough for carts, no shod animals, no bustle anywhere. Everything was hushed, strained, and even furtive.[5]

Modern Jidda is a thriving seaport and financial center with a population of around 1.5 million. The city can boast of a number of architecturally distinguished buildings, spectacular public art, modern hospitals, and several institutions of higher learning. It is the principal arrival point for most of the million and a half pilgrims who visit the Holy Cities of Mecca and Medina each year. Today Jidda is one of the most important business centers in the Arab world. It has grown more than 1,000 times the size of the town that Lawrence visited.

The Pyramid of Chephren at Giza, Egypt
Looking up at the mountainous pyramid, can you see where the fine dressed limestone cover remains? Most of the outer cover was removed by the Arabs and used by them to build their new city, Cairo.
Source: Joe Weatherby

In the eastern province of Saudi Arabia, a remarkable occurrence has taken place. On what were uninhabited beaches in the late 1930s, a great petrochemical complex has risen. Today this complex contains an almost unending area of marine terminals, refineries, and tank farms that support the new cities of Damman, Dhahran, al-Khubar, and Jubail.

Modern Jubail has been constructed since 1980. It is a planned industrial city built and populated solely because of oil. Jubail is the eastern terminus for the pipeline that crosses Arabia to the Red Sea port of Yenbu.

THE FERTILE CRESCENT

The Fertile Crescent is shaped like a bow that arches from the lower shores of the Eastern Mediterranean across the northern borders of Syria and Iraq to end at the edge of the Persian Gulf. Some geographers have included parts of the Nile Delta as part of their definition of the Fertile Crescent. This region was the location for some of the earliest known people. Sumerians, Assyrians, and various Semitic peoples called this home in ancient times. There is evidence that the first settlements took place here between 8000 and 7000 B.C.E.[6]

Perhaps no outside area has made such a contribution to the foundation of Western Civilization as has the Fertile Crescent. For this study, the Fertile Crescent begins in northeastern Egypt and includes parts of the Palestinian entity, Israel, Jordan, Syria, and Iraq.

Much of the drama of human history has been tied to this area. This land is the site of such ancient ruins as Baalbeck, Petra, and Palmyra. the Lebanese coastal village of Byblos is credited with originating the word "bible," because the village residents made the papyrus that was used to write early books. The ancient Greek word for book was "biblos" and the modern translation is "bible." Sometimes called "the land of prophets," the Fertile Crescent is the birthplace of Judaism and Christianity.

Geographically, this zone can be divided into the Mediterranean coast, the coastal mountains, and the desert interior. The coastal area closely resembles that of California. The climate of the northern part of Lebanon is like that of northern California. Haifa in Israel compares favorably with Monterey, California, and southern Israel resembles southern California.

The coastal range runs the length of Lebanon, parallel with the Mediterranean, into northern Israel. It is about one hundred miles long. The highest point is over 10,000 feet. Although the range is much lower than that high point, it has provided isolated refuge to people for centuries.

Once the coastal range has been crossed, the land flattens out. When leaving the sea and the coastal Lebanon Mountains, one encounters rich plains followed by the low Anti-Lebanon Range then the land eventually becomes a scrub desert. Two great river systems allow the desert area to be inhabited.

Humankind has misused much of the Fertile Crescent through poor irrigation techniques, charcoal burning, and overgrazing. Irrigation has resulted in some of the soil becoming unproductive because evaporation has covered the surface with salt. The overgrazing and cutting of wood for charcoal has caused severe erosion of the hillsides. The result is a Fertile Crescent that no longer looks like the lush region that it once was.

The coastal cities of the Eastern Mediterranean cannot compare in size with those of North Africa. Even the most important Israeli cities are relatively small compared with North African cities. Haifa has a population of 255,000, Jerusalem 591,000, and Tel Aviv, the largest city, has a population of 2.8 million inhabitants. In Lebanon, Beirut has a population of 2.0 million.

Damascus and Baghdad are the two great cities that dominate the interior of the Fertile Crescent. In 1895 the Victorian traveler Marion Harland wrote the following on first seeing Damascus:

> In spring-time, when the encompassing orchards are in bloom, Damascus may deserve, in the mind of the approaching traveler, some of the encomiums lavished upon it by poets and historians of a former age. At this season, the "pearl" is undeniably dingy.[7]

One hundred years later, Damascus, with a population of 2.3 million people, is the financial and political capital of the Syrian Arab Republic. Damascus is located on the Barda River.

Damascus is one of the oldest cities in the world. It was a city long before the time of the prophet Abraham and was the Muslim capital of the Omayyad Dynasty from 661 C.E. to 750 C.E. In more recent times, it was a regional headquarters for the Ottoman Empire. During and after World War I, Damascus became a "flashpoint" as Hashimite Arabs, Syrians, the British, and the French all vied for control of the city. When Syria became independent from French rule, Damascus was selected as the capital. Although it is a thoroughly modern metropolis, Damascus still retains many ancient monuments, including the Biblical "straight street," the Great Mosque, the bazaars, and the old Roman fortress.

Modern Baghdad has a population of 4.7 million. It is located on both sides of the Tigris River. Although rich in Islamic history as the capital of the Abbasid Dynasty, most of the old city has disappeared under the blade of the modern bulldozer. The city is largely the product of recent development. Today Baghdad is known for oil refining. Some traditional industries still survive, including the manufacturing of carpets, leather goods, and textiles.

Baghdad lost a great deal of its infrastructure during the Gulf War bombings of 1992. This included heavy damage to streets, water purification plants, and electric power-producing facilities. Because of United Nations sanctions, little of this has been replaced as the new century begins.

THE NORTHERN TIER

The Northern Tier is part of a great range of mountains that stretch from the European Alps in the west to the Himalayas in the east. Although the Trans Caucuses, Afghanistan, and Pakistan are sometimes included in this region, this discussion will be limited to Turkey and Iran.

Turkey Turkey and Iran are both states having interiors surrounded by mountains. Turkey has a geography that is a combination of East and West. The portions of Turkey north of the Bosporus are considered to be European. The part that includes the Anatolian Peninsula marks the beginning of Asia.

The northern and southern portions of Asian Turkey are mountainous. The center of the peninsula contains a large area called the Anatolian Plateau. The northern mountains are known as the Pontic or North Anatolian Range. The Pontics increase in height toward the east, with their highest point being 12,917 feet.

In the south, the Taurus chain extends along the Mediterranean coast for 350 miles. It, too, reaches heights of over 12,000 feet in the east. Both ranges converge to form a knot near the border with Iran. Here, near Lake Van, is the crowning jewel of Anatolia, Mt. Ararat, at 16,946 feet. Mt. Ararat provides some of the source water for the Euphrates River. It is the site identified in the Bible's Book of Genesis as the place where Noah's Ark landed after the Great Flood.

> And the Ark rested in the seventh month, on the seventeenth day of the month, upon the mountains of Ararat.[8]

Near the city of Rize, the northeastern mountains have a climate unknown in the rest of the Middle East. The mountain slopes along the coast of the Black Sea receive more than 100 inches of rain annually. Elsewhere, moisture is blocked from entering the interior Anatolian Plateau because of the height of the surrounding mountains. The average annual rainfall on the plateau is only 15 inches. Farming is marginal, and the population density is low. The plateau is best known as the site of the Turkish capital, Ankara.

Mustafa Kemal Ataturk transferred his capital from Constantinople (called Istanbul since 1930) to Ankara in 1923. He wanted to distance himself from the bureaucratic intrigues of the old capital city. Ankara also had the advantage of being isolated but having a central location. Today the capital is the second largest city in Turkey, with a population of almost 3 million people.

The area around Istanbul is the most historically and geographically important in the country. It is located astride the Bosporus at the entrance to the Black Sea in the east and the Sea of Marmara in the west. It is at this point that the West meets the East in Asia Minor. It was only natural that such an important contact point would become a major city. At times Istanbul has been the capital of the eastern Roman Empire, the Byzantine Empire, and the Ottoman Empire. It has always been a center of religion, learning, and trade.

Istanbul is a thriving metropolis with a population of 9.5 million. Situated on one of the most spectacular sites in the world, modern Istanbul boasts museums, palaces, and universities. Its chief monument is the famous Hagia Sophia. Originally a church built in 532 C.E., the building was converted to a mosque in 1453. The Hagia Sophia is now a museum.

Istanbul is also an important industrial center for the manufacture of textiles, glass, motor vehicles, and ships. Finally, it is the leading financial center for Turkey.

Iran Iran is larger than Alaska. Because it is surrounded by high mountains, little moisture penetrates to the interior. It is estimated that 50 percent of Iran is unproductive desert. The Zagros Mountains run down the west coast of Iran for 1400 miles. These mountains reach heights of 10,000 feet. They are an effective barrier, preventing Persian Gulf rainfall from penetrating the interior. There are few roads across these mountains, leaving the interior isolated. The Makran Mountains form a similar barrier to the southeast. The highest peaks in this range are around 9,000 feet.

The Elbruz Mountains run west to east along the southern coast of the Caspian Sea. These barriers reach heights of 10,000 feet for over 200 of the 400-mile length of the range. Mt. Demavend is an Elbruz volcano with a height of 18,934 feet. Located near the city of Tehran, Mt. Demavend is a popular ski resort during the winter months.

The low rainfall, few streams, and only one major river make water one of the major limits to Iranian agricultural development. Most of the people engaged in farming live on the northern side of the Elbruz along the coast of the Caspian Sea. This area has a climate similar to the Black Sea coast. There is lush vegetation in this region. Rice, cotton, flax, sugar cane, tobacco, oranges, and vegetables are all grown here in commercial quantities.

The interior of Iran contains two of the world's great deserts: the Dasht-e Kavir and the Dasht-e Lut. Popularly known as the "salt desert" and the "desert of death," these two adjacent areas comprise one of the most hostile environments on earth. They are distinguished for high summer temperatures and bitterly cold winters. The Dasht-e Lut probably has the highest average temperatures on earth. There is little human activity here. The land surface is crusted salt and mud flats. The central parts of these deserts are virtually impossible to cross in wheeled vehicles. It was the isolation of the Dasht-e Lut that tempted the Carter Administration to pick it as the base for the ill-fated American attempt to liberate the U.S. Iranian Embassy hostages in 1980. A sandstorm caused several of the rescue aircraft to crash, forcing the mission to be aborted.

Like many places in the Middle East, Iran has experienced a move of large numbers of unskilled people from the countryside to the cities. Urban areas have exploded in population during the recent years. By the year 2000, the capital city of Tehran had burgeoned to a population of 7.2 million. Other cities in Iran include Mashhad (2 million) and Esfahan (1.2 million).

Located in the foothills of the Elbruz, Tehran can be favorably compared to Salt Lake City, Utah. Both are built against major mountain ranges and slope dramatically downward onto a plain. They also have similar climates. Like Salt Lake City, Tehran is the dynamic urban center of the region. Its population is greater than the combined populations of Mashhad and Esfahan.

What Are the Important Rivers in the Middle East and North Africa?

Although thought of as a desert region, the Middle East contains two of the world's great river systems and also a river of great historical and political importance.

THE NILE

The Nile rises in two places: Ethiopia and Uganda. The Blue Nile and the White Nile flow from these areas to join in the Sudan at Khartoum. The river then passes into Egypt through Lake Nasser and the Aswan High Dam to reach the Mediterranean Sea. At 4,037 miles, the Nile is the world's longest river.

Mentioned on Ptolemy's map 2000 years ago, the source of the Nile became the subject of a bitter debate between two great 19th-century British explorers, Richard Burton and John Hanning Speke. In 1862, Speke correctly identified Victoria and Ripon Falls as the true source of the White Nile. Burton bitterly disagreed with Speke's findings. The dispute continued for some years after the original discovery.

Prior to the 20th century, the Nile had a flood period and a dry period each year. During the flood, silt from upriver was deposited in the Egyptian delta, creating rich farmland. The surplus water from the flood was trapped in basins for later use in irrigation. The dry period greatly reduced the river's size and depth, making river transportation difficult in places.

In the mid 1870s, Englishwoman Amelia B. Edwards made a Nile River trip during the dry season. She wrote the following comment about river travel during that time of the year:

> Our progress all this time is the slowest. The men cannot row by day; and at night the sand banks so hedge us in with dangers that the only possible way by which we can make a few miles is by sheer, hard punting. Now and then we come to a clear channel, and sometimes we get an hour or two of sweet south breeze; but these flashes are few and far between.[9]

The Nile was successfully dammed 550 miles south of Cairo in 1902. A dam at Aswan has been rebuilt several times since the first one was completed. In 1971 the Egyptians finished the construction of the famous Aswan High Dam. A dispute over the Western decision to withdraw funding for this project set in motion a series of events that eventually led to the Egyptian nationalization of the Suez Canal, followed by the 1956 Suez War. This war pitted Britain, France, and Israel against Egypt. Russian support for Egypt included funding and help with the construction of the dam, which led to a Soviet military and political presence in Egypt for twenty years.

A great deal has been written about the controversial environment implications of the High Dam project. Studies have shown that the changes caused by ending the Nile flood by damming the river have resulted in the depletion of delta soil for agriculture. Egyptian officials respond that there have been dams ending the flood since 1902. Furthermore, the Nile Delta's topsoil is very deep and, if need be, fertilizers can be applied to renew the land.

Other critics charge that artificial irrigation of rural lands has resulted in the accumulation of large amounts of stagnant water. This water has brought on an increase in water-related diseases such as bilharziasis.[10] They also complain that heavy silting in the standing water of Lake Nasser has reduced food and limited the fish catch downstream. The Egyptian response is that population growth dictated that they had no other choice than to build the dam. Without the dam, Egypt would run short of food. It is true there have been no Egyptian famines since the first dam was completed by the British at the beginning of the 20th century.

The Aswan High Dam has increased land under Egyptian cultivation by around 30 percent. Electricity generated by the dam's power provides lights for places where it did not previously exist. On balance, Egyptians believe the good produced by damming the Nile far outweighs any environmental damage that may have been caused.

THE TIGRIS

The Tigris and Euphrates make up the major parts of the second greatest river system of the Middle East and North Africa. The two rivers are always spoken of together when referring to this part of the Fertile Crescent. They flow parallel to each other until they and the Karun, from Iran, merge to form the Shatt al Arab before reaching the Persian Gulf.

The Tigris rises in the Taurus Mountains and flows 1,150 miles through Turkey and Iraq before reaching the sea. Because the Tigris has a fast current and irregular volume, it is subject to wide-scale flooding. To protect the city of Baghdad, the government has constructed a large system of dams, dikes, and canals. This scheme protects the city and provides a source of irrigation water for a large portion of the farmland around the capital city.

During World War I, the Tigris was the scene of one of the greatest defeats in British military history. A British force was sent up the river from Basra with the aim of capturing Baghdad from the Ottomans. Commanded by Major-General Charles Vere Ferrers Townshend, the British advanced all the way to Ctesiphon before being stopped 25 miles from their goal. The exhausted British began their famous retreat along the Tigris. After moving south 100 miles, General Townshend decided that he could not reach the safety of Basra. He positioned his troops on a peninsula in the Tigris River called Kut al-Amara to wait for a rescue from the south. After a siege that lasted 146 days, the British realized that help was not coming. The garrison was surrounded in April 1916. The surviving British prisoners were marched to work camps in Turkey. Few survived to return to their homes in England.[11]

The Tigris is navigable as far as Baghdad. Beyond that, the shallowness makes the river unsuitable for large boats. There is a rail line that carries freight along the Tigris from Baghdad through the oil center at Mosul to the Syrian border and beyond.

THE EUPHRATES

The Euphrates and the Tigris Rivers have origins near each other in eastern Turkey. The Euphrates, however, takes a winding route through Turkey and Syria before entering Iraq. The length of the Euphrates is almost double that of the Tigris, traveling 2,235 miles before reaching the Persian Gulf.

A great deal of work has been done in Turkey to harness the river to provide electric power and water for irrigation. This has caused some concern in Syria and Iraq. The Syrians, however, have also constructed a large dam at Tabqa. Most of the Euphrates is too shallow for navigation. In eastern Syria, the river is only a slow-shifting stream. Ancient flooding and overirrigation have caused large areas near the Euphrates to accumulate salt deposits on the surface, causing the land to become unproductive. In parts of Syria, the land remains much as Lady Jane Digby described it in 1854, when she is quoted as writing that it was "a desolate and burning country."[12]

Along the southern portions of the Iraqi Euphrates are the ruins of a number of ancient kingdoms that include Sippar, Kish, Uruk, Eridu, and Ur. Like the Egyptian settlements along the Nile, these kingdoms depended on the Euphrates and Tigris for existence.

THE SHATT AL ARAB

Created by the merging of the Euphrates, Tigris, and Karun Rivers, the Shatt al Arab is a slow-moving, meandering, ever-changing river. It flows through a rich marshland for about 120 miles before reaching the sea near the city of Basra. This area contains lush vegetation, including large groves of date palms. Basra at the mouth of the river is the major seaport for Iraq. Since the 1992 Gulf War, this port has lost much trade. In the long term, Basra and the Shatt al Arab should return to their former importance.

In the aftermath of the Gulf War, pockets of resistance to the central government emerged among the inhabitants of the Shatt al Arab area, who were called the Marsh Arabs. Sadam Hussein's response was to build a series of diversion channels to drain portions of the area. This action enabled the Iraqi forces to enter the drained marshes and take action to suppress these formerly isolated dissident groups.

THE JORDAN

When first visiting the Jordan River in 1895, Marion Harland remarked that,

> All visitors agree in pronouncing the Jordan a disappointment at first sight. It is, to put it plainly, a mere creek—by actual measurement, one hundred and ten feet wide, and seemingly not more than fifty.[13]

When compared with other well-known rivers, the Jordan is insignificant. Only 200 miles long, the Jordan flows from Lake Tiberius through the Jordan Valley to end in the Dead Sea. Along the way it is reduced to a small muddy stream. As it enters the Dead Sea it becomes salty.

The headwaters for the Jordan come from sources in Lebanon and Syria. These streams eventually find their way into Lake Tiberius, exiting to the south as the Jordan River. Throughout most of the year, the Jordan is hardly more than a shallow riverlet and is not navigable. During the months of winter rain, the river increases in depth and turbulence. The Jordan is the world's lowest river, flowing into the Dead Sea below sea level. The river forms the current border between Israel and Jordan.

The Jordan River
The far bank of the Jordan can be seen through the branches of the tree in the foreground.
Source: Joe Weatherby

The Jordan is more important for historic, religious, and political reasons than for its size. Historically, the Jordan is the site of the Biblical city of Jericho. Dating back to around 7000 B.C.E., Jericho is one of the claimants to being the oldest city in the world. It controlled the ancient route across the Jordan to Jerusalem. In Biblical times, the city fell to the army of Joshua, who opened the door to the "promised land" for the Israelites. The Biblical story states that the walls of Jericho collapsed, according to God's promise, leaving the city defenseless:

> And it came to pass, when the people heard the sound of the trumpet, and the people shouted with a great shout, that the walls fell down flat, so that the people went up into the city, every man straight before him, and they took they city.[14]

Modern Jericho is located on the Jordan near the site of the ancient city. By agreement, it was handed over to the Palestinian authority by Israel in 1994.

The Jordan is the traditional site for a number of events that Christians believe occurred during the life of Jesus. Perhaps the most important is the tradition that Jesus was baptized in the River Jordan. There are three sites that lay claim to being the location of the baptism. The best-known site is at the Kasar el Yehud on the western shore. This has been the traditional location visited by Orthodox Christians for more than one thousand years, and it is also the location of several Orthodox and Roman Catholic churches and monasteries. Pope John Paul II gave added legitimacy to this site by scheduling a visit to it during a tour of the Holy Land in March 2000.

A second possible West Bank baptismal site is near Kibbutz Kinneret about 40 miles to the north. It was opened to provide Christians access to the Jordan when the Kasar el Yehud location was declared a closed military area by the Israeli army. More than 500,000 Christian pilgrims visit the Kibbutz annually.

The newest proposed baptismal site is at Wadi Kharrar on the east bank of the Jordan just across the river from the traditional site. Jordanian archeologists say that their site is more likely the location for the baptism than the site of Kasar el Yehud because of the clear springs located at Wadi Kharrar. They believe that Jesus would never have selected the muddy water of the river itself for a baptism. The dispute is one of many that has developed along the Jordan. This time Jews and Muslims are competing for Christian tourist dollars.

Probably the most important issue involving the Jordan River today is political. There is a great deal of disagreement about how the water will be shared between three distrustful neighbors: Israel, Syria, and Jordan. Because there is very little water and because the land has little value without water, the resolution of this issue is critical to any lasting peace settlement between Israel and Syria. The sources of water for Lake Tiberius and the Jordan River are located in the Golan Heights, once part of Syria and now "annexed" by Israel, and the streams controlled by Lebanon. In 1955, U.S. Ambassador Eric Johnson negotiated a water-distribution plan. Although never implemented, this plan divided the "upper Jordan" water. As Syria and Israel discuss the provisions of a final peace, the old Johnson plan formula may provide a framework for discussing water rights along with the status of southern Lebanon and Golan Heights.

The Jordan River is the subject of several treaties and agreements between Israel, Jordan, and the Palestinian authority. These documents cover water-distribution issues, environmental issues, and access issues. The hard fact remains that the Jordan does not contain enough water for all of the parties to receive everything that they want. Until a new source of water can be developed, the River Jordan will continue to be a source of tension.

Where Are Some of the Famous Smaller but Important Cities?

Most readers are familiar with the great urban centers of the Middle East and North Africa. Cities such as Cairo, Istanbul, and Baghdad are mentioned in the world's newspapers daily. Included here are short studies of eight smaller cities and towns. Although some of these places are less well known, each plays an important role as a historic, political, or religious center.

BETHLEHEM

Bethlehem, population 100,000, is located about 5 miles from Jerusalem. The city has a special significance to Christians because it is the birthplace of Jesus and the center for numerous Bible stories. Christians believe Jesus to be the promised Messiah spoken of in the Old Testament Book of Micah.

> But thou, Bethlehem Ephratah, though thou be little among the thousands of Judah, yet out of thee shall he come forth unto me that is to be ruler in Israel; whose goings forth have been from old, from everlasting.[15]

The traditional site for the birthplace of Jesus is located in a grotto underneath the altar of the Church of the Nativity. First consecrated by the Emperor Constantine in 315 C.E., the church was rebuilt by Emperor Justinian in the 6th century. Saving this church was a major objective of the Christian army during the Crusades of the Middle Ages.

A dispute over Ottoman security at the church was one of the issues that led to the Crimean War of 1853. In 1852, a squabble over who had the right to protect the Christian holy places in Palestine broke out between France, Russia, and the Ottoman Empire. This dispute resulted in a war that eventually pitted the Ottoman Empire, Britain, Sardinia, and France against Russia. The war was largely fought in the Crimean area of the Black Sea. Although control of the Christian holy places was the trigger that started this conflict, the real objective was to block Russian attempts to expand their influence into the Eastern Mediterranean.

During the 1967 war with Jordan, Bethlehem was captured by Israeli forces. It was administered by Israeli military forces until turned over to the Palestinian Authority in 1995.

JERUSALEM

No city in the world provokes as much passion and conflict among Jews, Christians, and Muslims as does Jerusalem. Jerusalem is a holy city for these three great religions. All three claim the city as the source of their common heritage. In addition, Christians and Muslims identify parts of the city with events that occurred in the lives of both Jesus and Muhammad.

The Old Walled City is divided into quarters, each populated by a different ethnic group. The Muslim quarter contains the Dome of the Rock, located on Mount Moriah. Below the Dome is a large wall called the Wailing Wall, which is sacred to Jews. It is believed to be the only surviving portion of the temple built by King Solomon. The Christian quarter contains the Church of the Holy Sepulcher, where Christians believe that Jesus died, was buried, and arose from the dead.

Surrounding the Old Walled City is a modern one that is mainly populated by Jews. Today, Jews make up about three-fourths of the city's residents. Politically, Jerusalem is the official capital of the State of Israel. East Jerusalem has always been recognized as Palestinian territory by the Arab states. It, like the rest of the city, remains under Israeli control. Few states recognize the permanent status of the whole city as Israeli. Consequently, most foreign embassies are located in Tel Aviv.[16]

KARBALA

Karbala is a city of 180,000 people located 50 miles south of Baghdad. It is built on the site of the famous battle of the same name that took place in 680 C.E. This clash finally separated the Shiite and the Sunni branches of Islam. The battle was fought between two claimants for the title of successor to the prophet. Hussein ibn Ali was the leader of the Shiite faction in this dispute. During the battle, a large force of Sunni supporting the other claimant, Yazid, killed the grandsons of the prophet, Hussein ibn Ali and his brother Hasan.

According to Shiite thinking, the martyrdom of Ali can be compared with the Christian emotions concerning the death of Jesus. Like the Church of the Holy Sepulcher in Jerusalem, the tombs of Ali and Abbas Muhammad's uncle are, for the Shia, second only to Mecca as a pilgrimage place. The modern-day city of Karbala is an Iraqi provincial capital. It has an economy centered around Shiite pilgrimages. There is also important trade in dates and wool.

MECCA

Like Jerusalem, Mecca is an ancient city with a tradition as a religious center that predates Islam. Mecca is the birthplace of the prophet Muhammad. It is here that Muslims believe that Muhammad received his earliest revelations. From Mecca, Muhammad fled to Medina, an event marked to this day as the beginning of the Muslim calendar.

Mecca is located about 50 miles inland from the Red Sea. It is the principal pilgrimage site for Muslims throughout the world. The focus of the pilgrimage is the Great Mosque, which encloses a square, pre-Islamic building called the *Kabba*.

Today Mecca is reached by both sea and air transportation. The principal entry point for pilgrims is the Saudi Arabian port of Jidda. From Jidda, it is only a short drive over a modern highway to Mecca. Non-Muslims are not permitted to visit Mecca.

MEDINA

Medina is a Saudi Arabian city of around half a million people located 100 miles east of the Red Sea. It was to Medina that Muhammad fled when he was forced to leave Mecca. Medina is where the first large conversions to Islam took place. Medina was also the base for the Muslim conquest of Arabia. It was the site of Muhammad's death. Today, the Prophet's Mosque contains the tombs of Muhammad, his daughter Fatima, and the Caliphs Omar and Abu Bakr. Medina is also a pilgrimage site for Muslims. Like Mecca, non-Muslims are forbidden entry to Medina. In common use, a Medina is a city or town. It usually refers to the old quarter as opposed to the modern European districts of the city.

ESFAHAN

Located in south central Iran, Esfahan is one of the most historic cities in the country. Already important before the Arab conquest in 632 C.E., it reached its nadir when Shah Abbas came to power in 1587 C.E. The Shah made Esfahan the capital of Persia. For about one hundred years, Esfahan was one of the most important cities in the world. During this time, great public buildings, squares, parks, and mosques were constructed. The square of Meidun-e Emam Khomeini is recognized as second only to China's Tiananmen Square in size. Esfahan lays claim to having "invented the game of polo." It is certain that one of the earliest polo fields was located next to the royal palace.

KAIROUAN

Kairouan is considered by Muslims to be the most important holy city in North Africa. This Tunisian city is situated 40 miles west of modern Tunis. The glory of the city is the Great Mosque. Built in its present form between 836 and 875 C.E., this mosque served as the architectural model for Muslim buildings throughout North Africa and Spain. The structure features a large, open courtyard surrounded by covered passages. The square minaret is the oldest remaining minaret in North Africa. It was copied throughout the region. The most famous European example of this type of minaret is the Giralda Tower, which is now part of the gothic cathedral in Seville, Spain.[17]

MARRAKECH

Marrakech is a Berber city situated inland near the Atlas Mountains of Morocco. The city was the capital of Morocco from 1062 until 1147 C.E. It was also Morocco's capital during parts of the 15th and 16th centuries. It is famous for its beautiful gardens and impressive mosques.

Marrakech was an important political center during the French colonial occupation from 1913 to 1956. The French officials exercised their power through alliances with a local family headed by Thami el Glaoui. Under French guidance, el Glaoui built an empire in the Atlas Mountains that rivaled that of the Sultan of Morocco. More than any other Atlas chief, Thami el Glaoui profited from collaborating with the French colonialists.[18] When Morocco gained its independence from France and Spain in 1956, the power of the

Kairouan Tunisia

The entrance to the Great Mosque of Kairouan. Built between 836 and 875 C.E., the Great Mosque is considered to be one of the most important in Islam. The low entrance hides a magnificent open courtyard that is 65 meters by 50 meters. At the far end of the courtyard is a famous square minaret that is three stories tall. The stories are stacked one on top of the other, with each one above smaller than the one below.

Source: Joe Weatherby

Glaouis and other local Atlas chiefs was broken. The capital of the new kingdom of Morocco became Rabat.

Today Marrakech is a particularly interesting city of about half a million people. It retains the old walled town, the casbah, which is surrounded by a modern French city. Marrakech is still an important gateway to the Sahara, in the south, and to the capital, Rabat. Its warm, dry climate, beautiful gardens, and old casbah have made Marrakech an important tourist center in recent years.

Where Are the Famous Dead "Cities of the Sand"?

In 1972, Aubrey Menen used the term "cities of the sand" to describe a number of abandoned cities in the Middle East and North Africa. Today, it is startling to wander among the ruins of a once great city resting untouched and alone. Places like Volubilis in northern Morocco give the impression that they could be reroofed, electrified, and inhabited today. Standing in the ruins of Volubilis, one is prompted to ask why there are cities like this? Six ancient sites have been included here as examples of these sand cities.

CARTHAGE

Located only a few miles from the modern city of Tunis, the capital of Tunisia, the remains of Carthage are the least abandoned ruins among those in North Africa. Carthage is a suburb of Tunis. It is surrounded by modern, upscale housing. The remains of the Old

Old Morocco
This old casbah survives to dominate the village below. It and dozens like it evoke memories of el Glaoui and the other great chiefs who ruled this part of Morocco.
Source: Joe Weatherby

A Sand City
The ruins of Volubilis, built by the Romans in Northern Morocco.
Source: Joe Weatherby

City are largely Roman and not very impressive to the uninformed visitor. They indicate little of the greatness of ancient Carthage. Founded in the 9th century B.C.E., Carthage ruled most of the southern Mediterranean for hundreds of years. In 264 B.C.E., the Carthaginians and the Romans clashed in a series of wars that lasted for a hundred years. Called the *Punic War,* these struggles eventually resulted in the total destruction of Carthage.

The city was not rebuilt by the Romans until the 1st century C.E. Carthage then became the capital of Rome's most important overseas possession, called Africa Nova. This colony was the breadbasket of Rome. When the empire finally collapsed, Africa Nova was abandoned. Today, ancient Carthage is only a series of archeological sites overlooking the Bay of Tunis.

SBEITLA

It has been said that there are over three hundred abandoned ancient sites in Tunisia. More than fifty of these are of major importance to archeologists. Established by the Romans during the 1st century C.E., Sbeitla is typical of the abandoned sand cities of North Africa. Located in western Tunisia near the famous World War II battlefield at Kasserine,

Sbeitla is of interest because it was simply abandoned and nothing was built on top of it. Like many other sand cities, Sbeitla is largely untouched. Sitting on a deserted plain, Sbeitla's ancient columns, mosaic floors, spectacular gateway, and three main temples survive largely intact. Little archeological work has been done here. The modern visitor is surrounded by the emptiness of the place. Sheep and goats roam freely among the ruins of what was once a thriving city.

Little is known about Sbeitla's Roman past. It became part of Christian Rome for a time. Some stones from the ancient temples can be found in the remains of the nearby Byzantine churches that thrived before the Arab conquest. Today Sbeitla remains only an interesting footnote in the story of Rome's colonies that once fed the empire.

PETRA

Lost and forgotten for a thousand years, Petra was rediscovered in 1812 by John Ludwig Burckhardt. When visiting this site in 1839, the English traveler John Kinnear gave these first impressions of Petra:

> It is certainly one of the most wonderful scenes in the world. The eye wanders in amazement from the stupendous rampart of rocks, which surround the valley, to the porticos and ornamented doorways sculptured on the surface. The dark yawning entrances to the temples and tombs and the long ranges of excavated chambers, give an air of emptiness and desolation to the scene, which I cannot well describe. . . . [19]

Petra was established at a strategic point on the ancient caravan route that stretched from Oman and Yemen across the Arabian Desert to Baghdad. The principal trade going north was spices. At times, goods from as far away as the Orient passed through here. The Nabateans, who built the city, became rich because of this trade.

The city fell into decline after it was captured by the Romans during the 1st century C.E. Rome rerouted the caravans away from Petra. Later Petra was occupied by the Byzantines, and it was a Christian city until it fell to Muslim invaders during the Arab conquest. The city was again briefly held by Christians during the Crusades, but after the Christian withdrawal, Petra was largely abandoned by the Arabs and forgotten by the West.

There has been a great deal of speculation as to why this city was abandoned. Certainly the loss of the caravan trade destroyed the primary economy. Most believe, however, that a series of earthquakes devastated important parts of Petra. Don Belt has suggested that these earthquakes affected the complex series of aqueducts, dams, and pools that provided water for Petra. Without a reliable water source, this desert city could not survive.[20]

Petra is located north of the Gulf of Aqaba in an isolated part of Jordan and is difficult to reach. Once there, the visitor follows a deep, narrow passage through the rocks, which eventually opens out onto a large valley that is covered with monuments, temples, and tombs carved out of living sandstone. Although much of the city is still to be excavated, Petra is one of the most impressive cities of sand in the Middle East.

BAALBECK

Baalbeck is technically not a sand city because it is located 35 miles from Beirut in the beautiful Bekaa Valley. It ranks as one of the great abandoned ruins of the ancient world. Baalbeck is also not isolated, as it is adjacent to the modern town of the same

The Wonder of Baalbeck
The six remaining columns of the Temple of Jupiter are often used as the symbol for Lebanon. Note the size of the columns in relation to the adult standing to the right.
Source: Joe Weatherby

name. Baalbeck's temples, arches, and walls have the appearance of having been built for use by giants.

Founded in ancient times, Baalbeck became an important Roman city during the 1st and 2nd centuries C.E. The great temples were constructed during this time. Baalbeck was conquered and plundered on numerous occasions. Most of the temples were either damaged or destroyed by a great earthquake that occurred during the 18th century C.E. What remains includes six great columns of the Temple of Jupiter. These columns are one of the best-known symbols of modern Lebanon.

PALMYRA

Today Syrians use the more ancient name Tadmor for the town adjacent to the ruins of Palmyra. The ruins are located in an oasis in the middle of the Syrian Desert. Lady Jane Digby visited the place while escorting a party of English tourists in June 1864. Describing this visit, she is quoted as writing:

> We went the whole day without stopping, mostly trotting to get in before sunset, and, at last, as we attained the last hill an ever glorious panorama of Tadmor and its long-departed glories lay stretched before us. Alas, half hour too late for the sun no longer brightly illuminated the colonnade; the columns were white instead of golden as I wish them to be. Still, the party was astounded. . . .[21]

Palmyra grew to greatness during the 3rd century C.E. when it challenged Rome for the control of Mesopotamia and Syria. Under the legendary Queen Zenobia, Palmyra became a serious threat to the eastern empire of Rome. Eventually, Queen Zenobia was defeated by the Romans and the city of Palmyra was destroyed. Palmyra declined in importance and was forgotten by Europeans until it was rediscovered during the 17th century C.E. Today, several temples, a theater, and the great colonnade mentioned by Jane Digby still survive. Palmyra remains as it has for almost two thousand years: a true city of sand.

PERSEPOLIS

Located 30 miles from the modern Iranian city of Shiraz, Persepolis is the site of the "formal" capital of Darius the Great and Xerxes. The Persian Empire's political capitals were located at Susa in Iran and Babylon in Iraq.

Built on a huge stone platform, the ruins of Persepolis include massive carvings, majestic columns, a monumental grand staircase, a huge gate, and two large stone bulls that guard the site. The city was used more as a royal summer palace than as a major city. Persepolis probably had more than several thousand inhabitants. It was a huge palace for the Persian king.

Persepolis was most important between 520 B.C.E. and 420 B.C.E. The city was destroyed by Alexander the Great in 330 B.C.E. Although it was practically rebuilt, Persepolis did not survive the Arab period when the political and religious activities of Persia were moved elsewhere. Forgotten by the world, Persepolis became a city of sand until rediscovered in the 20th century.

During the 20th century Pahlavi Dynasty, the Iranian leadership sought to establish political legitimacy by linking their rule to the leaders of ancient Persia. Persepolis became a center for rediscovering the greatness of ancient Persia. Following the example of Mussolini in Italy, the Pahlavis gloried in the greatness of the Persian past. In 1972, Shah Muhammad Reza Pahlavi hosted the world's kings, queens, and other important leaders at a great celebration held at the Persepolis site. When the Shah was overthrown in 1979, the new Islamic government did not know what to do with Persepolis. Somewhat like the

Bolsheviks' approach to preserving the palaces in Russia, the Iranian government preserved, but chose to ignore, Persepolis. Today few tourists see this former great palace complex. Persepolis sleeps until it is again rediscovered by the outside world.

What Additional Terms Are Important to Know?

Short glossaries such as this will appear near the end of most chapters. Before beginning, several clarifications should be made. Two problems face anyone seeking to define terms used in the Middle East and North Africa: transliteration and geographically specific uses of words.

Transliteration is the process of changing the letters and words from one language to another during translation. In the Middle East and North Africa, the Arabic alphabet is used for writing Arabic and Persian. The sounds of Arabic, Persian, and Turkish differ from those of English. When translating from one of these languages to English, some transliteration is often necessary. Translators try to reproduce the sounds of the original language by using the process of transliteration into English. The problem is that there may be several ways to correctly spell the same word when it is transliterated. Beginners often become confused and incorrectly assume that these spelling differences indicate that they are reading words with different meanings. For example, the name of the Prophet Muhammad may be spelled in English at least four different ways: Mohammid, Muhammed, Muhammad, or Mahomet. Here, when known, I will use the most common spelling. Sometimes a secondary spelling will be placed in brackets.

The second problem occurs because the meaning of words often changes with geography. The region under discussion in this book stretches from the Atlantic Ocean to the borders of Afghanistan and Pakistan. Words change in meaning when used by people spread out over such great distances. Again, when possible, I will give the most common usages of words. Where there are major exceptions, they will also be added to the definitions.

CASBAH [KASBAH]

In popular usage, the casbah is the old quarter of North African cities like Algiers, Algeria. However, the word literally describes a walled city or fortress in North Africa. The Kasbah des Oudaia near Rabat, Morocco, is an example of a traditional casbah. It was built around the 12th century when Sultan Yacoub el-Monsour established his capital at Rabat. The casbah was used as a fortress to protect the harbor from attack. The Kasbah des Oudaia is interesting because it still stands walled and alone outside the main city of Rabat. Like the old walled cities of Europe, most North African cities have overwhelmed their casbahs. Although many have even lost their walls, they still are called casbahs. This is probably the source of some definitional confusion by visitors.

SOUK [SUQ, SOUQ]

A *souk* is a marketplace. Typically, the souk has a winding narrow street with specific areas allocated for selling certain items. For example, there may be areas for goldsmiths, rug sellers, and spice merchants. In North Africa many souks have covers of straw matting to shield shoppers from the sun. The terms *casbah, medina,* and *souk* are often used interchangeably to refer to the old quarter of a city. This is probably because in places such as Casablanca, Algiers, and Tunis, the old city has been engulfed by the growth of the new areas. Compared with the new city, the old town is very small, so no specific distinction between the casbah, the medina, and the souk needs to be made.

In the Arabian Peninsula, *souks* may refer to specific stores or groups of stores. For example, in new towns along the Persian Gulf, the gold souk may refer to a collection of shops that have the appearance of a European jewelry store.

BAZAAR

Similar to a souk, the *bazaar* is a marketplace. Cities like Istanbul and Damascus have vast covered bazaars that are hundreds of years old. In some of the new cities of Arabia such as Jubail, Dhahran, and al-Khubar, however, a bazaar can be anything from a large supermarket to a modern shopping mall. The use of the word *bazaar* is more common in the Middle East than in North Africa.

DASHT

Dasht is a Persian (Iranian) word meaning desert. It usually refers to a flat, gravel, or salt desert. The two most famous Iranian examples are the Dasht-e Kavir and the Dasht-e Lut, which were discussed previously in this chapter.

KAVIR

Kavir means salt in Persian. Thus, the Dasht-e Kavir is a salt desert.

DESERT

Surprisingly, there are a number of opinions as to what constitutes a desert. Not surprisingly, people from the region have a number of words that they use to describe various kinds of deserts. For example, they use the terms *col, dasht, hamad, harra, uruq, nafus, ramlah, riz, sahara,* and *zibarr,* among others, to identify various kinds of wasteland. F. J. Monkhouse defines a desert as "a land with scanty rainfall and therefore with little vegetation and limited human use."[22] Catherine Thompson defines the desert as "an arid area without sufficient rainfall and, consequently, vegetation to support human life."[23]

When flying over the Sahara in the early 1930s, the adventure writer Richard Halliburton probably agreed with Catherine Thompson when he described the desert as follows:

> I had pictured in my mind, in advance, what the center of the Sahara was going to be like . . . not one of my prearrangements came true. There were no black mountains, no gullies, no scars, no lions, and no Bedouins—only an endless, endless, ash-yellow sea of sandy gravel in which no human, animal, bird, insect, or vegetable, live or could live. Nothing ever moves but the sand. Nothing ever changes save the alternative light and darkness. In more than a million square miles, only a streak of scarlet and its two lonely passengers broke the vacuum.[24]

It is generally recognized that a desert is an area that receives less than 10 inches of precipitation annually. Thus, the rainfall is so low that human occupation is limited or transitory. It is usually restricted to isolated water holes or oases.

HEJAZ

Hejaz is a word used in Arabic to designate a boundary. Thus, the famous Hejaz of Saudi Arabia is the western province that forms the boundary between the Red Sea and the interior Nefud desert area.

JEBEL [JABAL]

Jebel refers to a mountain or large hill. This widely used word has become part of the name of famous mountains everywhere that Arabic speakers have lived. The following three locations are offered as examples of famous jebels.

On the Spanish coast lies the historic fortress of Gibraltar. Few people know that the name, Gibraltar, comes from the Arabic *Jabal-al-Tarik,* or Mountain of Tarik. It is named in honor of the Muslim leader who captured "the rock" in 711 C.E. Over time, the name has been corrupted by Europeans to the modern *Gibraltar.*

Jabal ash-Shaykh, or Mount Hermon, is a 9,000-foot peak located on the border between Lebanon and Syria. Since 1967, Israeli forces have occupied the southern slopes. It is considered by military authorities to be central to the maintenance of control over this volative region.

Jebel Druze (Jabal ad Druze, Jabel el Druze), the Mountain of the Druze, is a 5,000-foot mountain located on the southwestern border of Syria. Like Mt. Hermon, it is a strategic high ground that has been contested on many occasions by Israel and Syria.

SHATT

Shatt is an Arab word meaning river. The Shatt al Arab forms the boundary between Iran and Iraq. This river was the source of a boundary dispute that provoked the Iran-Iraq war of the 1980s.

WADI

Wadi is an Arab term used to describe a dry stream. Wadis are common in desert areas. They usually have deep, sharp banks. When rain falls in the hills, these dry stream beds can become raging torrents of water that cause a good deal of soil erosion, accounting for their deep channels. The word *wadi* often appears as part of a river's name when it carries some water throughout the year. One of the most important rivers in Spain was once called a wadi. The Guadalquivir was originally named the Wadi al Kavir by the Arabs.

Summary

The Middle East and North Africa form the traditional land bridge connecting Europe, Asia, and Africa. There is little agreement as to what constitutes the Middle East and North Africa. In this text, the region will include the states of North Africa, the Eastern Mediterranean, Arabia, the Persian Gulf, Turkey, and Iran.

The geography of the Middle East may be split into three parts: the plains of North Africa and Arabia, the Fertile Crescent, and the Northern Tier. Most people live along the coast of North Africa and the Eastern Mediterranean. Within this largely desert region lie two great rivers systems. The Nile is the most important river in Africa. The Tigris, Euphrates, and Karun unite to form the Shatt al Arab that flows into the Persian Gulf near the cities of Basra in Iraq and Abadan in Iran.

Review Questions

1. Can you locate the Middle East on an outline map?
2. Where is the Holy Land?
3. What is the Levant?
4. Why did the Trucial Coast acquire that name?
5. What are the Cities of the Sand?

Suggested Readings

Kenneth Davis, *Don't Know Much About Geography; Everything You Need to Know About the World But Never Learned,* Avon Books, New York, 1992.

Alexander McKee. *El Alamein; Ultra and the Three Battles,* Souvenir Press, Chatham, Kent, United Kingdom, 1991.

Alan Moorehead, *The White Nile,* Harper and Row, New York, 1971. *The Blue Nile,* Harper and Row, New York, 1972.

Matthew Rosenberg, *The Handy Geography Answer Book,* Visible Ink Press, Canton, Michigan, 1999.

Jennifer Westwood, *Mysterious Places; The World's Unexplained Symbolic Sites; Ancient Cities and Lost Lands,* Marshall Editions Ltd., London, United Kingdom, 1927.

Notes

1. John L. Stoddard, *Stoddard's Lectures,* Vol II (Chicago and Boston: George L. Shuman and Co., 1897), p. 113.
2. Bible, Zechariah 2:12
3. John Keay, *The Royal Geographical Society History of World Exploration* (New York: Mallard Press, 1991), pp. 116–118.
4. George Cressy, *Crossroads: Land and Life in Southwest Asia* (New York: J. B. Lippincott Co., 1960), p. 315.
5. T. E. Lawrence, *The Seven Pillars of Wisdom: A Triumph* (New York: Garden City Publishing Co., 1938), p. 72.
6. John Haywood, *Atlas World History* (New York: Barnes and Noble Books, 1998), Section No. 4.
7. Marion Harland, *Home of the Bible: A Woman's Vision of the Master's Land* (Chicago: Monarch Book Co, 1895), p. 110.
8. Bible, Genesis 8:4.
9. Amelia B. Edwards, *A Thousand Miles Up the Nile* (New York/Boston: H. M. Caldwell Co., 1877), p. 438.
10. Bilharziasis is a disease that attacks the internal organs in humans. It is spread by a worm that lives in fresh water snails until it finds a human host. Humans contract the disease by washing in or drinking standing water populated by the snails. If left untreated, this disease can cause death. The cost of treating bilharziasis is too high for many developing countries, so the disease is widespread. Although it has existed in the Nile Valley for thousands of years, bilharziasis has become a much more serious threat to humans in Egypt in modern times. The disease has spread because of the switch from natural flooding to permanent irrigation, which provides an ideal environment for the snails to multiply.
11. David Fromkin, *A Peace to End All Peace: Creating the Modern Middle East 1914–1922* (New York: Henry Holt and Co., 1989), pp. 201–202.
12. Mary Lovell. *Rebel Heart: The Scandalous Life of Jane Digby* (New York/London: W. W. Norton and Co., 1995), p. 178.
13. Harland, p. 263.
14. Bible, Joshua 6:20.
15. Bible, Micah 5:2.
16. More information on Jerusalem may be found in Chapter 7.
17. Henri Stierlin, *Islam Vol. I: Early Architecture from Baghdad to Cordoba* (Cologne, Germany: Taschen Publishing, 1996), pp. 169–170.
18. Douglas Porch, *The Conquest of Morocco* (New York: Alfred A. Knopf, 1983), pp. 290–291.
19. Wolfgang Schuler, *In the Holy Land: Paintings by David Roberts 1839* (London: Studio Editions Ltd., 1995), p. 21.

20. Don Belt, "Petra: Ancient City of Stone," *The National Geographic,* Vol. 194, No. 6 (December 1998), p. 122.
21. Lovell, p. 270.
22. F. A. Monkhouse, *A Dictionary of Geography* (Chicago: Aldine Publishing Company, 1965), p. 93.
23. Catherine Thompson, Editor, *Hutchinson Dictionary of Geography* (London: Brockhampton Press, 1993), p. 51.
24. Richard Halliburton, *The Flying Carpet* (Indianapolis: The Bobbs-Merrill Co., 1932), p. 28.

Chapter 2

The Geostrategic Middle East and North Africa

Introduction

Politics and geography have been linked since the dawn of history. For generations, students of Latin have translated the famous sentences from Caesar's *Gallic Wars:* "All Gaul is divided into three parts" and "Britain is an island." In modern times the study of politics and geography has become a subfield of geography, called *political geography.*

What is political geography? Perhaps the best definition for the purpose of this study was written almost 40 years ago by Lewis Alexander. He defined political geography as "the study of political regions as features of the earth's surface." He stated further that,

> By studying political phenomena in their association with other features of the earth's surface such as landforms, water bodies, or settlement patterns, political geographers are able to describe and analyze the diverse ways in which man organizes space for political purposes.[1]

Stated another way, political geography focuses on the geographic relations of states.

Why Are the Middle East and North Africa Geographically Important Areas?

The strategic importance of the Middle East and North Africa has been known for centuries. The ease of water transportation by way of the seas and straits of this region was well known to the Phoenicians, Greeks, and Romans. This geographic fact of life is no less important today.

The Middle East is surrounded by six seas: the Mediterranean Sea, the Black Sea, the Caspian Sea, the Red Sea, the Arabian Sea, and the Sea of Marmara. The region also contains five gulfs: the Gulf of Suez, the Gulf of Aqaba, the Gulf of Aden, the Gulf of Oman, and the Persian Gulf.

In spite of the ease of travel across the seas and gulfs, six easily blocked straits called "chokepoints" hamper entering and exiting the region by water. These narrow water passages are the Strait of Gibraltar, the Dardanelles, the Bosporus, the Strait of Hormuz, the Strait of Tiran and the Bab el Mandeb Strait. Several of these waterways are important enough to be described in more detail.

The Mediterranean Sea   The Mediterranean Sea is connected to the Atlantic Ocean by the Strait of Gibraltar, to the Black Sea by the Dardanelles and Bosporus, and to the Red Sea by the Suez Canal. Its location as the world's largest inland sea has made the Mediterranean a primary vehicle for commerce since ancient times. It provides easy access by calm water to southern Europe, Africa, and the Middle East. The main problem is that access by water to the ocean can be easily cut off at the Bosporus, the Suez, or the Strait of Gibraltar.

The Black Sea   Connected to the Mediterranean by the Bosporus and the Dardanelles, the Black Sea separates Europe from Asia. It is the only naturally ice-free access that the Ukraine and Russia have to the Mediterranean and beyond.

The Caspian Sea   Surrounded by Russia, Kazakhstan, Turkmenistan, Iran, and Azerbaijan, the Caspian Sea is the largest lake in area in the world. The Caspian's source of water is the Volga River. It is world famous as the source of fine caviar. Developed early in the 20th century, Baku, Azerbaijan, became one of the world's first major centers of oil production.

At the end of the 20th century, new discoveries of oil along the eastern shore of the Caspian Sea set off a new "oil race." Early surveys predicted that these discoveries could rival in size the reserves of the Persian Gulf.

The Persian Gulf   Long the dividing line between the Arab world and Persia, the Gulf was an object of competition and conflict during modern times. Even its name is disputed. Although generally recognized as the Persian Gulf by the world, Arabs usually refer to it as the Arab Gulf. The discovery of the largest oil reserves on the planet has made this region of "vital national interest" to the West. Outside of Europe, the Gulf is one of the few areas of the world that the United States has stated in advance that it will go to war to defend. In 1991 it did just that when it used force to liberate Kuwait.

The Gulf is oval shaped, with the Shatt al Arab serving as the northern entrance. The only southern exit to the Indian Ocean is through the Strait of Hormuz. This 25-mile-wide passage is a strategic nightmare. It is dotted with islands and has hostile neighbors on each side. Because most of the Gulf oil going to the West and Japan must pass through the Strait of Hormuz, it is one of the most potentially explosive passages in the world. To reduce the reliance on a passage that is in danger of being blocked during the time of conflict, Saudi Arabia has constructed a major pipeline that stretches from Jubil across Arabia to the Red Sea port of Yanbu.

The Red Sea   The Red Sea forms a narrow body of water stretching from the Gulf of Suez and the Gulf of Aqaba to the Bab el Mandeb Strait that separates Yemen and Eritrea. During the various wars between Israel and Egypt, the Gulfs of Aqaba and Suez along with the Suez Canal were heavily contested objectives. Today the entrances to both gulfs and to the canal are controlled by Egypt.

What Are the Politics of Geography in the Middle East and North Africa?

The study of political geography in the Middle East and North Africa involves looking at the region from two perspectives. First, the region should be viewed as part of a larger theory of global strategy. Second, there are numerous specific geographic disputes that cause problems in the region regardless of any connection to a greater whole. Both of these approaches to political geography will be discussed in this chapter. In other words, the Middle East plays an important role in "great power" global strategies. Whether linked to this role or not, these disputes can threaten regional peace and stability.

Who Are the Geographic Theorists Whose Ideas Have Influenced the Politics of the Middle East and North Africa?

Napoleon I Most historians date the modern involvement of the West in the Middle East and North Africa to the French invasion of Egypt in 1798. The stated French goal at the time was to establish order between the local princes and the Ottoman Empire. Napoleon, however, had an unstated strategic purpose for his action. He hoped that by occupying Egypt he could cut off the land bridge to the Red Sea from the Mediterranean. In this way, he planned to block British links to India. As a global thinker, he hoped to eventually expel the British from the Indian subcontinent. The French adventure in Egypt was cut short when their navy was defeated by the British Admiral Lord Nelson at the Battle of the Nile (Aboukir Bay). By 1801, the French had been forced out of Egypt and Palestine. France did not become seriously involved in the politics of the region for another 30 years.

Admiral Alfred Thayer Mahan It was the victory at the Nile combined with the ability of the British to move troops by sea to counter Napoleon's land invasion of Spain during the Peninsula War (1808–1814) that impressed a mid-century American naval officer, Alfred Thayer Mahan. First writing after the American Civil War, Mahan had seen his "mothballed" navy reduced to a few armed riverboats and obsolete wooden ships. As a naval officer in a navy that was being downsized, Mahan can be forgiven for being interested in developing a theory that would give the navy a prominent strategic role to play. In this effort, he was successful. He became convinced that the United States needed to imitate the strategy that the British were using for the preservation of their empire. His adoption of the British use of sea power as part of a global strategy eventually led to the creation of America's "Great White Fleet." His advocacy of the use of sea power to project influence made Admiral Mahan the father of the modern American navy.

Simply put, the British had adopted a policy of "gunboat diplomacy" to rapidly project power to any needed spot on the globe. Because 19th-century armies were limited to walking or to horsepower, the British stockpiled supplies and coal for ships at a number of strategic points around the globe. These preparations enabled the British to use their navy to move troops much faster than any opposing land-based army could march to the objective. The British created a network of strategic colonies in the Middle East and North Africa whose purpose was to secure the routes to their economic colonies in Asia. This meant the maintenance of bases at Gibraltar, Malta, Cyprus, Aden, and the Trucial States to protect the Indian Colony. Later the British purchased Egyptian interest in the Suez Canal and even occupied Egypt itself in 1882.

To Mahan, the Middle East and North Africa played a "life-support role" in a global strategy used to maintain the more important economic colonies of the Empire. At this time, the Middle East was important to the West as a means of protecting their more significant colonies in Africa, India, and Asia. The interesting question was: Would Mahan's theory of sea power and strategic colonies remain relevant if technology could be developed to counter the speed of ships?

Sir Halford Mackinder This Englishman believed that technological development was the weakness in Mahan's theory. Writing during the first half of the 20th century, Mackinder pointed out that the development of modern trucks and highways, and later aircraft, enabled land forces to counter the speed of ships. He believed that new technology had shifted power to land-based forces. He proposed that a land force could overcome a naval power by controlling the industrial interior of Europe, which he called the "heartland." He believed that a union of Germany and Russia would be immune to threats from any sea power. Furthermore, by establishing an interior heartland fortress, the land power could exercise control over the largest land mass in the world, Afro-Eurasia. Here the Middle East and North Africa were reduced to a peripheral role of providing a land bridge linking Europe, Asia, and Africa to the heartland. Mackinder's ideas changed the heartland's location during the 40 years that he revised his "land power" theory. His great fear was the German-Russian link that would pit the land powers against Britain and the United States, who were sea powers. In this scenario he believed that the sea powers would likely lose.

Nicholas Spykman The third political geographer whose theory of global strategy had an impact on the region was the American Nicholas Spykman. He argued that the heartland described at times by Mackinder could not control the world from the interior of Afro-Eurasia. He pointed out that the real power was not in the region from central Europe to Siberia. The power of Afro-Eurasia was in the belt of states that stretched from Europe in the west across the southern rim of Russia to China and Japan. In this belt were the masses of people, the resources, and the histories of civilization. The way to prevent a single power from dominating the Afro-Eurasian land mass was through the use of collective security arrangements between the states that form the rim around the heartland. This "rim land" theory called for the states to prevent the heartland from expanding into the Middle East and Africa.

Major Alexander de Seversky The final theorist that deserves brief mention here is Major Alexander de Seversky. A former military flyer and aircraft designer, de Seversky was a passionate advocate of air power. During the Cold War he opposed involvement in regional conflicts because they would weaken the United States. Instead he argued for the use of air power and its destructive capability to check the heartland power, Russia. He believed that the ability to project power through the use of aircraft was sufficient to contain any heartland power. Under his theory, overseas bases would be necessary only to act as fueling stations for aircraft fleets. His theory is useful to us in a discussion on the Middle East only because he correctly predicted that air power could be used to rapidly project power. Encouraging Americans to prepare for change because of the development of air power, de Seversky wrote,

> Admiral Mahan, our great theorist of sea power, long ago noted the lapse of time between technical advances and their strategic exploitation for sea power.

He then stated that because of the new technology of air power,

> Broad oceans will then be just so many English Channels, Skagerraks, and Sicilian Straits. Whether they are barriers to shield a nation or highways of destruction will depend entirely on the size and effectiveness of our air power.[2]

De Seversky was proved correct when the advances in technology enabled the United States to move a military force, largely by air, halfway around the world to the Persian Gulf in only weeks. This air-based force was able to defeat a land-based power in the 1991 Gulf War.

How Do These Four Theories of Global Strategy Apply to the Study of a Region Such as the Middle East and North Africa?

STRATEGIC GEOGRAPHY OF THE MIDDLE EAST AND NORTH AFRICA DURING THE EARLY YEARS OF WESTERN IMPERIALISM

During the past 150 years, the great powers of the West have involved parts of the Middle East and North Africa in the implementation of their strategies. The European takeover of the region during the 19th and 20th centuries is a complex story of conflicting interest coming into play. First, the British wanted to protect their lines of communication with their colonies in East Africa, India, and Asia. This meant that the British continued to use their superior naval power in the Mediterranean, the Red Sea, the Persian Gulf, and the Indian Ocean to protect the major colonies of India and Asia. In the Mediterranean, the British gained the active support of the Ottoman Empire to block French and Russian interest in the region. To maintain this advantage, Britain was required to establish a series of key strategic bases in the Mediterranean Sea and the Indian Ocean. The peace was maintained in the Persian Gulf through the implementation of a truce negotiated with local leaders.

In the 19th century, these bases allowed Britain to maintain a forward-deployed fleet to protect the trade routes and also keep the peace. If called on to fight, the British could use these bases to quickly mobilize the force necessary to defeat any challenger. Mahan's observations correctly analyzed the British strategy of using sea power to protect global interests.

In the 19th century, British power was used in the Middle East and North Africa to keep the trade routes open to places more important to their interests. Their principal strategy was to project enough power to prevent challenges by either France or Russia. Placing their superior battle fleet in strategic locations around the Mediterranean Sea, Indian Ocean, and Persian Gulf guaranteed British security.

In 1875, Britain bought an interest in the Suez Canal from Egypt. In 1882 they used the Ahmad Arabi Pasha riots as an excuse to occupy the Nile Delta. Calling it the "veiled dominion," the British worked behind the screen of Egyptian authorities to extend their control all the way down the western bank of the Red Sea to include the Sudan. By the end of the 19th century, the Sudan was ruled as an Anglo-Egyptian condominium. At this point it might be said that with the establishment of control over Egypt and the Sudan, British strategic interest had expanded past the mere establishment of strategic bases to protect trade with India. Egyptians, however, still say that the best British roads run from Cairo east to the Suez Canal rather than north to south where the people live. Even with Egypt, defense of the canal was a primary interest of the colonial troops. The British claimed that they were temporarily intervening in Egyptian affairs to give the state a sound fiscal administration. They remained in Egypt for 74 years.

Britain, France, and the Ottoman Empire became involved in a war with Russia from 1854 to 1856. This war was fought to prevent a change in the strategic balance in the Mediterranean by Russia. Fought mainly in the Crimea, the war confirmed Mahan's analysis of sea power. For the first time in history, steam-powered ships were able to transport 50,000 troops from Britain to Russia and land them in the Crimea. At the time, that was as difficult a technical feat as the American movement of a half million troops to Saudi Arabia during Operation Desert Storm.

No other 19th-century European rival had sufficient naval forces to implement Mahan's strategy. For the most part, they were forced to react to the British naval action. The United States would not possess that kind of naval power until the Great White Fleet days of the early 20th century.

After the defeats at the Battle of the Nile and at Trafalgar, the French were unable to challenge British sea power directly. In 1830, however, they intervened in Algeria because of a dispute with the French king. It was not until 1848 that the French gained complete control over Algeria, where they established the first French foothold in North Africa. For most of the rest of the 19th century, the French maintained a naval force sufficient to challenge everyone in the region but the British. Their strategy was regional rather than global. They could not have successfully implemented the kind of global program advocated by Mahan. During this period, Spain, Portugal, Germany, Italy, Asia, and the Ottoman Empire were not able to offer a successful challenge to either French or British imperialism in the Middle East and North Africa.

Germany had tried to defy British regional domination by sending a military mission to the Ottomans in 1880. Later they helped to construct the Constantinople-Baghdad Railroad, which was a direct challenge to British rule in India. The railroad was not actually completed until the end of World War I.

Just prior to World War I, the situation for Britain changed dramatically as Spain, France, and Italy made claims to parts of the Middle East and North Africa. The British continued their policy of protecting their routes to India. There were suggestions that the Ottomans might be able to provide a land route for Britain along the Tigris and Euphrates Rivers to India, but this idea was abandoned when the Ottomans sided with Germany and the Central Powers during World War I.

The other German threat was to France. During the occupation of Morocco by Spain and France, the Germans sent the gunboat *Panther* to the Moroccan port of Agadir. To avoid war with Germany, the French dropped their claims to part of the Congo in favor of Germany. The gunboat was then removed from Moroccan waters.

During World War I, the war in the Middle East and North Africa was a land war fought in the Dardanelles, Arabia, Palestine, and Mesopotamia. The Germans made no serious challenge to British bases outside these areas. Indirectly, one could argue that the campaign fought in Palestine was to protect the Suez Canal. The campaign in Mesopotamia was fought to secure the Persian Gulf. Viewed from this perspective, Mahan's theory on the necessity to protect regional strategic bases was alive and well. Mackinder's fears were not yet a factor because Russia fought against Germany. The collapse of Russia in 1917 did provoke an allied invasion, but it was probably more to stop communism and to tie down German troops in the East rather than to prevent any linkage between Germany and Russia.

The Middle East and North Africa were important in the strategic thinking of both sides in World War II. During the early years of World War II, first the Italians and then the Germans attempted to break Britain's chain of bases used to supply the Indian and the Asian colonies. Intense pressure was put on the British forces at Malta. In spite of air attacks, Malta survived and remained in British hands. Gibraltar and Cyprus probably avoided attack because of their close proximities to the neutral states of Spain and Turkey.

In North Africa, the early conflict was a "seesaw" battle largely fought across Libya and western Egypt. The German-Italian objective was to block access to the Suez Canal, which was the supply route to British-controlled India. In the best tradition of Mahan, Britain successfully preserved this chain of bases, thanks to General Bernard Montgomery's defeat of the Germans at El Alamein. U.S. troops secured the western links to North Africa when they invaded French Morocco. By May 1943, the German and Italian forces in Tunisia had surrendered. The supply lines to India had been saved.

THE ROLE OF GLOBAL THEORIES IN THE MIDDLE EAST AND NORTH AFRICA DURING THE LAST HALF OF THE 20TH CENTURY

As fear of an aggressive Soviet Union came to dominate the Cold War thinking of the United States and the Western allies, they began to see communist plots gaining ground throughout the developing world. In retrospect, it is probably more accurate to say that the limitations of the Soviet Union required the implementation of an opportunistic policy rather than the grand strategy attributed to it by the West.[3]

Outside events caused the post–World War II Western planners to develop strategies based on the combination of the ideas of Mahan, Mackinder, and Spykman. This period saw the Western influence of Britain and France in the Middle East and North Africa replaced by that of the United States. The Cold War moved the strategic interest of the West from North Africa to the Middle Eastern core. For most of his life, Mackinder had believed that the heartland of Afro-Eurasia would be controlled by an expanding Germany acquiring the resources of Russia. By the middle of World War II, Mackinder saw that his worst fears were coming to pass. Not Germany, but the Soviet Union, was going to win. An expansive communist state would control the heartland of Europe. In so doing, it was believed that the Soviet Union could threaten the entire land mass of Afro-Eurasia.

To counter such a threat, the United States embraced the rimland theory of Spykman. Renaming Spykman's theory "containment of communism," the United States proceeded to construct a series of military alliances that eventually would stretch from Europe in the west to Japan in the east. These alliances were designed to prevent communism from breaking out of the Eurasian heartland to infect the rest of the world. In one stroke the containment policy thrust the Middle East and North Africa onto center stage in the great struggle between the United States and the Soviet Union.

What Events Dragged the Middle East and North Africa into the Containment of Russian Communism Strategy?

The end of World War II saw the Soviet Union in military control of Eastern Europe. Soviet troops or their allies controlled all of the Black Sea except the southern Turkish coast. Yugoslav and Albanian communists held the eastern Adriatic. To most Western observers at the time, Mackinder's thesis was coming to pass.

Adoption of the containment of communism strategy was not a sudden thing. Rather, the United States and the Western Allies moved into their strategy by evolution in response to actions by the Soviet Union that were seen to be aggressive moves. The Middle East and North Africa, like much of the rest of the developing world, was to play a part in this struggle. In modified form, the theories of Mahan, Mackinder, and Spykman would all be applied to the conflict as it unfolded in this region.

The Russian Communist Threat to Iran At the beginning of World War II, Iran proclaimed neutrality. However, when the Soviet Union was invaded by Germany in June 1941, it became necessary to find a way to keep the Soviets supplied with war material. Turkey refused to allow Allied shipping to pass into the Black Sea. Moving supplies through the Arctic to Murmansk or transshipping them from the Pacific Ocean could not produce enough volume. It became necessary for the Soviet Union and Britain to occupy Iran to establish a supply route from the Persian Gulf to Russia. This occupation took place on August 25, 1941. The Soviets took the northern part of Iran, leaving the British in the south. Later, American troops were also sent to Iran. An agreement was signed between the Allies and Iran in 1942 that gave the Allies transit privileges across Iran, reaffirmed Iranian independence, and promised that all foreign troops would leave the country within six months of the end of the war.[4]

At the end of World War II both Britain and the United States honored the agreement and withdrew their troops. The Soviet Union did not. They proceeded to establish a pro-Soviet separatist republic in the northern part of Iran. The United States and Britain supported Iran's demands that the Russians leave. Iran agreed to several concessions to induce the Russian withdrawal. These included the establishment of a Soviet-Iranian oil company, subject to approval by the Iranian parliament, and the recognition of Soviet interest in the northern part of the country. Once Russian troops had been withdrawn from Iranian territory, these concessions to the Soviets were repudiated. The Soviet Iranian oil agreement was rejected by the Iranian parliament. Iranian troops were sent into the north to suppress the communist government there. By October 1947 the first crisis with the Soviets in the region had ended with a Soviet withdrawal from Iran and their diplomatic defeat.

The Russian Communist Threat to Turkey During most of World War II, Turkey had remained neutral. Turkish policy shifted with the changing fortunes of war. In spite of Allied pressure, Turkey did not declare war on Germany until February 23, 1945. Most observers agree that this declaration of war was made in order to meet the requirements for Turkey's admission to the United Nations.

For years, access to the Dardanelles Straits and the Bosporus was governed by the Montreux Convention. This agreement gave free passage for shipping to and from the

Black Sea in times of peace and provided for Turkish control of shipping in times of war. Turkish control and sovereignty over these waterways was clearly established.[5]

Citing the treaty, Turkey refused to allow Allied aid through the Dardanelles Straits to Russia during World War II, until January 1945. The Russians believed that Turkey should be punished for remaining neutral during World War II. In June 1945, the Soviet Union demanded concessions from Turkey. Among other claims, the Soviets called for a revision of the Montreux Convention and also the right to establish military bases along the Bosporus and the Dardanelles. What followed was almost a year of increasing Soviet political pressure applied to Turkey.

The Truman Doctrine Two events provoked the issuance of the Truman Doctrine: the near communist takeover of Greece during the Greek Civil War and the Soviet threat to Turkey. It is not within the scope of this study to look at the Greek Civil War except to say that the Communists in the Balkans came very close to toppling the post-war government in Greece.

Responding to these two threats, President Truman announced his "Truman Doctrine" before the Congress on March 12, 1947. This policy pledged United States economic and military aid to help Greece and Turkey resist the threat of Soviet communism. Congress approved the aid to Greece and Turkey that had been requested by the president. This action introduced American power and money into the Middle East and North Africa. The first blocks of the containment of communism strategy had been laid.

The Marshall Plan Almost simultaneously with the Truman Doctrine, the American government proposed the Marshall Plan (European Recovery Program) to aid selected countries in their efforts to recover from World War II. Although this plan was offered to the Soviet Union and the Soviet allies, it was refused. The Russians argued, probably with some justification, that this program would commit the Eastern bloc to an economic plan dictated by the United States. The program was extended to Greece and Turkey, both of which participated. In this way, Turkey became firmly tied to Western Europe, effectively checking Russian attempts to penetrate the Eastern Mediterranean.

The North Atlantic Treaty Organization (NATO) Created during the early part of the Cold War, NATO started as a Western European collective defense pact designed to block the Soviet Union's military threat. In 1952, the Truman Doctrine states of Greece and Turkey were added to this alliance. With this action, the second bloc of containment of communism was accomplished. Turkey became one of the states that played a key role in the prevention of communist expansion into the Middle East. NATO aid enabled the Turkish military to become one of the most powerful in the region.

The Baghdad Pact In an effort to mount an effective opposition to what was believed to be the threat of communist expansion into the Middle East and North Africa, several proposals were made before a solution could be found acceptable to the parties in the region. The problem was to contain communism without offending the peoples of the Middle East. Western relations with the new State of Israel further complicated this problem.

The first proposal was one supported by the United States and Britain to form a Middle East Defense Organization similar to NATO. Egyptian opposition stopped this plan. Policymakers in the United States and Britain finally embraced the strategy of containment when they decided to focus their efforts on building a defense system in the Northern Tier to be called the Baghdad Pact.

The Baghdad Pact evolved in several stages. First a mutual defense arrangement was concluded between Turkey and Pakistan. Turkey then made similar agreements with Iraq and Iran. These military alliances were strongly opposed by the southern Arab states, who felt that these actions violated Arab unity as expressed in the Charter of the Arab League.

After some delay, the Baghdad Pact became a reality in 1955. The states that joined were the Kingdom of Iraq, the Republic of Turkey, the United Kingdom, the Dominion of Pakistan, and the Kingdom of Iran. Although the United States was never a member, it strongly supported the effort by extending aid to the regional parties involved.[6]

Why did the Baghdad Pact fail? Almost before the ink was dry, the Baghdad Pact's strategy of containment was "leapfrogged" by the Soviet Union. A series of miscalculations made by the United States, Britain, France, Israel, and Egypt resulted in several crises, culminating in the Suez War of 1956. These events provided the Russians with openings to establish military and then economic ties with Egypt.

Syria had opposed the creation of the Baghdad Pact almost from the beginning. As events heated up in Egypt, anti-Western feelings increased in Syria. By 1957 the Syrians had signed military and economic agreements with the Soviet Union and the Eastern bloc.

The final blow to the Baghdad Pact occurred in 1958 when the pro-Western government of Iraq was overthrown. A new nationalist Iraqi government withdrew from the pact. Iraq proclaimed nonalignment but concluded several trade agreements with the Eastern bloc. These actions raised Western concerns that Iraq might go "the way of Syria and Egypt."

In an earlier effort to shore up the idea of containment, the president of the United States had issued the Eisenhower Doctrine. This proclamation, endorsed by Congress, stated that the United States would use force in the Middle East to block communist aggression. When the coup in Iraq occurred, President Eisenhower countered by sending the U.S. Marines into Lebanon as a warning to the Iraqis, Egyptians, and Syrians.

No matter how it was rationalized, the Baghdad Pact had failed by the end of 1958. There was a hole in containment through Syria and Iraq that led to Egypt. In the view of U.S. planners, this gap opened up the Arab core to Soviet penetration.[7] Britain and the United States attempted to shore up the non-Arab states of the Northern Tier through the creation of the Central Treaty Organization (CENTO). This alliance of the Northern Tier states linked the two Western powers with Turkey, Pakistan, and Iran. The Alliance expired in 1979.

With the Northern Tier containment of communism policy irretrievably breached, the United States adopted a triangular policy to contain the breach. Bolstering the CENTO agreement, the United States started a military aid program in Israel. Over time, with American support, Israel became not only the militarily dominant Middle East power but was also portrayed as the primary "bulwark against communism in the Middle East." Throughout the 1960s, Turkey, Iran, and Israel became the most important allies of the United States in the region.

The Nixon Doctrine In writing about the late 1960s and early 1970s, Henry Kissinger stated,

> The containment strategy of the early post-war period had projected America to the front line of every crisis; the soaring rhetoric of the Kennedy period had set goals that were beyond America's physical and emotional capabilities.[8]

The solution to this dilemma was the proclamation of the Nixon Doctrine on July 25, 1969. Among other things, the new policy stated that states threatened by communism would have to assume the primary responsibility for their defense. The implication of this statement was that while the United States would continue to furnish aid and arms, it would no longer provide combat troops. In proclaiming the Nixon Doctrine, the United States symbolically acknowledged the futility of overcommitment in places like Vietnam. Nixon reiterated that the United States would still continue to honor treaty commitments that had already been made.

In the Middle East, the Nixon Doctrine meant that a triangular containment policy would continue. Turkey would control Soviet access to the Mediterranean. Israel would remain powerful enough to contain communist threats in the Arab world. Iran would be built up to a point that it would prevent Soviet penetration into the Persian Gulf.

This policy failed when the Shah of Iran was driven from power by a popular uprising in 1979. Iran was invaded by Iraq in 1980, and the United States was estranged from both parties in the conflict. For several years the American attitude seemed to be one of allowing Iran and Iraq to exhaust themselves in a conflict that prevented them from causing mischief elsewhere in the region. However, when Iraq started to lose, the United States pursued a balance of power strategy by extending enough help to Iraq to prevent defeat. At the time, it was argued that an Iranian victory would lead to "Islamic radicals" extending their influence into the oil-rich Arab lands of the Persian Gulf. The American intervention led to the war's stalemate. The war ended in almost the same place where it began along the Shatt al Arab.

CONTAINMENT AT THE END OF THE COLD WAR

Shortly before the Soviet Union imploded in 1991, the weakened Soviet government of Russia was unable to maintain the global commitments made by the old communist regime. In most places the allies of the Soviet Union, left without their sponsor, had to make the best deal that they could with the West. Some leaders, however, misread the changing power relations that were occurring. This seemed to be the case when Iraq invaded Kuwait in August 1990. The Iraqi leadership made at least two miscalculations. First, they did not believe that the West would respond militarily to the invasion as long as the oil continued to flow. Second, they assumed that their old ally, the Soviet Union, would be able to offer strong support and thereby prevent the West and the other members of the alliance from responding militarily to their invasion. The members of the coalition did attack and defeat the Iraqi army. The Russians did not or could not come to Iraq's aid.

In retrospect it seems that the United States had adopted a neo-Mahan policy in the Gulf after the fall of the Shah in 1979. The United States, with the permission of the Gulf Arabs, prepositioned supplies and constructed the mothballed desert bases. No longer would bases for ships be needed as in the 19th century. By combining sea power with the air power, force could be quickly applied to Arabia by the United States. The only difference between this strategy and that employed by the British earlier was the speed in which the United States moved troops into the line of battle facing Iraq. Mahan would certainly recognize the use of a battleship to bombard the Iraqi defenses. In line with the same idea, the U.S. Navy launched missiles from the Red Sea and the Persian Gulf into the heartland of Iraq.

Another old strategy reappeared in a new form. De Seversky had always argued for the use of aircraft to project power. His concern was about the Soviet threat. However, the use of aircraft to move troops and to apply pressure on Iraq seemed to be neo-de Seversky.

DUAL CONTAINMENT OF IRAQ AND IRAN

The United States no longer pursued traditional policy containment. Rather, elements of Spykman's theory were merged with that of Mahan to secure the Persian Gulf. Like Britain during the 19th century, the United States moved to maintain overseas bases and the prepositioning of supplies. Nowhere was this strategy more apparent than in the Persian Gulf region. Not only did the U.S. Navy maintain a presence "just over the horizon," but the United States also placed supplies and ground forces in isolated spots on the Arabian Peninsula.

The United States and Europe applied a policy of containment to both Iran and Iraq. In the case of Iran this policy had been in place from the early 1980s and was still in force at the end of the 20th century. As the new century began, the U.S. allies in Europe had begun to soften their positions on Iran. Both Britain and France had resumed diplomatic and limited trade relations with Iran. Their view was that Iran was too important to be ignored indefinitely by the West. Furthermore, Europeans argued that more positive changes in Iran could be encouraged through trade than through the continuation of a policy of isolation. For its part, the United States was placed in the uncomfortable position of denying trade opportunities to its citizens trying to do business with Iran while simultaneously encouraging the same businessmen to trade with the communist People's Republic of China.

The United Nations embargo on trade with Iraq had remained in place since the 1990 invasion of Kuwait. Ironically these sanctions had lasted longer than anything imposed on Italy, Germany, or Japan after World War II. As time passed, support for this policy also started to erode. The Arabs of Arabia and the Fertile Crescent were particularly concerned. Many recognized that the borders of Jordan, Syria, Iraq, Kuwait, and, to a degree, even Saudi Arabia were artificial affectations of Western colonial rule. Arabs living outside Iraq had relatives and friends there. They didn't necessarily approve of the Iraq leadership, but they saw the embargo hurting average people who had little or no influence on government policy. Articles like the Associated Press story detailing the problems of the Abdul Rahman family were particularly upsetting to the Arab neighbors of Iraq. The story noted that Mrs. Abdul Rahman's 11-month-old son weighed only 13 pounds and that he was one of nearly 5000 malnourished children and mothers in one low-income Baghdad neighborhood.[9]

The United States and the United Kingdom continued to press the United Nations to pursue the containment policy until Iraq could be certified as having no weapons of mass destruction. Over time, U.S. allies in both Arabia and Europe changed their attitudes. Clearly, although containment had ruined Iraq's economy, it had not threatened the government's leadership or forced them to modify their policies. The danger was that the

United States would once again, as with Cuba, be left alone to enforce an ineffective, unpopular embargo.

After the Persian Gulf War, the Arabs in the small oil-rich states of Arabia were realistic about the future. They were quick to point out that the traditional powers in the Persian Gulf had always been Iran and Iraq. They warned that the United States, like the British in an earlier time, would eventually leave the Gulf. Geography dictated that because they had to stay, as residents of the Gulf, they would inevitably have to make their peace with both Iran and Iraq if they were to survive. To the careful observer, it seemed that the United States–sponsored strategy of dual containment would not last long without being modified by the new Bush administration.

What Are Some of the Most Important Geopolitical Flashpoints in the Middle East and North Africa?

THE DISPUTE OVER THE WESTERN SAHARA

The Western Sahara is located on the Atlantic coast of Africa. It is about the size of the State of Colorado and is bounded on the north by Morocco, on the east and south by Mauritania, and for a few miles in the east by Algeria.

The Western Sahara is an almost completely flat desert, devoid of rivers, that extends all the way to the Atlantic. The wadis remain dry most of the year, and only a few oases break up the brown landscape. Most of the interior is still unexplored. Until the 1970s, water had to be imported from the Canary Islands. More recently, a large underground pool near Dakia (Villa Cisneros) has been discovered and several deep wells have been drilled in the area.

The Western Sahara became known to Europeans when the ships of two private Spanish companies arrived to exploit the area in 1884. In 1885 Spain annexed the area and extended her protection to the handful of native residents. This Spanish action aroused the French opposition, which did not end until the boundaries were established in 1900. Effective Spanish control did not extend beyond the coast until 1934. Spain made some attempts to assimilate the local population during the rule of General Franco. In 1958 the region became the Province of Spanish Sahara. By 1961 the Province had been granted the same laws that controlled Spain. Legally, if not culturally, the native population became Spanish. For most of the period of Spanish rule, the territory failed to be economically profitable. There was practically no industry in the province, aside from a small amount of fishing. Shortly before the end of Spanish rule, the world's largest phosphate deposit was found near the dusty oasis of Bu-Cra. At the height of Spanish rule there were probably no more than 30,000 residents living in the province.

Beginning with Spanish Morocco in 1956, Spain began the process of withdrawal from Africa. By 1975, this process was largely accomplished. In that year, Spain held only a few enclaves along the North African coast and the Province of Spanish Sahara.

In a move to curry nationalist favor at home, the Moroccan king began to pressure the Spanish to give up the territory. The Spanish responded by offering the people of the Province self-determination. King Hussein called for a peaceful march of Moroccans to take the Province before independence could be established. Over 350,000 Moroccans crossed the border into Spanish Sahara in what was called the "Green March." Anxious to avoid a war, Spain withdrew from the territory in early 1976. Morocco claimed the northern two-thirds and Mauritania the southern one-third of the former Spanish Sahara.

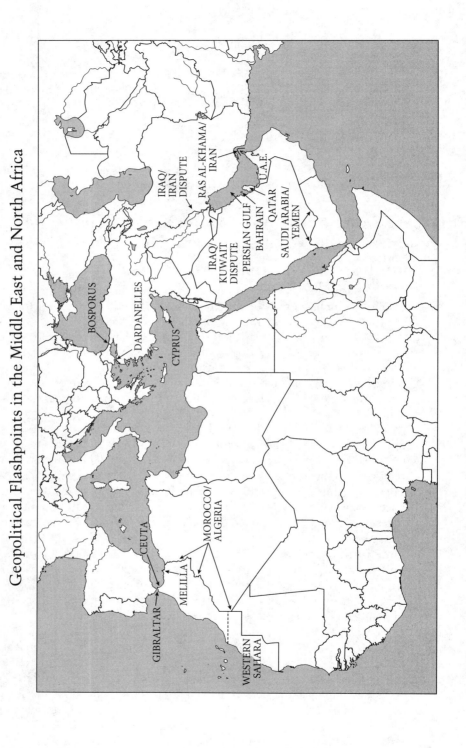

Large numbers of Saharan residents fled to Algeria, where they proclaimed the Sahrawi Arab Democratic Republic (SADR). The primary pro-independence exile organization was called the *Frente Popular para la Liberacion de Saguia y Rio de Oro* (Polisario) Front. This force, with Algerian support, began a guerrilla war against Morocco and Mauritania. In 1979, a frustrated Mauritania abandoned all claims to the Western Sahara.

In 1988, Morocco and the Polisario agreed to a United Nations peace plan, which included a referendum to decide the future status of the Western Sahara. A ceasefire was established in 1991. What had been agreed to by the parties had appeared to be straightforward. However, in practice, it was anything but that. The difficulty was determining who was a Saharan for the purpose of voting. Morocco had flooded the territory with settlers after 1976. When pressed on the question of voting rights, the Moroccan Minister of the Interior, Ahmed Midaoui, was reported by the British Broadcasting Corporation to have said that Morocco would not accept any referendum without the participation of all who could trace ancestry to the Sahara. Morocco refused to rule out citizens whose grandfathers and fathers had fled Spanish colonial rule.[10]

For their part, the Polisario insisted that only those people who were residents of the Spanish Sahara when Spanish rule ended should be allowed to vote. The problem was that since 1976 the numbers of Saharans in the area controlled by Morocco had grown from around 30,000 to 186,000. If the number of potential Western Sahara residents were to include exiles, the figure could now exceed one million. After years of dispute, the United Nations finally came up with a voter roll of members of the tribes that were recognized by the last Spanish census in 1974. By January 2000, the voter list contained only 86,381 names, more than half of the 147,000 applicants. Most of the names submitted by Morocco were rejected by the United Nations Electoral Commission. Morocco responded by filing 79,000 separate appeals. If each is fully investigated, it will take several more years before any referendum on independence is taken.

Moroccan strategy seems to be to steadily make the Western Sahara more Moroccan while at the same time delaying the referendum until a vote against independence can be ensured. The Polisario area is becoming more frustrated. Even though the Polisario government in exile has been admitted to the Organization of African Unity and is recognized by more than 70 countries, it does not control any territory. The Western Sahara remains firmly in the hands of Morocco. The two parties are separated by a Moroccan fortified sand wall that runs for 500 miles along the eastern boundary of the territory. Should the United Nations peace effort fail, the Polisario has threatened to resume fighting. The major Western powers are without a solution to the problem. On the one hand, they are for the general principle of self-determination. Morocco, however, is an ally and a key player in the maintenance of stability in the Maghreb. Sir Rupert Cornwell stated the dilemma this way:

> Do France, Spain, and the United States of America want to destabilize a promising young king of a strategically important country, just to secure independence for a patch of desert, rich in resources, which could fall into unfriendly hands?[11]

Speaking in defense of the Polisario position, President Thabo Mbeki of South Africa has been quoted as referring to the Western Sahara as "Africa's last colonial issue."[12] The result is the continuation of a stalemate in West Africa that could disrupt the uneasy peace between Algeria and Morocco. Should the referendum effort fail, the world's least known war, located in one of the world's most isolated places, could be resumed.

THE ARGUMENT OVER THE TERRITORIES OF GIBRALTAR, CEUTA, AND MELILLA

Known to the ancients as the Pillars of Hercules, the Straits of Gibraltar separate two mountains, the Rock of Gibraltar (Jebel-al-Tirak) in Europe and Ceuta (Jebel Musa) in North Africa. According to legend, Hercules placed the mountains there on one of his travels. Along with another Spanish outpost, Melilla, these territories are involved in a 21st-century dispute involving the United Kingdom, Spain, and Morocco. Gibraltar is a British Crown Colony situated in Spanish Europe and claimed by Spain, whereas Ceuta and Melilla are Spanish North African enclaves claimed by Morocco. All three areas are linked by history, geography, and politics to territorial conflicts that are centuries old.

Gibraltar Although geographically part of Europe, the fate of this crown colony is linked to the situation in North Africa. Gibraltar is a peninsula of southern Spain. It is only 2.5 square miles in size. It was first given the Arabic name Jebal-al-Tarik when captured by the Moors in 711. The Spanish took possession in 1462 and held it until the British captured it in 1704. Although continually challenged by the Spanish, Gibraltar has remained in British hands since that time. During the early years of British occupation, the Spanish population was expelled. Over the years, Italians, Jews, Maltese, and Portuguese settled there. Only about one hundred Spaniards remain out of the total population of 30,000.[13]

British rule in Gibraltar is based on two documents: the 1713 Treaty of Utrecht and the 1969 Constitution of Gibraltar. The Treaty of Utrecht granted Gibraltar to the British in perpetuity, with the one exception that if they ever decided to leave, the peninsula would be returned to Spain. The 1969 Constitution promised that any change in Gibraltar's status would require a vote of the people. In a 1967 referendum, 12,148 citizens of Gibraltar voted to remain British while only 44 voted to rejoin Spain. For their part, the British want Spain to apply the same standards to their enclaves in North Africa that Spain demands of the British in Gibraltar. The British are quick to point out that the Spanish will be able to rightfully claim what could be theirs, Gibraltar, if after a vote they are willing to cede Ceuta and Melilla to the Moroccans.

In reply, the Spanish make two arguments for the return of Gibraltar. First, they discount the 1967 referendum because the voter rolls did not include descendants of the Spanish who were expelled after the British occupation in 1704. Second, they argue that Gibraltar was taken from an existing sovereign state and should be returned to the same state. They cite the British return of Hong Kong to the People's Republic of China as a precedent for their claim. The British point out that Hong Kong was largely held by lease from China and had to be returned once the lease had expired. They are adamant that they will not surrender Gibraltar against the will of the current residents. Their actions with regard to the Falkland Islands remain as a reminder to all that Britain is capable of responding with force if needed. Spain is not China. Both sides make it clear that they wish to see a peaceful resolution to this problem.

CEUTA AND MELILLA

Spain's Gibraltar is the medieval fortress city of Ceuta. Located only about 12 miles across the Mediterranean from the British Crown Colony, Ceuta is a Spanish enclave on the coast of Morocco. This city of 65,000 has a border only 5 miles long. Ceuta fell to Portu-

IMPORTANT GEOPOLITICAL FLASHPOINTS IN THE MIDDLE EAST AND NORTH AFRICA

Spanish North Africa
The Moroccan coast near the enclave of Ceuta.
Source: Joe Weatherby

gal in 1415. Ceded to Spain in 1580, the city has withstood a number of attempts to drive the Spanish out. Today it is almost totally Spanish in architecture, religion, culture, and language. The thick walls and moat separating Ceuta from Morocco serve as a reminder to all of Spain's ancient determination to keep this foothold in Africa.

About 140 miles down the coast lies Melilla. Like Ceuta, Melilla has been mostly Spanish for 500 years. Today it has a population of 80,000. Elements of the Spanish Foreign Legion are based in both enclaves. To the casual observer, the Spanish claim to Gibraltar while denying the Moroccan demands for the return of Ceuta and Melilla would seem to be inconsistent.

The Spanish base their seemingly inconsistent position on the differing legal status of the three towns. They argue that because Gibraltar is a crown colony forcibly taken from an existing sovereign state in 1704 it is subject to being returned regardless of the wishes of current residents. On the other hand, Ceuta and Melilla are enclaves occupied centuries before Morocco was established in its present form. Furthermore, while the other Spanish colonies of Ifini and Spanish Sahara were surrendered to Morocco, a distinction has always been made concerning the status of Ceuta and Melilla. Even the European union failed to consider these enclaves colonies. The residents of Ceuta and Melilla have always believed themselves to be Spanish just as Alaskans or Hawaiians have considered that they are American. The Moroccan government has repeatedly denied the Spanish assumption that there was no government when Spain claimed Ceuta and Melilla five hundred years ago.

In 1999, Mr. Ahmed el Rhaid of the Moroccan Embassy in London stated,

> In fact, Morocco has existed as a sovereign nation since the 8th Century, when the Idrissids founded their dynasty in Fez. Two other dynasties, the Almoravides in the 10th and 11th Centuries and the Almohads in the 12th, conquered large areas of Spain.

He further stated that Morocco had committed itself to the recovery of Ceuta and Melilla since regaining its independence from Spain and France in 1956.[14]

All of the parties are publicly committed to resolving the status of these three small relics of a colonial age peacefully. Little progress toward the resolution of this dispute has been made, however. For its part, Morocco is too tied down with the conflict in the Western Sahara to apply much pressure on Spain. Furthermore, the 7,000 Spanish Foreign Legionnaires based in the enclaves serve as a Moroccan defense by offering an implied threat to Algeria not to press any border claims in eastern Morocco.

In spite of their desire to keep the issues separate, the Spanish are certainly aware that the day will come when they will have to choose between pressing their claim to Gibraltar and continuing to occupy Ceuta and Melilla. A lot depends on the internal conditions that develop in Spain itself. If membership in the European Community brings the hoped for prosperity to Spain, a reassociation of some type with Gibraltar might be possible. For their part, Gibraltarians have, at times, hoped for a change to special status within the European Community or a change in the 1969 Constitution from the Crown Colony to a relationship similar to the one that Britain has with the Channel Islands. Neither of these expressed desires has been met. Morocco has proposed granting dual citizenship to the residents of Ceuta and Melilla without drawing much interest on the part of the Spanish. Presently the Spanish policy seems to be playing for time in North Africa while pressing the British for a change in the status of Gibraltar. Their strategy is to push for a resolution on the Gibraltar situation before they are forced to take the opposite position with regard to Ceuta and Melilla.

In the final analysis, the solution of one issue probably will depend on the solution of the other. Spain and Morocco have close economic ties. Spain has become Morocco's second largest trading partner after France. The two states are planning to construct a rail tunnel that will run under the Straits of Gibraltar between Morocco and Spain. Gibraltar has become a booming port since the British military withdrew from their bases. It has become the largest ship-fueling station in the Mediterranean, handling over 35,000 ships a year. The average income of Gibraltarians is slightly more than that on mainland Spain. Over time the economic benefits of cooperation may move Spain, Gibraltar, and Morocco to overcome their present policies and help the parties to find a solution that will benefit all. A failure in this effort will hinder economic development on both sides of the Western Mediterranean.

TENSIONS ALONG THE MOROCCO-ALGERIA BORDER

Disagreements over the border between Algeria and Morocco go back at least 175 years. At the beginning of the 19th century, the Sultan of Morocco claimed a vast territory that stretched from the Mediterranean across the Sahara and included parts of Algeria and

Mauritania. This "Greater Morocco" was based on historic assertion rather than effective control. The idea of tribal lands without specific boundaries was a concept familiar to North Africans but alien to Europe. In Europe, specific boundaries were marked and defended or deemed not to exist.

With the arrival of French colonization of Algeria in 1830, the French proceeded to negotiate parts of the border with Morocco. Areas in the southern desert, however, remained undefined. As the French established their control in Algeria, they built a line of forts stretching along the border that they claimed as Algerian. Moroccan tribes often raided French Algeria, seeking horses, camels, and slaves. The French authorities responded by expanding their forts into areas that the Moroccan Sultan still claimed. Nowhere was this problem more acute than in the area around the desert oasis of Bechar. Operating from this base inside the area claimed by Morocco, the tribes could freely move back and forth across the unmarked border to attack French positions and supply columns in southern Algeria.

Clearly marked borders between Algeria and Morocco did not extend much further than 100 miles south of the Mediterranean. The northern border was settled by treaty in 1845. This agreement recognized that tribal custom would govern the status of territories further south. By the beginning of the 20th century, the situation along the southern border was out of control. French interests were continually threatened by tribal attacks from Morocco. The French solution was to move into Moroccan-claimed territory to occupy Béchar. They renamed the oasis Colomb, which was an Algerian name. It was to become the famous Foreign Legion post of Colomb-Béchar. When Richard Halliburton visited Colomb-Béchar in the early 1930s, he wrote,

> The Foreign Legion quarters at Colomb-Béchar are surrounded by a wall. . . . But at the time of our visit, in the back wall, there was a break in the masonry where bricks had been removed for the extension of a pipeline . . . and this very convenient exit was wide open . . . any Legionnaire who chose could walk out of camp. . . . There was just one little catch. He had no place to walk to except out across miles and miles of more clean sand.[15]

From Colomb-Béchar, the French began a gradual incursion into Moroccan territory. This action eventually resulted in the partition of Morocco between France and Spain in 1912. Morocco did not regain its independence until 1956.

Because they controlled both areas, the French imposed a border called the "Varnier Line" between Algeria and Morocco.[16] During the period of French rule, the authorities made several attempts to get the Moroccans to agree to a boundary settlement in the south. The Moroccans refused to agree to any settlement until they gained full independence. When the French were forced out of Algeria, the Moroccan army quickly moved to occupy those desert areas that had been lost earlier to the French. A border war between Morocco and Algeria was fought in 1962 and 1963. A final agreement on the border was not reached until 1970. Algeria retained Colomb-Béchar and much of the disputed territory. From north on the Mediterranean to Colomb-Béchar all the way to Tindauf, near the Western Sahara, the border remained a source of tension between Morocco and Algeria.

Basic problems between Algeria and Morocco have been reflected in the continuing strains along their common border. First, the parties found themselves in opposing Arab camps during the Cold War. Algeria was largely secular and pro-Soviet, whereas Morocco was Islamic and closely tied to the West. Second, the conflict between the two states over the Western Sahara caused most cooperation to be put on hold. As long as Algeria gave safe haven for the Saharan rebels, it was hard for Morocco to cooperate on border issues. In the 1980s the parties agreed to disagree on the Sahara. The King of Morocco and the President of Algeria met and agreed to reaffirm the 1970 border agreement. This provided a decade of relief for people living in the border region.

There was an attack, however, on a Moroccan hotel that killed two Spanish tourists in 1994. Moroccan authorities charged the attack was carried out by Algerians. They responded by requiring that all Algerian nationals obtain visas before entering Morocco. Algeria promptly closed the common border and suspended cooperation with Morocco in the Arab Maghreb Union.

Algeria also had several long-standing disagreements that focused on the border that transcended the immediate dispute. It was believed in Algeria that Islamic militants who were engaged in a virtual civil war in Algeria were using eastern Morocco as a base, supply source, and bank. These concerns in the north were balanced by similar charges made by Morocco about Algerian interference in the Western Sahara dispute.

In the late 1990s, the "closed border" also aided both sides, who were trying to slow down the tide of illegal African immigrants using Algeria and Morocco as a pipeline into Europe. These immigrants crossed Algeria and Morocco to reach the Spanish-controlled enclaves of Ceuta and Melilla. This problem provoked objections from Europeans.

At the beginning of the new century, there were signs that relations might improve between the two states. Both stated publicly that they wished to resolve the border problem. They recognized that in an era of open borders in Europe this kind of dispute was "out of date." It can be expected that the border, closed for six years, is likely to be reopened. Until both the Western Sahara issue and the internal conflict in Algeria are resolved, Moroccan-Algerian relations will remain shaky.

THE DISPUTE OVER CYPRUS

Cyprus is an island located in the Eastern Mediterranean. Its closest neighbors are Turkey, 40 miles to the north, and Syria, 60 miles to the east. People have lived on Cyprus for at least 6000 years, during which the island has been ruled by Minoans, Mycenians, Greeks, Phoenicians, Assyrians, Persians, and Venetians.

The modern story of Cyprus began with its capture by the Turks in 1571. The island remained under Ottoman Turkish rule until it was handed over to the British at the Congress of Berlin in 1878. The British used the island as a naval base to check Russian attempts to penetrate the Mediterranean during the last quarter of the 19th century. Because Greece remained part of the Ottoman Empire from 1466 until 1830, there was no conflict over Ottoman-controlled Greeks in Greece and Ottoman-controlled Greeks on Cyprus. Even under British rule, the Cypriot Greeks maintained close ties to Greece. The island remained culturally Greek but geographically near Turkey.

Although the British granted Cyprus the status of a crown colony in 1925, the desire of the Greek majority was to establish closer ties to Greece. After World War II, the movement for the establishment of an independent Greek Cypriot state increased. After a great deal of anti-British agitation and violence, the Cypriots gained their independence in 1960. During the negotiations that preceded independence, the Greek majority called for a union with Greece. The Turkish minority wanted to partition the island between Greeks and Turks. What emerged was a powersharing agreement that pleased no one.

During the next 10 years, there was a good deal of unrest instigated by extremists on both the Greek and Turkish sides. Greek nationalists overthrew the government on July

15, 1974. The new Greek Cypriot authority moved to formally unite with Greece. This action caused Greece and Turkey to mobilize their military. On July 20th, the Turkish army invaded northern Cyprus. They quickly occupied over 30 percent of the island. About 200,000 Greeks and 100,000 Turks were forced to flee from their homes. Following the Turkish invasion, the United Nations, which had maintained peacekeepers on the island since 1965, had them redeployed between the new Greek and Turkish-held territories. The United Nations peacekeepers have divided the two parties since that time.

By 1983 Cyprus had been partitioned. The United Nations occupied a buffer zone. Turkey retained most of the land that it had captured. Turkish military forces remained deployed in the northern portion of the island. With Turkish support, this area became the Turkish Republic of Northern Cyprus. Recognized only by Turkey, the Republic controlled about one-third of the island, with a population of about 134,000. The Greeks occupied two-thirds of Cyprus, which had a population of 754,000.

Since their invasion in 1974, the Turkish government has actively encouraged the resettlement of Turks from the mainland to the island. Perhaps as many as 60,000 people from the Turkish mainland have been settled in the Turkish Republic of North Cyprus. This mass population resettlement has caused much bitterness throughout the island. In 1996, Greece and Turkey almost went to war over an island dispute in the Aegean Sea. This dispute also heated up the tensions on Cyprus. It is generally agreed that a settlement on the Cypriot dispute is the key to improving relations between Greece and Turkey on other matters.

Greece has objected to the admission of Turkey for membership in the European Community until the Greek Cypriots gain their objective. The Greek Cypriots call for the re-creation of a multiethnic state in Cyprus similar to the one that existed before 1974. The Turkish Cypriots demand recognition for the Turkish Republic of North Cyprus as a precondition for peace talks. Both Greece and Turkey back the positions of their clients on the island.

The Turks on Cyprus continue to build closer ties, both economically and politically, with the Turkish Cypriots. Both parties on Cyprus continue to press for the adoption of their version of a solution to the dispute. In March 2000, the Northern Cypriot government announced that a campus of Turkey's Middle East Technical University would be located in the town of Guzelyurt. At the same time, the Greek Cypriots are actively pursuing possible membership in the European Community with or without northern participation. Although offers have been made to the Turkish Cypriots allowing them to participate, they have been rejected because it would imply a recognition of Greek legal dominance of the island.

Fearful that two NATO allies might end up fighting over Cyprus, the United States intervened in 1999. Under pressure, both sides, along with their sponsors, agreed to conduct a series of talks aimed at finding a solution to the dispute. President Clinton made the U.S. position clear in a message that he sent to the Congress:

> The United States remains actively engaged in efforts to promote a negotiated settlement of the Cyprus dispute, under UN auspices and on the basis of a bizonal, bicommunal, federal solution.[17]

Essentially the U.S. objective in the talks was to recognize two Cypriot states but to require that they have a common structure for dealing with third parties. If accepted in a final settlement, a plan such as this would fall short of participation as demanded by the

Turks but would not reunify the island as called for by the Greeks. Both sides could move toward a final settlement while at the same time saving face.

Failure to resolve this dispute will have consequences that extend far past the conflict itself. For Turkey, it is clear that there will be no chance of a European Community admission without a settlement on Cyprus. The Greeks also understand that issues with Turkey over the Aegean Sea cannot be resolved until there is movement on Cyprus. In the meantime, the United Nations peacekeepers remain on guard on one of the potentially most explosive areas in the Mediterranean.

THE IMPORTANCE OF CONTROL OVER THE DARDANELLES AND BOSPORUS

Previously mentioned in the discussion of the Truman Doctrine, the Dardanelles and Bosporus along with the Sea of Marmara make up a 190-mile-long passage between the Mediterranean and the Black Sea. At the Gallipoli Peninsula, the narrow passage between Kilid Bahr and Chanak has a width of less than 3,000 feet. As the outlet for Russia's only warm water ports, the Straits are among the most important strategic water passages in the world.

The Ottoman Empire gained full control over the Straits in the mid 15th century. Since that time, the Turks have been able to threaten Russian shipping in the Black Sea. Over the centuries the disputes over the control of the Dardanelles and Bosporus have been the cause of a number of conflicts between the Turks and Russia.

It was a British attempt to supply Russia through the Dardanelles during World War I that led to the British defeat at the Battle of Gallipoli in 1915. The initial plan had been to capture the Dardanelles by using the bombardment by ships alone. However, the Allies

A Strategic Waterway
This is a view of the Gallipoli peninsula taken from a ship passing through the Dardanelles Strait.
Source: Joe Weatherby

were unable to get past the Turkish defenses. In March the British, Australians, and New Zealanders committed troops to action on the Gallipoli Peninsula itself. In spite of great sacrifice on the part of the Allied troops taking part in the invasion, they were never able to make any significant headway against the Turkish forces defending the heights above the beaches. Without the destruction of the Turkish forts guarding the Dardanelles, the British navy could not break through the Black Sea. The operation had to be abandoned in 1916.[18]

The modern State of Turkey was created out of the wreckage of the Ottoman Empire at the end of World War I. As one of the defeated powers, Turkey briefly lost control of the Straits under the provisions of the 1920 Treaty of Sèvres. By 1923, with the Treaty of Lausanne, Turkey had regained some control. This agreement returned the waterway to Turkish administration but kept it demilitarized. In 1936 Turkey was able to replace the old agreement with the Montreux Convention, which still governs the administration of the Straits. The Montreux Convention permitted Turkey to remilitarize the waterway. States bordering the Black Sea had passage for both military and merchant shipping during times of peace. Turkey could close the Straits to all warships and merchant vessels during periods of war with or without threats. States not bordering the Black Sea itself had to limit military vessels to 15,000 tons. The idea was to prevent non–Black Sea powers from introducing battleships and aircraft carriers into the area.

Turkey was neutral during World War II. Although there were allied complaints that Germany violated the provisions of the Montreux Convention, Turkey generally engaged in an even-handed banning of all belligerent shipping during the war years. The allied use of alternate routes to supply Russia through Iran has already been discussed. The immediate post-war problems with Russia have also been covered under the discussion of the Truman Doctrine.

During the Cold War, there were periodic incidents that occurred either in the Straits or the Black Sea. In the 1970s, NATO officials accused the Soviets of shipping "hidden" arms as cargos on merchant ships sailing through the Bosporus and Dardanelles on their way to Africa. Perhaps the most serious Cold War incident occurred in 1988 when Soviet ships actually hit two United States destroyers while they were passing within the 12-mile territorial limit claimed by the Russians.

Throughout the Cold War the Soviets had maintained that the Americans were violating the spirit of the Montreux Convention when they entered the Black Sea with missile-carrying, intelligence-collecting destroyers. They asserted that the 15,000-ton limit could not have anticipated the technical advances and destructive capabilities of missile-carrying destroyers. They also rejected U.S. claims of free passage through Russian waters on the grounds that those waters could be easily avoided since the American ships were not sailing to any Russian destination. The Americans countered that they were free to sail in any waters within three miles of the coast because they only recognize a three-mile limit. The Americans periodically tested their right of passage by sailing close into potentially hostile states like the Soviet Union and Libya. On occasion, these actions provoked hostile responses like the 1988 ship-bumping incident. The Turkish authorities were often blamed for allowing the American Naval vessels to enter the Black Sea in the first place.

Although the Cold War is over, Russia and Turkey continue to disagree over the administration of the Straits. Using the powers under the Montreux Convention to regulate traffic and to control sanitary conditions, the Turks have limited Russian shipments of oil from the Black Sea. The Russians have charged that Turkey is trying to force the construction of an oil pipeline from the Caspian oil fields through Turkey. In 1997, the Turks used the same inspection loopholes to stop ships in an effort to prevent Russian air-defense missiles from being sent to the Greek part of Cyprus. In the 21st century, the Turkish control of the Dardanelles, the Sea of Marmara, and the Bosporus will remain just as important as it has been in the past.

THE DIFFERENCE BETWEEN THE PERSIAN GULF AND THE ARAB GULF

In terms of geography, there is no difference between the Arab Gulf and the Persian Gulf. That two different names apply to the same body of water reflects one of the many geographic disputes that exist there. Arabs refer to the Gulf as the *Arab Gulf* and Iranians use the name *Persian Gulf*. Most Western sources refer to it as the Persian Gulf. The most neutral way to refer to this body of water is to call it the *Gulf*.

The Gulf is a shallow sea with an area of 3,000 square miles. Over 600 miles long, the Gulf varies in width from around 200 miles at its wide point to only 35 miles in the south. Until the 19th century, little was known about the Gulf in the West. British sea charts of the time showed Doha as an island rather than a town located on the large Qatar Peninsula.

The 19th century tribal rivalries became state border conflicts when oil was discovered throughout the area during the 20th century. What had been desert land and a shallow sea with few boundaries suddenly had value. This area was situated on top of the largest pool of oil in the world. There had been a long-standing dispute between Arabs and Iranians over control of the Gulf. The discovery of oil made matters worse as the states surrounding the Gulf disputed each other's claims to this new source of wealth.

SOME OF THE MORE IMPORTANT BOUNDARY DISPUTES IN THE GULF REGION

The Island Dispute Between the Sheikdom of Ras al-Khama and Iran Abu Musa, Greater Tunb, and Lesser Tunb are small islands located at the southern end of the Gulf. They are in strategic locations controlling the entrance to the Gulf from the Strait of Hormuz. All three islands are claimed by the sheikdom of Ras al-Khama and by Iran.

For over one hundred years the British Navy policed the Gulf as part of a strategy of protecting the trade routes to India. After Indian independence, this mission evolved into the containment of communism effort mounted by the Western powers against the Soviet Union. By the 1960s, however, the British had begun a pullback of forces to areas "east of Suez." On November 30, 1971, one day before the British withdrew from the Gulf, Iran sent troops to occupy these three small islands. Iran asserted that the islands had been considered to be Iranian until the British arrived in the 19th century. The Iranian occupation was protested by Sharja and Ras al-Khama. Later, as members of the United Arab Emirates, the Union restated the Arab claims to the islands. There were continuing attempts by the United Arab Emirates and Iran to reach a settlement over the status of the islands, but all ended in failure. After the downfall of the Shah and the creation of the Islamic Republic of Iran, the Western powers became more concerned over Iran's control of this island group. During the Iran-Iraq War, the Gulf islands controlled by Iran were used as bases to intercept neutral ships that were believed to be aiding the Iraqi war effort. The

United States responded to these Iranian actions by allowing Kuwaiti ships to fly the U.S. flag while in the Gulf. They also sent naval vessels to protect this pseudo-American shipping against the interference by Iran.

When oil was discovered at Ras Al-Khama in 1983, it became apparent that the control of Abu Musa and Greater and Lesser Tunb also meant access to offshore petroleum fields. These discoveries added to the strategic importance placed on these islands by the contending parties.

The dispute over the three islands carried over into the 1990s. In 1995 the United Arab Emirates proposed an agenda for resolving this issue with Iran. This agenda called for the withdrawal of Iranian troops from the islands, followed by a negotiated settlement. Failing in this effort, the members of the United Arab Emirates threatened to carry the matter to the International Court of Justice at the Hague. Iran again rejected these claims. In 1999 the United Arab Emirates established a permanent committee to deal with border-related issues. One of the first business items was to discuss the dispute over the three islands. Simultaneously, the Gulf Cooperation Council announced that it supported the United Arab Emirates' sovereignty claims in the border dispute with Iran. This issue is the chief impediment to Iran improving relations with the Emirates. It is hoped that the 2001 election of a more moderate government in Tehran may lead to some kind of resolution of conflicting claims to Abu Musa, Greater Tunb, and Lesser Tunb Islands.[19]

The United Arab Emirates When it was established, few observers expected the Emirates to last. During the 19th century, the British spent a great deal of time keeping peace between the sheikdoms that now made up the union of the Emirates. During the colonial period, the British had been forced to maintain a mobile military force, called the *Trucial Oman Scouts,* to prevent fighting in what was then called the Trucial Oman States. Initially, there were real geographic disputes between the member states. Abu Dhabi controlled most of the territory of the Emirates. The second state in size was Dubai. Both had been involved in a border war in 1940. All of the other members had border disputes with sheikdoms making up the union. However, after 30 years, the United Arab Emirates have continued to survive in spite of these problems, many of which remain unsolved. This is remarkable because the discovery of oil has made what once appeared to be worthless sand very valuable to the sheikdom who owns it. The United Arab Emirates have also worked hard to resolve disputes with their neighbors. In 1999 the Emirates concluded an agreement with Oman that marked almost the entire disputed border between the two. Covering 350 kilometers, the agreement signaled that both sides were satisfied with the new frontier. Officials hoped this agreement would demonstrate to the Iranians that the United Arab Emirates could also be trusted to negotiate in good faith over the status of Abu Musa and the Greater Tunb and Lesser Tunb Islands.

Perhaps the chief factor contributing to the union's survival was a fear of its powerful neighbors, Iran and Saudi Arabia. Iran's conflict with the Emirates has already been discussed. Saudi Arabia claimed large areas of what became the United Arab Emirates. Specifically, the Saudis asserted their rights to the large portion of the Emirates that extended from Qatar all the way to Buraimi Oasis on the border with Oman. At stake in this border demarcation was billions of dollars worth of oil reserves. In 1955, the British had sided with Abu Dhabi in the Buraimi Oasis dispute. At that time, Abu Dhabi and the Sultanate of Oman gained joint control. After the union was established, Abu Dhabi reached a further border settlement with the Saudis that included the return of an oil field to Saudi Arabia.

The United Arab Emirates are small, rich sheikdoms flanked by powerful neighbors. To survive, they must remain on good terms with both Saudi Arabia and Iran. In spite of continuing border disagreements with both, the Emirates can be expected to avoid pushing either to a point that it would provoke conflict.

Qatar and Bahrain North of the United Arab Emirates lies the peninsular state of Qatar and the island state of Bahrain. Both remained under British protection during most of the 19th and the first half of the 20th centuries. Bahrain was one of the earlier Gulf states to exploit oil. Qatar remained a poor, largely forgotten backwater country until the largest deposits of natural gas in the world were discovered in what is now called the North Field. It is expected that this gas deposit will remain a source of revenue for the next century.

Qatar and Bahrain have been involved in a boundary dispute since the 1930s. Both states claim the Hawar Islands, Shoals of Daibel, and Jerada Reef. In addition, Bahrain also claims the Zubarah region of the Qatar Peninsula. This claim is based on the pearling activity there that the ruling family of Bahrain was engaged in during the mid 18th century. Qatar gained control of the Zubarah region in 1937 while unifying the peninsula. Bahrain exercises control over the offshore islands. The Gulf Cooperation Council has put a great deal of pressure on the parties to reach a settlement, but without success. Qatar has taken the case to the International Court of Justice, whereas Bahrain has called for a mediated settlement.

In recent years, there has been an improvement in relations between the two parties that has overshadowed the dispute. Qatar and Bahrain established diplomatic relations with each other for the first time in 1997. Since that time, the parties have made halting progress toward resolving their border problem. A committee was formed in December 1999 to try to solve the dispute. The heads of state met in March 2000 to discuss the issue.

Gulf Sailboats
Traditional fishing dhows in the harbor of Doha Qatar.
Source: Joe Weatherby

The fate of these islands and of the coastal strip of Qatar remains one of the major impediments to Arab unity in the Gulf.

Kuwait and Iraq The story of the establishment of Kuwait depends on who is telling it. Although the Greeks had settlements in this area during the time of Alexander the Great, the first modern occupation of the bay, now Kuwait City, occurred only 300 years ago. The ancestors of the present ruling Al-Sabah family probably arrived from central Arabia during the 18th century. They initially went to Basra, which was under Ottoman control, before settling along the Bay of Kuwait. Over the next 200 years, the Al-Sabahs became the dominant family in the northern Arab side of the Gulf.

Although the Ottomans claimed sovereignty over the Al-Sabah Emirate, they never actually exercised control. At times, Al-Sabah emirs had close relations with the Ottomans, but they managed to avoid being absorbed into their empire. Like many parts of the Ottoman Empire, the emirs acknowledged some Ottoman authority so long as the Ottomans did not attempt to exercise any actual control.

During the second half of the 19th century, the British signed agreements with the Al-Sabah rulers that were similar to the ones that they negotiated with the other Arab rulers in the Gulf. By the century's end, the British were interested in blocking German entry to the Gulf through the Ottoman Empire. Measures were taken by the British to separate Kuwait from any Ottoman ties. In 1913, the British established the border between Kuwait and the Ottoman Province of Basra, making the separation formal.

At the end of World War I, the British were given control over the Ottoman territory that was to become Iraq. This area included the province of Basra. Because they controlled Iraq and were allies of Kuwait, there was no challenge to the status of Kuwait. Iraq gained independence from Britain in 1932. At that time it was forced to accept the border with Kuwait. When the 1958 revolution occurred in Iraq, however, the new military government renounced the earlier agreements that had recognized Kuwait as an independent state. They asserted that Kuwait had always been part of Iraq because it had been linked to the Ottoman Province of Basra prior to Iraqi independence. Like Basra, Kuwait should still be part of Iraq.

A number of small incidents occurred during the 1950s and 1960s, after oil was discovered along the border. The Iraqi claim became more strident when Kuwait gained full independence from Britain in 1961. There were several serious incidents where the parties actually moved troops to the border. Many of the disagreements that led the Iraqi leadership to invade Kuwait in 1990 will probably never be known, but the dispute over the border between the two states was a major factor. The border ran through oil fields that were shared by both parties.

When Kuwait was liberated in 1991, the United Nations established the Iraq-Kuwait Boundary Demarcation Commission. The Commission's job was not to change the boundary but to set out the precise location of the border between the two states. The United Nations Security Council accepted this work when it passed Resolution 833 in May 1993. Since that time the United Nations has maintained an observer force to monitor the border and accompanying demilitarized zone. From time to time the Iraqi leadership has appeared to be ambiguous in its acceptance of both the border and the legitimacy of Kuwait itself. In 1999 Tariq Aziz, the Deputy Prime Minister of Iraq, was quoted as describing Kuwait as "an entity created by Britain to weaken Iraq and deprive it of its historic coast."[20]

The Gulf states, including Saudi Arabia, have been firm in their support of the sovereignty of Kuwait. While some may disapprove of the United States–sponsored United Nations sanctions policy regarding Iraq, they can be expected to remain united on the issue of the Kuwaiti border. As long as this position is backed by a firm commitment of U.S. military power, the present borders of Kuwait will remain secure.

THE BORDER DISPUTE BETWEEN SAUDI ARABIA AND YEMEN SETTLED

Near the Red Sea, the southern border of Saudi Arabia and the northern border of Yemen is made up of a knot of mountains reaching heights of 12,000 feet. This rugged highland area has been a source of tension between Yemen and its northern neighbor since the end of World War I. Initially the peninsula was under the nominal control of the Ottomans. When they withdrew after their defeat in World War I, this mountainous area became a point of contention. Yemen had the backing of the British. During the consolidation of what was to become modern Saudi Arabia, Saudi forces attempted to invade Yemen. The British quickly stopped them.

The 1934 Ta'if Agreement fixed the northwestern boundaries between Saudi Arabia and Yemen.[21] The Ta'if Agreement established the Yemeni side of the border on a line that followed the top of the mountains. Over the years there have been a number of skirmishes between the two sides.

During the 1990s, the exploration for oil began on the Yemeni side along an unmarked area bordering the Rub al-Khali. It is believed that the prospect of a new oil field sparked a renewed Saudi interest in making claims to parts of the border area. Saudis called for a change in the border that would give them control of the mountaintops and would restrict Yemen to the southern base of the peaks. The Saudis justified their position by stating that Yemeni forces constituted a threat to southern Saudi Arabia by their holding of the high ground. Yemen responded that the modern Saudi military had missiles and jet aircraft and that these modern arms rendered traditional assessments about holding strategic high ground obsolete. They pointed out that the Ta'if Agreement should continue to govern the northwestern boundary location. Saudi Arabia and Yemen have had strained relations for a number of years. When the latest incident flared up in 1999, the Saudis expelled over 4,000 Yemeni nationals, stating that their papers were not in order.

In June of 2000, a breakthrough occurred at a meeting of the two parties held in the Saudi port of Jidda. There, the representatives of Saudi Arabia and Yemen signed an agreement to allow an outside company to mark the entire border. It was considered significant that Saudi Crown Prince Abdullah and the Yemeni President were present to witness the signing ceremony.

Under the terms of the new agreement, both sides have agreed to temporarily demilitarize the area while an outside party, still to be selected, marks the border. The foreign ministers of both states have been given the task of implementing the Jidda agreement.

Yemen is a poor, weak state in relation to Saudi Arabia, and the Yemeni side must tread carefully when dealing with the Saudis. In this case, there is hope that if the border dispute can be finally resolved, other outstanding grievances against the Saudis can also be eliminated. Better relations with Saudi Arabia reduce some of the objections to Yemen's admission to the Gulf Cooperation Council (GCC).

In the past, border disagreements have come and gone in this part of the world. The area in question is poorly marked and mountainous, and tribal conflicts are common. Relations between Saudi Arabia and Yemen have historically been correct but unfriendly. It will take good will on both sides to make the implementation of this settlement work. Failure to successfully accomplish this task has an explosive potential that could destabilize the southern part of the Arabian Peninsula.

Words Commonly Used in Describing the Politics of Geography in the Middle East and North Africa

Enclave An *enclave* is a part of a state surrounded by the territories of another state. The two Spanish towns located on the Mediterranean coast of Morocco, Ceuta and Melilla are enclaves.

Sheikdom (Shaykhdom) Although some are religious, one of the definitions of *sheik* is political. In traditional Arabian society the sheik (shaykh) was the leader of an extended collection of families or a tribe. The sheik was selected by the heads of families at a meeting or a council. In this loose form of tribal democracy sheiks were selected on the basis of both wisdom and power. Although this was not an inherited position, it was not uncommon for sons to succeed fathers. As the tribes became more settled, however, it became common to refer to the established territory controlled by the tribe as a sheikdom.

Over time, loose family rule became established states. Old nomadic boundaries tended to overlap, causing modern border disputes. The selection process of the Gulf sheiks also changed. It had become a dynastic process in practice. Sometimes the word *emirates* is substituted for the old word *sheikdoms* to describe the Arab states of the Gulf. There is further discussion of the title of sheik in Chapter 3.

Emir (Amir) Originally a commander, the title *emir* evolved into one of regional governor. Today it can have a broad meaning that includes commander, prince, or ruler. Most of the rulers of the sheikdoms of the Gulf use the title *emir*.

Sultan The Turkish title *sultan* meant supreme ruler of the state as opposed to a religious title. In the Gulf, the ruler of Oman uses the title "Sultan Qaboos." His dynasty can be traced to the 18th century.

Bab This is the Arabic word for gate. When included with other qualifiers, it takes on several different meanings. For example, the Bab-I Ali of the Ottoman Empire literally meant the "high gate," but in politics it referred to what was called the Sublime Porte. It was the European name given to the government of the Ottoman Empire.

The word *bab* is also used to describe a strait or narrow passage. The best-known geographic "bab" is the famous Bab al-Mandeb (Gate of Tears), located at the southern end of the Red Sea. The Bab al-Mandeb has a width averaging only 20 miles. Its name reflects the fact that Bab al-Mandeb's narrow channels cause swift currents that have always been hazardous to mariners attempting to use the passage.

It is possible for states bordering Bab al-Mandeb to close the passage, thus denying access to the Red Sea from the south. During the Cold War this threat affected access to both the Suez Canal and to the states of Israel and Jordan. The Soviet Union and the United States maintained naval forces in the area during times of tension.

Although the passage remains important, the use of supertankers that cannot transit the Suez Canal when loaded and the completion of the Saudi oil pipeline to the Red Sea port of Yanbu have reduced its strategic importance. Nevertheless, control of the Bab al-Mandeb will remain significant so long as the Red Sea is used to transport goods.

Condominium   Although little used today, condominiums have been proposed as compromise solutions to disputed territories in many parts of the world, including the Middle East and North Africa. A condominium is an area where two or more powers share sovereignty over the same area. The degree of control does not have to be equal. The Anglo-Egyptian Sudan was administered as the condominium of Egypt and the United Kingdom from 1898 until the Sudan gained independence in 1955. Recently condominium status has been suggested as a way to solve the disputes over both Cyprus and the status of Jerusalem. Neither of these proposed condominiums have been accepted by the parties involved.

Convention   A convention is an international agreement or contract between states. Conventions, like acts, declarations, and protocols, are agreements less formal than treaties. Between the end of World War I and 1936, the status of the Dardanelles and Bosporus was governed by two treaties and one convention. The present 1936 Montreux Convention governing access to the Dardanelles and Bosporus superseded the earlier treaties.

The Gulf States   Eight states stretch along the coastline of the Persian Gulf. Technically all are Gulf states. However, the term *Gulf states*, as it is understood, refers to the Arab states of the western and southwestern coast of the Persian Gulf. Specifically, the Gulf states include monarchies of the United Arab Emirates, Bahrain, Oman, Qatar, Saudi Arabia, and Kuwait. Iran and Iraq are not generally linked with the other six when using this term.

Spanish Sahara   This was the name of the Spanish colonial territory along the Atlantic south of Morocco. When the Spanish withdrew, the land became the disputed territory of the Western Sahara.

Strait of Tiran   Forming a "V" with the Gulf of Suez, the Strait of Tiran is a narrow chokepoint between the Gulf of Aqaba and the Red Sea. Only 12 miles wide at places, the Strait controls traffic between the Suez Canal and the Red Sea to the Israeli port of Elat and the Jordanian port of Aqaba. During the wars between Egypt and Israel, control of the Strait became a primary objective of both parties. The 1979 treaty of peace between Egypt and Israel guaranteed free passage for Israeli ships through the Strait in return for an Israeli withdrawal from the Sinai Peninsula.

Summary

The politics of geography in the Middle East and North Africa include both a theoretical base and specific points of dispute. The involvement of North Africa and the Middle East in the global strategic thinking of the major powers occurred first because of the region's important role as a bridge between the Afro-Eurasian continents. More recently, it became important because of the vast petroleum deposits that exist there. The legacy of colonialism has also contributed to disputes over territory in many parts of the region. Some of the more important territorial disputes have been discussed. Finally, a number of terms useful in the understanding of the policies of geography in this region are briefly explained.

Review Questions

1. What is the theory of sea power?
2. Who was the great advocate of sea power?
3. What is the theory of land power?
4. Why did the Middle East and North Africa become involved in great power struggles that were centered outside the region?
5. How does the author see that some of these geographic theories are still being applied to the region?

Suggested Readings

Peter Calvocoressi, *World Politics Since 1945,* 6th Edition, Longman, New York, 1991.
Irene M. Franc and David Brownstone, *The European Overland Routes,* Chapter 5, Facts on File, New York, 1990.
Martin Glassner, *Political Geography,* John Wiley & Sons, New York, 1992.
Colbert C. Held, *Middle East Patterns: Places, Peoples, and Politics,* Westview Press, Boulder, Colo., 1989.
Geoffrey Kemp and Robert E. Harkavy, *Strategic Geography and the Changing Middle East,* Brookings Institution Press, Washington, D.C., 1997.

Notes

1. Lewis M. Alexander, *World Political Patterns,* 2nd Edition (Chicago: Rand McNally and Co., 1963), pp. 1–2.
2. Major Alexander de Seversky, *Victory Through Airpower* (New York: Simon and Schuster, 1942), p. 13.
3. The global threat of Soviet communism may have been exaggerated by the United States and its allies because of the events taking place in the early Cold War years. Looking back on that period, many scholars now believe that the Soviets did not have the capability to expand on the global scale so feared by the West.
4. George Lenczowski, *The Middle East in World Affairs,* 3rd Edition (Ithaca, N.Y.: Cornell University Press, 1962), p. 190.
5. For a copy of the International Regulations governing the Turkish Straits: The Montreux Convention, July 20, 1936, see Ralph Magnus, *Documents on the Middle East,* American Enterprise Institute for Public Policy Research, Washington, D.C., 1969, pp. 42–53.
6. Ralph Magnus, *Documents on the Middle East* (Washington, D.C.: The American Enterprise Institute for Policy Research, July 1969), pp. 81–83.
7. Today most observers would acknowledge that the Baghdad Pact failed because of events in the region that had little to do with the Cold War. The Soviet threat was an opportunistic move more than a planned expansion of influence.
8. Henry Kissinger, *Diplomacy* (New York: Touchstone Books, 1994), p. 707.
9. "Iraqis Struggling Despite Oil Prices: Many Still Hungry Despite U.N. Sanctions," Associated Press Dateline Baghdad, *The Dallas Morning News,* February 23, 2000, p. A10.

10. British Broadcasting Corporation, BBC, Worldwide Monitoring Report from the Moroccan News Agency, MAP, January 19, 2000.
11. Sir Rupert Cornwell, Frontline La'Ayone, Western Sahara: Democracy at Its Most Confusing: Organizing an Election for Nomads, *The Independent* (London), p. 13.
12. Jean-Jacques Cornish, "South Africa," *Business Day,* January 25, 2000, p. 12.
13. Michael Knipe, "The Rock's on an Economic Roll," *The Times of London,* Features Section, November 17, 1998.
14. Ahmed el Rhaidi, Minister Councellor, Moroccan Embassy, London, Letter to the Editor, *The Daily Telegraph* (London), February 23, 1999, p. 23.
15. Richard Halliburton, *The Flying Carpet* (Indianapolis: Bobbs-Merrill Co., 1932), p. 83.
16. Thomas Pollsen, *Nations and States: A Geographic Background to World Affairs* (Englewood Cliffs, N.J.: Prentice Hall, 1995), p. 207.
17. William Clinton, from the letter released by the White House on June 3, 1999, from the President to the Speaker of the House of Representatives and to the President of the Senate on the Cyprus Dispute Report.
18. R. Hill, *The Illustrated History of the Royal Navy* (Oxford, England: The Oxford University Press, 1995), p. 303.
19. Lewis Alexander, *World Political Patterns,* 2nd Edition (Chicago: Rand McNally and Co., 1963), p. 387.
20. Michael Theodoulou, "Iraq Threatens to Flout 'Unjust' UN Resolutions," *The Times* (London), Overseas News Section, January 11, 1999.
21. Officially known as the Treaty of Muslim Friendship and Arab Fraternity, the Ta'if Agreement ended a six-week Saudi invasion of Yemen in 1934. The Saudis defeated the tribal forces in Yemen but had to accept peace when Britain, France, and Italy sent warships to the Yemeni coast. Yemen regained about half of the territory that they had lost during the initial invasion.

Chapter 3

The Politics of Religion in the Middle East and North Africa

Introduction

The story is told that a wise man and an atheist were standing on a beach when the atheist asserted that there was no God. The wise man then pointed to a ship sailing on the horizon. He said that the ship appeared to sail itself. He then said that the answer to the question of whether there was a God could be found when the ship arrived at the shore. Eventually the ship arrived and the captain and crew disembarked. The atheist laughed, pointing out to the wise man that the ship needed a captain and a crew. It could not sail itself. The wise man replied, "If for one vessel you need a captain and a crew, what do you need to guide the entire universe?"[1]

The world's three great monotheistic religions (Judaism, Christianity, and Islam) arose in the Middle East. All three religions are interconnected historically. They share the same basic world vision that there is no god but God.

At the beginning of the 21st century, many modern religious and political leaders recognize this commonality of belief. Interestingly, they stress the similar values of Judaism, Christianity, and Islam rather than their differences. When Iranian leader Muhammad Khatami met with Pope John Paul II in the Vatican, he said,

> The hope is for the final victory of monotheism, ethics, and morality together with peace and reconciliation.

Then, speaking to the Pope directly, he stated,

> May God protect you.[2]

Later, when visiting Mount Nebo, where it is said that Moses was allowed to view the Promised Land, Pope John Paul II said,

> In sight of the city of Jericho, our gaze directed toward Jerusalem, let us lift up our prayer to almighty God for all of the people in the Promised Land: Jews, Muslims and Christians.[3]

The Metropolitan of the Antiochan Orthodox Archdiocese of North America, Philip Saliba, recently said,

> The messages of Islam and Christianity are about 90 percent the same.

He further stated that,

> There are people who call themselves Christians in North America today who do not believe in the Incarnation and who do not believe in the Resurrection. Islam is closer to us than these so-called Christians.[4]

Egyptian President Hosni Mubarak welcomed the Pope to Egypt, stating,

> In today's world, where God is tragically forgotten, Christians and Muslims are called in one spirit of love to defend and always promote human dignity, moral values, and freedom.[5]

When the Pope made a March 2000 visit to Israel, Prime Minister Ehud Barak echoed this same religious theme by saying, "This historic visit is important for the relations between Jews and Christians."[6]

Unfortunately for the stability of the region, these statements of religious understanding represent only the aspirations and tolerance of some. Past and present history makes the prospect of an understanding and tolerance of each other's religion based on the common belief in one God unlikely. As revealed truths given by God, the religions of each of the three view the others as either inferior or false. Jews, Christians, and Muslims each assert that there is only one truth, theirs! Under the circumstances, there is little purpose in dialogue. The political and religious tensions are so bitter that few Muslims, Christians, or Jews would welcome the chance to sit around a table talking about God. This kind of discussion is largely limited to ecumenical meetings in places outside the Middle East and North Africa.

Why Is Religion Important in the Middle East and North Africa?

Along with nationalism, religion is one of the two great forces shaping the modern character of the region. As practiced there, the three monotheistic religions do have a number of common elements. First, religion in the Middle East and North Africa is far more important in the daily life of the individual than is generally understood in the West. Perhaps in former centuries, the practice of religion in the West was as pervasive in daily life as it currently is in the Middle East and North Africa, but the role of Western religion changed after the Age of Enlightenment. Much of the day-to-day activities of Western society became secular. Religious activity became individualistic and private. Public demonstrations of religion became limited to gatherings held for one or two hours each week. This is not to say that belief in God declined, but rather that public demonstrations of religion declined. In the Middle East and North Africa, religion plays a far more public role in the life of believers. This is true not only for Muslims but also for Christians and some Jews as well.

Second, life for many in this part of the world is difficult. Religion allows the individual believer to accept life with all of its hardships in the expectation that there is a better existence to come. This dependency on a better life in the "hereafter" produces a religious composure that is difficult for secular Westerners to understand. This reliance on the security found in an all-encompassing religion is the core of all Middle Eastern religions, whether Jewish, Christian, or Muslim.

Third, religion in the Middle East and North Africa, like religions in the West, has a miraculous element. To appreciate this key feature, religion must be understood to exist on two levels: the academic religion and the popular religion. The orthodox doctrine of the three monotheistic religions is not too different in the Middle East and North Africa from that practiced elsewhere. The development of the official religion of synagogue, church, and mosque is the job of the scholar, lawyer, and preacher. Like their counterparts in the West, these theologians work in universities, seminaries, and sanctuaries. Much of this scholarship will be analyzed later in the chapter.

Far more difficult to understand are the popular religions of Judaism, Christianity, and Islam. Although officially hostile toward each other, these religions have developed in the same geographic area. They draw on the same cultural source for their existences. Both Christianity and Islam claim a historic linkage to Judaism. It should not be surprising that the popular religiosity of these three religions would tend to overlap. Although most people would deny it, many popular practices of the three religions are similar. Often the three even venerate the same geographic locations. All have sacred places—wells, rocks, rivers, and mountains—that tend to overlap. Among other things, believers practice the wearing of crosses, stars, or Islamic verses as jewelry. They all fear unknowns such as "the evil eye." They venerate the tombs of holy men who were often from competing religions. They commonly use certain colors on houses to guard against evil. They carry religious charms, wear special clothing, and observe customs that to the Westerner might seem to be more tribal than religious. The distance between this popular religiosity and the formal religion of the scholars is often great.

Religion plays an important role in understanding the history and culture of any society, but in the Middle East and North Africa, religion defines history and culture. It is impossible to have any understanding of the events taking place in that area currently without taking into account the impact that religion has on its culture.

If one is to understand current political events, one must view them through "the eyes" of the residents. Part of that perception can come only through an understanding of the influence that religion has on decision-making. To appreciate a religion with which one is unfamiliar, it is necessary to replace preexisting opinions and prejudices with understanding and respect. Muslims are fond of saying that to understand Islam, one must enter by the door. Unless this transition of thinking can be made by the reader, many political events in the Middle East and North Africa will seem irrational and without purpose. For many of us schooled in the secular societies of the West, an open-minded analysis of the importance that different religious cultures have in political decision-making is difficult because we have not been conditioned to think about it. Nevertheless, the journey is well worth the effort. Better understanding of political events that occur in the region is the prize.

What Is the Most Influential Religion in the Politics of the Middle East and North Africa?

Islam is the youngest of the three great monotheistic religions that originated in this area and has been the dominant religion for over 1000 years. Today more than 90 percent of the population is Muslim. To understand political events in the Middle East and North Africa, it is necessary to have some knowledge of Islam.

Islam is a dynamic religion. Arguably the world's fastest growing religion, Islam is dominant in at least 40 countries. In Europe, Islam is second in size after Christianity. In

Cultural Similarities
Displayed, left to right, on an oriental carpet are Roman Catholic beads, Greek Orthodox beads, and Muslim beads.
Source: Joe Weatherby

the year 2001, the United States has more Muslim citizens than either Jews, Episcopalians, Latter Day Saints, Lutherans, Presbyterians, or members of the Churches of Christ!

WESTERNERS DON'T KNOW MUCH ABOUT ISLAM

Islam has over 1 billion members. One in five people on the planet is a Muslim! Yet most people in the West know more about the ancient religions of Central America than they do about Islam. Is this a plot? Not exactly.

For most of the 20th century, the perceived threats to the survival of Western civilization and values were fascism and communism. Ironically, both of these philosophies were Western in their origin. During the last millennium, however, the primary threat to the West came from the Muslims of the Middle East. Whether it was the Islamic invasions in the Sagas of Roland, the Crusaders striving to capture Jerusalem, or the central Europeans fighting to stop repeated assaults from the Ottomans, Europeans have always believed that the greatest danger to Western Christian civilization was coming from the Muslim East. The fear of Islam is deeply ingrained in Western culture.

In literature, art, and the development of the Western view of history, the Islamic threat has always been emphasized. In more recent times, a constant barrage of negative images spread by the popular media has reinforced this portrait of Islam and Muslims.

Certainly, some Muslim political and religious leaders have not helped this image. Through their comments, the end of Western colonialism has often been portrayed to Westerners as the beginning of a new Muslim assault on the West. This fear has been reinforced by the rapid growth of Islam in Western society. In some places in the West, these new immigrants and their converts have been treated with harassments similar to those that were formerly reserved for people accused of being "reds" during the "Cold War."

Certainly the few acts of terrorism by Muslims that have been directed toward Western targets are real. It should be understood, however, that attacks such as these are not new and they are not exclusively from Muslim sources. While the Qadaffis, the Khomeinis, and the Bin Ladens are well known, they represent only a small fraction of Muslims worldwide. They probably no more represent Islam than fascists like General Peron and General Franco represented Christian views during the 1940s. Although most of these "leaders" have claimed that they are acting in the name of religion, they were usually pursuing political objectives.

To truly appreciate the importance of Islam to civilization, it is first necessary to change the popular idea that Islam is a problem and recognize that it is a solution to the problem for millions of people around the world. It should also be made clear that any religion with a billion adherents is not and cannot be monolithic. There are hundreds of positions held by Muslims on the political events of the day. It is a grave mistake for Westerners to assume that all Muslims are determined to destroy the Western way of life.

THE REASONS FOR THE POPULARITY OF ISLAM

It should be understood that all major religions have a geographic and cultural base. The three great monotheistic religions, however, have transcended their geographic origins to gain a worldwide following. This phenomenon is particularly apparent in Christianity and Islam. Both of these religions are noted for aggressive missionary activity in areas far from their origins. Of the two, Islam is the fastest growing and will likely overtake Christianity in absolute numbers during the 21st century. As previously mentioned, Islam is second after Christianity in terms of adherence in many Western countries. However, it is in the developing world, especially in Africa, where Islam has shown the most spectacular growth. It is fair to ask, first, What has been the appeal of Islam to people in the developing world? Second, Why has Islam experienced such a resurgence in the Middle East and North Africa?

There are several answers to the first question. Islam offers a simple and straightforward path to life after death. Unlike Christianity, there is no catechism, no complicated theology, and no professional priest dispersing sacraments. Islam's call is clear and can be understood by anyone. There is no god but God and Muhammad is his messenger. This salvation based on the belief that there is only one God has a universal appeal.

The second great truth in Islam is equality before God. All believers are considered equal. This truth is ritually reenacted each year during the pilgrimage to Mecca. There, every male participant wears the same seamless sheet of white cloth. In the same fashion, the religion's position on racial equality has had great appeal in societies that have suffered discrimination based on race. The Muslim view on race has been especially effective in Africa where Christianity is often identified with the racial injustice perpetuated by Western colonialism.

It should be pointed out that, like other religions, Islam has experienced periods when racism was practiced. In early Islamic history, Arabs asserted superiority over non-Arab Muslims. Even in modern times there have been cases of discrimination against both people with dark skin and also people with white skin. However, these practices were part of popular culture and have never been condoned by Islamic teaching.[7]

THE BELIEFS OF MUSLIMS

Islam requires that the believer acknowledge that there is no god but God. Muslims also believe that Muhammad is the prophet of God. The word *Islam* means "submission." The word *Muslim* means "submitter." Thus, a Muslim is a believer who has submitted to the will of God. The word *Qur'an* (Koran) means recitation. For Muslims, the Koran is Islam's holiest book. They believe that the Koran is the literal word of God revealed to Muhammad by the angel Gabriel. Through the Koran, God tells humankind that there will be a day of judgment when all persons will have to answer for their deeds during life. Simply stated, Muslims believe that there is no god but God, Muhammad spoke the truth in reciting the Koran, there will be a final judgment day, and there will be life after death. Unlike Christianity, the great disputes in Islam do not focus on what is true; rather, they look to what is good.

Islam is not only a religion in the Western sense; it is a way of life. Unlike the Western tradition where religious life and secular life are divided, Islam prescribes the individual believer's behavior in all aspects of daily existence. Religious disputes focus on what is good for the community of believers. Such questions as how society should be governed, how leaders should be selected, how business should be carried out, how people should behave, and what should be included within the scope of Islamic law are hotly debated. It is on these cleavage points that Islamic society fragments into the various branches of the religion.

WHY ISLAM IS A MONOTHEISTIC RELIGION

Monotheism is the doctrine that there is only one God. Muslims are uncompromising monotheists. To them, God is eternal and beyond description, the creator of the universe. In Arabic, God is called Allah. To state, as is often done in the West, that Muslims worship a God called Allah is incorrect because it implies that the God worshipped by Muslims is different from the God of Christians and Jews. Arabic-speaking Jews and Christians may also use the word Allah to refer to God. The Muslim affirmation that there is no god but God more accurately states their strict concept of monotheism.

Although God is beyond description, here are two references to God in the Koran:

> Yea, to God belongs the dominion of the heavens and the earth; and to God is the final goal (of all).[8]

> It was he who created man and we know what dark suggestions his soul makes to him: for we are nearer to him than (his) jugular vein.[9]

Simply put, Islam is a God-centered religion. Muslims believe that Christians have departed from strict monotheism by asserting that Jesus is the Son of God. Furthermore, many Muslim theologians believe that the use of the concept of a trinity and the creation of saints by some Christians has caused them to break with the correct idea of a God-centered religion.[10] This is one of the most important differences in the views of Islam and Christianity.

MUSLIMS LIVE THEIR FAITH

It is not difficult to make the simple profession of faith required by all Muslims. Because Islam is an all-encompassing way of living, however, it requires a great deal of commitment to be a good Muslim. To help guide the believer through earthly life, all Muslims are called on to observe five obligations, which they call the Five Pillars of Islam. In popular culture, some Muslims use the hand to symbolize these five obligations.

THE FIVE PILLARS OF ISLAM

The Profession of Faith (Shahadah)   This affirmation of faith is simple, but the implications are great for the believer. If one is sincere and attests that "There is no god but God and Muhammad is the Messenger of God," one becomes a Muslim. This profession of faith is the single most important act in the Muslim religion.

The profession must be taken without reservation. If it is not, then it has no validity. True acceptance is to attest to the oneness of God, that Muhammad spoke the truth, and that the Koran is the final, complete, and perfect word given by God through Muhammad to humankind.

Muslims believe that human beings may do both good and evil in their lives but that this true affirmation of faith will keep them in the blessing of God. By making the profession of faith, Muslims are accepting the principles of Islam set out in the Koran. They also are acknowledging the obligations of the faith set out in the traditions and practices of Islam. As these cover most activities of a person's earthly existence, these obligations require a major commitment if they are to be observed.

Ritual Prayer (Salat)   The second obligation that all Muslims must accept is prayer that takes place five times each day. While facing toward the Kaaba in Mecca, the prayer is given in a prescribed way at specific times of the day. The dawn prayer (Subh) begins shortly before the sunrise, the noon prayer (Zuhr) occurs just after the sun has reached the high point in the sky, the afternoon prayer (Asr) takes place when the body's shadow is approximately two body lengths, the sunset prayer (Maghrib) happens just after the sunset, and the evening prayer (Isha) is performed in the evening just before going to bed. The Muslim day begins at sundown.[11]

Depending on circumstances, the prayer may be carried out in a group or individually. What is important is that the performance of prayer and the formal process of praying are a great collective activity done by Muslims everywhere.

The prayer requires the believer to participate in three phases of ritual. First, he must prepare by erasing all evil or selfish thoughts from his mind. This allows the worshipper to focus entirely on the glory of God. Second, the prayer area must be cleaned. Finally, the believer must wash. This cleansing of the body includes the hands, mouth, nose, ears, neck, arms to the elbows, feet, and ankles. The architectural tradition of running water associated with mosques was developed to facilitate this ritual purification. However, Muslims can be seen washing in this prescribed manner almost anywhere that water is available. In the absence of water, believers are permitted to use sand to perform this cleansing.

The prayer itself takes place with several distinct actions occurring in order. The following are directions for the prayer:

- First, shut eyes to aid in the concentration of the greatness of God. Keep eyes shut throughout the prayer cycle.
- While standing upright, bring hands up to the level of the ears with the palms forward.
- While in the same position, drop hands to waist, crossing the right hand over the left.
- Bend forward at the waist, placing hands on the knees.
- Resume standing position with hands at side.
- Go to kneeling position with knees, toes, forehead, and hands touching the prayer mat.
- Assume seated position with hands placed on thighs, rising on feet, with men raising the right heel.
- Return to the former kneeling position.
- Return to the sitting position.

After repeating the prayer several times, it ends in the sitting position. Prescribed oral recitations are said in each position of the prayer. This very formal prayer sequence is one of the great unifying features of Islam.

Unlike the prayers of Christians, Muslim prayer is made in obedience to the command of God.[12] It is a daily acknowledgement of the believer that there is no god but God and Muhammad is his prophet. This prayer cycle may take place anywhere during the appointed times. Muslims are commonly seen leaving important business meetings in modern office buildings to pray, praying in the aisles of jet aircraft, praying on street sidewalks, praying in schools, and praying in small shops. This kind of regular public demonstration of faith is virtually unknown in Western religions. In addition, Muslims are enjoined to make the Friday prayer in the mosque where they are together. Men and women pray in separate places. In many places this prayer is primarily a male activity and women make the Friday prayer in their homes. It should be noted that private prayer is considered to be admirable. However, it is not required as part of the Five Pillars.

Before leaving the subject of ritual prayer, two questions should be addressed. First, why do Muslims pray in the direction of Mecca? During the early days of Muhammad's ministry, Muslims were called to pray toward Jerusalem. At the time, it was assumed by Muslims that, as monotheists, Jews and Christians would see the Koran as the perfect word of God. They would understand that the other divinely revealed books, the Torah, the Psalms, and the Gospels had, over time, been corrupted by humankind and should be superseded by the Koran. When Jews and Christians failed to accept the truth of the Koran and become Muslims, the faithful turned and began to pray toward Mecca, the birthplace of Muhammad.

All mosques have a pointer, or qibla, to direct the prayer act toward Mecca. The quibla is no altar as in a Christian church. It has no significance other than to point the direction in which to pray. Thus, a Muslim in North America would pray to the east, in China to the west, and in Yemen to the North.

The second question is: Why are Muslims called by a muezzin to pray? Since the time of Muhammad, Muslims have assembled together to pray. Tradition holds that as the crowds grew too large for this informal prayer activity, Muhammad asked a believer from Africa named Bilal to call the people to prayer. In so doing, Bilal became the first muezzin. A muezzin is a person who gives the call to prayer.

Tunisian Mosque
This unusual mosque has an eight-sided minaret.
Source: Joe Weatherby

Almsgiving (Zakat)   Muslims are obligated to pay a percentage of their income to help the poor and needy. This form of religious taxation is called *zakat*. Zakat is an act of monetary worship. It is different than state taxes as they are understood in the West. Part of the Muslim's religious duty is to practice benevolence. The funds from this collection are usually dispersed by the state to the disadvantaged. Even when the state does not make this collection, Muslims are expected to make the donation to the needy as a personal gesture.

In addition to the zakat, Muslims are urged to engage in a form of spontaneous voluntary almsgiving called *sadaga*. In this case, the process often involves passing a few coins into the hands of a needy person on the street.

To be meritorious, both zakat and sadaga should be given without fanfare and without calling attention to oneself. Those who do good work are also giving alms. For example, a physician who works in a free clinic during his spare time is also giving alms. As a religious observance, the key is that the act is freely given for the glory of God and not for the aggrandizement of the individual.

Muslims also have a different attitude from some Christians toward the needy. Need is considered to be a condition in life that is beyond the control of the individual. It is a Muslim's duty to help the unfortunate. They do not believe that poverty is evil. For Muslims, there is little or no stigma attached to the individual who accepts this form of religious welfare.

Throughout the Middle East and North Africa there are a large number of religious charities engaged in all sorts of activities to help the poor. One reason why Islam has enjoyed such a resurgence in this part of the world is that these voluntary charities have filled the social service vacuum left by the failure and corruption of the secular states of the region.

Fasting (Sawm)   It is common for adherents of religions in many cultures to fast. Both Christians and Jews engage in fasting during designated times of the year. In part, Christian fasting is usually done as a way of atoning for sin.

In Islam, the fast is done for an entirely different reason. Muslims fast during the ninth lunar month of Ramadan to clear the believer's mind of earthly wants in order to gain a richer perception of God. This fast is a personal commitment made by each member of the community to share together the hardship of the most underprivileged. It is designed to discipline the believer while giving one freedom to contemplate the glory of God.

The month-long fast takes place in the daylight hours from the time that one can see a thread in the morning until the evening prayer time. During this period, Muslims are enjoined from eating, drinking, smoking, or engaging in sexual activity. The month of Ramadan is selected because it was during this period that Muhammad received the first revelation from God.

Muslims are expected to engage in the fast with a positive frame of mind. Just as believers abstain from food, they are also expected to avoid evil acts such as lying, envying, stealing, or quarreling. To commit these acts violates the spirit of the fast. During this period Muslims are expected to actively aid the poor.

This fast is longer in duration and more intense than anything practiced by Jews or Christians. In spite of the hardship of fasting, Muslims believe that it teaches self-denial and moderation. They also believe that the community of believers is brought closer to the understanding of the greatness of God during Ramadan.

Islam is a practical religion. Those on harsh journeys, the sick, pregnant women, and others who would be endangered by this rigorous activity are not required to fast. If possible, they are called to make up their lost fasting time at a later date.

Pilgrimage to Mecca (Hajj)   One of the most moving events in a Muslim's life is the pilgrimage to Mecca. Here Muslims, both male and female, with males wearing the ritual white, from every country in the world and from every station in life, pray as equals before God.

According to Muslim tradition, this pilgrimage dates back to the time of Abraham. Muslims believe that it was Abraham who reconstructed the Kaaba where it is located within the court of the Great Mosque of Mecca. It was near Mecca that Abraham was ordered by God to sacrifice his son. Muslims believe that the son was Ishmael, not Isaac. Jews and Christians believe that Isaac was to be sacrificed and that the event took place in Jerusalem. Arabs believe that Ishmael was the father of the Arab people. Muhammad validated this tradition by himself making the pilgrimage to Mecca. If able, all Muslims are called to make the pilgrimage to Mecca once in their lifetime. This religious act takes place during the twelfth month of the Muslim calendar. Like the prayer, the ritual of the pilgrimage is carefully prescribed. Although the process is not difficult to do, each step has great religious significance for the believer. Perhaps the most impressive aspect of the pilgrimage is the sight of millions of people of all backgrounds performing the same rituals.

There are no priests or leaders; each participant performs the sequence of events individually but within the context of the great Islamic community.

The pilgrimage consists of several rituals that take place on a strictly prescribed route to be valid. These include, first, the donning of the pilgrim's garment, which is white and seamless for men. For women, the garment is only a simple white head covering and a dress. While wearing this garment, the pilgrim is considered to be in a special state of grace.

Second, pilgrims make the journey to the Plain of Arafat for the "standing." Here participants pray and meditate near the spot where Muhammad preached his last sermon before his death. Pilgrims are expected to repent of their sins and offer prayers during this period. At sunset, the pilgrims depart.

The feast of sacrifice is the third ritual. First pilgrims toss stones that they have gathered at three pillars representing the devil. Muslims believe that it was on this spot Abraham resisted the temptation of Satan, who called upon him to disobey God's command to sacrifice his son Ishmael. To the pilgrims the act of tossing stones signifies a personal commitment to resist wickedness.

After the stoning, those pilgrims who are able sacrifice a sheep. They then give a portion of the meat to the needy. According to Islamic tradition, Abraham was stopped by an angel from sacrificing his son and a sheep was substituted. This act signifies Abraham's willingness to obey God's command. For Muslims this act is one of thanksgiving for God's mercy.

The "circling" is the fourth act of the pilgrimage. Participants proceed to the Great Mosque of Mecca. Here they pray and circle the Kaaba seven times. The Kaaba is a square black building located in the center of the courtyard of the Mosque. They complete the ritual by praying on a spot in the courtyard where Abraham is believed to have prayed. These acts complete the pilgrimage.

There are other rituals that most pilgrims also try to complete while in Arabia. The "running" is an important event during the pilgrimage. Participants cross through a covered passage between two small hills. This ritual is to commemorate the search of Ishmael's mother for water. The angel Gabriel appeared and created a spring for them to drink. Pilgrims drink the water of the spring and then fill small bottles to take home. Pilgrims return to the stone pillars to again cast stones before beginning the journey to their homes. Each pilgrim who completes these rituals is honored by others with the title *Hajji*. While still in Arabia, many pilgrims also visit the city of Medina. There they pray at the tombs of Muhammad and his early successors.

This pilgrimage was formerly very dangerous and took great bravery and sacrifice to accomplish. With modern transportation and the facilities provided by the Saudi government, many of the hardships formerly experienced by pilgrims journeying to Mecca have been eliminated. Today the pilgrimage is the largest single gathering of humanity on earth.

Holy Struggle (Jihad) Sometimes called the sixth pillar of Islam, this duty is often misunderstood in the West. Jihad has both a personal and a communal meaning. The personal meaning calls for Muslims to always resist their own evil inclinations. This inner struggle is less known in the West but plays a significant role in the believer's daily life. The external meaning of jihad calls on all Muslims to further the cause of God. This command promises a place in heaven for those believers who fight to spread the universal Muslim doctrine expressed in the profession of faith. The confusion over the external aspects of jihad arises because many leaders, to further their own agendas, have used the term *jihad* in a political manner. This manipulation of the call for jihad has been a familiar theme throughout the centuries.[13]

Paul Coles writes that,

> Ottoman Sultans of the 16th century were obliged to magnify their role as standard bearers of the jihad in order to mobilize enthusiasm among their Muslim subjects for a long series of wars against Europeans in the Mediterranean and Eastern Europe.[14]

Robert Lacey pointed out that this same call was given during the October war between Israel and Egypt:

> On 20 October 1973, King Faisal of Saudi Arabia declared jihad (holy war) on Israel and on all the countries who supported her, as part of that holy war he imposed a total oil embargo on the Kingdom's oil shipments to the United States. The world has not been the same since.[15]

The medieval Christian calls for a crusade to liberate the Holy Land, for the reconquest of Spain, and for the conquest of Mexico and Latin America were similar to the Muslim idea of jihad. Even the 19th-century Western idea of the "white man's burden" often had elements of a Christian crusade.

Muslims do believe in the principles of jihad both as individuals and as a community of believers. The conflict occurs when the community attempts to apply the concept to the real world. Should jihad be used only against the enemies of Islam? Are Muslims who do not strictly observe all aspects of Islamic law subject to jihad? Are secular states in the Muslim world subject to jihad? Are Muslims who wish to modernize society along Western lines subject to jihad? These and many other questions are being raised within the context of jihad as Muslims are confronted with problems that are common to modern societies everywhere.

The Koran (Qur'an)   The Koran is the holy book of Islam and is believed to be the literal word of God revealed to Muhammad. The Koran was revealed in Arabic and was first written down in Arabic. Although many translations have been made into other languages, the Arabic version is considered by Muslims to be the only true version. Even when translations are made, they often are printed with an accompanying text in Arabic.

The Koran is about the size of the Christian New Testament. It is divided into 114 chapters that are called *suras*. The organization is by length of the sura. The longest sura is first and the shortest is last. It is believed that this order has no relationship to the time that they were revealed to Muhammad. It should not be forgotten that Arabia during Muhammad's lifetime was a society where memorization was valued. During the years of Muhammad's ministry, his followers memorized these suras exactly as they were revealed by God. There was no need to worry about sura order. However, only a few years after Muhammad's death, the Caliph Uthman had the suras written down. Since that time the Koran has remained unchanged. As it is the revealed word of God, written in Arabic, there are no revised editions as are commonly found with the Christian Bible.

The Koran is intended to be memorized and recited orally. There is no attempt to analyze these passages. The believer accepts each sura. As God's word is beyond questioning, the Koran is not subject to debate or modification. This is why the tradition of memorization and recitation is still so important for a Muslim's act of faith. The believer is embracing the words of the Koran by the heart instead of the head.

Muslims hold sacred the divinely inspired books of the Torah, the Psalms, and the Gospels. As the Koran is the word of God and not something that someone has said about God, they believe that it is the only perfect revelation. As such, all Muslims accept it without question. The Koran is the primary guide for living for all believers.

THE PRINCIPLES USED TO GUIDE THE MUSLIM COMMUNITY

For Muslims, there is no concept of original sin as it is understood in Christianity. The Koran provides the directions for the believer to follow on the path that leads to final judgment. If the Muslim departs from these directions, however, he is left alone outside the community without a moral compass. The Muslim is expected to offer unquestioning obedience to the commands of God. For guidance, Sunni Muslims also rely on traditions and rulings developed by theological and law schools. These principles are drawn from a hierarchy of authority, collectively called the "shariah," or correct path. In descending order of importance, this path includes: the Koran, the traditions of Muhammad (Hadith), the consensus of religious scholars (Ijma), and analytical deduction (Qiyas). Shiite Muslims do not accept this hierarchy in its entirety.

Disagreement over what could or could not be used in determining the direction of the community eventually led the Sunni majority to accept four major schools of Islamic law. Taking the names of their founders, these schools are still recognized today. The Hanafite School accepts reason as a proper source of decision-making when other more important authorities cannot provide answers to current issues. Founded in the 8th century, the Hanafite School has a strong influence in modern Turkey and Pakistan. The Malikite School stresses the traditions of the Prophet and the consensus of Islamic scholars to decide problems. This 8th-century school is important in Iraq, Syria, Egypt, and North Africa. The Shafite School originated between the 7th and 8th centuries. Shafites accept consensus only when it has broad community support. They oppose traditions that do not have an Islamic basis. They will use analogy to reach a decision only when no other source exists. Shafite schools of law exist in Indonesia and other parts of Southeast Asia. The most conservative approach to decision-making is found in the Hambalite tradition. Founded in the 9th century, this school only accepts the Koran and the traditions of the Prophet as a basis for legal decision-making.

Islam is a religion of law. These laws govern all aspects of Muslim life. Some of the more important laws prohibit earning interest on loans, engaging in unequal business arrangements, and speculation to gain advantage over others. Laws also cover marriage, divorce, inheritance, racial equality, and the rights of both men and women. For Muslims, the shariah covers the practical application of sacred law to real events of everyday life.

Muhammad Like many of the early prophets, little can be documented about Muhammad's early life. His given name, Ahmad, is only known by tradition. Muhammad is an honorific title meaning "praised." In speaking of the earlier prophets of the Hebrew and Christian Bible, the Koran states,

> Muhammad is not the father of any of your men, but [he is] the Apostle of God and the Seal of the Prophets. And God has full knowledge of all things.[16]

Muhammad was born in Mecca around 571 C.E. He was born into the ruling Quraysh tribe and was a member of the Banu Hashin clan. The modern Hashemites, the current rulers of Jordan, claim descent from the same clan. Orphaned at an early age, Muhammad

A Moroccan Mosque
This mosque has a square minaret, which is common in North Africa.
Source: Joe Weatherby

was first raised by his grandfather and then later by his uncle. Although linked to powerful Meccan leaders by both tribe and clan, Muhammad's youth was difficult because he was both without parents and poor in a society where family was important.

At about the age of 25, Muhammad began to work for a rich widow named Khadija, whom he later married. Mecca was located on the rich trade route from Yemen to the Mediterranean. At this time, Mecca was not only a center of commerce but also a pilgrimage center. Pilgrims came to Mecca to visit a small square building located in the center of town. This building housed hundreds of Arab tribal gods. The pilgrimage was a source of wealth for the Quraysh tribe, who controlled the access to this pilgrimage site. It is believed that Muhammad went with Khadija's caravans possibly as far as Syria. If he did, he certainly came in contact with both Christians and Jews who may have told him of the one God.[17]

When Muhammed was 40 years old, he started to receive revelations commanding him to tell the world that there was no god but God and that he, Muhammad, was the final messenger of God. He was also told to warn humankind that there was going to be a day of judgment when every person would stand to answer for his or her actions before God. Muhammad continued to receive other revelations from God, one verse at a time, during the rest of his life. Muhammed's biography is well documented from the time that he started to have revelations.

It is natural to assume that the monotheistic message of a minor member of a great tribe like the Quraysh would not be welcomed by people who owed their prosperity to the worship of hundreds of tribal gods that were under their guardianship. Muhammad and his few followers were subjected to all kinds of threats and trials. Finally, in September 622, he and a few trusted friends fled Mecca for exile in Yathrib (later known as Medina). There he was invited by the city's quarreling clans to be the leader of this small city-state. In Muslim history the date of the flight from Mecca (Hijra) begins year 1 in the calendar.

Muhammad lived to see the people of Medina, the tribes of Arabia, and even Mecca itself converted to Islam before his death in 632. It was a great disappointment to Muslims that Christians and Jews rejected Muhammed's message. Before his death, Muhammad told Muslims to pray toward Mecca instead of toward Jerusalem. He also directed that the pilgrimage to Mecca was to be continued. This time the old tribal gods were to be banished in favor of the one true god, God.

Muslims understand that the Prophet Muhammad was only a man. Unlike Jesus, he did not perform miracles or raise the dead. Muslims affirm only that Muhammad was God's messenger. They also believe that he had a perfect life and therefore he should be imitated in the daily life of believers. When he died, some said he was in hiding and would return. However, Abu Bakr, who was to become the first caliph, said,

> Whoever worshipped Muhammad let him know that Muhammad is dead, but whoever worshipped God, let him know that God lives and dies not.[18]

From that point on, Islam became the uncompromising monotheistic religion that it is today.

The Rightly Guided Caliphs When Muhammad died, there was no clearly defined line of succession. The person to be selected as Muhammad's successor or "caliph" was an important issue. Without strong leadership, Islam might not have survived the early years. Some clans and tribes of Arabia maintained that their allegiance to Islam ended with Muhammad's death. Unlike Christianity, Islam did not have a formal priesthood or religious hierarchy. It was important for Muslims to formalize some aspects of what had been an association centered around the personal leadership of Muhammad. There were four candidates, and in time each would be caliph. The candidates were Abu Bakr al-Siddig, Ùmar ibn al-Khattab, Ùthman ibn 'Affan, and 'Ali ibn Abi Talib. Each man had supporters, but traditionally Abu Bakr was selected because he had been asked to lead the faithful in prayer during Muhammad's last illness. He was also supported by Umar. Abu Bakr was selected by the faithful as the first successor of Muhammad.

It was Abu Bakr who had ridden out with Muhammad on the flight from Mecca to Medina in 622. It was Abu Bakr who sustained Muhammad throughout his ministry. And it was Abu Bakr, once he was caliph, who held the Muslim community together during the early years when others had begun to doubt. He reassembled the tribes of Arabia into a unified force that was destined to spread the religion of Islam throughout the rest of the world. He was noted for his simple, modest life style. H.G. Wells has described Abu Bakr as follows:

> There can be little doubt that if Muhammad was the mind and imagination of primitive Islam, Abu Bakr was its conscience and its will. . . . Abu Bakr was a man without doubts, his beliefs cut down to acts cleanly as a sharp knife cuts.[19]

Abu Bakr endorsed the second caliph, Umar. In two ways, Caliph Umar's life parallels that of the Christian leader Saint Paul. Both began as strong opponents of the religions that they later embraced. Both were largely responsible for their faiths expanding to areas that were geographically distant from their original base. Both were responsible for the respective faiths becoming world religions instead of regional cults.

During Umar's rule, Islam expanded out of Arabia to Syria, Egypt, and Persia. In 638, Umar conquered Jerusalem. He was known to be tolerant of Christians and Jews so long as they paid their taxes and remained loyal to the Islamic state. He allowed the conquered peoples to maintain their own culture and laws. This tolerance of Christianity was expressed in the promise that he made to the leaders of Jerusalem when it was captured. His peace treaty with them stated, "You have complete security for your churches which shall not be occupied by the Muslims or destroyed."[20] He did oppose assimilation with subject peoples and built the camps of Kufa and Basra to isolate the Arab armies. He feared that social contact with the sophisticated people of the Fertile Crescent would dilute the Arab faith in Islam. He was assassinated by a slave in 644. Before his death he appointed a committee to select his successor.

Uthman was appointed to succeed Umar. During the Caliphate of Umar, the tensions between the aristocratic "new believers from Mecca" and Muhammad's first supporters in Medina emerged into the open. Uthman was a member of a powerful Mecca clan. During his caliphate he was accused of favoring relatives who were new converts from Mecca over the early Medina converts. He appointed a relative, Mu'awiya, governor of Syria. This appointment was eventually led to the most important division in Islamic history.

During Uthman's rule, he completed the conquest of Persia and overran Libya. However, his most important contribution to the future of Islam occurred when he ordered that the Koran be written down in a common version. This act avoided the problems that have plagued Christians and Jews who have repeatedly argued over the proper wording and what should be included in the sacred texts of the Bible. The fact that the Koran was standardized within 15 years of the Prophet's death gives it a currency that is beyond dispute. Uthman was assassinated in 756.

Although Ali had been successful in controlling most of the opposition to his caliphate, the conflict over his selection as fourth caliph caused the most important split in Islam. It led to the establishment of the Sunni and Shiite branches of the religion. Ali was one of Muhammad's earliest followers. He was Muhammad's cousin, and he was married to Muhammad's daughter, Fatima. Although Muhammad failed to leave clear instructions concerning who his successor would be, many believed that the natural choice should have been Ali. Supporters of the claim of Ali have always asserted that through his actions, Muhammad indicated that he expected Ali to succeed him.

The followers of Muhammad selected three caliphs before the residents of Medina elected Ali caliph. This election was opposed by Mu'awiya, the powerful governor of Syria. Ali was successful in controlling most of the opposition after his victory at the "Battle of the Camel" in 656. He failed, however, to defeat his rival Mu'awiya in 657 at the Battle of Siffin.

In the aftermath of the battle, Ali agreed to defer his claim in favor of Mu'awiya. Some of his followers who were dissatisfied with his agreement with Mu'awiya assassinated Ali in 661. Ali left two surviving sons, Hasan and Husayn. It was Husayn's death at the "Battle of Karbala" in 680 that finally split the supporters of Ali, the Shiites, away from the majority, the Sunnis.

The Sunni and the Shiite Muslims In most important issues there are few differences between the Sunni and Shiite branches of Islam. They observe similar rituals and follow the Five Pillars: profession of faith, prayer, fasting, alms, and making the pilgrimage. Both follow the teachings of the Koran. Both accept the same version of this holy book. The important differences lie in how the successor to Muhammad should be selected and how the community of believers should be governed. Just as most Protestants and Roman Catholics identify themselves as Christians, Sunni and Shia consider themselves first to be Muslims.

The Sunni branch of Islam is by far the largest in number, accounting for about 90 percent of all Muslims. Sunnis believe that the successor to Muhammad should be selected by an election of the faithful. To them, God would never allow the Muslim community to make a mistake. They also have incorporated the Arab tradition of equality into their conception of sacred law. They have limited the interpretation of that law to the four schools previously mentioned in this chapter.

In practice, the idea of a divinely guided election of the caliph ended when Caliph Mu'awiya nominated his son Yazeed to succeed him. He justified this decision on the grounds that it was better to predetermine succession than allow the community of believers to drift into another conflict. The result of this decision was a war between Yazeed and the followers of Ali that ended in the death of Ali's son at the Battle of Karbala. This event caused a split that remains until the present. To the Shia, the martyrdom of Ali's second son, Husayn, has special significance that is not unlike the importance that Christians place on the crucifixion of Jesus. In the 1400 years that have passed since Karbala, many other differences have developed between the Sunni and the Shia. However, the two parties are in complete agreement on the basic articles of faith.

Although much smaller in number, the Shia have exercised a great impact on Islam. Shia believe that Muhammad intended that Ali become the first Imam. *Imam* is a word used by Shia instead of caliph to refer to Muhammad's successor who descended from Ali. They also believe that since the community of the faithful could make mistakes in the election of the Imam, the Imam should come from Muhammad's extended family and specifically from a descendant of Ali.

Because they have the blood of both Muhammad and Ali, these Imams are believed to have had a close connection to God. Shia believe that a divine connection has been passed in the chain of leadership reaching from Muhammad through Ali and his son Husayn to the eldest male successors who then become Imams.

Most Shia follow the tradition of "twelvers." This means that they see a progression through the first twelve Imams. The eleventh Imam, Hasan al-Askari, died in 874. Most twelvers believe that his son went into hiding and will eventually return as the Mahdi, or rightly guided one, to bring justice to the world.

A second group of Shia are called "seveners." The seveners maintain that on the death of the Imam, the eldest son always becomes the new Imam. These minority Shiite Muslims eventually became the Ismailis. The current Ismaili leader carries the title Aga Khan. Twelvers disagree on the succession, arguing that the sixth Imam's younger son, Musa al-Kazim, became the legitimate Imam. They see the chain continuing until the disappearance of the twelfth Imam.

At least two major differences distinguish the Shia of all persuasions from the Sunni. Unlike the Sunni, Shia maintain that because of the special connection between Muhammad, Ali, Husayn, and the succeeding Imams, their opinions could be relied on to guide the Shiite community. Sunni believe that this reliance on innovation by the Imams is a dangerous departure from the original teaching of Islam.

Since the disappearance of the twelfth Imam, his place has been vacant. Religious scholars called mujtahids or ayatollahs, acting as the twelfth Imam's deputies have asserted that they can exercise religious authority. Shia believe that these leaders can continue to make decisions involving sacred law until the Imam returns as the Mahdi. The Sunni are more conservative in their approach to the interpretation of sacred law. They continue to rely on the established traditions of the Sharia.

The second difference with the Sunni concerns the Shiite tradition of martyrdom. Because the Shia rejected the legitimacy of the caliphs after Ali, they were always in opposition to the majority in Islam. In most conflicts with the majority, Shia were often persecuted. Because most Shiite leaders, including Ali and Husayn, were killed, a tradition of martyrdom developed. The Shia came to accept martyrdom as part of an earthly trial in the spirit of Imam Husayn. This tradition was also reinforced because the strongest centers of Shiism were among non-Arab Muslims who were the ones most often discriminated against. Shia form large minorities in Lebanon, Syria, Yemen, Bahrain, Pakistan, and India. They are the majority believers in both Iran and Iraq.

The Sufis   The Sufis are the mystics of Islam. Most authorities believe that the word *Sufi* comes from the Arabic *suf,* which refers to wool. The early Sufis were known for the rough woolen garments that they wore. The religious philosopher Edward Bray has written that,

> Every true religion is born from a mystical experience. But as it grows and attracts increasing numbers of followers, this mystical aspect is lost or hidden. It becomes secret teachings to which only selected people may become initiates, like the Sufis within Islam.[21]

Because there are so many variations of Sufism, this form of mysticism is one of the most interesting but least understood elements of Islam.

Some claim that Sufism's origins predate Islam. Certainly some of the Sufi brotherhoods resemble the monastic orders found in both Christianity and Buddhism. Sufis have also absorbed popular traditions from cultures that were alien to the early Arab converts. Nevertheless, it is generally accepted that true Sufism emerged sometime during the 8th century. The most famous brotherhoods flourished between the 13th and 16th centuries.

Sufis recognize that the traditional Islamic orthodoxy that most Muslims practice is fine for most believers. Sufis, however, seek a closer relationship with God. They seek to go far past mere orthodox ritualistic submission to the will of God. Through a complex series of steps or passages, they seek to eventually transcend the earthly and reach a direct knowledge of God.

Organized into brotherhoods, each Sufi order has a master, or sheik. Most orders are linked to an early founder or saint. The members are initiates who study under the direction of the sheik. The specific rituals of each order may vary widely, ranging from verbal repetitions, dancing, and meditation to more exotic and flamboyant practices that can include fire walking and body piercing. Today there are at least forty Sufi brotherhoods, each with different rituals, that are active around the world. Recently Sheik Hasham Kabbani al-Haggani recognized this Sufi diversity when he said, "Sufism changes with every master. In every century there must be reviving and reforming."[22] Because Sufis often shun traditional Islamic practices, they have frequently been opposed by orthodox Muslims.

The Sufis are called the missionaries of Islam. As Islam expanded out of the Arabian Peninsula to become a world religion, it was the Sufis who were most willing to accept cultural practices that previously existed in the newly acquired territories. New subjects were able to become Muslims without surrendering all of their old traditions. Many people in Asia and Africa were open to the acceptance of Islam because of the flexibility of the Sufis.

Sufism represents a major departure from mainstream Islamic practice. Because of the Sufi willingness to accept local traditions, it has enjoyed more popularity with the common people than with the religious scholars. In modern times, Sufism has been opposed by Islamic reformers and modernizers alike. Both see Sufism as a force corrupting Islam. Saudi Arabia has even banned the practice of Sufism as anti-Islamic.

WORDS AND TOPICS COMMONLY FOUND IN ISLAM

Sheik (Shaykh) *Sheik* has different meanings in different parts of the Middle East and North Africa. It is always an honorific title of respect. In some places the master of a Sufi brotherhood is called a sheik. Among the Arabs, tribal leaders are called sheiks. In many places, religious scholars are designated sheiks. In Saudi Arabia, an elder, respected leader of a family is referred to as sheik by those wishing to show their respect.

Shirk *Shirk* is sin. Unlike Christians, Muslims do not believe that humankind is damned by original sin. They do believe that people sin. As strict monotheists, they see anything that makes a comparison or competes with God as a sin. Thus, a word, action, or even a thought can be *shirk* if it interferes in any way with the worship of the one God.

Dar al-Islam Meaning the House of Islam, *Dar-al-Islam* refers to the community of believers. In practice, that includes those states and lands that are under Muslim rule. Muslims have described this condition in terms of circles: the inner circle, Dar al-Islam, is surrounded by a hostile outer circle called Dar al-Harb.

Dar al-Harb This refers to the House of Unbelievers, who oppose Islam. It is the duty of Muslims to constantly oppose Dar al-Harb by expanding the faith.

Prayer Beads (Subha) Probably originating in India, prayer beads are commonly used by both Muslims and Christians. The full Muslim string contains 99 beads arranged in groups of 33. Although there are several ways that these beads can be used, the 99 represent the beautiful names of God. There are also smaller strings that contain only 33 beads.

Popularly called "worry beads," they are commonly seen being carried in men's hands as they go about their daily business.[23]

The Mosque   This is the building where collective worship takes place. Unlike most churches and synagogues, mosques are almost devoid of furniture, allowing room for the faithful to pray. Their architectural style varies according to culture. In North Africa they are noted for their openness. In Turkey and Islamic lands further east, many are covered and have richly decorated domes.

Regardless of architectural style, all mosques contain a qibla or mark identifying the direction of Mecca. They also have a place where the leader gives the sermons, called the minbar. Finally, mosques usually contain a minaret. The minaret is a tower that rises above the mosque. It is the place where the call to prayer is given. Minarets vary from the famous square towers found in Spain and North Africa to the more common round ones that exist in the rest of the region. While the mosque is used daily for prayer, the Friday prayer is the most important.

The Kaaba   As has been previously stated, the Kaaba is a cube-shaped temple situated in the center of the courtyard of the Great Mosque in Mecca. However, it is much more! The Kaaba is the most important religious building in Islam. Tradition holds that the Kaaba was built by the prophet Abraham. The Kaaba is made of a dark stone that comes from near Mecca. In one corner is placed a black stone that is ritually touched by pilgrims. Just as each mosque has a "pointer" to Mecca, the Kaaba is a spiritual pointer that unifies all Muslims in their belief that there is no god but God.

For centuries the Kaaba was covered by a black cloth brought from Egypt. This cover is crowned by inscriptions from the Koran. The cover is replaced by a new one each year during the pilgrimage season. Since the establishment of Saudi Arabia, protection for the Kaaba— the cover—has been furnished by the Saudis.

The People of the Book

> Say we believe in God and in what has been revealed to us and what was revealed to Abraham, Ishmael, Isaac, Jacob, and the tribes, and in [the Book] given to Moses, Jesus, and the Prophets, from their Lord: We make no distinction between one and another among them, and to God do we bow our will [in Islam].[24]

In this Koranic passage, Muslims assert that their belief is in one common truth. They see the same truth being communicated by God to a number of prophets and peoples prior to Muhammad. However, they believe that truth in an uncorrupted form has come to humankind through the revelations that God gave to Muhammad in the Koran. They recognize that earlier people were singled out by God to receive revelation. Along with Muslims, those people are called "People of the Book." In the early days, this status was limited to Jews and Christians. Later, Zoroastrians were added to the protected list. When conquered, Zoroastrians, Jews, and Christians were given a special status within the Muslim community. They were allowed freedom to worship and continue their communities as they had always done. They were required to pay a special tax but would remain unmolested so long as they remained loyal to Muslim rule.

The degree of tolerance exercised by Muslims to the People of the Book varied by time and place. When compared to Christian treatment of non-Christians in Europe during the same period of history, however, Muslims exhibited a great deal more tolerance.

During the Ottoman period, the relationship between People of the Book was institutionalized by the Millet System. Each recognized minority culture was allowed to preserve traditions, dress, and religion. These communities ran their own civil and religious affairs. Leaders of each Millet were also members of the Ottoman government. Respect for this form of tolerance of the People of the Book was considered to be an act of faith for Muslims.

The Millet System established an organization of divided rule at the local level. In the long run, it allowed small communities of Christians and Jews to survive in a region dominated by Muslims. They still exist as minorities there today. In the name of Christian orthodoxy, many similar groups, along with the Muslims, were ruthlessly stamped out in Europe.

Today the minority People of the Book living in the region include a little more than 6 million Jews, 7 million Christians, and less than 5 thousand Zoroastrians. Although small in numbers, Jews and Christians have exercised a political, economic, and cultural influence in the region that is in excess of their numbers.

NEW RELIGIONS THAT HAVE EMERGED OUT OF ISLAM

The Druze (Druse) The Druze have around a million followers throughout the world. They are the product of a split that occurred in Islam during the 10th century. Essentially, the Druze took some of the elements of Shiism concerning the Sixth Caliph and incorporated some non-Islamic ideas to create a new religion. They were prosecuted as Islamic heretics. Most of their current ritual is secret and only known to believers. The Druze have a strong presence in Lebanon, Syria, Jordan, and Israel. They are the only non-Jews allowed to serve in the Israeli Army.

The Bahais This religion emerged out of Shiite Islam during the 19th century. It has elements of Babism, which was an earlier Iranian religion. The Bahais believe that God has made himself known throughout human history through a number of prophets including Abraham, Moses, Jesus, and Muhammad. They believe that all religions are ultimately united in their moral teachings. Bahais advocate world peace, the use of a common international language, and world government. They believe in simple living and service to others. After their leader was exiled from 19th-century Persia, the Bahais established themselves in the city of Haifa in what is now Israel. Later the leaders' sons carried the religion to the United States. As a global religion, modern Bahais live in places as diverse as Iran, Israel, and the United States.

WHAT IS THE HISTORY OF CHRISTIANITY IN THE MIDDLE EAST AND NORTH AFRICA?

Most readers of this book will be familiar with the teachings of Judaism and Christianity as these religions exist in the West. This chapter will focus on these religions as they are practiced in the Middle East and North Africa. It may be surprising to learn that, once a few general principles are assumed, the specific beliefs and traditions of Middle Eastern religions often differ greatly from their Western counterparts. This is especially true with Christianity.

In order to understand the different paths taken by Christians in this part of the world, it is necessary to go back to the very beginnings of the movement. The problem is that very little is known about this period. The Gospels were not written until later. Most authorities assume that little was written down during the early period of Christianity for several reasons. First, many early Christians assumed that the end of the world was near so there was little need to write anything down. Second, the early Christians had an oral culture. Third, as an oppressed minority, early Christians may have been uneasy about making written documents available that might later be used against them. Finally, people did not need to rely on written documents; they became believers because they heard the words of disciples who had known Jesus.

It is believed that Christianity went through a transition period as it moved from being merely another Jewish sect into a religion with a global message. During this period there were a number of believers who pulled the fledgling religion in different directions. It was the late convert Paul who laid the basis for the modern Christian religion when he carried the message of Jesus to people outside of Palestine. By preaching to the Gentiles, Saint Paul gave a worldview to the Christian faith. The importance of Saint Paul's mission was firmly stated by D. C. Somervill when he wrote,

> The future of the civilized world for two thousand years, perhaps for all time, was determined by his missionary journeys and his hurried writings. It is impossible to guess what would have become of Christianity if he had not lived; we cannot even be sure that the religion of Europe would be called by the name of Christ.[25]

During the first years of Christianity, it is believed that there was little established dogma. Each church, bishop, and teacher adhered to a loose set of beliefs but may have disagreed on specifics that were to become a source of great conflict later on. Many ideas that were popular would eventually become heresy when the church developed an orthodox theology. The emphasis was placed on establishing broad areas of agreement. This strategy was used to convert as many as possible to the new religion before the world came to an end. Over time it became apparent that the world was not going to end. A number of church leaders started to press their views as orthodoxy. By the end of the 1st century, Bishop Ignatius became the first church father to use the epitaph "heretic." He used it to describe anyone who "confused the true understanding of Christ."[26]

Emperor Constantine adopted Christianity as the state religion of Rome during the 4th century. This was an attempt to bring unity to the Roman Empire. As time passed, the theological arguments surrounding specific Christian beliefs grew to a point that they threatened to split the church itself! The historian H. G. Wells argued that there were three major factions seeking to impose their version of orthodoxy on Christianity:

> The Arians followed Arius, who taught that Christ was less than God. . . . The Sabellians taught that he was a mode or aspect of God—God was the creator, savior and comforter. . . . The Trinitarians taught that the Father, the Son, and the Holy Ghost were three distinct persons but one God.[27]

It became clear that if the Church was to play a role in unifying the Empire, the dissentions within it would have to be resolved. To accomplish this task, Emperor Constantine ordered the Church leaders throughout the Empire to meet in Nicaea to resolve their differences. This council resulted in a victory for those supporting the Trinitarian point of view. The adoption of the famous Nicene Creed was the result. The views of the churches from Palestine and the East did not prevail.

In 451 another council was held at Calcedon. There the nature of Jesus was debated. Again, believers from the eastern parts of the Empire lost. The council agreed on the position that Jesus was both divine and human but joined in one person. This view of Jesus is the position taken by the Roman Catholic, Protestant, and Eastern Orthodox Churches today.

The Christians of the Eastern Mediterranean rejected the position taken at Chalcedon. They held that Jesus had only one nature while on earth, which was divine. Today they are known as Monophysite Christians. Other Christians who rejected the creeds of Nicea and Chalcedon were called monotheletists. The Maronite Church that survives in the Middle East today evolved from these early dissenting Christians.

The second major split affecting Christians in the region came in the 11th century when the Eastern Church refused to recognize the authority of the Western one headed by the Pope. During the fourth crusade, Western crusaders actually sacked the orthodox Christian capital of Constantinople. Today the Orthodox Eastern Church has 123 million members worldwide. It still has a strong presence in Turkey and the Levant.

CHRISTIANS OF THE MIDDLE EAST AND NORTH AFRICA

The Christian churches with the longest presence in the region are the products of those early theological disputes that split the Church. Most follow one of the two great dissenting views of the nature of Jesus, monophysitism, or monotheletism. Both have been branded as heresies by Eastern Orthodox and Western Christians who are strict trinitarians.

Monophysites Monophysites believe that Jesus did not have a divine and a human nature as claimed by Christians in the West. They believe that while in human form, he had only one nature, which was divine. By the 7th century, the monophysites had completely separated from the majority of Christians who had adopted as their creed the trinity of God, Son, and Holy Ghost. Three Middle Eastern churches have emerged from this dispute. These churches are the Coptic Church, the Syrian Orthodox or Jacobite Church, and the Armenian Orthodox Church.

The Coptic Church Copts trace their origin back to the missionary work of Saint Mark the Evangelist, who founded the church during the 1st Century C.E. For several hundred years their great school at Alexandria produced some of the most important Christian thinkers. The Coptic Church lost its preeminence when it refused to accept the decisions of the majority at the Council of Calcedon. The Church was branded as a heresy and still remains outside the Western Christian community.

Persecution of the Copts by Western Christianity started when Christianity became the religion of Rome. To escape Christian persecution, many Copts retreated into the Egyptian desert and further south to the Sudan and Ethiopia. This exodus resulted in large numbers of conversions in those two places. The conflict between Western Christianity and the Copts so weakened the cause of Christianity that it was easy for the later Islamic conquest of Egypt to occur.

What survives today are believers who make up the largest Christian church in the Middle East. At about 10 percent of the total population, there are over 6 million Copts in Egypt. The Copts have disproportionate influence in the Egyptian professions, teaching, and finance. Because of their reputation for having foreign contacts and because of their relative prosperity, Copts have often been the targets of Muslim militants. A small number of Copts have accepted the sovereignty of the Catholic Church and are recognized by Rome. Called Unites, these Copts maintain Coptic religious positions but are in association with Rome.

Syrian Orthodox Church Popularly called Jacobites because of their 6th century founder, Jacob Baradaeus, the Syrian Orthodox Church has been declared a heresy by both the Roman Catholic and the Eastern Orthodox Churches. Although most of the members live in Iraq, the Patriarch of Antioch has his residence in Damascus, Syria. Today there are about 160,000 members of the Syrian Orthodox Church.

Like the Copts in Egypt, the Jacobites have lived under Muslim rule since the conquest. Many Jacobites hold government positions in both Iraq and Syria.

One Unite branch of the church has had an association with Rome for several hundred years. Their recognized "Patriarch of Antioch" lives in Beirut. Since the defeat of Iraq, many Iraqi Jacobites have immigrated to Europe and the United States.

The Syrian Orthodox services are conducted in the ancient Syriac language. As part of their service, they use only one finger when making the sign of the cross to strongly emphasize their belief in monophysitism.

The Armenian Orthodox Church Armenians make the claim that Armenia was the world's first Christian kingdom. The Armenian or Gregorian Orthodox Church was established in the late 3rd century by Saint Gregory. Early disputes with the church authorities in the West caused the Armenian Church to become autonomous shortly after being established. A final break came when, like the other monophysites, the Armenian Orthodox Church was declared a heresy for rejecting the orthodox positions of the Council of Calcedon.

Today the Armenian Church has an important presence in Armenia, Turkey, and Israel. Their religious services are similar to those of the other Eastern churches. The worship is conducted in Armenian. Like the previously mentioned churches, there is a branch of the Armenian Church that has reestablished relations with the Roman Catholic Church.

The Monotheletists Monotheletism emerged in the 7th century as a compromise between the positions held by Orthodox Christians and Monotheistic Christians over the human or divine nature of Jesus. This doctrine maintains that although Jesus had two natures, human and divine, he acted with only one while on earth. By the early part of the 8th century, this doctrine had been rejected by Western Christians. Today only the Maronite Church supports this point of view.

The Maronite Christians emerged as a separate body as a result of the 7th-century split over monoelitism. They returned to communion with the Roman Catholic Church during the 12th century. The ritual also resembles that of other Eastern churches. This is primarily an Arab Christian Church. The services are held in Syriac. Maronites place special emphasis on the cross. Today the Maronite Church has approximately 1 million members around the world. Most live in Lebanon, but there are Maronite Churches in Israel, Egypt, Cyprus, South America, and the United States.

During the 19th century, the massacres of Maronite Christians in Lebanon provoked an intervention by France. This unhappy period also caused the exodus of a large number of Maronite Christians to the United States. These early arrivals formed the basis for what was later to become the Arab American community in North America.

Other Christian Churches in the Middle East and North Africa The most important Western Christian bodies in the region are the Eastern Orthodox Church, the Roman Catholic Church, and the Protestant Church. The various theologies of these predominantly Western churches should be familiar to the reader. It should be noted that both the Eastern Orthodox Church and the Roman Catholic Church have maintained a foothold in the region since the Middle Ages.

The Eastern Orthodox Church This is an umbrella title representing a number of churches that follow the orthodox tradition in their services. These churches are most important in Russia, Serbia, Greece, Bulgaria, and Cyprus. In the Eastern Mediterranean, the Greek Orthodox Church has around 2 million members in Turkey. There are a million Arabs who are members of the Orthodox Church in Syria and Lebanon. One hundred thousand Palestinians are also Orthodox Christians.

The Roman Catholic Church The Roman Catholic Church has had a presence in the Holy Land since the Crusades. Today there are Roman Catholics in most Eastern Mediterranean countries. The Catholic Church plays an important function in the administration of the Christian pilgrimage sites in the Holy Land. The worldwide power of the Roman Catholic Church has given the Middle Eastern Catholics a role that is disproportionate to their modest numbers.

The Assyrian Church Commonly called the Nestorian Church after its founder, the Abbot of Antioch Nestorius, the Nestorians believed that Jesus was conceived by God but was born a man and lived on earth as a man. They rejected the majority Christian view that Mary was the Mother of God. They opposed the findings of the Council of Chalcedon. Nestorianism was opposed as heresy throughout the Roman Empire. It survived outside the areas of Roman control in Persia and the Fertile Crescent. Before the rise of Islam, there were Nestorian Churches in Arabia, India, and even Mongolia. The Assyrian Church does not allow paintings or sculptures in churches. The services are still held in Aramaic, the language of Jesus. Although at one time widely spread, the Assyrian Church is now the smallest ancient Christian Church in the region.

The Protestant Churches Almost every modern Protestant church has some kind of representation in the Middle East and North Africa. The Protestant presence came as a result of European colonial involvement in the region during the 19th and 20th centuries. Missionaries found that they could make few conversions within the Muslim community so they focused their efforts on converting non-Protestant Christians to their particular churches.

Culturally, the Protestants had a great influence on the development of the modern Middle East. They set examples for the majority Muslims by playing leading roles in the establishment of universities and hospitals in Lebanon, Palestine, and Egypt. Generations of Middle Eastern leaders have studied at the American Universities of Beirut and Cairo since their founding.

There are only a few hundred thousand Protestants in the Middle East and North Africa. Presbyterians have traditionally been active in Lebanon and Syria. Episcopalians have had a presence in Jordan and Palestine. Both Episcopalians and Presbyterians have a long history of work in Egypt. In the political struggle between the Arabs and the Jews over Palestine, the Christian churches with old roots in the region, whether Roman

Catholic, Eastern Orthodox, or Protestant, have tended to sympathize with the plight of the Palestinians. The evangelical Protestant churches that are relatively new to the region have been more supportive of the State of Israel. They view the establishment of a Jewish state in the Middle East as a fulfillment of prophecy. Today, as in the past, Christians seem to be as divided as ever.

The Future for Christianity in the Region   In a sense, Christianity has been under siege in the region since the rise of Islam. Certainly Christian–Muslim relations were strained by the Muslim conquests, the Christian Crusades, and the Christian reconquest of Spain. The centuries of conflict between Christians and Muslims in the Balkans and in Russia also created negative images that make ecumenical understanding difficult. Christians point to the repeated Muslim threats to Western civilization. Muslims reply by objecting to the harm done by centuries of Western imperialism.

A combination of Muslim political pressure, the charge that Christians represent only Western colonial interest, and the ability of Christians to move is causing more and more people to leave the region for the West. In Israel and Palestine this pressure comes from both Muslims and Jews. Nowhere is this tension more acute than in the Old City of Jerusalem where the Christians are pressured to leave by all sides. The result is a steady decline of the Christian presence in the land where Christianity was born.

Beliefs that Muslims and Christians Share   There are many areas of common belief or similar belief that are part of the religions of Christianity and Islam. First and foremost, both believe in monotheism. They trace their roots back to the Hebrew scriptures. Some events of the Hebrew Bible are part of Christian and Muslim traditions, too. For Muslims these events may occur in different places with different participants. Christians and Muslims honor many of the same prophets. Both honor Jesus as a prophet, although Muslims reject the claim that he was the Son of God. Both believe that Mary played a special role in giving birth to Jesus. They believe in many of the same angels although they may have slightly different views of tasks that the angels perform. Christians and Muslims believe in heaven, hell, and Satan. They acknowledge that there will be a day of judgment for all humankind. Finally, Muslims and Christians believe in the concept of salvation by faith.

What Is the History of the Jews of the Middle East and North Africa?

Christians and Muslims trace their origins to the revelations described in the Jewish holy books. Judaism traces its history back 3000 years to the time of the prophet Abraham. It is not the intention here to repeat that well-known history. The story of the important political role that Jews have played in the development of the modern Middle East and North Africa is a recent one.

At the beginning of the 20th century, relatively few Jews lived in this region. Of those who did, most lived in North Africa, Egypt, Syria, and Persia (Iran). Very few Jews lived in Palestine until the 20th century. Since the Babylonian captivity "of ancient times" there have always been more Jews living outside of Palestine, in the "Diaspora," than in the land of Israel.

Traditionally the Jews of the Diaspora, outside of Palestine, have been more prosperous than the Jews of Israel. Since its creation in 1948, the State of Israel has become a center of Jewish culture, but it is not yet the center: There are nearly twice as many Jews living in North America than in Israel itself. Some Jews have even referred to North America as the "new Israel."

At the beginning of the 21st century, most of the Jews of the Middle East and North Africa live in the new State of Israel. Although a Jewish presence survived in the vicinity of Jerusalem for over 2000 years, most of the current population arrived during the past century. Of these, the overwhelming majority has arrived after the State of Israel was established in 1948.

To understand Jewish immigration patterns, it is necessary to know something about Jewish history. Most people know that the Jews were last dispersed after losing in a revolt against Rome in C.E. 135. The survivors were forced to join earlier exiles in many parts of the ancient world. In the Christian world, Jews were repeatedly discriminated against. This discrimination took many forms, including prescribed dress, jobs, and living areas.

It must be said that Jews did much better under Islam. As strict monotheists, they seemed to have more in common with Islam than with Christianity. Many Jews rose to senior positions in states under Muslim rule.

By the 18th century, the Jews living in the Diaspora had developed into two cultures: the Sephardim and the Ashkenazim. Some of the characteristics of the Sephardim included speaking the Ladino language and using Spanish and Arab traditions. The Sephardic Jews lived first in Spain. In 1492 they were expelled by the Christians and moved to the lands controlled by the Ottoman Empire. It was said of this period that in one act the Spanish Christians sent their enemies, the Ottomans, their most valuable asset, the Sephardic Jews.

The Ashkenazim lived in Germany, Western Europe, Eastern Europe, and Russia. They spoke a combination of Hebrew and German called Yiddish. Eventually they also became the largest Jewish group in North America. It was Ashkenazi pioneers from Europe, Russia, and America who founded the modern State of Israel.

It should be emphasized that Judaism is a religion of law and ritual. Both the Sephardim and the Ashkenazim follow similar laws and rituals. The Torah and the laws have remained the same for both communities. Their differences with each other are in their respective histories. The two communities have cultural and not theological differences.

There is one small but historically important Jewish tradition that has survived in Palestine since Roman times. The Samaritans live near the Israeli town of Nablus where they have maintained their own distinctive form of Judaism for more than 2000 years. They even built their own temple, refusing to recognize the one in Jerusalem. Because they tend to marry within their own community, they are in decline. Today there are only a few hundred surviving members of this once important Jewish sect.

During most of their European history in Christian Europe, Jews were forced to live in isolated or segregated communities. Throughout this period Jews maintained their traditions. They were subject to Jewish laws as interpreted by their religious leaders. They tended to marry within the Jewish community. This isolation allowed Judaism to maintain both a cultural and a religious presence. The religious leaders were able to exercise strict control over their congregations.

At the beginning of the 19th century, an event occurred that was to shake the Ashkenazi community to its very roots: the French Revolution. One of the basic principles of that revolution was equality. For a brief time Jews were not restricted by Christian Europe. Many Jews took advantage of this opportunity to move away from their insular past and into the European mainstream.

This 19th-century process caused Jews who wanted change to follow several paths: Jewish reform, assimilation into Gentile society, Marxist socialism, and Zionism or humane socialism.

Jewish Reform Advocates of the reform movement argued that traditional Judaism was out of step with the times. They followed two courses to renew Judaism as a religion.

The Reform Jews believed that it was necessary to modernize the religion by abolishing ritual Hebrew, adding organ music, and changing the day of worship to Sunday. Sunday was the common worship day for Christians in Europe and North America. As a minority, Jews needed to fit into the work schedule of the majority. They continued to generally follow Jewish law. By choosing to observe only some Jewish rituals, this movement allowed believers to adjust their life style to the modern world while remaining religious. They drew their greatest support in England and North America.

The second alternative to traditional orthodoxy emerged at the end of the 19th century as a compromise between the approach of orthodox Judaism and the relaxed reform version. Called Conservatives, they continued to emphasize studying Hebrew and the Torah. They focused on keeping the traditions of Judaism while avoiding the isolation of orthodoxy.

Today the United States of America is home for the largest Jewish community in the world. Within their group, most Jews who are religious practice the reformed tradition. Orthodox Jews make up the smallest Jewish community in the United States.

Modern Israel has been established as a Jewish democracy. Within that context, only the orthodox tradition has been given a place in the governing of the country. The paradox of this situation becomes obvious if one recognizes that even in Israel itself most Israelis do not follow that tradition.

Reformers and conservatives argue that in order to attract the many Israelis who are only culturally Jewish and who are opposed to orthodoxy, the Israeli government will eventually have to recognize their traditions. They believe that only through using modified Judaism as a bridge will secularists be returned to the faith.

Judaism and Revolution During the 19th century the breakup of the hold that orthodoxy had on the Jewish community led some Jews to reject religion entirely as being out of touch with the modern world. They also moved in two directions. One was economic and social reform and the other was Zionism. Sometimes the movements were hard to separate.

Jewish revolutionary movements often emerged from the oppression of the Jews in Eastern Europe and tsarist Russia. These movements had the goal of making a better world by eliminating economic and social inequities through socialism and communism. These so-called "red diaper" Jews rejected the old religion's controls and worked to establish a new secular utopian world. Foremost among these movements was the famous Jewish Bund. As a workers movement in Eastern Europe and Russia, the Bund sought to link Jewish aspirations with those of other workers. Members of the Bund also believed that they were being held down by the leaders of Jewish orthodoxy. The Bund promoted a secular form of Jewish culture while rejecting the religion's orthodox traditions. They believed that religion had contributed to the enslavement of Jewish workers.

Other secularists took a more radical course and became communists. In Russia and Eastern Europe, some of the earliest communist activists were secular Jews, including Trotsky, Zinoviev, Kraganovich, and Rosa Luxemburg.[28] They played key roles in the Russian and Eastern European revolutions. Shortly before World War II, many Jews actively participated on the side of the Republic in the Spanish Civil War.

Modern political Zionism is a Jewish form of nationalism that developed because of the anti-Jewish feelings that emerged in Christian Europe at the end of the 19th century. Zionism is based on an age-old Jewish tradition of a return to Israel. Founded in Basel, Switzerland, in 1897, political Zionism called for the establishment and maintenance of a Jewish State in Palestine. Over the years, the specifics of this call were modified to fit the changing needs of the movement. Today Zionism means that the survival of the State of Israel is the guarantor of the survival of the Jewish people. Zionists believe that it is the duty of all Jews to support this effort.

Initially Zionism was a largely secular movement. Still it did support some Jewish religious traditions. For example, Zionists supported the establishment of the Jewish home in Palestine, rejecting other suggested locations. Nevertheless, many early Zionists were secular socialists. Some had participated in the revolutions in Russia, Germany, and other parts of Europe. In Israel they hoped to establish a new form of humane socialism that had not been achieved by the Marxists. Israel was to be a special place that would serve as a symbolic home for Jews everywhere.

This idealism was dramatically expressed by Joseph Schlossberg in the foreword of a 1947 book on the labor movement in Palestine. He wrote,

> Eight and nine centuries ago the Crusaders came from Europe to conquer the Holy Land. The Jewish crusaders came to rebuild, with their own brain and brawn, the neglected and wasted land; to give health and vitality to the disease-ridden soil and people.[29]

Prior to World War II and the Holocaust, Zionism was a minority view in world Jewry. Since the establishment of the State of Israel, however, the principles of Zionism have been almost universally embraced by both religious and secular Jews.[30]

Assimilation into Gentile Society   As a result of the liberating effects of the French Revolution, some Jews abandoned their religious traditions as being obsolete and out of touch with the openness of the new Europe. Thus, they exchanged Judaism for nationalism. They sought to become immersed in the new traditions of the 19th-century nation state. Toward the end of the century their hopes for Jewish assimilation were dashed by the emergence of another period of European anti-Semitism that centered around the trial of the French staff officer, Colonel Alfred Dreyfus. Although Colonel Dreyfus was eventually acquitted, the fact that, as a Jew, he had been singled out and tried for treason was a clear blow to those who had hoped that assimilation into European society would shield them from anti-Semitic attacks.

In modern America, assimilation has taken a different turn. Because of the relative freedom of association that exists, a new form of assimilation is occurring. More and more Jews are marrying outside of their religion. This process has had the effect of weakening the established forms of Judaism. It also has led to an increase in the number of Jews who consider themselves to be Jewish in cultural rather than religious terms.

Who Are the Zoroastrians?

Before the arrival of Islam, Zoroastrianism was the most important religion of Persia (Iran). After the Muslim conquest, the new rulers forced most Zoroastrians to flee. Eventually these people reestablished themselves in India, where they are now called Parsis. Today only a few Zoroastrians remain in the Middle East, most of whom live in Iran.

Although not monotheist, the ancient Zoroastrians had certain religious beliefs and practices that later appeared as traditions in Judaism, Christianity, and Islam. They are considered by most Muslims to be "People of the Book."

Zoroastrians pray five times a day toward a source of light. They perform a ritual of cleansing before prayer. They believe in the battle of good and evil, with the eventual triumph of good. They also believe that at death each individual will have to cross a bridge over hell to reach the light. If one's sins are too great, that person will fall off the bridge and perish.

It should be noted that one of the Roman mystery religions is believed to have emerged as an offshoot of Zoroastrianism. Called Mithraism, this religion was a great rival of early Christianity. When Christianity became the Roman state religion, Mithraism withered away.

Summary

The Middle East is the birthplace of the three great monotheistic religions: Judaism, Christianity, and Islam. Islam is the youngest of the three. It has dominated the life of people in the Middle East and North Africa for more than 1000 years. Today, more than 90 percent of the population is Muslim.

Both Christianity and Islam consider Judaism to be a source for their beliefs. They draw heavily on the teachings of the Torah, sometimes called the "Jewish Bible." All three religions profess to be monotheistic. They all assert that they worship the same god who is God. Christianity and Islam each claims the truths found in their respective holy books, the New Testament or the Koran, are the revelations given by God to humankind. Although their teachings are similar in many respects, believers in each of these three religions consider theirs to be exclusively correct and the other two to be misguided and inferior.

Review Questions

1. What are the three great monotheistic religions with origins in the Middle East?
2. What branch of Islam has the most followers?
3. Name the Five Pillars of Islam.
4. Who are the Copts?
5. Who are called the People of the Book?

Suggested Readings

Peter Clark, "The World's Religions; Understanding the Living Faiths," *Reader's Digest*, 1993.
Kenneth C. Davis. *Don't Know Much About the Bible,* Eagle Brook, New York, 1998.
Henri Sterlin, *Islam: Early Architecture From Baghdad to Cordoba,* Vol. I, Taschen, London, 1996.
Desmond Stewart, "Mecca," *Newsweek*, 1980.
David, Waynes, *An Introduction to Islam,* Cambridge University Press, Cambridge, 1998.

Notes

1. Story attributed to the Sufi Master, Sherif Hisham Kabbani al-Haggani. Mart Abley, "A Mystical Tradition in Islam Is Finding Wide Appeal," *The Gazette* (Montreal), October 22, 1994, p. B1.
2. Alessandra Staley, "Pope and Iranian Leader Hail Talks As An Opening: Khatami Speaks of Religion's Common Bonds," *International Herald Tribune* (Nevilly-sur-Seine, France), March 12, 1999, News p. 5.
3. David Warren, "His Faith Is Not in Vain: This Rock, This Peter, Has Endured Everything From Totalitarianism to the Bullet of an Intended Assassin. Yet His Face Radiates Pure Kindness," *The Ottawa Citizen* (Ottawa, Canada), March 26, 2000, A16.
4. Harvey Shepherd, "Christianity Meets Islam: Messages of Both Religions Much the Same, Antiochian Prelate Says," *The Gazette* (Montreal, Canada), September 18, 1999, Religion J7.
5. Drusilla Menaker, "In Egypt, Pope Condemns Violence in Name of Religion," *The Dallas Morning News* (Dallas, Texas), February 25, 2000, p. 10A.
6. Marius Schattner, "Pope Faces Conflicting Hopes from Israel, Palestinians," *News Release Agence France Press*, March 21, 2000.
7. Charles Lindholm, *The Islamic Middle East: An Historical Anthropology* (Blackwell Publishers: Oxford, England, 1996), p. 219.
8. Sura XXIV, 42, *The Holy Qur'an,* 2nd Edition, Translation and Commentary, A. Yusuf Ali (American Trust Publication for the Muslim Students Association of the United States and Canada, 1977), p. 911.
9. *Ibid* 6, Sura L, p. 1412.
10. Shia, Sufis, and followers of the popular religion in parts of the Muslim world pay devotion, make a pledge to, and intercede at saints' tombs. Many Muslim theologians regard such practices with suspicion. "This is particularly the case with those influenced by the Wahhabis." Ian Richard Netton, *A Popular Dictionary of Islam* (Curzon Press: Richmond, Surrey, UK, 1992), pp. 256–257.
11. This form of prayer is practiced by every Muslim regardless of culture and race throughout the world. This very formal prayer sequence is one of the great unifying features of Islam.
12. Central to Christian worship is prayer that is a personal conversation with God. For Christians this prayer can be public in a church or private. Through prayer Christians attempt to communicate their innermost thoughts to God. John McCollister, *The Christian Book of Whys* (Testament Books: New York, 1983), Chapter 5.
13. Laurence Ziring, *The Middle East Political Dictionary* (ABA-clio Information Services: Santa Barbara, Calif., 1984), p. 57.
14. Paul Coles, *The Ottoman Impact on Europe* (Coles and Thames and Hudson: London, 1968), p. 68.
15. Robert Lacey, *The Kingdom: Arabia and the House of Saud* (Avon Books: New York, 1981), p. 9.
16. Sura XXXIII, 40, *The Holy Qur'an,* 2nd Edition, Translation and Commentary, A. Yusuf Ali (American Trust Publications for the Muslim Students Association of the United States and Canada, 1977), p. 1119.
17. There has been much speculation about the influence of events during the early part of Muhammad's life. Albert Hourani puts it this way: "Before the end of the 7th century, this

Arab ruling group was identifying its new order with a revelation given by God to Muhammad, a citizen of Mecca, in the form of a holy book, The Koran, a revelation which completed those given to earlier prophets or messengers of God and created a new religion, Islam, separate from Judaism and Christianity. There is room for scholarly discussion about the way in which these beliefs developed." Albert Hourani, *A History of the Arab Peoples* (The Belknap Press of Harvard University Press: Cambridge, Mass., 1991), pp. 14–15.

18. Ismail I. Nawwab, Peter C. Speers, and Paul F. Hoye, Editors, *Saudi Aramco and Its World: Arabia and the Middle East* (Saudi Arabian Oil Company: Dhahran, Saudi Arabia, 1995), p. 50.
19. H. G. Wells, *The Outline of History*, Vol. I (Garden City Books: New York, 1961), p. 486. Also see: Ismail I. Nawwab, Peter C. Speers, and Paul F. Hoye, Editors, *Saudi Aramco and Its World: Arabia and the Middle East* (Saudi Arabian Oil Company: Dhahran, Saudi Arabia, 1995), p. 53.
20. Ismail I. Nawwab, Peter C. Speers, Paul F. Hoye, Editors, *Saudi Aramco and Its World: Arabia and the Middle East* (Saudi Arabian Oil Company: Dhahran, Saudi Arabia, 1995), p. 53.
21. Edward Bray, "Face to Faith: Christians Also Have a Mystic Journey to Make," *The Guardian* (London), September 28, 1996, Features, p. 17.
22. "Sufi's Choice: A Mystical Tradition in Islam Is Finding Wide Appeal," *The Gazette* (Montreal, Canada), October 22, 1994, Weekly Review Section, p. B1.
23. Netton, *op. cit.*, p. 236.
24. Sura III, 84, *The Holy Qur'an*, 2nd Edition, Translation and Commentary, A. Yusuf Ali (American Trust Publications for the Muslim Students Association of the United States and Canada, 1977), p. 145.
25. D. C. Sumerville, *A Short History of Our Religion: From Moses to the Present Day* (Macmillan Company: New York, 1922), p. 99.
26. Joan O'Grady, *Early Christian Heresies* (Barnes and Noble: New York, 1985), p. 5.
27. H. G. Wells, *The Outline of History*, Vol. II (Garden City Books: New York, 1961), p. 433.
28. Ronald Clark has described Lenin's views on Zionism in the following way: "Although his Jewish ancestry always remained in dispute, Lenin's views on Jewry were decided if complicated. Always taking a strong line against anti-Semitism, he was an almost equally fervid anti-Zionist, once writing that Zionism appeared to be a greater enemy to social democracy than anti-Semitism." Ronald W. Clark, *Lenin: The Man Behind the Mask* (Faber and Faber: London, 1988), p. 73.
29. Samuel Kurland, *Cooperative Palestine: The Story of Histadrut* (Sharon Books: New York, 1947), p. 50.
30. For a short but interesting account of the evolution of political Zionism, see "Dreaming of Altneuland," *The Economist* (London), U.S. Edition, December 23, 2000, Christmas Specials Section.

Chapter 4

The Politics of Culture in the Middle East and North Africa

Introduction

When I hear the word culture, I reach for my gun.[1]

Culture is one of the most difficult concepts to define. By the mid-20th century, anthropologists had developed more than 150 definitions for culture. Used here, culture simply refers to the shared values and traditions that distinguish the peoples of the Middle East and North Africa from other societies.

Culture is a controversial subject for almost everyone because it involves the very core of what people believe. Any threat to modify culture will always be resisted. Like societies in many other parts of the world, the people of the Middle East see assaults on their culture at almost every turn.

There is a popular description of people in the region that characterizes the soldiers as Turks, the people of literature as Persians, and the people of religion as Arabs. This cultural stereotype may be an overgeneralization, but it illustrates an attitude held by many about others.

This author once heard the following exchange between an Iranian professor of the Persian language and his Arab student. Student: "Professor, why do you say that all great literature except the *Qur'an* [Koran] is written in the Persian language and not Arabic?" Professor: "What of literary value could we expect to come from Bedouin tribesmen?" This attitude is an example of the tensions that still remain between the cultures that co-exist in the Middle East and North Africa.

The reader should recognize that one of the difficulties in understanding the culture of a place like the Middle East and North Africa is the ability to identify and separate what has become an intermingling of pre-Islamic, Islamic, and tribal traditions. Here, the religious traditions have absorbed other practices to become a way of life. Everything is said to have a religious origin whether or not that is historically accurate. Still, these practices have become the basis of the culture.

Arab Dress

Today many Arabs in the cities wear a form of Western dress. In rural areas, however, and on occasion in cities, traditional dress is seen. Traditional Arab dress for both men and women is similar throughout the Middle East and North Africa. There are many regional differences and names for individual clothing items, but the visitor will see that there is a general conformity in dress. Men wear long, flowing, loose-fitting gowns. Headwear may vary from small caps, to variations of the fez, to a head cloth secured by a double cord.

Women are enjoined by the Koran to dress modestly. They generally wear an inner and an outer garment. The inner one is for the home, whereas the outer one is for wearing on the street. The degree of cover varies according to local custom.

In general, Middle Eastern dress is sensible clothing for the climate. There is nothing more amusing than to see a foreign visitor in Western clothing standing in the heat alongside a Saudi counterpart. The Saudi looks cool and dignified in his white flowing robes, whereas the Western visitor is wilting in his rumpled business suit.

A Hat Maker in Tunisia
Similar to the more famous fez, these felt hats are being sized and left to dry on wooden forms before being sold to the public.
Source: Joe Weatherby

Traditional Saudi Dress
This Saudi is demonstrating proper use of an incense burner
Source: Joe Weatherby

> Saudi Arabian dress can be used as a model for traditional Middle Eastern attire. Men wear a loose-fitting, floor-length, long-sleeved garment called a *thawb*. In other parts of the region it may be called a *jallabiyah*. Sandals or Western shoes are used to cover the feet. Some men, especially on more formal occasions, wear a dark cloak over the thawb. Often the cloak is trimmed with a gold border. For a head cover, Saudi men wear a skullcap and over that a head cloth secured by a black cord.
>
> Saudi women also wear dark, loose-fitting outer clothing. Elsewhere this outer cover varies greatly in color and style. In Morocco, the garment is an elegant hooded affair with a separate veil. In other parts of the region, it can even be a covering for the entire body. In Egypt and Turkey, it may be only a cloak with a scarf tied under the chin. In the house, women wear colorful clothing that ranges from long elaborate gowns to the latest Paris fashions. Nothing is more surprising for an outsider than to leave Arabia on a jet aircraft filled with veiled women only to see most of them arrive in New York or London dressed in the latest Western business attire and carrying designer briefcases ready for the morning's work.

An example of custom becoming a religious duty is the confusion over the veiling of women. Veiling was not required by the teachings of the Koran. The Koran enjoins women to dress modestly. In point of fact, veiling existed in the Mediterranean world long before the advent of Islam. The wearing of a scarf to cover a woman's head is still a common practice in rural areas of the Mediterranean from Spain to Turkey. Even upper class Northern European women were commonly veiled in public until the 18th century.

Today the veil is associated with a religious duty, but it is more likely to have an origin in local tribal custom. For this reason, the term *veil* refers to a great variety of coverings ranging from a simple scarf on the head used in Turkey to the complete body cover that is commonly seen in Arabia and Iran. In Morocco, the veil and hooded cloak are often quite elegant and exotic. To most residents of the region, the veil is simply a demonstration of modesty in public, much like "proper business dress" is worn by Western women outside the home. The important point to understand is that veiling is a custom like many other aspects of local culture that has become "established" by placing it in a religious context. Although many arguments can be made for and against veiling, few Muslims would argue that it is without any religious justification. Over time this custom has become a practice of Islam. Veiling is only one example of the way hundreds of traditions have become part of the religious milieu of the region.

Is There a Single Race of People in the Middle East and North Africa?

There is a popular misconception that there is a homogeneous race of people in the Middle East. This notion is fostered by some of the region's religions whose traditions allude to Arab, Jewish, or even Aryan races. These terms have little meaning unless they are limited to linguistic or cultural associations.

The term *people* means a community united by common culture, history, religion, or language. If one uses *people* to describe linguistic and cultural rather than racial attributes, there are three major peoples in the region. Based on language, most Middle Easterners are Semites, Turks, or Persians.

The largest linguistic group in the Middle East and North Africa is the Semites. People speaking Semitic languages emerged in the area of the Tigris and Euphrates valleys more than 4000 years ago. Over the centuries, Amorites, Canonites, Phoenicians, and Hebrews spread Semitic dialects from the Fertile Crescent to Arabia. There, Nabateans and pre-Islamic Arabs who were living in the Sinai, parts of modern Jordan, and Saudi Arabia were speaking a Semitic dialect at least 2500 years ago. Other forms of Semitic languages are still spoken in places as diverse as Malta and Ethiopia.

THE MODERN SEMITES

Although these peoples spoke Semitic languages in ancient times, the only large Semitic groups that survive today are the Arabs and the Jews. Hebrew and Arabic are closely related Semitic languages. Arabic is spoken by about half of the people who live in the region. Hebrew is a language of ritual that has been revived in common speech as a symbol of nationalism by the Jews living in Israel.

THE ARABS

The focus in this chapter is on the Arabs. They are the largest cultural group in the area. The written form of the Arabic language unifies them. Because Arabic was exported from Arabia to large parts of the Middle East and North Africa, it became the vehicle that caused over 200 million people to consider themselves to be Arabs. Most have adopted Islam as their religion, but all have absorbed enough of the language of the original desert people to identify with a common set of values and traditions that are associated with the Arab civilization.

The Domination of Arab Culture Throughout Most of the Middle East and North Africa Arab culture now dominates an area from the Fertile Crescent across North Africa to the Atlantic. This area is also the Arabic-speaking part of the region.

The ancient world had highly developed cultures that were associated with this area. Starting with the Fertile Crescent, great empires developed in Babylon, Egypt, Persia, and Byzantium. Each of these cultures played a significant part in the history of the world. With the exception of the Persian language, all that is left for the modern observer to see are the impressive ruins from these early civilizations. Why does the influence of the Arabs touch on almost everything in the region? The Middle Eastern scholar John Bandeau has provided an answer to this question. He states his thesis this way:

> The Arab conquest of the ancient world in the 7th and 8th centuries produced two momentous and enduring effects. The more immediate and dramatic was the creation of a new world state in the Mediterranean Basin and the Near East. The second effect was the development of a new world culture within this state.[2]

Within 100 years of the beginning of the Arab State, its boundaries had stretched from the Pyrenees in the west across Spain, North Africa, and the Fertile Crescent to include the old Persian Empire in the east. Although there were later retreats, no Arab-occupied land remained untouched by Arab culture. This fact is all the more amazing when the reader considers that prior to the Arab conquest, Arabia had remained largely a "backwater" untouched by the earlier great civilizations. The Arabs were largely a nomadic

Arab Names

In Arabic, names are much more than simply a form of address. Among other things, names convey family history, social status, and origin. Full Arab names consist of five parts: the kunya, ism, nasab, nisba, and lagab.

1. The *kunya* is the part of an Arab's name that indicates descent. In the case of males, the word "abu" literally means "father of sons." When referring to female descent, the word "umm," or "mother of," is used. Some examples are: Abu Hanifa, Abu Bakr, Abu Al-Saud, Abu Salem, etc.
2. The *ism* is the equivalent of a person's given name in English. Examples of given names could be Aub, Job, Muhammad, Ahmed, Ali, Abdellah, Mahmoud, Saleh, Salman, etc.
3. The *nasab* refers to an Arab's lineage. Because bloodlines are considered to be very important, the nasab is a significant social qualifier. In referring to male lineage, the word *ibn* is used; for female lineage, the word is *bin*. Names often carry the pedigree back several generations. Some examples are: bin Salman, bin Abdul-Aziz, etc.
4. The *nisba* describes the place of origin, the profession, or any other distinguishing characteristic. For example, a person from Afghanistan might be called al-Afghani. Some examples are: Al-Masri (from Egypt), Al-Maghrebi (from Morocco), Al-Sodani (from Sudan).
5. The *lagab* originally signified an honorific title. In more recent times it has also referred to the family name. Examples of honorific titles would be the scientists, the preacher of the two holy places, or the protector of the religion. The full name would never be used except possibly in print. The *kunya,* or *lagab,* is commonly used. The ism is almost never used except by close friends or relatives: Al-Kurdi, Al-Harazi, Abdul-Aziz, Al-Hajjri, etc.

A formal Arab name might look like this: Muhammad Abu Bakr bin Salman Abdul-Aziz.

---

tribal people. Few, prior to the Arab conquest, would have predicted that a movement that would change the world would emerge out of the Arabian Desert. But it did.

The Arab nation began as a small isolated people living in Arabia. The great expansion of the Arab state took only a short period of time. Although other empires had passed the same way, it was the Arabs who were able to make their civilization permanent.

Most authorities agree that the linkage of language with the Islamic religion was the unique factor that led to the importance of Arab culture in the Middle East and North Africa. Arabic is the language of the Koran and therefore of Islam. As the religion spread across the region, so did the language. After religion, the most important aspect of Arab culture is the language.

The Arabic Language Helped to Expand the Arab Culture All would agree that belief is a matter of "the heart" and that it is not necessary to speak Arabic to be a Muslim. Nevertheless, the knowledge of Arabic is believed to be an advantage in understanding the Koran because translation into other languages distorts God's word.

Arabic was an invaluable tool in the spread of Arab culture. As a Semitic language, Arabic appears in three versions: spoken "street" Arabic, literary or modern standard Arabic, and sacred Arabic. As might be expected of any spoken language, spoken Arabic has many dialects and varies widely across the region. A dock worker in Casablanca might have as much difficulty understanding a farmer in Iraq as a Texas cowboy would find trying to speak English to an Irish resident of County Cork. Literary Arabic can be read by all educated Arabs. It is the language of newspapers and books. Sacred Arabic is the language of the Koran. It is largely unchanged from the time of Muhammad. Most educated Arabs can read both modern standard and the sacred form of Arabic. Arabic is written and read from the right to the left.

The unique alphabet and script of Arabic have been imported to cultures that do not speak the language. Modern Iranians write using a modified form of the Arab alphabet. They also have many Arab words that have crept into their language. Although Turks, like Iranians, retained their own language, it was written using altered Arabic script until the nationalist leader Mustafa Kemal Ataturk abolished the practice and substituted a version of the Latin alphabet early in the 20th century. In Catholic Spain, it is said that Arabic has influenced the development of the Spanish language more than any other foreign tongue except Latin. Although slightly fewer than 200 million people speak Arabic, probably 800 million Muslims around the world understand portions of this language.

As Islam expanded out of Arabia to become a world religion, Arabs carried other aspects of their culture along with their language and religion. Initially, conquered Christians, Jews, and Zoroastrians were allowed to remain faithful to their own cultures and religions. It was not long, however, before the dominant religion linked with Arabic began to supplant the indigenous cultures. As people abandoned their traditions, the growth of an Arab civilization based on language continued. Even people who did not become Muslims slowly became Arabs. An example of this evolution occurred in Egypt. After the conquest, traditional Egyptian culture declined in favor of Arab culture. By the end of the Middle Ages, even the language of Egypt had been abandoned in favor of Arabic. After modern Egypt gained independence, President Gamel Abdul Nasser formally proclaimed that the Egyptians were Arabs. Today both Christians and Muslims in Egypt speak Arabic and identify with the Arab world. They may consider themselves to be Egyptian first, but they also are culturally part of Egyptian Arab civilization. A similar process took place elsewhere in North Africa, the Eastern Mediterranean, and the Fertile Crescent. That is the region that eventually became the Arab world. Today the Arab language and culture unite Muslims and non-Muslims as part of a common civilization.

Other Aspects of Culture That Came to the Region from the Arabs The Arabs emerged from Arabia as a desert people with the values of that harsh place. Although Muhammad and most of the other early Muslim leaders were city dwellers, they were guided by traditions that emerged from the desert tribes that had existed prior to Islam. The traditions of the desert still influence Arabs throughout the region. In describing the cultural impact that the people of the desert had on the Arab world, the astute Western observer Eleanor Nicholson wrote,

> The Bedouin of the Arabian Peninsula produced a culture complete in itself, and as timeless as the desert that influenced it.[3]

An Old Tunisian Home
This traditional Tunisian home has a simple outside with a beautiful inner courtyard. This Arab idea is now common in many "Spanish" homes all over the world.
Source: Joe Weatherby

A number of Arab virtues have evolved out of this harsh existence. These include the love of freedom, the sense of equality, pride, subservience to no man, and fear of God. The desert also forced a reliance on group solidarity for survival. Family, clan, and tribe were more important than the individual. The dishonor of one member of the group dishonored everyone.

Arab Art Especially during the early period of conquest, Arab art was part of a greater Muslim art. It observed the same limits and rules that were imposed on all Muslims. Arab artists scrupulously avoided representing the human figure. Re-creating human figures was believed to lead to the sin of worshipping something other than God. This practice is still true in most of the Arab world. Stylized figures do appear as exceptions in the Islamic art of Persia, India, and parts of Asia.

The Arabs focused on art that they believed would aid in the contemplation of God. They evolved a geometric-based form of abstract art that is now world famous. It appears in sculpture, ceramic tiling, and painting.

In handwriting itself, the written form of Arabic became a religious expression. Calligraphy became an art form. The calligraphy of old Korans rivals the beauty of the medieval illuminated texts of European Christians. Today the art of beautiful calligraphy is still prized throughout the Arab world.

Arab Architecture As a community of believers, Arab architects focused their efforts on providing buildings for group and family rather than individual ostentation. Their buildings, whether for public or private use, are usually plain on the outside and richly decorated inside. The famous Alhambra Palace in Granada, Spain, may be considered the ultimate example of this type of architecture. As the visitor climbs the hill through a series of beautiful gardens, at first sight the palace is a disappointment. Plain yellow walls pierced by a beautiful gate are all that indicate what is to be found inside. On entering the palace, the eye is overwhelmed by the beauty of the wall carvings, the ceilings, the views, and the fountains. Everywhere beauty graces rooms and courtyards. Although the Alhambra is the finest expression of this kind of secular architecture, it exists in modified form across the Arab world. Perhaps more importantly, this style of architecture has spread to Latin America, Mexico, and the western United States, where people would be surprised to learn of its origin.

Arab mosques are at least as distinctive as European cathedrals. They follow general features in that all have pointers toward Mecca. They may have great open-air courtyards or be covered. However, they have maintained a similarity in style, within these categories, from the earliest days of Islam.

The Arab Oral Tradition At the time of Islam's beginning, the Arabs maintained their literature and history by means of an oral tradition. Storytelling was a primary means of conveying news and information. Although Arab writing became important, the oral tradition remains a significant part of Arab culture. The Arabs have a number of stories and fables, including the famous tales of the Arabian nights that have been told and retold for centuries. Arab storytellers are still common throughout the region.

In addition to storytelling, recitation from memory is a prized art form. From a very early age, young boys and now some girls are taught to memorize the passages from the Koran. There are many Arabs and other Muslims who can recite the Koran from the first sura to the last. In the Arab world great reciters of the Koran achieve the kind of fame that surrounds sports heroes in the West. It is believed that memorization goes to the heart, not the intellect. The Koran as accepted by the heart as God's word can never be analyzed by the head.

The tradition of memorization still exists in the modern world. Western teachers new to the region have been shocked when they started to grade their students' exams to find that parts of the textbook had been repeated verbatim. In recent years, modern Western education methods have de-emphasized this form of learning. Unfortunately, much of Western literature and poetry have been lost to the student in the process.

Where Do Arabs Live Although many of their idealized traditions emerged from the nomads of the desert, most modern Arabs are residents of the towns and cities. Along with

The Alhambra Palace in Granada, Spain
Once the home of Muslim kings, the Alhambra is one of the finest examples of Islamic art in stone and plaster. The channel in the floor allows the visitor to always hear the relaxing sound of running water that is carried from nearby fountains to rooms throughout the palace.
Source: Joe Weatherby

the Bedouins of the desert, residents of the towns and cities form an interlocking, mutually dependent society.

The Bedouins The Bedouins are the nomadic peoples of the desert. They live an idealized free existence that many see as the way of life of the original Arabs. Although they exist in almost every Arab state, they are best known as a symbol of traditional life in Saudi Arabia. There the Bedouin values of freedom, honor, and loyalty to family, clan, and tribe are cherished by all Saudis.

Like the "urban cowboys" found in the American Southwest, urban Saudis often leave their modern homes in the city for weekend visits to their Bedouin past. In the desert they can park their four-wheel-drive recreation vehicles, pitch their tents, and sit around the evening campfire just like their grandfathers did. Most Saudi luxury hotels even have a tented area inside the lobby where the men can have coffee and sit and talk. Some Saudi

Mosque of Muhammed Ali
Located on the Citadel towering above Cairo, this mosque was begun in 1824. Today, it remains the most imposing landmark in the city.
Source: Joe Weatherby

families still send their sons to live for a time with their Bedouin relatives in order for them to learn the values of their desert past.

One of the paradoxes of this life style is manifested in the common Arab attitude toward formal government. Although it is true that Arabs adhere to an informal form of equality and democracy at the family, clan, and perhaps even tribal level, there has been little transference of this tradition to formal government. By Western standards, most Arab governments are inefficient, corrupt, and authoritarian. The tradition of Western democracy is as alien in this region as it is in most of the developing world. Real decision-making still occurs informally in the traditional way. Recommendations are discussed within the family, the clan, and the tribe before being formally ratified by the actions of government.

Honor also plays a role in the enforcement of the rules of society. In the West where individualism is stressed, society deals with lawbreakers through the instruments of government. In the Arab world where individual guilt affects family honor, the members of the group often administer a rough form of justice outside of the governmental apparatus. In this way the dishonor of a family member is kept within the family. Families tend to punish their own for transgressions to avoid public disgrace. It can be said that the basic Bedouin ideals of honor, hospitality, and loyalty to the family, clan, and tribe are now deeply rooted throughout the Arab world.

The romance and free spirit of the Bedouin were captured over 100 years ago in the words of Lady Jane Digby, who married a Syrian tribal chief. She is quoted as writing,

> The moment when my heart fails me is when I am obliged—as is the custom—to give the sheik his lance or other arms, when he mounts his magnificent mare to go off with his tribe against some rival, one that approaches to seize our camels and tents.[4]

This ideal had remained unchanged when Eleanor Nicholson met a Saudi Bedouin in 1961:

> He rides at a lopsided gait, colored tassels swinging from the saddle and cloak behind. The white camel halts, and from its great height the man gazes down on us. . . . The Bedouin holds me with his gaze, piercing, direct. Then a smile breaks the fierceness of his countenance, and his response gives us the peace of Allah.[5]

Today most governments of the Middle East and North Africa are interested in establishing a strong central authority. The Bedouins, with their independent ways, are a hindrance to this process. They recognize no borders or nationalism except the traditional ones. Concerted efforts are being made to first count and then induce the Bedouin to cease their migrations and settle on the land. This process may be resisted by some, but it seems inevitable that the free life of the Bedouin will soon disappear into the mist of a more romantic past.

The Village Although the specific patterns of village life vary widely with the conditions in the region, several generalizations can be made that are common to most. The villagers have traditionally been held in low esteem by both the Bedouins and the city dwellers. When she entered the village adjacent to the ancient Palmyra in 1854, Lady Jane Digby expressed this commonly held view. She is quoted as stating that the villagers were,

> Unmitigated barbarians . . . permitted by the Bedouins to live within the town, on condition of their acting as purveyors to the tribes.[6]

In the 19th century the Bedouin supplemented their income by raiding others. These raids were often visited on the defenseless villagers. In modern times the balance of military power shifted as villagers armed with modern weapons were able to successfully defend themselves against Bedouin attacks.

The city dwellers also have exploited the villagers. Absentee landlords have taken portions of the harvest, while the central government took taxes and the army took the sons. Villagers furnish raw materials to the cities in return for receiving high-cost finished products. The result is an urban dominance over village life that has increased with modernization.

Villages usually encompass a cluster of small houses made of stone or mud brick and are located near a water source. The village economy is based on agriculture supplemented by crafts. People usually live in the village and work in nearby fields. The village economy is run as a family affair. Everyone is part of a perceived extended family. Like the Bedouin, villagers surrender individualism for the collective good of the community.

In some places, electricity, radios, and even television have brought political awareness to the village. These technological advances have brought many villages into the mainstream of state life. However, there are still villages where traditional loyalties to family, clan, and tribe dominate. In these places the capital city and the state may even be considered to be the same. Governmental representatives are often viewed with suspicion and distrust.

The modern world has steadily encroached on the autonomy of the village. The central government has adopted the Western model of sending experts on agriculture, education, and health care from the cities to work in the villages. With their arrival has come the process of modernization, which will eventually change the customs and life in the village.

A Typical Village in Central Morocco
The single street cuts through few small houses and shops. Note that the village now has modern street lights.
Source: Joe Weatherby

The City   Part of the Arab world has always identified with city dwelling. Muhammad grew up in a city. There are ancient cities that still exist in southern Yemen. During the Middle Ages, Baghdad was perhaps the most important city in the world. Although influenced by rural culture, city dwellers had their own distinct traditions, including religious societies, trading associations, and governmental institutions. It was in the cities with their schools and universities where the orthodox religious traditions of Islam were preserved. Until the 20th century, most of the cities of the region were comparatively small. Compared to other cities, Cairo is relatively new. Still, Cairo can be taken as an example of how fast the process of change has occurred. When the French invaded Egypt in 1798, Cairo had a population of only around 250,000 inhabitants and was a few square miles in size. Today, Cairo (9.5 million) and the suburbs may have as many as 13 million inhabitants. This gives Cairo a larger population than Egypt had in 1830. The city stretches east from the old city for about 8 miles to the edge of the Pyramids at Giza.[7]

Cairo exhibits many of the settlement patterns found in the major cities throughout the Middle East and North Africa. The old city is surrounded by a modern European-style area, with broad boulevards framing endless rows of apartment buildings. The outskirts of the city contain largely self-built shantytowns, or "tin-can cities." These slums are the "no man's land" areas common in cities throughout the developing world. They are inhabited by the poor from the villages who have arrived seeking work. Most new arrivals are uneducated and without skills. They are reduced to carrying out the most menial, unpleasant tasks in the city.

Cairo also has an additional infamous slum. Located in the center of the Old City, it is the burial ground of the medieval Mamluk rulers. For centuries this area has been called

A Squatter's Town
A common sight in many parts of the developing world, squatters have built a tin-can and cardboard town on the side of the highway leaving the Moroccan city of Tangier.
Source: Joe Weatherby

"the City of the Dead." Here, some of the poorest of the poor scratch out an existence while living inside the old tombs. Modern visitors often assume that this slum area has been settled solely because of the growth of the modern city, but this is not so. The city's poor have inhabited the City of the Dead for more than a hundred years.

In describing the City of the Dead when he visited it at the end of the 19th century, John Stoddard wrote,

> . . . incredible as it seems, bats and lizards now infest the beautifully sculptured walls, and families of Egyptian beggars make their homes within the tombs of Muhammad's successors.[8]

The Old City of Cairo is like others in the region. It is made up of a maze of twisting, narrow passages. Open-fronted shops face directly onto the street. Generally the shops are located by product. There are streets for gold sellers, spice sellers, leather goods sellers, and rug sellers. In the past, there has also been an ethnic division of labor. Since many shops manufacture their goods on the spot, this means, for example, that if the Greeks are the goldsmiths, their shops are in the gold market or souk, whereas other ethnic groups manufacturing other items will locate on the streets in the Old City where their products are sold. In most cities, like in Cairo, there are no ghettos in the European sense of that word. They are common areas of manufacture and sales. Here people of all religions come and go to do their business. In the modern portions of the city, the shopping takes place in much the same way as it is done in any large city in the West.

Cairo represents a process that is taking place throughout the Arab world. As governments attempt to modernize, their bureaucracies expand in size, governmental spending is concentrated on the cities, industry is established in the cities, and the centers of education and social services are located in the cities. People from the countryside flock to these areas hoping to take advantage of the new opportunities that are becoming available, and growth soon outstrips services. Many new arrivals do not have the skills to compete for the available jobs and so they drift into a poverty worse than what they left in the village. The result is a dispossessed, alienated poor that are vulnerable to political and religious movements that promise change.

One other group that is a source of tension in the cities should be mentioned. There are literally hundreds of thousands of educated, minor functionaries in government and industry who have been reduced to meaningless, bureaucratic jobs with little or no future. Frustrated because education had promised them upward mobility that had been available to educated people in the past but is now no longer possible, they have become a source of unrest. These educated dissatisfied bureaucrats have been influenced by movements promising radical change and social justice. A stereotypical person in the group is the university graduate who is now a low-paid minor ministry clerk serving under an uneducated corrupt ministry head who has obtained the top job through the informal ties of his family, clan, and tribe. These people are aware of the injustices of their situation. They are often unwilling or unable to rely on the traditional support systems to resolve their problems.

There is at least one major exception to the urban patterns just described. The new cities of Saudi Arabia and the Persian Gulf do not fit the traditional model. Although a few of these cities may be quite old, all have undergone their primary development since the discovery of oil. Cities like Jidda, Riyadh, and Dhahran in Saudi Arabia and their counterparts in the Gulf have literally exploded in size since the oil industry was created. With almost unlimited funds available, these "planned cities" boast beautiful public art, wide thoroughfares, and housing that is superior by any standards in the world.

In these cities the problems are quite different from those found in places like Cairo. Rapid development has meant the destruction of much of the old parts of cities like Jidda and Riyadh. Only in recent years have preservationists started efforts to save what is left of the past for future generations to see. Jidda has been one of the more successful cities to preserve its old parts by acting to establish a preservation district in the Old Town. Facing a growth from only a few thousand people during Word War I to an astounding 1.5 million inhabitants by the end of the 20th century, city planners in Jidda were faced with a formidable task to be able to save anything. As the city underwent a growth boom, the land along the seafront became a very valuable spot for new development. Much of the old seaport was lost. However, there is now a strong effort to save and rehabilitate those structures that remain. The result is an interesting blend of the ultramodern and the old in the city. In Riyadh, parts of the mud walls and palace have been saved. Unfortunately, there are more examples of urban decay than of restoration in most of the Middle East and North Africa.

There was very little significant urban settlement along the shores of the Persian Gulf prior to the discovery of oil. Even here, however, the palaces and forts that remain are being preserved. In Doha, Qatar, the government has even preserved several fishing boats, called *dhows,* in a local park to serve as examples of what the economy was like before oil. It should be pointed out that in Qatar and other parts of the Persian Gulf, dhows are still used for trading and fishing.

New prosperity has led to some unusual problems in this part of the Arab world. Although most people now live in cities, many Bedouin values remain. The idea that it is dishonorable to work for wages in jobs with low status is prevalent among many educated

A Street in the Old City of Jidda, Saudi Arabia
The wooden screens on the sides of the houses are used to catch the breeze while giving the residents privacy.
Source: Joe Weatherby

young Saudi men. Their reluctance to take low prestige jobs has forced the government to rely on foreigners to fill the vacancies. However, the Saudi government and the Gulf States learned a hard lesson about "guest workers" during the Iraqi invasion of Kuwait. Although guest workers were well paid by outside standards, they had a much lower status than the native population. In the case of Kuwait, large numbers of guest workers openly sided with Iraq during the occupation. They accepted the promise that the wealth of Kuwait would be redistributed and guest workers would be included.

To combat the threat that foreign workers might pose for the state, the Saudi government has initiated a program to gradually replace guest workers with Saudis. The problem is that few Saudi males seem willing to step forward to take the low-status jobs that will soon become available under the Saudization program. This leaves governmental planners with a dilemma. How can educated Saudi males be persuaded to accept jobs that their Bedouin culture scorns? On the other hand, if educated Saudi women are used to fill these positions, what will happen to the traditional role of women as homemakers? If both of these alternatives fail, what will happen to the Saudi culture when guest workers, with their differing values, are hired to do the work?

A second problem exists in the western part of Arabia. During the annual pilgrimage to Mecca, millions of Muslims from all over the world visit the Kingdom. Many are from states that are poor. At the end of the pilgrimage, a significant number of visitors do not return home. They remain illegally in the Kingdom, hoping to find jobs. Like undocumented aliens in Europe and North America, these laborers live a precarious existence, working at the jobs that no one else will do.

In the oil-producing regions of the Persian Gulf, a different situation has developed. Here cities like Dhahran, Damman, and Jubail simply did not exist before oil. These are completely planned urban areas. Because of the large number of foreigners and the strategic importance of the oil fields, these areas are virtually military districts. Here guest workers are closely regulated. European and American specialists live in guarded, self-contained compounds where the housing, stores, and recreation facilities are almost indistinguishable from those in their home countries. Some of the largest public works projects in modern history are taking place along this coast.

THE TURKS

The Turks are a people who speak the Turkish language and consider themselves to be Turks. They make up about 80 percent of the population of the modern state of Turkey. The Turks are said to have immigrated to Anatolia from central Asia. Over time they overran and then dominated the population there. Eventually the Turkish language replaced Greek and other indigenous languages. Today the Turkish language is the primary unifying element that separates Turks from other Muslims in the Middle East. The Turkish contributions to the Muslim world include a military tradition, a system of bureaucratic government rich in documents, and the works of great builders and architects. The important influence that the Turks had on the history of Islam is discussed in Chapter 5.

THE PERSIANS

The Persians are an Indo-European people who live in Iran.

> The term Indo-European refers to a broad group of people who date back to the Stone Age. As a group, they are known to have anthropological and linguistic similarities but are nevertheless diverse in detail.[9]

The Persians are also considered to be culturally Aryan. As used here, this term does not imply racial unity. About two-thirds of the inhabitants of the modern state of Iran speak some form of Persian. Persian is an Indo-European language that is spoken in Iran and parts of Afghanistan. A dialect of Persian was spoken in this region as early as the 6th century B.C.E. Modern Persian evolved around the 10th century C.E. Compared to the Semitic languages, Persian has a simple grammar and is considered to be rather easy to learn. Since the arrival of Islam a number of Arabic words have been incorporated into the language. A modified form of the Arabic alphabet is used to write Persian. Like Arabic, Persian writing is read from the right to the left.

Persian-speaking Iranians dominate the cultural life of Iran. After the first century of Islam, Persians began to dominate the political life of the Muslim world. In Baghdad, Persian scholars raised Muslim science, literature, and philosophy to heights unknown at that time in the rest of the world. Although Persian influence on the Middle East was reduced after the fall of the Abbassids, the Persian tradition of kingship lasted until the Iranian Revolution in 1979. Modern Iranian culture is still recognized for its literature, art, and scholarship. In acknowledging the importance of this cultural heritage, some outside observers have referred to the Iranians as "the French of the Middle East." Further discussion of Persian cultural influences on the region are detailed in Chapter 5.

IMPORTANT CULTURAL MINORITIES OF THE MIDDLE EAST AND NORTH AFRICA

The Armenians Armenians believe that their people originated near Lake Van in what is today eastern Turkey. Their tradition holds that they are the descendants of one of the sons of Noah. Armenians claim that they established the first Christian kingdom during the 3rd century C.E. The Armenian Church has been out of communion with Western Christianity for most of the time since its founding. Like other minorities in the region, Armenia has had the misfortune of being located between traditionally powerful neighbors. Consequently, Armenian history is full of stories of massacres and persecutions.

Probably the saddest period of Armenian genocide occurred between 1894 and 1914. At that time, Turkish nationalism was evolving out of the old multicultural Ottoman Empire. Having an alien Christian people located in the heart of the Turkish-speaking Muslim land during this time provoked outrage, resulting in a number of massacres of Armenians. The most devastating occurred during World War I when the Armenians were accused of siding with Russia against the Ottomans. The Ottoman government moved to expel the Armenian population from their homes in eastern Anatolia. More than half a million Armenians are believed to have lost their lives during their dispersal by the Ottoman Turks.

Since that time, exiled Armenian communities have established themselves in Lebanon and Iran. There are also large numbers of Armenians who settled in the United States. Their bitterness toward the Turks for their actions during this period remains a central issue in modern Armenian politics.

At the end of World War I, an Armenian Republic was established in the Caucasus Mountains. After the Russian Revolution, this republic became part of the Soviet Union until the fall of communism. Since 1991 the Armenian Republic has been independent of Russia. This state has slightly less than 4 million inhabitants. There is little remaining of the Armenian culture that once thrived in eastern Turkey.

The Berbers Unlike most North Africans, the Berbers are not Arabs. The Berber language is part of the Hamitic group. Many Berbers also speak Arabic and French. They are Sunni Muslims, like their Arab neighbors. They have their own unique dress, which is different from that of the Arabs. Unlike Arab women, most Berber women do not wear the veil. Numbering fewer than 10 million, the Berbers live in Libya, Algeria, and Morocco.

The Berbers are famous for their warrior traditions. During the Riff War of the 1920s, the Berbers of the mountains defeated the Spanish and held off the French for years before finally succumbing to Western Imperialism in 1925. Berber irregulars were also instrumental in helping Arab nationalists to force the French to withdraw from Algeria in 1962.

The Circassians Originally from an area stretching from the Black Sea to the Caucasus, the Circassians of the Middle East now live in Turkey, Syria, and Jordan. They were a

A Berber Market in Northern Morocco
Note that, like most Berber women, the woman in the photograph does not wear a veil.
Source: Joe Weatherby

Christian people from the 6th century until they came under Ottoman rule. The Circassians converted to Islam while they were governed by the Ottomans.

During the 19th century, the Ottoman Empire was forced to surrender the Circassian homeland to Russia. The Circassians actively opposed the Tsarist armies prior to the Ottoman surrender. Rather than live under Russian authority, many Circassians elected to move to safer areas in the Ottoman-controlled Fertile Crescent. Since that time, the Circassians have been famed for their military ability. Many professional officers in the Jordanian Army are Circassian. Circassian women are known throughout the Middle East for their beauty.

The Kurds With a population of around 20 million, the Kurds are one of the lesser-known large minorities. It might surprise the reader to learn that there are more Kurds than there are inhabitants in Ireland, Jordan, Lebanon, Syria, Israel, or Tunisia. There are more Kurds in the Middle East than Jews in the world.

The Kurds are found in eastern Turkey, eastern Syria, northern Iraq, western Iran, and in parts of Azerbaijan and Armenia. All but about 5 million Kurds live in a mountainous geographic region called Kurdistan. The Kurds have been in a struggle for their independence since the end of World War I.

The geographic location of Kurdistan, an area that stretches across several hostile states, has led to a great deal of disunity among the Kurdish people. Each country with a Kurdish minority has tried to use their historic disunity to destabilize the neighboring states. The result has been a continuous internal struggle among the Kurds themselves that rivals their fight for independence.

The Kurds are Sunni Muslims. They have their own language and cultural traditions. Most of Kurdish history has been a struggle against outside rule. The lack of road and rail communications into Kurdistan has allowed the Kurds to survive with their culture largely unchanged.

Summary

By any standard, a culture is hard to define. As used in this chapter, culture involves those characteristics of society that separate the peoples of the Middle East and North Africa from others.

There is no homogeneous race in the Middle East and North Africa. More than 90 percent of the inhabitants are Muslim. People there also divide along linguistic lines. There are three major languages spoken: Persian, Turkish, and Arabic. Of these, Arabic has had the most lasting influence on the region as a whole because it is the language of the Koran and Islam. As the Islamic faith has spread throughout the region, so have Arabic and the accompanying Arab culture. Because of the importance of the Arabic language to Islam, even those parts of the Middle East that do not speak Arabic have been profoundly influenced by Arab civilization.

Review Questions

1. What is culture?
2. Who are the semites?
3. What two elements helped to spread Arab culture throughout North Africa and the Middle East?
4. Who are the Bedouins?
5. Do all Muslim women wear a veil?

Suggested Readings

Elizabeth Warnock Fernea, *Guest of the Sheik: An Ethnography of an Iraqi Village,* Doubleday and Co., USA, 1990.
Sarah Graham-Brown, *Palestinians and Their Society 1880–1946,* Quartet Books Ltd., London, 1980.
Mary S. Lovell, *Rebel Heart: The Scandalous Life of Jane Digby,* W. W. Norton and Co., New York, 1995.
Naquib Mahfouz, *Midaq Alley,* Bantam Doubleday Dell Publishing, USA, 1991.
Abdelrahman Munif, *Cities of Salt,* Vintage Books, USA, 1989.

Notes

1. Gregory Titelman, *Popular Proverbs and Sayings,* Gramercy Books (New York: 1996), p. 4.
2. John S. Bandeau, "The Arab Role in Islamic Culture," *The Genius of Arab Civilization: Source of Renaissance,* New Edition, B. Winder, Editor, Europa Publishing (London: 1983), p. 5.
3. Eleanor Nicholson, *In the Footsteps of the Camel: A Portrait of the Bedouins of Eastern Saudi Arabia in Mid Century,* Transworld Arabian Library, Riyadh, Stacey International (London: 1984), p. 9.

4. Mary S. Lovell, *Rebel Heart: The Scandalous Life of Jane Digby,* W. W. Norton and Co. (London: 1995), p. 211.
5. Nicholson, *op. cit.,* p. 23.
6. Lovell, *op. cit.,* p. 167.
7. William R. Polk, *The United States and the Arab World,* Harvard University Press (Cambridge, Mass.: 1965), p. 19.
8. John Stoddard, *John Stoddard's Lectures,* Vol. I, George L. Shuman and Co. (Chicago/Boston: 1897), p. 262.
9. George B. Cressey, *Crossroads: Land and Life in Southwest Asia,* J. B. Lippincott Co. (New York: 1960), p. 4.

Chapter 5

The Politics of Islamic History, Colonialism, and Nationalism in the Middle East and North Africa

Why Study the Political History of Islam?

As previously stated, in the Muslim world there is no concept of the separation of mosque and state. To a Muslim, Islam through the Koran and the sacred law provide the believer with a complete, perfect guide for living. Because Islam is now the religion of more than 90 percent of the people, it is logical that the history of Islam and the history of the region overlap.

For most of Islam's existence, the history has been one of the rise and fall of dynasties. Some of the dynasties were more religious than others. All, however, claimed to be governed by the teachings of Islam. It is not the purpose here to discuss the fate of dozens of regional dynasties that have appeared on the scene. Instead, a "broad brush" will be used to paint a picture of the three most famous and well-known Muslim dynasties: the Umayyads, the Abbasids, and the Ottomans. Several minor dynasties will be briefly mentioned to illuminate the richness of Islamic political history.

How Did the Three Major Islamic Dynasties Develop?

Muhammad was recognized as the representative of Allah by all believers during his lifetime. He failed, however, to clearly designate his successor before his death. A series of tribal defections and struggles for power began soon after Muhammad's death. The most serious of these disputes eventually led to the great Sunni–Shiite split, which exists to this day.

Initially the faithful chose Muhammad's successor, called the caliph, through a rough form of tribal democracy. The leaders among the faithful elected the person who they believed was most qualified to be caliph. The first four Muslims selected were called the "rightly guided caliphs." Each of these caliphs was linked to Muhammad by friendship and family. Although there is disagreement as to which caliph should have been chosen first, there is no disagreement as to the worthiness of these leaders.

Muslims look with fondness to the period of the rightly guided caliphs as a time when Islam had a purity of purpose that has been lost. Believers stress the acknowledged virtues of the time, the missionary zeal, the justice, and the humanity. Many ignore the struggles for power and the conflicts that led to the assassinations of three of the four rightly guided caliphs.

During this early period, the political center of Islam was Arabia. However, there always was a rivalry between the towns of Medina and Mecca. Islam became a real movement with the flight of Muhammad from Mecca to Medina. The first mass conversion to Islam occurred in Medina. The Mecca elites opposed and persecuted the early Muslims. Once Islam had triumphed in Arabia, there began a competition for leadership between the "old believers" from Medina and the "new believers" in Mecca.

This tension became an open struggle during the rule of the third caliph, Uthman. Although Uthman had been one of the first converts to Islam, his Mecca clan, the Umayyads, had been in the forefront of those opposing the new religion. Once Mecca fell to Islam, however, the members of the clan quickly converted. Under Caliph Uthman, Mecca Umayyads were given places of authority. To the early converts, this elevation of the Umayyads seemed to be unfair.

HOW THE UMAYYADS CAME TO POWER

Uthman was assassinated in C.E. 656. His successor was Caliph Ali. The murder of Uthman, followed by the selection of Ali as caliph, brought the tensions between the various factions of Islam into open conflict. Ali was forced by dissidents, including members of the Umayyad clan, to fight for his place as the successor of Muhammad.

Foremost among the opponents of Ali was the Umayyad governor of Syria, Múawiya. He was an aggressive, dynamic leader. Eventually Múawiya fought Ali to a standoff. Both he and Ali asserted rival claims to the caliphate until Ali was assassinated in C.E. 661. After Ali's death, Múawiya became the fifth caliph and the first Umayyad ruler.

Most Muslims view the rule of the first four caliphs as special. After that, the rule becomes different. Múawiya established his capital in the city of Damascus. From this time onward, the political center of Islam was never to return to the southern part of Arabia.

The Umayyads are described as establishing the first Muslim dynasty. Until this period, Muslims had elected their leaders from men who had actually known Muhammad. Now the caliphate was to be passed through the Umayyad clan. Succession was not to be a strict passage from father to eldest son as found in Europe. In some cases that form of succession occurred, but in others leadership might fall to a distant clan member. What is important is that the title of caliph remained in the hands of the Umayyads for 100 years. This dynasty ran through the rule of at least thirteen caliphs before being overthrown in C.E. 750.[1]

Like their predecessors, the Umayyads took advantage of the disunity and overconfidence of their Christian, Zoroastrian, and Hindu rivals to create the largest empire in the world. Muslim lands stretched from Spain and Sicily across North Africa, the Fertile Crescent, Arabia, Persia, Afghanistan, and parts of India. The Arabs did not have an administrative structure to rule this vast territory. They were required to rely on the more sophisticated conquered administrations of Byzantium and Persia to make the system work. This meant Persians became the indispensable civil servants of the ruling Arab Umayyads.

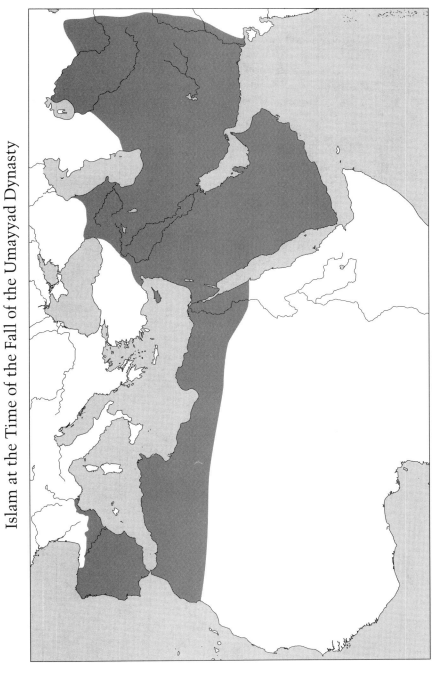

Islam at the Time of the Fall of the Umayyad Dynasty

Source: Adapted from *The Arab World*, Time Life Publishers, *The Atlas of World History*, Barnes & Noble Atlas of the Middle East, Hammond

Some Muslims have criticized the 100-year rule of the Umayyads as being un-Islamic. They charge that, like some of the early Christian popes, Umayyad caliphs behaved more like Byzantine kings than religious leaders. They have been accused of living in splendor and engaging in drunkenness and debauchery.

Much was accomplished during the Umayyad period, however. The lands under Muslim rule were expanded to their greatest extent, and Islamic architecture reached a high point. This period was especially noteworthy for the construction of the Dome of the Rock in Jerusalem and the mosques at Kairouan, Damascus, and Cordova.

THE DOWNFALL OF THE UMAYYAD DYNASTY

It might be said that success destroyed the Umayyads. As they expanded to become the largest empire in the world, the Umayyads proved incapable of controlling the territories they acquired. Over time the Arab tribal traditions gave way to the more sophisticated administrative practices of the Greek and Persian converts.

Although the teachings of early Islam had stressed the equality of all Muslims, the Umayyads attempted to place the Arabs of Arabia above other Muslims. In much the same way that George Orwell's book *Animal Farm* states that, "all animals are equal, but some animals are more equal than others," the Arabs claimed superiority over the non-Arab converts.[2]

The paradox was that the non-Arabs were running the empire for the Arabs. They were performing the same administrative jobs that they had done for their former Byzantine and Persian masters. When they were barred from the top Umayyad positions of authority, they became dissatisfied. In the eastern territories of what had been Persia, the Persians, the Shia, and many dissident tribes rose in a series of rebellions against Umayyad rule. By the year 747, these revolts were an open threat to Umayyad survival. Arab descendants of Muhammad's uncle, Abbas, became the unifying force behind a rebellion, which succeeded in overthrowing the Umayyads in C.E. 750. The new rulers called themselves Abbassids after their founder, Abbas.

The Abbassids set out to exterminate all members of the Umayyad Dynasty. In a story worthy of a Hollywood movie, it is said that a large group of Umayyad survivors were invited to a banquet by the new Abbassid Caliph. During the dinner, they were slaughtered. There is a legend that only one Umayyad escaped. Abd al-Rahman fled across North Africa to become the leader of Muslim Spain. He established a new Umayyad Dynasty that was to survive until 1031.[3]

THE ABBASSIDS

The Abbassid Dynasty lasted from C.E. 749 to 1250. It is impossible to identify any single family, tribe, or people who held onto power throughout the entire period of Abbassid rule. However, certain periods of rule within the whole time frame can be identified. The successful overthrow of the old order was accomplished through the unification of a number of diverse peoples. They only agreed on one common issue, which was opposition to Umayyad rule. The coalescing of this opposition around an Arab family descended from the uncle of Muhammad gave the movement the legitimacy that was required for it to be successful.

As time passed, the influence of non-Arabs increased until the Arabs had largely been displaced from power. The Arabs would never return to dominate the politics of the region in the same way that they had during the early days of Islam. Their lasting legacy was the Islamic religion, the beauty of the Arabic language, and the Arabic system of writing. They also bequeathed many cultural traditions, including a strong sense of honor, chivalry, and respect for sacred law.

The Abbassid Dynasty was made up of a polyglot mixture of believers. Persians dominated the early centuries of Abbassid rule. Instead of the simplicity of the tribal democracy of the Arab caliphs, the splendor of the ancient Persian court increasingly became a feature of the Abbassid Caliphate. Instead of a reliance on tribe and family connections, access to power was largely based on merit.

THE ABBASSID PERIOD IS CALLED THE GOLDEN AGE OF ISLAM

In C.E. 762, the Abbassids founded a new capital city, called Baghdad, located on the Tigris River. In time, Baghdad became the most important seat of learning outside of China. Scholars, both Muslim and non-Muslim, were attracted to the free atmosphere that existed there. In Baghdad they were encouraged to revive ideas that were becoming "forgotten" in Europe. The writings of the great thinkers of the classical world of Greece survived because they were translated into Arabic. Pagan philosophy in Europe was banned by the Church during this time. Much of what is now known about the writings of the philosophers of Greece and Rome is due to the work of the Abbassids.

During this period, great advances were also made in science and mathematics. Abbassid scholars adopted the Indian decimal system and numbers. They adopted a Hindu symbol for zero. These innovations allowed mathematicians to develop the branches of algebra, geometry, and trigonometry. While the few Europeans who could were trying to add, subtract, and multiply Roman numerals, Abbassid scholars were performing mathematical functions with ease.[4]

Because the Empire had absorbed vast territories and peoples with different cultures, it was inevitable that new ideas would have an influence on religion. During this period, the great Sufi order emerged.

The Abbassids adopted a system of banking and used an exchange procedure similar to modern checking. They adopted the Persian custom of using tables for eating instead of the Arab tradition of sitting on the floor. Other Persian activities, including polo, chess, and backgammon, became popular.

Poets became famous for their epic poems. Using the new Chinese import of rag paper, books became more common. They covered subjects on literature, science, and medicine. It is said that some of these efforts became the sparks that ignited the flame of the later European Renaissance.

The Abbassid Dynasty can be viewed like a skyrocket. In the first several hundred years, it shot into the air, exploding with a great flash of stars, only to quickly fade into the darkness. By the 11th century, the Empire was in decline. The caliphs had become little more than figureheads. Mercenary troops often controlled the caliphs, disposing of them at will. Other leaders, called *viziers* and *sultans,* had emerged to hold real political power. In the provinces on the fringes of the Empire, local leaders established mini-empires, virtually ignoring the authorities in Baghdad. William Polk described this disintegration when he wrote,

> In Egypt the Turkish governor began to lay the foundations for what became an empire within the larger Abbassid Empire, and in Iran, the Saffarids carved out another kingdom.[5]

The Empire was on "borrowed time." In 1215, the Mongol armies moved against China. This began a steady process of conquest that resulted in the capture of Baghdad

Muslim Kingdoms, Including the Abbassid, about C.E. 900

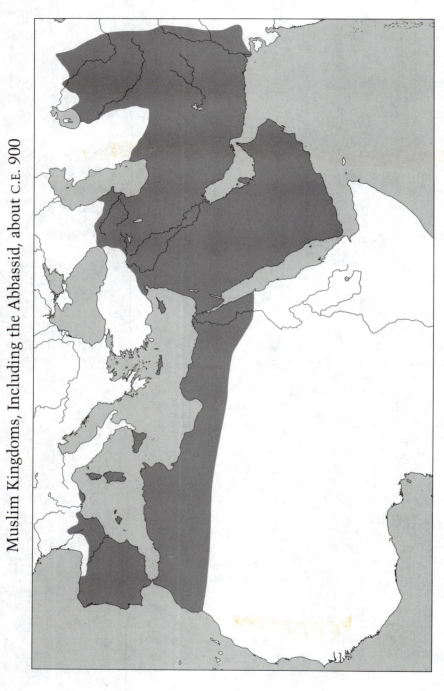

Source: Adapted from *A History of the Arab People*, Harvard University Press; *Middle East Patterns*, Westview Press; *Atlas of World History*, Barnes & Noble; *Atlas of the Middle East*, Hammond

and the execution of the last Abbassid Caliph in 1258. The Mongols were not stopped until they were defeated at Ayn Jalut, now located in modern Israel, by Mamluk forces in 1260.

With the destruction of the Abbassid Caliphate, the region was left without any central authority. The Middle East and North Africa would witness several centuries of turmoil with petty regional powers vying for control before a strong authority could be reestablished. This time the new power would emerge further north in the Anatolian Peninsula with a Turkish dynasty called the Ottomans.

THE OTTOMANS

During the last centuries of Abbassid rule, areas at the edge of the Empire started to move away from the center. In Anatolia, Turkish tribes, migrating from central Asia, established a string of small buffer states that separated the Muslim lands from Byzantium. When the Empire finally fell to the Asiatic invasions in 1250, these petty states remained. There was a period of struggle as rulers tried to take as much of the old Abbassid territories as they could absorb. In the Anatolian Peninsula, the House of Osman managed to overcome the other Turkish rivals to establish the Ottoman Empire. This Empire was to become the dominant power in the Middle East and North Africa for 600 years.

Taking advantage of the power vacuum left in the Middle East, the Ottomans moved north into the Balkans. At the Battle of Kosovo in C.E. 1389, the Serbs were decisively defeated, ending centuries of Christian rule there. In 1453 the Ottomans captured Constantinople, ending the Byzantine Empire. Ottoman forces also seized parts of Persia, Kurdistan, and the Fertile Crescent. By the mid-16th century, Suleyman I, called Suleyman the Magnificent, expanded the Empire to a size that rivaled ancient Rome. Ottomans controlled an empire that stretched from the Danube to the Euphrates, from the Alps to the Caucasus, and across North Africa to the Atlas. Within that vast territory lived twenty different peoples practicing fifteen religions.

Given the size and diversity of the Empire, it should not be surprising that Ottoman rule often changed the lives of the people very little. The Ottomans were interested in taxes, trade, and conquest. In most parts of the Empire, subjects were allowed almost complete autonomy as long as tax revenues and trade were not interfered with. Over time, an ethnic division of labor emerged with a mixed Muslim leadership at the top, a disciplined Muslim army, Christian, Jewish, and Muslim traders in the middle, and a rural Muslim peasantry at the bottom.

Organization of the Ottoman Empire The Ottoman Empire reached its high point of power during the sultanate of Suleyman the Magnificent (1520–1566). During this period the imperial structure produced an impressive administrative and military system. Like the Roman Empire, the Ottomans were borrowers and adaptors of other cultures rather than originators.

They developed a multicultural empire that centered around the Ottoman ruling house. The leader took the title of sultan. It was assumed that, although the title caliph was not used, the sultan was leader of both secular and religious matters. The sultan was a military leader and a lawgiver, and, within the constraints of Islam, a religious official. In 1538, the sultan institutionalized this system by becoming the caliph also.

Under the sultan was a council of four advisors, the Grand Vizier, the Judge Advocate, the Minister of Finance, and the Secretary of State. Of these, the Grand Vizier was the

The Ottoman Empire about 1690

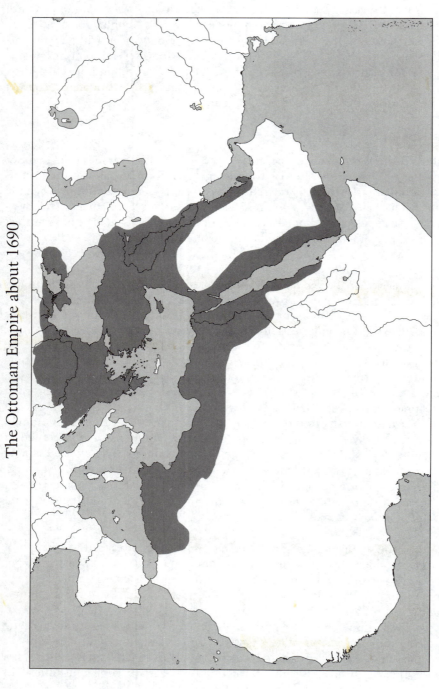

Source: Adapted from *A History of the Arab People*, Harvard University Press; *Atlas of World History*, Barnes & Noble; *Atlas of the Middle East*, Hammond

most important. He not only had the powers of a European chancellor or modern prime minister, he was also expected to lead armies in the field. Although not formally part of the government, the Grand Mufti or Sheik-al-Islam was the top religious advisor to the sultan. As a religious judge, the Mufti had a great deal of authority over the religious activities of the Empire.

Senior military, governmental, and religious judges were members of a great council called the Divan. This council was not a legislative body. It advised the sultan on matters involving the Empire.

One of the unique aspects of the Ottoman Empire was the use of slavery. Often this system is misinterpreted by Westerners who are reminded of the system of slavery in North and South America. In the Ottoman Empire, slaves played an important part in almost every aspect of the government and the military. The use of slaves in government and the military was designed to ensure loyalty to the sultan by preventing the rise of a landed aristocracy. They were slaves in the sense that they were entirely dependent on the will of the sultan for their status. For example, the army's famed Janissary Corps was made up of boys drafted from Balkan Christian or converted villages. Raised as Muslims in special military schools, in the beginning these soldiers did not marry or own land. The slave administrative counterparts could rise to quite high ranks in the sultan's household. Few freeborn Turks were given positions of authority in the administration or the army.

The army also contained a free Muslim Cavalry Corps. The officers, called Sipahis, were able to hold land, collect taxes, and gain booty from conquests. They and the Janissaries were used to check each other and prevent the army from becoming a threat to the sultan.

The ethnic diversity of the Empire was recognized through the Millet System. This system allowed the religious communities to maintain internal autonomy. Officially, the three major Millets were the Armenian Orthodox, the Greek Orthodox, and the Jewish community. Modern scholars recognize that the Muslims were also considered to be a Millet.[6]

Within the Millet System, the religious heads of each community were charged with maintaining law and collecting taxes. They were considered to be officials of the Ottoman government.

Factors Leading to the Decline of the Ottoman Empire The Ottoman Empire lasted for a period that is greater than the Europeans have lived in North America. Given the length of Ottoman rule, the decline of the Empire occurred at an almost imperceptible pace over several hundred years. The modern Western perception of the Empire is usually based on the conditions that existed when the Ottomans had reached a point of collapse. It should not be forgotten that for most of Ottoman history it was the West that was the more backward. It was the militarily superior Ottomans threatening the capital cities of Eastern Europe and not the other way round.

Several factors seemed to have caused a slow reversal of the power relationship between the Ottomans and the West. These include the end of the period of Imperial conquest, an extended period of governmental misrule, the failure to adapt to the changing conditions in Europe, and the failure to trade. Taken together, these seemingly unrelated events led to the Empire's decline and final destruction in the aftermath of World War I.

The End of the Conquest During the period of growth, the Ottoman Empire functioned as a military system geared to conquest. Along with the spread of Islam, Ottoman soldiers could expect to acquire the spoils of war. Captured booty became a major source of wealth in the system. Without the income from victorious wars, the Empire was not very productive. After the Ottoman victories of the 16th century, the expansion of the Empire was blocked by the Christians in Europe and the Persians in the East. As the empire was forced into a defensive system, the fundamental weaknesses of the military became apparent. With no booty, the military evolved into a caste system. The ability to successfully resist the Empire's rivals steadily declined.

Governmental Misrule Few sultans who succeeded Suleyman the Magnificent showed much capability to govern. In many cases, the Grand Vizier or the "slave" establishment exerted real power. They led the Empire in several directions that proved disastrous. As the establishment lost its reason for existing, it became increasingly rigid and conservative. The religious leaders moved the Empire into a strictly Sunni Islamic state, causing the weakening of the Ottoman hold on the eastern Shiite territories.

As revenue declined, the Imperial authorities developed a system of "tax farming." Individuals were given the right to collect Imperial taxes for a fee. This system was extremely corrupt. It introduced a tradition of unfairness and bribery that undermined the credibility of the administration of the Empire. Over time, all of these actions completely discredited the Ottoman administration.[7]

Failure to Adapt The bureaucracy and military failed to recognize the importance of the Renaissance taking place in Europe until it was too late. It is ironic that after earlier Muslims had spread the "ideas of the Renaissance," the Ottomans were completely unprepared for the changes that were occurring in Europe. As Europeans moved into the modern world, Ottomans retreated into a closed system. Few knew or cared to even learn the languages of Europe. Only the minority Christians and Jews maintained an interest in the outside world. Europe's move into the modern age had changed the rules for state power. In the future, technology would be used by Europeans to offset the personal bravery of individual Ottoman warriors. When the Ottoman system failed to respond to this change in Europe, it was doomed to failure.

Failure to Trade The Ottoman system valued only three professions, and Muslims engaged in only four. At the top was governmental service, followed by the military, and the religious status of the Ulama. Most of these posts were filled by a high class of non-Turkish "slaves." They owed personal loyalty to the sultan. At the bottom, Muslim peasant farmers were engaged in agriculture. All of these activities were quickly being rendered obsolete by the more modern institutions evolving in Europe.

The issue of commerce was mostly left to minority Christians and Jews. They alone were particularly equipped to take advantage of the changes taking place in Europe. So while a small minority of traders began to look to the West, most of the Empire continued to fall further and further behind.

What Is the History of Western Colonialism, Neocolonialism, and Imperialism in the Middle East and North Africa?

Before beginning, the terms *colonialism,* *neocolonialism,* and *imperialism* should be defined. *Colonialism* simply describes a mother country's settlements or colonies. Often the words *colonialism* and *imperialism* are used interchangeably to describe the control of one state over another.

Technically, *colonialism* and *imperialism* have slightly different meanings. Colonialism refers to a relationship where a people of one country are subject to the authority of another country. This control may be direct, as in traditional colonialism, or indirect, as in neocolonialism. In neocolonialism, the subjected state may have formal independence but has vital elements of society controlled or influenced by another state. The subject state appears to be independent, but it is, in fact, a client of another state. Imperialism describes the process of extending the control of one state over another.

This story focuses on the penetration of the West into the Ottoman Empire. It is representative of Western imperial activities that occurred throughout the Middle East and North Africa. The French and Spanish imperial activities in North Africa have already been discussed in Chapter 2.

To understand how the imperial powers of the West came to control the Ottoman Empire, it is necessary to look at the relations between the "two worlds" over a long period of time. During the Ottoman expansion in the 16th century, the Ottoman Empire was considerably more powerful and advanced than Europe. The decline began with the death of Suleyman the Magnificent in 1566. As time passed, the European powers gained military parity with the Ottomans. By the end of the 18th century, Ottoman military power was inferior to that of Europe. During the 19th century, the Ottoman Empire became "the sick man of Europe." By using this time line, it is possible to see how decisions that were correct when Ottoman power was at its height became disastrous for the Empire once it became less powerful.

SPECIFIC EVENTS CONTRIBUTING TO THE RISE OF WESTERN POWER

The Capitulations At the height of Ottoman power, Sultan Suleyman entered into an alliance with the French king, Francis the First. Called the Capitulation Agreement, this treaty was signed by the parties in C.E. 1535. At the time, this agreement was considered to be weighted in favor of the powerful Ottomans. France needed Ottoman help in fighting off other European rivals. For their part, the Ottomans wanted access to the new military technologies of France. In matters of trade, the French would be allowed to trade in the Empire. They would enjoy reduced customs duties and would be subject only to French law. This meant that French businessmen would have a status something like a diplomat when doing business in the Empire. Ottomans were given the same rights in France, but there was little that the French had that the Ottoman traders wanted. Except for the acquisition of military technology, the Ottomans were not interested in French trade. This treaty lasted over 300 years. As the Empire became weaker, other states demanded the same extraterritorial status for their subjects doing business with the Ottomans. By the end of the 19th century, a number of European powers had exacted capitulation agreements from the Ottoman authorities.

Next, the Europeans demanded the right to "protect" the minority Millets of the Empire. To accomplish this, a series of "protégé" agreements were concluded, which allowed minority Christians and Jews to assume the status of Europeans. This meant that they also became exempt from most Ottoman laws. Finally, even Muslims were able to purchase protégé status from some European states, allowing them to assert exemptions from Ottoman law. The result was that a large segment of the Empire's population was able to argue that it was no longer subject to Ottoman authority. No society could survive with a large portion of the population not adhering to its laws. The fact that, as businessmen, most protégés were the progressive outward-looking members of Ottoman society made the situation worse.

When the authorities attempted to crack down on the abuses of the capitulation and protégé agreements, the Europeans responded with "gunboat diplomacy." They threatened and, on occasion, intervened to protect their clients in the Empire. Because the Ottoman military was no longer able to stand up to the European Imperialist, the fabric of the Empire was steadily weakened.

The French Invasion of Egypt in 1798   The Ottoman Empire had always been a loose arrangement where powerful governors controlled regions. As long as the tax revenues went into the sultan's treasury, everyone was satisfied. As the Empire declined during the 18th century, governors at the fringes of the Ottoman Empire became semiautonomous leaders within the Empire itself. In Egypt a class of "slave" landholders called the Mamluks ruled in the name of the sultan.

In 1798, a French army under Napoleon Bonaparte defeated the sultan's Mameluke army at the Battle of the Pyramids. Although the French were in Egypt for only three years, their presence was a warning that more Ottoman territory was likely to come under European control if something was not done. Other losses to Europeans soon occurred in the Balkans and Black Sea.

Regional Objectives of Western Power Politics During the 19th Century   The question might be asked, why did the Empire survive the 19th century? The easy answer is that the Ottoman Empire, in its weakened condition, served the interests of Britain and France. The Ottoman control of the Dardanelles and Bosporus prevented tsarist Russia from being able to break out of the Black Sea into the Mediterranean. There was a fear that the Russian influence over the Orthodox Christians in the Empire could allow Russia to become a power in the region. The so-called great game of the 19th century was designed to contain Russian influence in the region.

The British and French used a strategy of applying pressure on the Ottomans to reform, followed by Ottoman concessions, leading to growing internal weakness, to pursue their policies. Defeated militarily and weakened internally, the Ottoman Empire continued the relentless slide to destruction.

Western Involvement in Colonialism in the Middle East and North Africa   The French occupation of Egypt signaled a new European ability to pursue their imperial objectives into the heart of the area. During the 19th century, Britain, France, Italy, and Spain established footholds in the Middle East and North Africa. Germany and Russia were not involved only because their ambitions were blocked by the military power of the British and the French. The British first established a presence in the Persian Gulf. Their alliances there were designed to protect access to India. The French occupation of Egypt also alerted the British to the dangers to India that existed in a hostile power occupying territory in the Eastern Mediterranean. Although Britain opposed the French construction of the Suez Canal in 1861, the British purchased a major interest when the personal stock of the Egyptian head of state became available. In 1882 the British occupied Egypt to ensure that defaulted loans made by Egypt to foreign investors be paid. The British maintained the "fiction" that the occupation of this nominally Ottoman state was temporary. They kept some presence there until 1956. By the end of the 19th century, Britain controlled colonies stretching from the Persian Gulf through the Red Sea to include the Mediterranean islands of Cyprus and Malta. Britain was the European state with the most extensive presence in the region.

After withdrawing from Egypt, the French established a colony in Algeria. French immigrants were encouraged to settle in Algeria, and the colony was eventually incorporated into metropolitan France. Tunisia was occupied as a colony in 1881 but was never considered part of France.

The other colonial participants did not become involved in a major way until the 20th century. Spain had maintained the Moroccan enclaves of Ceuta and Melilla for hundreds of years. They also occupied the desert territory of the Spanish Sahara during the latter half of the 19th century. However, Italy did not become involved in Middle Eastern imperialism until the 20th century.

Western Colonialism During the 20th Century Italy took Libya from the Ottomans in 1911. Spain and France acquired holdings in Morocco in 1912. These territories were administered as colonies by their mother countries.

The most important territories were not "colonized" until the breakup of the Ottoman Empire at the end of World War I. Claiming that they were "temporarily" administering the former ottoman holdings as mandates for the League of Nations, the British occupied Iraq, Transjordan, and Palestine and the French took Syria and established Lebanon.

The Motives for Western Colonialism in the Middle East and North Africa The period of Western colonialism had begun with the French invasion of Egypt. Some would assert that Western neocolonialism continues. Even if one only considers traditional colonialism, the Western penetration of the Middle East and North Africa lasted for over 150 years. During such a long time, it should not be surprising that the motives for colonialism changed from time to time.

What Was Unique About the 19th-Century Colonial Motives for Colonialism in the Middle East and North Africa? Unlike other parts of the colonial world, the acquisition of natural resources did not play a great part in the decisions of Westerners to establish colonies there. With the exception of Algeria, a large population transference from the mother country to the colony did not occur. Colonies in the 19th century were established for strategic and prestige purposes. The Middle East and North African territories were recognized as important land bridges to other colonies. The British were especially concerned that the communications to India be protected. Both Britain and France wanted to block Russian influence in the Eastern Mediterranean. Outside of Algeria, most European colonial activity was limited to establishing strategic bases and influencing the

CHAPTER 5 • HISTORY, COLONIALISM, AND NATIONALISM

	Egypt	Turkey	Iran
1800	1798 French occupied Egypt 1801 French evacuation of Egypt 1805 Muhammad Ali goes to Egypt		1794–1925 Kajar Dynasty Weak government allowed concessions to foreign business n return for modernization
1810	1811–1818 Muhammad Ali leads Ottoman campaign against Wahhabis		
1820			
1830		1826 Sultan's massacre of Janissaries while in their barracks	
1840	1839–1840 Invaded Asia Minor; stopped by United Europe 1841 Sultan made Ali's rule over Egypt heredity	Young Ottomans' 12 Reforms a. Edict of Gulhane 1839 b. Hatti-Humayun 1856 c. Constitution of 1876	
1850			
1860	1863–1879 Ishmael ruled a. 1867 Suez Canal built b. Sold Canal 1875 to UK		
1880			
1880	1880–1881 Arabi Pasha threat to cancel foreign debts 1882 British occupation		
1890		1889 Young Turks established demanded implementation of dormant 1876 constitution 1890s Armanian massacres; brought threats of foreign intervention 1896 Young Turks suppressed by sultan	
1900			1900 Oil concession to D'Arcy
1910		1908 Coup brought return of Young Turks 1909 Counter coup failed; Sultan removed by Young Turks; new sultan selected 1914 Turkey joined central powers and lost World War I 1918 Defeat of Ottomans; Treaty of Mudros disposed of Ottoman Empire	1906 coup to weaken Shah–brought on constitution (like French of 1875 1907 Occupied and partitioned between UK & Russia 1909 Shah with Russian support tried to end new constitution. Shah was expelled 1911 Russian army occupied Iran for one year WWI Iran Pro-German forced UK & Russian occupation 1919 UK attempted to establish Protectorate in 1919
	1914 UK proclaimed Protectorate		
1920	1922 Ended Protectorate; gave internal sovereignty; opposed by nationalists 1924 UK Commander assassinated and UK reoccupied country	1920 Treaty of Sevres divided Turkey between France, UK & Greece & Italy (Greece had invaded 1919 1920 First Grand National Assembly met in Ankara 1921 Greeks were defeated outside Ankara by Turks 1922 Turks drove Greeks into sea at Izmir 1922 Sultanate abolished 1923 Turkish Republic proclaimed 1924 Mastafa Kemal abolished caliphate 1928 Islam abolished as Turkish state religion	1920 Russia attempted to establish communist republic in Azerbayjan & Gilan–failed after 1 months 1921 Nationalist uprising; Russian-trained Cossack brigade came to power. Its commander became minister of war. 1925 Cossack Brigade Commander seized power and became Reza Shah
1930			
1940	1936 Anglo Egyptian Treaty UK could take over in case of war; would rule canal for 20 years 1942 Germans defeated at Battle of El Alamein	1936 Montreux Convention establishes rules for shipping for Dardanelles and Bosporus 1947 Truman Doctrine aids Greece and Turkey	1941 Russia, UK, and later USA occupied Iran 1941 Reza Shah deposed; son Muhammad Reza becomes shah 1951 Mosaddeq comes to power; nationalizes oil 1953 Mosaddeq overthrown with CIA help
1950	1952 Egyptian Revolution of Revolutionary Command Council establishes leadership Nasser 1956 Egypt nationalizes Suez Canal to pay for Aswan Dam		
1960	1956 Israel with British and French support invades Egypt 1956 U.S. cancels loan for Aswan Dam 1957 Israel withdraws from Egypt	1960 First military coup in post war	
1970			
	1973 Egypt and Syria attack Israel	1974 Turks intervene in Cyprus	
1980	1979 Camp David peace between Egypt and Israel 1981 Anwar Sadat assassinated; Hosni Mubarak becomes head of state	1980 2nd military takeover 1982 New constitution limited civilian role	1979 Shah flees Iran 1979 Ayatoliah Khomeini returns to Iran 1979 Islamic Republic established 1979 U.S. Embassy hostages taken 1980–1988 Iran-Iraq War 1981 U.S. Embassy hostages returned
1990	1990s Government battles fundamentalists; economic and social problems continue	1990s Kurdish problem; Islamic fundamentalism; Cyprus problem; move to join European union fails	1990s Move for improved relations with West

WESTERN COLONIALISM, NEOCOLONIALISM, AND IMPERIALISM

	Saudi Arabia	Israel	Arabs
1800	1803–04 Wahhabis capture Makkah		
1810			
1820			1820s British pacts with Persian Gulf Sheikhs
1830			
1840			
1850			
1860			
1870			
1880		1881 First Jewish new settlement in Palestine	
1890		1896 Political Zionist movement founded	
1900	1900–1908 Hejaz Railway built 1902 Ibn Saud captures Riyadh		
1910			1911–1912 Ottoman-Italian War over Libya 1916 Secret Sykes Picot Agreement to partition Middle East among Allies
1920	1915 McMan papers agreed to 1916 Arab revolt in Hejas against Ottoman rule 1916 British recognize Hussein as King of Mecca 1919 ibn Saud defeated troops of Husayn of Hejaz 1924 Hussayn of Makkah (also Hejaz) abdicates in favor of his son Ali 1925 Ali also abdicates 1926 ibn Saud proclaimed King of Hejaz 1932 Kingdom of Hejaz and Nejd becomes Saudi Arabia	1917 British issue Balfour Declaration 1917 British army captures Jerusalem 1922 British mandate established in Palestine 1925 Hebrew University established 1930s Jews and Palestinians clash	1918 British and Arabs capture Damascus 1920 Faysal proclaimed King of Syria and Palestine (blocked by French) 1920 French create Lebanon from part of Syria 1920 British make Faysal King of Iraq 1922 League of Nations approves British and French mandates in Middle East
1930			
1940		1939 British White Paper limits Jewish settlement	
1950	1946 Oil production begins	1947 U.N. Partition Plan 1948 State of Israel established 1948 War with Arabs; Israel victorious	1945 Arab League created 1948 Transjordan becomes Jordan
1960		1956 War with Egypt	1958 U.S. Marines briefly occupy Lebanon
1970	1964 Faisal becomes king	1967 War: Israel attacks Egypt; eventually captures Sinai, West Bank, Jerusalem, and part of Syria 1973 War with Egypt and Syria	1964 PLO established 1973 OPEC cuts off oil to U.S. and Netherlands for supporting Israel
1980	1975 Faisal assassinated; Khalid becomes king 1982 Khalid dies and Fahad becomes the current ruler of Saudi Arabia	1982 Israel invades Lebanon; does not completely withdraw until 2000	1982 U.S. intervenes in Lebanese Civil War 1982 Christian forces massacre Palestinian camps at Sabra and Shatila in Lebanon 1983 U.S. withdraw from Lebanon 1987 First intifada in occupied West Bank and Gaza
1990	1991 Saudi Arabia plays a major role in Gulf War to liberate Kuwait 1990s U.S. forces remain stationed after the liberation of Kuwait	1990s Several limited peace agreements with the Palestinians 1995 Assassination of Prime Minister Rabin 2000–2001 Second Intifada blocks peace talk progress	1990 Iraq invades Kuwait 1991 Kuwait liberated 2000–2001 Second Intifada against Israel

A Symbol of British Imperialism
A membership card for the Gezira Sporting Club in Cairo, Egypt. Once an exclusive British club, the Gezira now hosts Egyptian elites.
Source: Joe Weatherby

existing governments rather than exercising rule. Spain maintained small colonies in Morocco for prestige purposes.

The 20th-Century Motives for Colonialism The 20th century was the century of the internal combustion engine. With the discovery of vast supplies of high-grade, inexpensive petroleum in the region early in the century, the battle to control natural resources became a major motivation for colonialism. The British were active in Iran, Iraq, Kuwait, and the rest of the Persian Gulf. Americans became involved in Saudi Arabia and later in Iran and Kuwait. In each case the Western powers operated behind the chairs of local rulers. They always denied that they were engaged in colonial activities.

The Western efforts to maintain strategic controls over the Middle East and North Africa continued during the Cold War. Containment of communism replaced "the great game" in major power politics. Even when formal colonialism had ended elsewhere, the Western powers continued to pursue their strategic objectives in the region.

In evaluating the conduct of the West during this period, it is possible to state that the method and timing of this form of colonialism were particularly harmful to the development of the region. It caused a great deal of bitterness, which continues to the present. The major colonial period for most of the Middle East and North Africa occurred during the 20th century. This process continued when even the colonial powers no longer believed in it. Europeans attempted to mask their efforts by the use of "mandates" granted by international organizations. They also engaged in what is now called *neocolonialism* by using agents who acted as advisors to local client rulers and elites. Thus the Western powers engaged in a hypocritical and self-serving penetration of the region. Author David Fromkin stated it this way:

> The long-expected European adventure in the Middle East had therefore begun too late. Europeans could no longer pursue it either with adequate resources or with a whole heart.

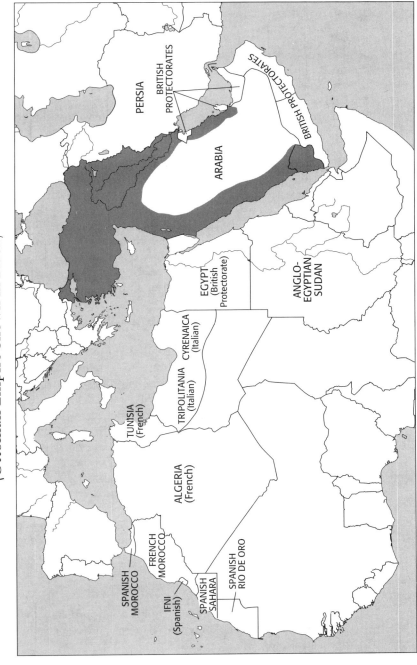

European Colonization and the Ottoman Empire around 1914
(Ottoman Empire Shown in Black)

Source: Adapted from *The Atlas of World History*, Barnes & Noble, *Atlas of the Middle East*, Hammond

He then wrote,

> . . . to a growing number of Europeans, imperialism seemed out of place in the modern age.[8]

Since World War II, Middle Eastern suspicions of Western motives have been compounded by the almost unquestioning American support for the State of Israel. At the present time, Arab nationalists also object to the stationing of U.S. troops in Saudi Arabia, the land of the Muslim holy places. To them the American military presence is a repeat of 19th century British colonial practices. They believe that the Americans are there to protect Western access to the oil fields of Arabia rather than to defend the independence of Saudi Arabia and the Persian Gulf States. Arabs see the Israeli occupation of Jerusalem and the American presence in the land containing Islam's most holy sites as part of a great neocolonialist plot to dominate the Muslim world. Although few Americans would agree with this analysis, they have not had to live under 150 years of Western domination.

In judging the hostile actions toward the West, it should be remembered that during the past century and a half almost every area has suffered under some form of Western colonial or neocolonial control. Because many of these areas fell under Western influence after World War I, they experienced the worst forms of colonialism. At times the Western powers even denied that this occurred. Nowhere has Western colonialism been implemented in a more hypocritical or cynical fashion.

The Most Important Documents to Have Influenced the Current Status of the States of the Middle East There are three famous sets of documents that have shaped the politics of the present Middle East. Depending on one's personal view of the modern history of the region, one of these documents can be cited to justify that position. In their defense, the Allies during World War I were in a desperate situation and would have probably made an "agreement with the devil" if the devil would have opposed the Central Powers. In order of their dates, the documents are the Hussein-McMahon letters of 1915–1916, the Sykes-Picot Agreement of 1916, and the Balfour Declaration of 1917. Each of these documents made promises of territory once World War I was concluded.

The Hussein-McMahon correspondence is a series of letters written as part of a British strategy to get the Arabs in Arabia to revolt against Ottoman rule. In this way it was hoped that the Ottoman Empire would be diverted from supporting other Central Powers during the war. For their part, the Arabs under Sherif Hussein were promised financial and military support for the revolt. What is most significant today is that the British promised independence for "Arab lands under Ottoman rule". Over the course of the correspondence the question of what were Arab lands continued to be raised. For example, in a letter from McMahon to Sherif Hussein dated October 24, 1915, McMahon is quoted as formally stating the British position:

> The two districts of Mersin and Alexandretta and portions of Syria lying to the West of Damascus, Hama, and Aleppo cannot be said to be purely Arab and should be excluded from the limits demanded.

In the assurance section of the letter, McMahon is further quoted,

> Subject to the above modifications, Great Britain is prepared to recognize and support the independence of the Arabs in all regions within the limits demanded by the Sherif of Mecca.[9]

The specific Ottoman-controlled areas marked for independence varied throughout the correspondence. Earlier, in August, McMahon is quoted as writing the following:

> With regard to the questions of limits and boundaries, it would appear to be premature to consume our time discussing such details in the heat of war . . .[10]

All of this gave the Arabs the impression that the British would support the independence of a greater Arab state once the war had been won. Whether this correspondence was a result of Arab wishful thinking or a series of promises being made by the British depends on the viewpoint of the reader. In any case, the establishment of a single Arab state did not occur.

The Sykes-Picot agreement was a secret pact concluded between Britain, France, and later Russia, which called for the partition of the Ottoman Empire after the war had been won. Under this arrangement, Greece and Italy would get a portion of the Empire located in Libya and the Eastern Mediterranean in return for their participation in the war. Tsarist Russia was to obtain parts of Anatolia and the city of Constantinople (Istanbul). France would control Syria and the Levant. Britain was to have Iraq, Transjordan, and parts of Palestine while retaining control of Egypt.

Finally, the Balfour Declaration promised support for the "establishment in Palestine of a national home for the Jewish people."[11] The reasons behind the issuance of this document are hazy. It is known that the famous Zionist chemist Chaim Weizman approached his friends in the British cabinet with such a request. It is believed that the Balfour Declaration could be justified on at least three grounds. First, finding a home for the Jewish people was believed to be morally correct. Second, the issuance of the document would energize American Jews in their efforts to persuade the United States to support Britain during the war. Third, it was hoped that the Balfour Declaration would cause Jewish unrest in Germany.

As so often happens in diplomacy, events moved past the negotiations over the declaration. Before the Balfour Declaration could be issued, other German actions provoked the United States to enter World War I on the British side. There was no Jewish uprising in Germany. German Jews remained completely loyal to their country's war effort. What is important is that the new British policy gave official support to a Zionist policy for Jews in Palestine. Aaron Margalith quoted the Balfour Declaration in the notes of his book on international mandates as follows:

> His Majesty's Government views with favor the establishment in Palestine of a National Home for the Jewish People, and will use their best endeavor to facilitate the achievement of this object, it being clearly understood that nothing shall be done which may prejudice the civil and religious rights of existing non-Jewish Communities in Palestine or the rights and political status enjoyed by Jews in any other country.[12]

Clearly, all three documents are in conflict. The British had bargained the same lands to three different parties. It was not until the end of World War I, however, that the British and French duplicity became apparent. The only agreement actually implemented by the victorious powers was a modified form of Sykes-Picot. Because Russia had become a communist state, the Russians were denied their claims in Anatolia and Constantinople.[13]

The French occupied the Eastern Mediterranean and drew the boundaries of modern Lebanon and Syria. Britain oversaw the creation of Iraq and Transjordan and the internationalization of Palestine. The British territories were to eventually become Iraq, Jordan, and Israel. Earlier, the British had carved a small enclave out of the Ottoman Province of Basra to establish Kuwait.

Although Hussein's sons were to become British-established kings in Iraq and Jordan, the Sherif never became the ruler of Arabia. After a short period as King of the Hejaz, he was defeated by Ibn Saud, who united the tribes and created the modern Kingdom of Saudi Arabia.

The Development of Nationalism in the Middle East and North Africa

Nationalism is a Western invention. Until the rise of the 18th century nation state, Europeans held traditional loyalties to family, tribe, church, and crown. After this time, European leaders were no longer able to rely exclusively on the ties of blood, divine right, or papal decrees to rule. Europeans started to confer legitimacy on a new entity that was called the nation-state. The nation-state held authority over a large group of people who believed that they had a common identity, called *the nation*. It is important to note that the "belief" did not have to be true; it only had to be believed.

The popular symbols of the nation included race, language, religion, and history. These features separated one nation from another. In time, nation-states adopted symbols of nationhood that included flags, songs, uniforms, emblems, and special days that were substitutes for the "totems" of the past.

Modern nationalism represents something greater than the sum of its parts. The individual's personal interests are subordinated to the abstraction of the state. What is different from states of the past is the transference of people's loyalties away from traditional authority of family, religion, and crown to the abstraction, the state. Nationalism also is based on the idea of exclusivity. It focuses on unity based on the difference between one's nation and others. The "foreign devil" is one of the primary motivations of nationalism. Thus the perception of a Saddam Hussein, Bill Clinton, or Tony Blair as a hero or a foreign devil depends on one's location. These and other symbols of nationalism are commonly manipulated by leaders to secure legitimacy for state policies.

HISTORICAL UNIQUENESS OF THE NATIONALISM IN THE MIDDLE EAST AND NORTH AFRICA

Before beginning, it should be pointed out that true nationalism, as a mass movement, has been a late comer to the Middle East and North Africa. The idea of the nation-state is largely the product of the post–World War I world. Some would argue that parts of this region have yet to adopt this form of association. This should not be surprising if one considers that nationalism did not emerge in Europe until the 19th century. Germany did not become a single, unified state until 1871. Many of the nation-states of Eastern Europe did not exist prior to 1919. Although there were 19th-century individuals and even groups of elites that yearned for statehood, most people of the region still based their loyalties on family, clan, tribe, and religion.[14]

Despite specific differences, all of the states of the Middle East and North Africa have suffered the indignities of Western colonialism or neocolonialism. The experience of being dominated by the Western powers caused the people of the region to reassess their ability to resist. This reassessment was the first step that led to the rise of nationalistic movements everywhere. It was the means of resistance to Western colonialism.

The first goal of Middle Eastern and North African nationalism was independence. This aspiration did not come suddenly. It evolved over a period of over a hundred years at different speeds and in different places. The short studies in this chapter demonstrate that, here, nationalists used a variety of approaches to gain independence. Some came to reject the political and religious institutions of the past while others embraced them. Some sought to chart a middle course between rejection and repetition. Some have even tried to fit the traditions of the desert into a modern framework.

There Were at Least Four Factors That Contributed to the Rise of Nationalism
These components included the arrival of European military advisors, the government sponsorship of military science students at Western universities, the establishment of Western educational institutions in the region, and British intrigues in Arabia during World War I.

If one accepts the conventional view that nationalism and the modern nation state were exported from the West to other parts of the world, then it is worthwhile to briefly explore the conditions that led to this development in the Middle East and North Africa.

The decline of the Ottoman military power and the defeat of the Egyptian forces by France got the attention of the leadership in the Ottoman Empire. Their hope was to keep the Empire intact while updating the military. During the early years of the 19th century, they tried a number of strategies aimed at achieving "defensive modernization." In other words, they wanted military modernization but no real change in Ottoman society. Some efforts were very superficial, such as adopting European uniforms. However, after Napoleon's defeat, a number of unemployed former French officers were hired in Egypt and other parts of the Ottoman Empire to train the military in the techniques of modern warfare. After the American Civil War, defeated Confederate mercenaries performed similar tasks. It is ironic that Western military "advisors" continue to fulfill this role today. Then, as now, these outsiders introduced new ideas to the region that threatened the traditional values of society.

Both in Egypt during the early 19th century rule of Muhammad Ali and later throughout the Ottoman Empire, the authorities selected the best and the brightest to learn the modern military arts in schools in Europe and the United States. Unfortunately, once they arrived overseas, many started to read more than artillery manuals, and they ended up rejecting the oppressive regimes they were hired to serve. The 19th century Middle Eastern elites studying abroad started to read Hobbes, Locke, Rousseau, and Jefferson. They began to question and to compare Western and Middle Eastern societies. Worst of all, they became acquainted with the new ideas of the nation-state and nationalism. Some went home as revolutionaries. Then, as today, it was impossible to compartmentalize knowledge.

During the mid-19th century, American missionary activity penetrated the Levant. When these missionaries failed to "convert" Muslims to Christianity, they turned to "influencing them by example." Missionaries built schools and hospitals, and in 1866 they founded the Syrian Protestant College, which was to become famous as the American University of Beirut. This great university was later followed by the French-sponsored Jesuit Université, St. Joseph, and the American University of Cairo. It was in these schools that thousands of Ottoman subjects first learned of the American and French

Revolutions. Some of the early nationalistic stirrings came from elites who had attended these schools.

The beginnings of rural Arab nationalism did not develop until World War I. During the war, the British sent agents, including Lawrence of Arabia, to the major tribal leaders of Arabia. Their objective was to foster a rebellion against the Ottoman Empire. It was hoped that unrest in Arabia would cause the Ottomans to divert troops away from the British to put down the revolt. By allying themselves with Arabs who controlled the Holy Places of Arabia, the British also hoped to prevent the Ottoman Sultan from being able to incite unrest among the Muslims living in British India.[15]

British agents carried the famous McMahon letters to the Sherif of Mecca. The unification of a large portion of the Arabian tribal leaders under the banner of the Hashemites against the Ottomans encouraged the Sherif to seek the reestablishment of a great Arab state with an Arab caliph as its head.

In a letter dated August 30, 1915, addressed to the Sherif, Sir Henry McMahon wrote,

> We declare once more that His Majesty's government would welcome the resumption of the Caliphate by an Arab of true race.[16]

The famous Arab revolt against Ottoman rule began on June 15, 1916. Although the exploits of the Arabs and of Lawrence of Arabia have captured the imaginations of people in both the East and the West, it is difficult to justify the grand claims that were made by their supporters. There were military successes in Arabia and in what is now Jordan and Syria. But there was no wide-scale Arab revolt against Ottoman rule. The eventual victory over the Ottoman forces was gained by British troops taking the major population centers of the Levant. At a time when the carnage on the Western front was appalling, it served allied interest to focus public attention on the romantic figures of the revolt. Today there is even some question of whether this was a nationalist revolt at all. Some would assert that the Sherif of Mecca, Hussein ibn Ali, was simply using British money and military support to grab Ottoman territory for the Hashemite family. A contemporary historian puts it this way:

> Hussein was not a revolutionary in the service of national self-determination but rather an imperialist aspirant seeking to substitute his Empire for that of the Ottomans. If he had ever truly subscribed to the notion of "Ottomanism," which he had not, he discarded it not for the high ideals of "Arabism" but rather for the self-serving cause of "Hasheimism."[17]

Arab sources, however, have always maintained that the revolt was much more important to the Ottoman defeat than the West was willing to admit.[18] What can be said is that regardless of motives and military value or historical accuracy, the desert revolt was captured by later Arab Nationalists as a symbol of the Arab struggle to throw off the chains of foreign domination.

The Young Turk Movement in the Ottoman Empire The Ottoman Empire was successful because it was able to maintain unity in a multicultural society. Emphasis was placed on loyalty to Ottomanism. In this way, all peoples of the Empire had a place through the Millets. Islam was paramount, but Christians and Jews also held important positions in society. The idea of a nationalism, which pits one group against another, would have been a mortal blow to the Empire. The authorities ruthlessly suppressed early attempts by students and writers, including Armenians and Jews, advocating ethnic separation. It is beyond the scope of this short account to discuss the evolution of the national movement in the European portions of the Ottoman Empire.

The Young Turk movement was the first real nationalist effort that had any broad support in the Middle East. Founded in 1889, the Committee for Union and Progress, or Young Turks, was made up of elites coming from the Ottoman army and intellectuals living in Europe. Their original objective was to preserve the Empire while reorganizing it along modern lines. They wanted a modern European state organization. Because of the multicultural nature of the Empire, they flirted with the ideas of basing the Empire on loyalty to Ottomanism.

In 1908 the Young Turks used the fear that the Empire was about to be destroyed by Western powers to seize control. During their initial period of rule they were viewed as young intellectuals who were opposed to the out-of-date leadership of the Ottomans. Because of their proclamation that all Ottomans were equal, the Young Turks had initial support from the minorities of the Empire. This good feeling toward the movement did not last. The Young Turks' attempts at reform included centralization of power. Eventually the stress of a series of territorial losses in the Balkans forced a crackdown on minorities, which doomed the inclusive Ottoman policy. This caused alienation of the minority supporters, including Jews and Armenians, which was followed by unrest among the Arabs. Taking a page from the Young Turks' own history, a number of small prenationalist organizations started to spring up throughout the Empire. They were to be significant forces when the Young Turk movement failed in the aftermath of the Ottoman defeat in World War I.

The Young Turk revolution produced a paradox. The basic objective of the movement was to save the Empire by freeing it of European domination. A secondary objective was to reform the Empire along modern lines. These conflicting policies produced a love/hate relationship with the West. Author David Fromkin puts it this way:

> Ambivalent in attitude toward Europe—scorning it as non-Muslim while admiring its modern ways and achievements—the Committee for Union and Progress intended to throw off the shackles of Europe in order to imitate Europe more closely.[19]

With the 19th century loss of Greece and some Christian territories in the Balkans, the Empire had become increasingly Muslim and Turkish by the time of the Young Turks' revolution in 1908. Their failure to follow the pre-revolution goal of ensuring equality throughout the Empire was a major mistake. Once in power, the Young Turks focused on unifying the Turkish-speaking Muslims. But, in so doing, they lost the support of many Ottomans and thus doomed the chances to preserve the Empire.

Finally, the greatest mistake that the Young Turks made was to bring the Empire into World War I on the side of Germany and the other Central Powers. In doing so, they went to war against Russia, France, and Britain. Their action would have gained them little if they were victorious, but it ensured the death of both their movement and the Empire when they lost.

Modern Middle Eastern Nationalism

The idea of the nation state and the accompanying nationalist movement emerged with the Ottoman defeat in World War I. Until that time, few people in the region had identified with a true nationalist ideology. Even though the Young Turks may have come close, their objectives had been to preserve a multicultural Empire along traditional lines.

The rise of true nationalism has been primarily the product of the cities. In much of the countryside, people still have the loyalties found in pre-nationalistic places elsewhere. Villagers still give their first loyalty to the family, tribe, and religion. Government is often viewed with hostility as a source of exploitation. In many parts of the Middle East and North Africa, the central government has little or no legitimacy.

Most of the states of the Middle East and North Africa have been independent for more than 50 years. Prior to independence, their nationalism called for the creation of a classless society, a democratic political system, and an effective challenge to Israel. Today, most of these goals remain unfulfilled dreams.

In the following case studies, the reader will see examples of strikingly different approaches to nationalism. In one way or another these examples of nationalism included an aspiration for independence. This has been followed by opposition to what is interpreted as neocolonial interference. All of these relatively new states, including Israel, are deeply sensitive to perceived Western interference in their affairs. This is partially due to their recent history and partially a result of insecurity. There is also little more than lip service given to the larger regional movements such as pan-Arabism or pan-Islamism. Often the opposition to Western imperialism or even Israel is a cover for disagreements between "friends." As the recent Gulf War demonstrated, co-religionists were quite willing to ally with infidels against fellow believers if it served a political purpose.

What Are Some Examples of Nationalism in the Middle East and North Africa?

The evolution of nationalism in Turkey, Iran, Egypt, Saudi Arabia, the Arabs, and Israel has been selected as an example of the differing approaches nationalists have followed. Each example is unique, but taken together they should give the reader some insight into the complexity of politics in the region. Nevertheless, there are common themes running through each example. All of these efforts sought independence from outside interference. All used cultural traditions and symbols as part of their strategy to achieve political goals.

Turkey The Ottoman defeat in World War I contributed to the successful birth of Turkish nationalism. When the victorious powers partitioned the Empire, they left the Turkish-speaking portions largely intact. Those Turkish areas of Anatolia held by foreigners were liberated during the postwar period. In a short period of time, the Turkish people were freed of the burdens of controlling a multicultural empire. Turkish nationalists were then able to draw on the unifying aspect of the Turkish language and Turkish identification to create a new movement. This idea succeeded for the same reason that the similar Young Turk movement had failed. The nature of the Ottoman Empire rendered the appeal to being Turkish ineffective. The modern nationalists succeeded because the geographic area of postwar Turkey coincided with areas where people identified with being Turkish rather than with being Ottoman.

The new movement was led by a military hero, Ataturk (Mustafa Kemal). He called for the abandonment of the past and the creation of a modern, secular, Eastern European republic. Only in this way could Turkey compete on equal terms with the West. At the time, Ataturk's revolution was considered to be as significant as those of his contemporaries: Lenin, Mussolini, and Hitler. Eighty years after the founding of modern Turkey, Ataturk's reforms are not considered as far reaching as they once were.

Ataturk sought to bring Turkey into the modern world by abandoning the symbols of the Ottoman past. His reforms included the abolition of sacred law to govern, the separation of mosque and state, the introduction of a modern education system, the developing of a modern Western-style economic system, the adoption of a modified Western form of writing, and the emancipation of women. On a more superficial level, the fez was abolished in favor of the Western hat, and women were no longer veiled.

Since the 1950s, Turkish nationalism has abandoned some of its more controversial themes. For example, Islam is a resurgent force in what was once considered to be a secular state. Ataturk's Republican Peoples Party is no longer the dominant political movement in modern Turkey. Nevertheless, as they have done for more than half a century, Turkish nationalists continue to turn away from their Middle East past and look toward Europe for their future.

As the 21st century begins, two opposing nationalists' visions of the future are contending for power in Turkey. One is represented by the governmental establishment, the residents of the cities and the university-educated elites, who support the original principles of the republic that Ataturk founded in 1923. They defend Westernization, including secularism; they want Turkey to remain a member of NATO; and they wish to be admitted to the European Community. Others, including Islamic traditionalists and conservative rural Turks, believe that the country has deserted a rich Middle Eastern heritage. These conservatives support efforts to control what they see as excesses of modern Turkish society. Under their influence, more mosques are being constructed than at anytime since the days of the Ottoman Empire. The result of this struggle is a Turkey torn between the secular establishment and a population that is 99 percent Muslim. Today Turks are deeply divided over the direction that nationalism should take. Should Turkey continue to push for a place in Europe or should Turks return to their traditional place of leadership in the Islamic Middle East?

Iran Like the Ottoman Empire, the Persian Empire was an Islamic monarchy except that Shiite Islam was the state religion. Iranian nationalism developed as a reaction to the Anglo-Russian interventions in Persia during the early part of the 20th century. The history of nationalism in Iran can be divided into three periods: the reign of the Pahlavis, the Mossadeq Crisis, and the Islamic Revolution.

The first Pahlavi, Reza Shah, was an army officer who seized power in 1921 and had himself crowned king (shah) in 1925. His rule lasted from 1925 to 1941. Reza Shah believed that a modern state could be created in Iran, like in Turkey. Although many of his changes emulated those of Ataturk in Turkey, Iran was far less Westernized and results came slowly. Unlike Ataturk and Lenin, who destroyed the old to create a new system, Reza Shah wrapped himself in the traditions of the old Persian monarchy to establish his legitimacy. In the late 1930s, he indicated a sympathy for Adolph Hitler that provoked a Russian-British-American intervention in Iran once World War II began. Reza Shah was deposed, and with the approval of the Western powers, his young son, Muhammad Reza, was placed in power.

Muhammad Reza's reign was uneventful until the Iranian oil crisis of 1951. At that time, a popular nationalist leader, Muhammad Mossadeq, formed a political organization known as the National Front. He gained control of the government and then nationalized the British-owned Anglo-Iranian Oil Company. The Western oil powers responded by boycotting Iranian oil. Deprived of oil revenue by 1953, the Iranian economy was in such bad shape that the Shah used this crisis to attempt to have Mossadeq removed. The Shah's action failed and he was forced into exile in Switzerland. In one of the most interesting periods in modern history, supporters of the Shah were persuaded—it is now believed with CIA help—to stage a counterrevoltion.[20] Mossadeq's allies failed to respond effectively, and the Shah was returned to power within days. The downfall of Mossadeq ended the rule of one of the only truly popular, secular nationalist leaders in modern Iranian history. Returned to power, the Shah ruled in an increasingly arbitrary manner until he was forced into exile in 1979.

When the Ayatollah Khomeini assumed power in Iran, he enjoyed the support of both the secular nationalists abroad and the religious nationalists at home. The Western-educated elites who accompanied him on his return flight from exile in France carried foreign passports. Khomeini's first cabinet was made up of these secular nationalists. Many of these officials expected to bring liberal democratic rule to Iran. Within three years, all of these officials had disappeared from the political scene. Ayatollah Khomeini built his political base among the poor and the dispossessed who also happened to be the religious conservatives. In this way, he was able to shape the Iranian revolution into a struggle that was both religious and class oriented.

Totally reversing the two millennia of Iranian monarchy, the Islamic Republic of Iran has represented, at the very least, a temporary victory for the religious nationalists over the secular nationalists of the 1950s. The leaders make effective use of the symbols of Shiite Islam to maintain their authority over the Iranian people. According to the rhetoric of the regime, this movement represents an attempt by Shiism to gain the leadership of the Islamic world. The progress of the Islamic revolutionary model developed by Iran is being watched with interest by many.

Both the nationalisms of the Pahlavis and the Islamic Republic have drawn on the past to legitimize their rule. They have capitalized on longstanding Iranian traditions to mobilize popular support for the government in power. Whether using kingship or Shiite Islam, the leadership of the day has been able to utilize powerful emotional symbols from Iran's past to rule. Unless the living conditions of the average Iranian can be improved, however, the intensity of the Islamic revolution and its accompanying nationalism cannot be sustained. Although it is unlikely that Iran will return to the nationalism of the Pahlavis, it is equally unlikely that the continuation of the role by the Islamic nationalists can survive without undergoing change.

Egypt   Egyptian nationalism emerged as a reaction to Napoleon's invasion in 1798. A national movement of the same sort is almost as old as the French Revolution. Experiencing both peaks and valleys during the 19th century, nationalists championed the call to end the British occupation of Egypt that had begun in 1882. In the 1920s a middle-class anti-British political movement called the *Wafd* emerged to dominate Egyptian politics until the rise of Nasser in 1952.[21]

Probably no man in the history of the modern Middle East has successfully captured the hearts and minds of those of all social classes and political philosophies as did Gamal Abdul Nasser. Espousing a militant nationalism of Arab socialism abroad and social reform at home, Nasser also called for independence from foreign domination, opposition to Israel, and Arab unity abroad. He is best remembered by Middle Easterners for his successful challenges to the policies of the United States and the former colonial powers of Western Europe. It is important to note that Nasser's continuing contribution to Egyptian nationalism is symbolic and transcends specific successes or failures of his policies while he was the country's leader. Following Nasser's death in 1970, Anwar al-Sadat assumed control.

Anwar al-Sadat's eleven-year rule over Egypt is extolled in the West as an example of what an enlightened third-world nationalist can accomplish. Sadat expelled the Russians in 1972, fought Israel to a standoff in 1973, and then went to Jerusalem to begin a process that resulted in the 1979 peace agreement with Israel. Sadat's assassination in 1981 is still viewed in the West as a great setback to peace efforts in the region. Surprisingly, Egyptians rarely discuss the tenure of Sadat. In Egypt, he is considered to have frustrated the cause of Arab unity by stressing the separateness of Egypt and peace with Israel over the greater good of the Arab people. Sadat's virtual surrender of the Egyptian economy to Western investment raised new fears of a return to neocolonial status. The danger of an erosion of independence, whether direct or indirect, became central to the thinking of many Egyptian nationalists who were opposed to Sadat.

President Hosni Mubarak sought to develop a nationalism that steered a middle course between the economic excesses of Sadat and the political adventurism of Nasser. He worked hard to end Egypt's isolation in the Arab world. Expelled after the Camp David agreement, Egypt was eventually restored as a member of the Arab League and the League's headquarters was returned to Cairo. The Egyptians continued to honor the peace

River Transportation
A passenger felucca on the Nile at Aswan, Egypt.
Source: Joe Weatherby

agreement with Israel. They reestablished diplomatic relations with Russia and remained a close Arab ally of the United States. The thrust of all of these diplomatic efforts was aimed at establishing Egypt as a bridge between competing states in the region.

Since Nasser's rise to power, Egyptian nationalists have sought to steer a middle course between totally abandoning the past as in Turkey and totally embracing it as in Iran. Since the death of Nasser, both of his successors, Anwar al-Sadat and Hosni Mubarak, have tried to move the national movement away from Arab socialism toward a form of state-regulated capitalism. From once trying to lead the Arab world, Egyptian nationalists now focus on building up Egypt economically. Few outside observers would hazard a guess as to whether they will be successful.

Of all the states of the Middle East, Egypt is the one that authorities speak of in the most pessimistic terms. Beset by a population explosion that is uncontrollable without using unacceptably draconian measures, no Egyptian government can hope to make significant improvements in the lives of the people in the foreseeable future. The question being asked by all who look at Egypt's problems is: How long will the Egyptian masses wait before turning to more radical solutions to their problems? Since Egypt is the most populous Arab state, the direction that it takes will determine the future of much of the Middle East. Is time for Egypt growing short? Egypt's leaders have many problems and few solutions. The miracle is that Egypt continues to limp on, surviving each gloomy forecast.

Saudi Arabian Bedo-Nationalism It is popular to speak of the British royal family as "the family business." Perhaps no better example of a family business exists than that of the House of Saud. Since the alliance between a clan chief, Muhammad ibn Saud, and Muhammad ibn Wah-hab in 1744, the House of Saud has played the defining role in Arabian politics. Whether in or out of power, Sauds have always been a force to be reckoned with.

The modern story of Saudi Arabia began in 1901 when the famous leader Abdul Asiz Ibn Abdul Rahman Al-Saud (Ibn Saud) rode out of desert exile in Kuwait to capture the fortress of Riyadh. From that base he gradually increased his hold on the Arabian Peninsula until he was able to unite all the major tribes and their territories to create the present state of Saudi Arabia (called the Kingdom) in 1932.

In 1933, Ibn Saud rejected British advice and granted a 60-year petroleum concession to Standard Oil of California. When a great pool of oil was discovered, this arrangement became one of the most profitable business deals in history. The oil company first evolved into the Arabian American Oil Company (Aramco) and later, under Saudization, into Saudi Aramco.

Ibn Saud's greatness was a result of his ability to first win military victories and then to consolidate power by linking his family through marriage and alliances to the other major families in the region. This tribal linkage has remained intact to the present day. Saudi nationalism centers around the embracing of desert tribal traditions to build a national consensus.

Using the Kingdom's vast oil wealth, Ibn Saud and his sons were able to wrench the Arabian people out of a rural Bedouin life into the modern world. All of this was accomplished without sacrificing the region's traditional values. Saudi Arabia became the world's best example of the premise that a state did not have to be Western to be modern. Because of the leadership from the House of Saud, residents of the Kingdom were able to enjoy the benefits of the modern world while remaining true to the religious and cultural traditions of their Bedouin roots.

At first glance the Saudi government is authoritarian. But this is a misleading impression caused by substituting Western models of government for the complexities of Arabian politics. Politics in Arabia are true to the traditions of that region. The West separates religion from government and focuses on problem-solving strategies. The Kingdom combines religion and government by placing all issues within an Islamic context. These issues are dealt with on the basis of personal relationships backed by family honor. The ties maintained by the family, clan, and tribal loyalty to the ruling family form the basis of Bedo-Nationalism.

Arab Nationalism The political scientist Karl Deutsch once said, "A nation is a group of people united by a common dislike of their neighbors and a common misconception about their ethnic origins."[22] If one looks at the spirit of the nation from the perspective of the Arabs, it is clear that Deutsch's observation applies to the Middle East.

Arab nationalism is often characterized as xenophobic, negative in international outlook and dependent on a historical past that is often more myth than fact. Arabs are suspicious of others because of what they perceive to be more than 200 years of lies and deceit by the colonial powers. Throughout the 19th century and well into the 20th, this pattern repeated itself with cynical regularity. For example, the British promised the Arabs independence during World War I, only to carve up the region into colonial mandates when the war was over. Arab nationalists from Gamal Nasser to Saddam Hussein have seen this event as a treacherous act, ensuring that the Arabs would remain a divided people who could be controlled by outsiders. Many Arab nationalists see U.S. support for the State of Israel as a fresh attempt to divide and dominate the Arab people.

Higher Education
The courtyard of a modern university in Saudi Arabia. This university is typical of a large number of institutions of higher learning that have been built with the revenue from oil.
Source: Joe Weatherby

The history that forms the basis of Arab nationalism is characterized by the gap between aspiration and reality. The aspiration is the reestablishment of a single, united Arab nation similar to that which is believed to have existed during the early days of Muhammad. The reality is that this kind of unity has never existed. Even during its early days, the Islamic state was characterized by civil wars and assassinations. In modern times, the aspiration has been to free the Arab people from foreign domination. The reality has been a reliance on foreign influence, aid, and military support to accomplish Arab political goals. For example, Arab opposition to Israel caused nationalists to embrace almost any outside power that was perceived as being willing to aid in this effort. The reality of this approach has been to mortgage Arab sovereignty to external obligations. The aspiration that oil can be used to achieve Arab economic independence has clashed with the reality that Arab oil must be sold to the West for hard currency. Instead of unifying the Arabs, wealth generated by oil has divided rich and poor Arabs across the region. Although Arab nationalism is a potent force, it has failed to meet the hopes of those who seek the rebirth of a great, unified Arab nation.

Israel Israel may be described as a settler state with a European ideology transplanted into the Middle East. This impression may be less true today than it was in the past. Modern Israel is more conservative, militaristic, sectarian, and Middle Eastern than it once was. With U.S. financial aid more important than ever before, Israel reflects many of the same neocolonial fears and suspicions that are found in other Middle Eastern states.

Founded in Basel, Switzerland, in 1897, modern political Zionism is a form of nationalism that calls for the establishment and maintenance of a Jewish state in Palestine. The return to Palestine is based on Jewish traditions that go back 2000 years. The specifics of this call have been modified to fit the changing needs of the movement. Today, Zionism generally means that the survival of the State of Israel must be guaranteed as a symbol or refuge for Jews everywhere, whether they choose to immigrate or not.

Over the years, two factions of nationalists emerged to contend for power. Secular nationalists who were interested in the establishment of a modern state with viable borders were represented by the Israeli Labor Alignment. These nationalists included some of the great names of Israeli history such as David Ben Gurion, Golda Meir, and Abba Eban. They represented the ideas of the European founders of Israel, and their party alignments dominated the policies of Israel from the nation's founding until 1977.

In 1977, the demographic changes in the Israeli population tilted politics in favor of non-European Jews. Continuing Palestinian hostilities and new demographics created conditions that brought a conservative coalition, called the Likud, to power. The Likud represented the second direction taken by the Zionists. Their view argued for the creation of a "Greater Israel" or a "Promised Land" that would include those portions of the Middle East that tradition held were promised by God to the ancient Hebrews. In recent years, non-European Jews had experienced Arab domination; they also tended to support Likud's hard-line policies toward the Arabs.

At the beginning of a new century, Israeli nationalism is in a state of transition. No one can predict with certainty the final direction that the movement will take. On the one hand, Israel can pursue the maximalist Likud goal of recovering and then holding all of "the land of Israel." To the outsider this course seems to be not only impractical but also sure to doom the state to entering into an endless cycle of debilitating wars with the

Arabs, followed by costly occupations. To many this is a process in which Israel cannot hope to prevail.

The other nationalist approach is accommodation with Israel's neighbors. This choice is also dangerous and difficult. It involves making painful concessions on issues that are of primary concern to most Israelis. This course is made all the more difficult because it means that Israel will have to give up the most when exchanging "land for peace." It is analogous to sacrificing several chess pawns in order to win the game. Here, winning for Israel is survival as a Jewish state with secure borders and peaceful neighbors. There are indications that some Israelis are willing to give peace a chance. In 1999, elections resulted in a landslide victory for the Labor Party and Ehud Barak. A decorated general, Barak ran on a program of reaching a final peace settlement with the Arabs. This meant the abandonment of some deeply held territorial goals by some nationalists. Since the 1999 election, Barak's peace efforts were overtaken and discredited by the events discussed in Chapters 6 and 7. New early elections brought the Likud leader, Ariel Sharon, to power. It is still too early to determine if the hard line nationalists in Israel and those on the other side are willing to make the ideological sacrifices that will be necessary to see the peace progress through to a successful end. At this point there is little room for any optimism that a peace can be reached with the Palestinians in the foreseeable future.

The Holy Land
A terraced hillside near Jerusalem. Centuries of overgrazing and woodcutting have caused much of the topsoil to be washed away, leaving the hills bare.
Source: Joe Weatherby

What Are Some Other Events, Organizations, and People Important to the History of Islam, Colonialism, and Nationalism?

EVENTS

The Sassanian Empire This was the last truly Persian rule before the Muslim conquest. The Empire lasted from 224 B.C.E. to C.E. 640. The Sassanians practiced Zoroastrianism. In the latter period of Sassanian rule, a series of wars with Christian Byzantium dissipated their strength. This weakness contributed to the Sassanian defeat by the Arabs. When the Pahlavi Dynasty was established, the Shah drew on Sassanian traditions to establish legitimacy; Iranians still look with nostalgia to the Sassanian period as one of the times of Persian greatness.

The Safavid Dynasty The Safavids rose to power in Persia at the beginning of the 15th century. They are noted for making Shiite Islam the state religion, as was mentioned in Chapter 1; Shah Abbas I made the city of Esfahan the empire's capital. He expanded the Empire to include the cities of Karbala in present day Iraq. Even in the 21st century the Shia dominate the lower portions of Iraq. The Safavids were eastern rivals to the Sunni-dominated Ottoman Empire. Their fixation on the western portions of the Kingdom caused them to fall to an invasion from Afghanistan in 1722. Today the borders of Iran correspond roughly to the borders of Shiism established by the Safavids. The only major exception is in Iraq, where the Shia are about 60 percent of the population.

The Mamluks Meaning slave in Arabic, the Mamluks started, like the Janissaries, as warriors drafted from children living in the Muslim-controlled, Christian territories. They were converted to Islam and trained as cavalry. They appear at different times in Islamic history from the Middle Ages to the early part of the 19th century. The Mamluks are best known for their activities in Egypt. They were first brought there as an army to defend the province. Over time, they became both the rulers and largest landowners. The first period of Mamluk rule ended with their defeat by the Ottomans in 1517. As the Ottoman Empire started its decline during the 18th century, the Circassian Mamluks rose to power in Egypt. They were finally defeated by Emperor Napoleon I at the Battle of the Pyramids in 1798. They were noteworthy for their cavalry skills and their swordsmanship. They were defeated by the modern weapons of the French, which rendered their "dash and courage" obsolete.

The Agadir Incident During the rush to establish colonial empires in North Africa in 1911, both the French and the Spanish moved to partition Morocco. The Germans attempted to counter these moves by sending the gunboat Panther to the Moroccan port of Agadir. This action caused an international crisis that threatened to provoke a war between Germany and France. The crisis was defused when France made concessions to the Germans in southern Africa.

The Treaty of Sevres After suffering defeat during World War I, the Ottomans were forced to sign the humiliating Treaty of Sevres. The Treaty forced the Ottomans to surrender the non-Turkish portions of the Empire. Portions of Anatolia were to be occupied by the victorious allied forces, including Greece. The Dardanelles and Bosporus were to be internationalized. The Turkish population united behind Ataturk to reject many of the conditions imposed by the treaty. They went to war to free their country of foreign rule. They drove the Greeks out of Anatolia and abolished the Ottoman Suleynate. Their reaction to the Sevres Treaty can be said to have led to the establishment of the modern Turkish Republic. In 1923, the allies were forced to accept the more favorable Treaty of Lausanne, which recognized Turkish independence.

ORGANIZATIONS

The Assassins A subordinate branch of Shiism called the *Nizaris* (the Assassins) got the name from Europeans during the Crusades. They were noted for their total obedience to their leaders. They often used murder to achieve political objectives. They had followings in what is now Iran and Iraq. Their activities caused them to be feared throughout the Muslim world. They were defeated during Mongol invasions in 1256. After that time the Assassins ceased to be a major factor. Small groups of Nizaris are said to still exist in Syria. They have been given the word "assassin" as a title. Used today, an assassin kills for political motives.

Syrian Nationalism Through the latter half of the 19th century, there were small groups of elites in the Ottoman Arab provinces of the Fertile Crescent who advocated some form of autonomy within the Empire. Some Christians and Jews talked of a common Arab heritage. True nationalism, however, did not emerge until the Young Turk movement appeared in the decades before World War I. The Young Turks' seizure of power in 1908 meant that leadership in the Empire would be tilted toward the Turks and against the Arabs. The Arab reaction was to form groups that, at first, called for more freedom for Arabic-speaking peoples within the Empire. Later, after the Empire imploded and the Europeans had partitioned the region, Syrian nationalists called for complete independence from foreign rule.

The Wafd Meaning delegation, the Wafd emerged from the Ottoman defeat of World War I. It was a nationalist delegation calling for complete independence from Britain. It eventually evolved into a nationalist political movement that dominated Egyptian policies during the postwar period. Because the Wafd reform policies included limiting the powers of the Egyptian king, friction between the palace and the government was a feature of policies during the 1920s and 1930s. During World War II, the party supported the British in the struggle against Germany. This policy was resented by many Egyptians who saw a German victory as the only way of getting the British out of Egypt. By the time of the 1952 revolution that brought Nasser to power, the Wafd was discredited as being too corrupt and too pro-British. The party ceased to exist in the aftermath of the revolution.

Ba'ath Party The Arab Socialist Renaissance Party is an Arab nationalist party that is in power in both Syria and Iraq. The common ideological principles of the Ba'ath include secularism, socialism, and Arab unity. The parties in both states have a history of ideological struggle between the socialist left and the extreme nationalist. For some years the parties of Syria and Iraq have been bitter enemies. These positions reflect the often hostile governmental relations between the two states. Today the Ba'ath rules both Syria and Iraq as one-party states.

PERSONALITY

Muhammad Ali   Sometimes called "the Father of Modern Egypt," Muhammad Ali was sent to Egypt by the Ottoman Sultan. Eventually he became independent in all but name from the Ottoman Empire. Taking advantage of the defeat of Napoleon I by the British, he used French mercenaries to reorganize and modernize the Egyptian army. He continued to expand his influence until he became a military threat to the Ottoman Empire itself. Fearful that an Ottoman collapse would invite Russian expansion, the French and British united to oppose him in 1839. In return for his withdrawal from the Eastern Mediterranean, the Ottomans awarded him the hereditary title Khedive, or Viceroy of Egypt. For the rest of his life, Muhammad Ali devoted his efforts to modernizing the Egyptian economy, education system, and infrastructure. To some, he is considered to be a leader with early nationalist beliefs. To others, he failed to meet that test because he was a foreigner who relied on foreigners to administer his policies.

Summary

The story of the Middle East and North Africa has been colored by two great "events" in Islamic history, a colonial experience, and the evolution of nationalism. This chapter emphasizes the history of Sunni Islam because it has had the most influence on the region. Although Western colonialism influenced all parts of the region, the Allied World War I and postwar decision established the states of the Middle East as they currently exist. Because of this, the allied agreements, treaties, and commitments are briefly discussed. The colonial story in Morocco and Algeria was noted in Chapter 2. Finally, the long prenationalist and nationalist periods of the Ottoman Empire are followed by capsule summaries of the nationalisms of Turkey, Iran, Egypt, Saudi Arabia, the Arabs, and Israel to illustrate the different forms that nationalism has taken.

Review Questions

1. Who were the Abbassids?
2. Who were the Young Turks?
3. Why is 1798 an important date in the history of the Middle East?
4. Discuss the features of nationalism as it developed in Turkey, Iran, and Egypt.
5. Define these terms: Zionism, the land of Israel, and the State of Israel.

Suggested Readings

Jere L. Bacharach, *A Middle East Studies Handbook,* Cambridge University Press, Cambridge, 1984.
Albert Hourani, *A History of the Arab Peoples,* Harvard University Press, Cambridge, Mass., 1991.
T. E. Lawrence, *Seven Pillars of Wisdom: A Triumph,* Doubleday and Co., Inc., New York, 1991.
Raphaela Lewis, *Everyday Life in Ottoman Turkey,* Dorst Press, New York, 1971.
Anthony Nutting, *The Arabs,* New American Library, New York, 1964.
Dan Perry and Alfred Ironside, *Israel at Fifty,* General Publishing Group, Santa Monica, Calif., 1998.
Daniel Pipes, *Greater Syria: The History of an Ambition,* Oxford University Press, Oxford, 1990.

Notes

1. Jere Bacharach, *A Middle East Studies Handbook,* Cambridge University Press (Cambridge, England: 1984), p. 18.
2. George Orwell, *Animal Farm,* The New American Library (New York: 1964), p. 123.
3. Anthony Nutting, *The Arabs: A Narrative History From Muhammad to the Present,* The New American Library (New York: 1964), p. 97.
4. The discipline of mathematics was far behind in the West. Pope Sylvester II first introduced Arabic numerals to Europe at the end of the 10th century. This system was not commonly used until 1202 when John Holywood's book, *Algorismus,* popularized the use of Arabic numerals. See pp. 138–141, Marjorie Rowling, *Life in Medieval Times,* G. P. Putnam's Sons (New York: 1968). Abbassid scholars were also leaders in the sciences of astronomy and navigation.
5. William R. Polk, *The United States and the Arab World,* Harvard University Press (Cambridge, Mass.: 1965), p. 61.
6. Bacharach, *op. cit.,* p. 142.
7. The practice of paying bribes to have governmental agents do their duty still exists in the region.
8. David Fromkin, *A Peace to End All Peace: Creating the Modern Middle East,* Henry Holt and Company (New York: 1989), p. 561.
9. Ralph H. Magnus, Editor, *Documents on the Middle East: United States Interest in the Middle East,* American Enterprise Institute for Public Policy Research (Washington, D.C.: 1969), p. 17.
10. Magnus, *op. cit.,* p. 14.
11. George Lenczowski, *The Middle East in World Affairs,* Cornell University Press (New York: 1962), p. 81.
12. Aaron M. Margalith, *The International Mandates,* John Hopkins Press (Baltimore: 1930), pp. 139–140.
13. After the Russian Revolution of 1917, the new Soviet government distanced itself from the efforts of their predecessors by publishing the Sykes-Picot Agreement. This was considered to be further proof that World War I had been an imperialist war. See David Fromkin, *op. cit,* p. 257. Soviet historian V. Lutsky emphasized the duplicity of the British in this affair when he wrote, "One of the sayings of British diplomacy is that you can promise anything that you like because the situation is bound to change." V. Lutsky, *Modern History of the Arab Peoples,* Progress Publishers (Moscow: 1969), p. 393.
14. Albert Hourani has described the rise of nationalism this way: "a series of writers . . . began to put forward new ideas about the way in which society and the state should be organized. It was in this generation that the idea of nationalism became explicit among Turks, Arabs, Egyptians, and Tunisians. There had been some stirrings of national self-consciousness earlier, and behind them there lay something older and stronger, the wish of long-established societies to continue their lives without interruption, but as an articulate idea animating politics it became important only in the last two decades before the First World War." Albert Hourani, *A History of the Arab Peoples,* The Belknap Press of Harvard University Press (Cambridge, Mass.: 1991), pp. 308–309.
15. It is interesting that the Germans attempted to infiltrate agents into British-controlled Afghanistan in order to destabilize British interests in Afghanistan, Persia, and India. Sometimes called "the German Lawrence of Arabia, Lieutenant Oskar Nredermayer crossed pro-Allied territory in Persia to Afghanistan. His mission was to stir up the independence movement there. Although the mission failed and Afghanistan remained neutral, it shows that both sides of the conflict were willing to introduce nationalist ideas into the region if it helped further their objectives. See George Lenczowski, *The Middle East and World Affairs,* Cornell University Press (Ithaca, N.Y.: 1962), p. 43, and David Fromkin, *op. cit.,* p. 208.
16. Ralph Magnus, *op. cit.,* p. 14.

17. Efraim Karsh and Inari Karsh, *Empires of the Sand: The Struggle for Mastery of the Middle East,* American Enterprise Institute for Public Policy Research (Washington, D.C.: 1969), p. 14.
18. Note: Arab sources have always maintained that the revolt was much more important to the Ottoman defeat than the West was willing to admit. The following quotes from author Suleiman Mousa take this position: "Foreign sources have habitually attributed any Arab military successes to the British or French officers on the scene. Even if the Arab party consisted of a thousand men led by senior Arab officers, these sources would only mention them as a marginal appendage to the heroics of the foreign officer. . . ." He states further, "Western sources, of course, have ample excuse for their partiality, for they obtained their information from the reports which the British and French officers habitually made about the activities in which they had taken part." Finally Mousa states, "At the peace conference, Feisal declared that the Arabs had put a hundred thousand troops into the battle field, of whom ten thousand died for the cause they cherished." Suleiman Mousa, *T. E. Lawrence: An Arab View,* Oxford University Press (London: 1966), pp. 61, 62, 260.
19. Fromkin, *op. cit.,* p. 46.
20. Although never officially acknowledged by the U.S. Government, there is little doubt about the CIA involvement in the episode. See Kermit Roosevelt, *Counter-Coup: The Struggle for the Control of Iran,* McGraw-Hill (New York: 1979), Chapters 11, 12, and 13, and R. G. Grant, *M15, M16: Britain's Security and Secret Intelligence Services,* Gallery Books (New York: 1989), pp. 113–114.
21. Edward Mortimer and Michael Field, "Nationalism, The Steel of the Arab Soul," *Financial Times* (London) August 18/19, 1990, Section 11.
22. Mortimer and Field, *op. cit.,* Section 11.

Chapter 6

The Politics of Issues

Introduction

What follows is a series of editorially oriented essays on contemporary political issues in the Middle East and North Africa. Their purpose is to stimulate your interest in these issues rather than to tell you what you should think about them.

The Dispute Between Arabs, Palestinians, and Israelis

WHY DO WE BLAME THE VICTIMS?

There is a popular Middle Eastern story told here in a different context. One day a scorpion met a frog on the east bank of the Jordan River. The scorpion said to the frog, "Brother, let me ride on your back while you swim the Jordan so that I can visit the home of my ancestors in Jerusalem." The frog replied to the scorpion, "Brother, I would like to help you, but if you jump on my back you will sting me and I will die!" The scorpion answered, "That cannot happen, because, while in the river, if I sting you and you die, you will sink and I shall drown." The frog said, "That is reasonable, hop on my back and we will cross the River Jordan together." Halfway across the river, the scorpion stings the frog. As he is dying, the frog says to the scorpion, "Why did you sting me? Now I shall die from your sting, but you are going to drown!" Before he sinks for the last time, the scorpion shouts, "Yes, but this is the Holy Land!"

Time and time again the parties to the Palestinian-Israeli dispute have taken stands on what they perceived to be matters of principle even when their action had the effect of working against their own self-interests. To put it another way, the parties to this dispute never fail to choose conflict instead of the alternative peace.

Before discussing the specifics of the conflict, several assumptions should be made. First, the leaders on both sides have raised some of their objectives to the heights of irreducible principles. By painting themselves into ideological corners, both the Palestinian and the Israeli leaders have ensured that peace is impossible without the ideological surrender of the other side.

Second, during more than a century of conflict, both sides have suffered grievous injustices at the hands of their opponents. Peace will require a new way of thinking in which the old animosities will have to be forgiven and forgotten.

Third, because Israel has been victorious in every war fought with the Palestinians and other Arabs since 1948, the Israelis have acquired all of the "chips." Peace will require Israel to give up the most to take a chance on ending the conflict. Palestinians have nothing to bargain with except the threat to continue a bitter, costly, low-intensity war against Israel indefinitely.

Fourth, Israel can only hope to win the battles, but the Israelis can never win the war. Without peace, the Jewish State will be overwhelmed by the demographics of Palestinian population growth. Peace accompanied by ethnic separation is Israel's only hope to maintain a Jewish democracy over the long term.

Finally, it will take cooperation between the Israelis and Palestinians for either of the two cultures to prosper. Neither is large enough or rich enough to go it alone without outside support.

WHAT ARE THE MOST IMPORTANT ISSUES THAT MUST BE ADDRESSED BEFORE PEACE CAN OCCUR BETWEEN ARABS, PALESTINIANS, AND ISRAELIS?

Land The issue of land is one of the oldest, most contentious disputes between Jews and Palestinians. It involves cultural misunderstandings on both sides.

The first troubles started with 19th century Jewish land purchases. During most of the period of the Ottoman rule, land title had not been too important. Country people lived on the land by tradition and there was common land for grazing. In 1858, the Ottoman authorities enacted a land code that required registration of agricultural land. This was a new idea for peasants who were using land that had no official owners. Fearful that registration meant taxation or the drafting of their sons for military service, many Palestinians either failed to register or had merchants in the cities or towns register the land in their names. With the stroke of a pen these peasants moved from the status of independent farmers, to tenants of absentee landlords. Later, some of these absentee "owners" sold their land to Jewish groups. Following European custom, the Jewish immigrants holding legal titles proceeded to occupy the land by expelling the Palestinian residents. To the Europeans, this action was a reasonable step for a landowner to take. For the evicted Palestinians, their expulsion at the hands of the new arrivals was land theft. This conflict over land titles continued from the late 19th century until well into the 20th century.

During the Israeli War for Independence, large numbers of Palestinians were either expelled or fled their lands, never to be allowed to return. During this period, Israel expanded to twice the size proposed in the first United Nations partition plan. In the aftermath of the 1956 war, Israel held 8,000 square miles of Palestine. That figure increased to 30,000 square miles after Israel's victory in the 1967 war.[1]

During the early years after Israel's independence, Israeli authorities promised that Palestinians who had lost property in Israel would be compensated after there was a peace treaty with the Arabs. Unfortunately, after more than fifty years, the idea of a full compensation to the Palestinians seems to be both an economic and practical impossibility. As an example of the complexity surrounding this issue, just look at one property: the proposed site for the American Embassy should it be moved to Jerusalem. In a study reported by the *International Herald Tribune*, Walid Khalidi of the Institute for Palestine Studies at Georgetown University found that part of the site set aside for the future American Embassy in Jerusalem belongs to exiled Palestinians. Their number has grown in the last half century to include 90 United States citizens.[2] Khalidi asserts that to place the American Embassy on land taken from American citizens would be to endorse the land seizures that have taken place since 1948. In fairness, it should be pointed out that the Israeli authorities dispute the facts in this case. What is important is that the dispute over title to the proposed embassy site is typical of the complexity surrounding land ownership in Israel and the occupied territories.

There is little hope that any significant amounts of land within the present borders of Israel will ever be returned to their former Palestinian owners. The question of compensation is still to be resolved. In the occupied territories, the Israelis have agreed to return land in increments. To date, the Palestinians have regained slightly less than half of the West Bank land captured in 1967. The Palestinian land there is in isolated parcels. There is no contiguous Palestinian-controlled territory.

Water In all Arab land, water and water law are important. In the Middle East, water is the region's major deficit. Nowhere in the region is this issue more contentious than in the Jordan River Valley. As states modernize, the claims of Lebanon, Syria, Jordan, and Palestine will challenge those of Israel. The harsh fact of life is that the Jordan River is a historically important but minor river. In most places it is no more than a hundred yards wide. There is no hope of securing the region's future water needs from Lake Tiberias, the Jordan, or the Dead Sea. To illustrate the difficulty here, both Israeli and Palestinian experts say that there is not enough existing subsurface or surface water to supply present consumption levels let alone account for usage based on an increased population. At the present time, Israel controls most of the water. Israeli settlers average a daily use of 74 gallons of water per person. They live lives similar to those in Israel proper. Their Palestinian neighbors are limited to less than 20 gallons a person per day. It is estimated that more than 200,000 West Bank Palestinians have no running water at all.[3]

There are also water disputes with Syria and Jordan. Unless some alternative sources of water can be found, an equitable solution to the future distribution of water will become an increasing impediment to the peace process.

Refugees One of the most controversial episodes of Israeli history was the flight or expulsion of almost half a million Palestinians from their homes in 1948. It is not the place here to pass judgment on an event that happened during a life and death struggle for survival where atrocities occurred on both sides. However, the Palestinian exodus was the beginning of one of the world's best known refugee problems. In 1967, the Israeli occupation of the West Bank and Gaza resulted in the flight of another half million Palestinians. These and other deportations have earned the Palestinians the unenviable title of "Jews of the Middle East."

One of the reasons that some of the surrounding Arab states have resisted moves to assimilate the Palestinian refugees is that the continuation of this problem has helped to fuel the Arab opposition to Israel. Caught in the middle of a struggle between powerful neighbors, the Palestinians have languished in squalid refugee camps for over 50 years.

The current refugee problem is an extension of this old, sad story from the past. In the intervening half century, the refugee population may have grown to as many as 2 million Palestinians living outside of Israel and the occupied territories.

Certainly no Israeli government would seriously consider such a large repatriation to Israel because that would effectively end the Jewish State. In response *The Economist* quotes a Palestinian refugee as saying, "I am willing to forego any implementation of the right of return. But I will not accept an agreement that gives up my right of return. Israel was responsible for my exile, and it must recognize that responsibility."[4]

The problem is that the Palestinians, for whatever was the original cause, are now being asked to accept a state of about 20 percent of what was historic Palestine. They are having to recognize the rest of the territory as "the homeland for the Jewish people." In order to resolve this issue, some Palestinians, if even a token number, need to be repatriated and a reasonable compensation plan developed for the rest if this sad historic memory is to be removed as an obstacle to peace.

There are also potential Jewish refugees living in Israeli settlements all across the occupied territories. Regardless of how they got there, there will have to be some displacement of Israeli settlers in any major return of land to the Palestinians. This will be a painful process but one that must take place. There is precedent for a withdrawal with compensation. When Israel withdrew from the Sinai, some Israeli settlements were forcibly removed by the military. The way Israel handles abandonment of the settlements that they lose in a Palestinian peace agreement can serve as a model for negotiating with Syria over the Golan Heights.

Palestinian Prisoners in Israeli Jails The prisoner issue is another thorny one. No one knows exactly how many Palestinians are being held in Israeli jails. Some are classified as detainees, whereas others are called prisoners. Some have been tried and convicted, whereas others have been held without trial for indefinite periods ranging from months to years. This issue is a sore point for both Palestinians and Israelis. The Palestinians want to see the speedy release of people who they consider to be freedom fighters. However, Israeli families who have lost loved ones to what they consider to be terrorist acts deeply resent the release of people who they believe to be cold-blooded killers. There are precedents for prisoner releases such as those in Ulster, Northern Ireland. There, prisoner releases occurred after the peace agreement was signed between the Protestant and Catholic sides.

Jerusalem The future status of Jerusalem is the most serious issue dividing Arabs, Palestinians, and Jews. Leaders from all groups have made inflammatory demands from which it is difficult if not impossible to retreat. Here religion is now mixed up with the nationalist aspirations of each side. The religious symbols of Judaism, Christianity, and Islam have been manipulated by various leaders to serve their own ends. The following statements illustrate the difficulty of resolving the question of who controls Jerusalem.

> No Israeli prime minister could agree to let the Palestinians have sovereignty over the Temple Mount, which is the holy site for the Jewish people for generations.[5]

> No one is entitled to say that Jerusalem, or al-Aksa Mosque, is under Israeli sovereignty. We put ideas to the Palestinian side and ask that they discuss them from all angles. It is up to the Palestinians to make the decision compatible with their interest and which is simultaneously acceptable to the Arab and Islamic world.[6]

Never has a Muslim leader, in the history of Islam, willingly abandoned sovereignty over holy places . . . that would make Arafat a pariah in all the Arab and Muslim world.[7]

All of this is complicated by the close proximity of the holy sites of Muslims, Christians, and Jews. They are literally stacked one on top of the other in a walled old city that is about the size of an American university campus. It has been said that all of the other issues involving disputes between Palestinians and Israelis are less important than this one. It is this kind of sectarian nationalism that so frustrates the outside observer. Nevertheless, if some equitable sharing of the city cannot be found, there will be no peace.

The irony is that the city is already being shared in all but law right now. The Palestinian Authority exercises defacto influence in the Arab quarters of the Old City. In spite of creative redrawing of the city's boundaries, the percentage of Palestinians in the city continues to increase. According to journalist Lee Hockstader, the Arabs now make up more than 30 percent of the city's population.[8] Muslim authorities control activities on the Temple Mount restricting non-Muslims from prayer. Elsewhere, secular, religious, and indifferent Palestinians, Jews, and tourists peacefully pass each other daily.

Palestinian Independence For some time, Palestinians have threatened to unilaterally declare their independence. Probably the main reason that this has not taken place is because of the Palestinian fear that Israel would then have an excuse to freeze everything under negotiation. That would leave Palestine with an unviable territory of isolated communities that would be impossible to govern effectively. Thoughtful Palestinians know that time is on their side and Palestinian statehood is inevitable. These Palestinians assert that patience and compromise will be the key to independence, not confrontation leading to a war that Palestine, even with Arab help, cannot hope to win.

WHAT ARE THE PEACE PLANS FOR JERUSALEM?

There have been hundreds of "peace plans" that seemed reasonable to well-meaning people who do not live in the region. These plans have been offered by people who extend from former President Jimmy Carter to popular journalists with experience in the region. What seems clear in the aftermath of the failed year 2000 Camp David talks is that agreement can be reached on everything except the final status of Jerusalem. Can this hurdle be overcome through compromise? Perhaps, if one realistically looks at the facts. During the past 2000 years, Jerusalem has always been a multicultural city. It has never been wholly Jewish, Christian, or Muslim Arab. Until the post–World War II period, the three religions grudgingly shared the holy places and segregated themselves socially in quarters. In commerce, they functioned and still do function together to make up the economy of the Old City. Even the founders of Zionism recognized this fact of life when they discouraged the Jewish expansion into the Old City by building a new modern Jerusalem outside the city walls.

Certainly the bitterness surrounding the separation of the city by the Jordanians cannot be forgotten by most Israelis. However, they should recognize that the Jordanians were understandably bitter about being forced to absorb a substantial portion of the Palestinian refugees who were also separated from their homes in the new Israel. There are enough charges made by both sides to prevent peace.

Jews, Christians, and Muslims have a history of wishing to exclusively control Jerusalem. History has demonstrated that this kind of control is impossible over a long period of time. Perhaps a new starting place for everyone might be to return to the thinking of the past. In the past, there were two Jerusalems. One was spiritual and above politics and nationalism while the other was administrative. If the parties to the dispute can be persuaded to make this distinction, then the religious and the secular nationalist issues can be dealt with.

The Camp David discussions seem to have made progress on administrative issues concerning the areas of the Old City with large Arab and Jewish populations. There may even have been agreement on the establishment of a Palestinian capital to be located in a suburb of Jerusalem with a view of the Dome of the Rock.

What needs to be decided is how to share the spiritual sites of the Old City. Former President Carter has laid out a simple, practical plan for overcoming this roadblock to a larger peace. He suggests that a strategy be devised that avoids a direct conflict over final sovereignty. He puts it this way,

> This is still the only basic approach that can succeed concerning Jerusalem: to negotiate practical agreements on unlimited access to and control of the holy places and a joint administration of the city's more mundane affairs.[9]

This approach would allow Yasser Arafat and the Israeli prime minister to avoid the issue of final legal authority. Over time the practicality of this arrangement accompanied by the enforcement of a demographic status quo in the Old City will cause the issue of secular nationalist-inspired sovereignty to fade away. That strategy could give the prospects for peace between Israelis and Palestinians a chance.

WHAT ARE SOME OTHER PROPOSALS, PERSONALITIES, ORGANIZATIONS, AND MEMORIES INVOLVED IN THE DISPUTE BETWEEN ISRAELIS AND PALESTINIANS?

Peace Proposals

An American Framework for Iraeli-Palestinian Peace As his administration came to an end, President Clinton offered a plan to resolve the differences between Palestinians and Israelis. Hoping to build on the earlier Camp David effort, President Clinton proposed a "framework for negotiation." He insisted that he would not convene the parties unless they accepted his conditions in advance. His plan called for the Palestinians to receive some sovereignty over the Temple Mount and Arab portions of the Old City of Jerusalem. They would also gain control over about 95 percent of the West Bank and Gaza territories. In return, they would have to abandon their right of return for all refugees wishing to return to their former homes in Israel. In addition, the price for formal independence would be peace with Israel. Eventually, both sides accepted the framework but with reservations that made the framework unacceptable. Although the peace conference did not resume on the Clinton watch, the plan did state an official American position on some of the most important points dividing the parties.

This plan is not without its critics. In an editorial opposing the Clinton framework, columnist Charles Krauthammer stated: "For three decades the United States supported a united Jerusalem. The Clinton plan now divides Jerusalem. For three decades the United States held that Israel should withdraw to secure, defensible borders. The Clinton plan has Israel giving up its critical Jordan Valley buffer zone." He continued, "Thus the first order

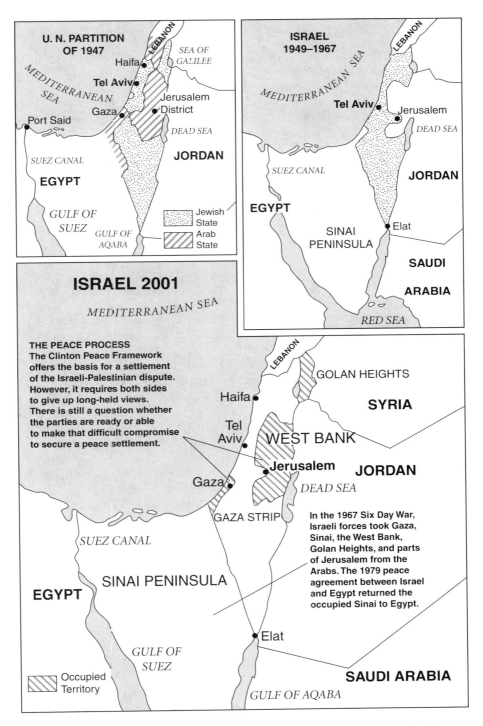

The Changing Boundaries of Israel: The boundaries of Israel have changed as a result of wars fought with Arab neighbors in 1948, 1956, 1967, 1973, and 1982.

Source: Adapted from *The Other World* 4th ed., Longman Publishers, Joe Weatherby et al., 2000

of business for the Bush Administration should be to declare itself not bound by the desperate eleventh hour measures and to fire the entire peace team. . . . "[10]

On the other hand, many critics charged that the Clinton plans apparent acceptance of "illegal" Israeli settlements, rejection of the Palestinians right of return, and the acceptance of annexation of most of East Jerusalem flew in the face of basic principles of International law and a series of United Nations resolutions including some backed by previous United States presidents. In fairness to the Clinton plan it should be remembered that it was only a beginning framework for negotiation that would require compromise from all sides.

The Sharon Plan Prime Minister Sharon has proposed a radical departure from the approaches of the past. His formula is to freeze any further return of the occupied territories to Palestinian control, which will result in the Palestinian Authority controlling a little more than 40 percent of the West Bank and Gaza. Jerusalem is to remain undivided and under Israeli sovereignty. The Palestinian right to return to their homes in Israel is flatly rejected. Finally, no Israeli settlements will be abandoned. Some settlements will be expanded.

Even the most optimistic observer of this conflict can see that this proposal is a recipe for further conflict. Senior Palestinian negotiator Saeb Erekat has been quoted by the Associated Press in Jerusalem as offering the following negative response to the Sharon plan: ". . . if he says that he is going to keep 58 percent of the West Bank and Gaza, we'll meet in the next life."[11]

The George W. Bush Administration Approach to Peace Between Israelis and Palestinians When President Bush entered office on January 20, 2001, he brought with him one of the most experienced foreign policy teams in recent American history. From the very beginning the new administration made it clear that they would not be as aggressive as the Clinton policymakers had been in pursuing a comprehensive peace between Palestinians and Israelis.

This was probably a realistic policy considering the deterioration of the situation since the beginning of the second intifada. The new Israeli prime minister had publicly announced that the earlier issues discussed at the Camp David summit and those elaborated in the Clinton framework were no longer subjects for negotiation. Furthermore, he said that there would be no discussions with the Palestinians until the intifada was called off. For their part, the Palestinians were just as adamant, stating that they would resume discussions with Israel only by taking up the issues on the table at Camp David and summarized in the Clinton framework. The first short-term approach for the Bush team was to work for a series of interim agreements designed to end the violence and buy time until conditions between the parties to the conflict improved.

Events in the Middle East, however, have a way of dragging U.S. policymakers into the conflict whether they like it or not. Less than a month after taking office, events in Iraq caused President Bush to bomb, command and control sites near Baghdad. Both allies and opponents of the United States condemned this action. Saddam Hussein used the attack to link the fate of Iraq with that of the Palestinians when he charged that it was a U.S. Zionist plot. One thing was certain: President Bush was going to have to be very careful in his dealing with the Palestinians and Israelis if a major conflict in the Middle East was to be avoided.

Is Any Comprehensive Peace Worth the Price? The former Israeli prime minister made offers to the Palestinians that had never been proposed before and may never be discussed again. Still, the Palestinian leadership rejected them out of hand. Former Israeli Foreign Minister Abba Eban is often quoted as saying that the Palestinians have never missed the opportunity to miss an opportunity. In this case the rise of Ariel Sharon reflects the inability of both sides to make the extremely difficult concessions necessary to achieve a comprehensive peace.

For the foreseeable future a grand settlement may be beyond the ability of the parties to accomplish. In the meantime, the best that can be hoped for is a return to discussions, with the aim of stopping the violence and then reaching interim agreements that will improve the atmosphere for the future.

It is clear that both sides will experience a great deal of pain before this conflict is resolved. It is also clear that there are simply too many Palestinians and Israelis for one or the other to go away. Regardless of who leads the contending parties, the previously mentioned issues that have divided Israelis and Palestinians for over half a century still remain to be settled.

Personalities

Sir John Bagot Glubb (Glubb Pasha)   Glubb was a British officer sent to Iraq after World War I. Later, when he was no longer with the British army, he became a member of the famous Arab Legion of Transjordan. As its commander in World War II, he led the Arab Legion when it played an important part in putting down nationalists and Vichy French attempts to establish pro-Nazi movements in both Syria and Iraq. During the Israeli War for Independence in 1948, Glubb Pasha successfully directed the Arab Legion occupation of the West Bank and the Old City of Jerusalem. In the aftermath of the overall defeat of the Arabs, he was charged by nationalists of being an agent of Britain. By the late 1950s, nationalist pressure on the King of Jordan forced him to send Glubb Pasha into retirement. Like his predecessor, Lawrence of Arabia, Glubb Pasha remains one of the more romantic adventurers of the 20th century. His importance to the Israeli-Palestinian dispute lies in his leadership in the Jordanian occupation of the West Bank and the Old City of Jerusalem. This action deprived the Palestinian leadership of the lands still held by the Arabs, which could have been used to found their state.

Chaim Weizmann   A famous professor of chemistry, Professor Weizmann was of great help to British scientists during World War I. Because of his fame as a scientist, Weizmann had access to the highest circles of the British government. Using his position, he was instrumental in pressing Britain to issue the Balfour Declaration in 1917.

Weizmann was part of the moderate wing of the Zionist movement. He advocated cooperation with both the British and the Arabs. Eventually, he came to the position of supporting the establishment of two states in Palestine: one Arab and one Jewish. His conciliatory policies put him in conflict with other Zionist leaders. Nevertheless, he was elected as the first president of the new State of Israel in 1949. He established the precedent that the president of Israel does not play an active role in policy-making.

Ehud Barak   Following the Zionist tradition, Ehud changed his name from the Eastern European Borq to the Hebrew Barak. He had a distinguished military career, becoming the youngest army chief of staff in Israeli history. He became active in Labor Party politics on retiring from the army in 1994. He became the Labor Party leader in 1997. In 1999 he decisively defeated the Likud Party candidate while campaigning on a program to make peace with the Palestinians.

His administration started with great hope that he could reach an agreement to end a century of conflict with the Palestinians. Early on in his administration, he successfully withdrew Israeli troops from Lebanon where they had been tied down since the 1980s.

At the July 2000 Camp David Conference, Barak made a number of new concessions in an attempt to draw Yasser Arafat into a peace agreement. When Barak's efforts failed and his concessions became known, his political standing with the Israeli public declined. After the second Intifada, violence erupted, his government coalition fell apart, and a new election for prime minister was scheduled for February 2001. In that election the Likud brought an early end to Barak's leadership. It was doubtful that the specific peace efforts that he championed would be supported by his successor.

Ariel Sharon Like many Israeli politicians, Ariel Sharon had a military career before entering politics. He participated in some capacity in all of Israel's wars with the Arabs. During the 1973 conflict, the forces under his leadership trapped the Egyptian 3rd Army, making him a national hero. A paradoxical man, Sharon was a cofounder of the right-wing Likud Bloc in Israeli politics. As Minister of Defense, he was one of the main forces behind Israel's invasion of Lebanon in 1982. He was blamed by many for allowing Lebanese Christian forces to massacre Palestinian refugees during that conflict. He resigned from the defense ministry partly over that scandal. He remained in the parliament and since that time has served in several cabinets in a number of positions. As Minister of Housing during a Likud administration, Sharon worked to increase Jewish settlements in the West Bank and Gaza territories.

After the Likud defeat in 1999, Sharon assumed leadership of the Bloc. He was active in his opposition to Barak's proposed concessions to achieve peace with the Palestinians. When that peace effort failed, his popularity with Israelis rose as Barak's fell.

His late September visit to the Temple Mount set off a series of violent confrontations that became the second Intifada.[12] As this conflict hardened positions on both sides, Sharon was elected prime minister. As prime minister, he announced that he was repudiating most of the recent peace proposals made by both Barak and Clinton. During his term as prime minister, a question remains of whether Ariel Sharon is willing or able to move from being an active opponent of the Palestinians to being able to make peace with them.

Yasser Arafat Although born in Egypt, Arafat was from a Palestinian family and spent his early years in Palestine. Leaving with his family in 1948, Arafat, in exile, graduated from Cairo University as a civil engineer. In 1958 he was a co-founder of a clandestine organization called Fatah. During the 1960s Fatah launched a number of guerilla actions against Israel. Mastering the intricate politics of the various Palestinian exile organizations, Arafat eventually emerged as the leader of the umbrella organization called the *Palestinian Liberation Organization* (PLO). He led that organization to Arab recognition of the PLO as the sole legitimate representative of the Palestinian people. After years of ups and downs, Arafat was recognized by Israel as the Palestinian spokesman when the 1993 Interim Agreement was signed. In 1994 he shared the Nobel Prize with the Israeli leaders. In 1994 he also returned to the Gaza Strip to head the Palestinian Authority.

The great test for Chairman Arafat is to make the transition from Palestinian revolutionary to statesman. That is a difficult task. Others, including former Israeli Prime Minister Menachem Begin, have done it. Thus far, Arafat has failed to meet that test. Whether he has the ability to accept a compromise in the foreseeable future, for Arafat the question remains whether the "struggle against Israel" has become more important than a compromised resolution of that dispute.

Organizations

Irgun Zavi Leumi (IZL)   The Hebrew title means national military organization. It was a paramilitary underground resistance organization prior to the establishment of Israel. During the 1930s the Irgun split off from the moderate Zionists. Irgun bands engaged in terrorist attacks on both the Arabs and the British. After the end of World War II, the Irgun continued to engage in violence. On July 26, 1946, the Irgun bombed the British army headquarters in the King David Hotel in Jerusalem. That attack resulted in the deaths of 91 people. The Irgun rejected the United Nations partition plan of 1947. It was blamed for the massacre of Arabs in the village of Deir Yassin. Other incidents led to the forcible disbanding of the Irgun by the Israeli Defense Forces in September 1948. The Irgun leader, Menachem Begin, eventually became prime minister of Israel.

Haganah   The Haganah, or defense, was established in 1920 in the wake of Arab riots in Jerusalem. The Haganah was linked to the Histadrut labor movement. It was considered to be more moderate than the Irgun because it advocated dealing with the British and the Arabs politically rather than militarily. The positions of the Haganah leadership caused its more militant members to split off and to form the Irgun. The Haganah and the Irgun maintained an uneasy alliance until Israel gained its independence. Between 1946 and 1948, both organizations ran a British blockade to smuggle Jews from Europe into Palestine. Dissolved after the 1948 war, the Haganah formed the basis of the Israeli army, now called the Israeli Defense Force.

Fatah (Movement for the Liberation of Palestine)   Founded in 1958 by Yasser Arafat and others, Fatah maintained that a mass, armed struggle was the only way to liberate Palestine and defeat Zionism. For years, Fatah refused to cooperate with more moderate Palestinian movements, including the Palestinian National Council. During the 1960s, Fatah carried out a number of actions against Israeli targets that included attacking the national water carrier in 1965. A major battle was fought against the Israeli army at Karameh near the Jordanian border in 1968.

At the end of the 1960s, Fatah ideology changed. Its new objective was to establish a single democratic secular state over all of Old Palestine. Fatah theorists argued that such a state would provide equal rights for Jews, Muslims, and Christians. They also agreed to attend meetings and cooperate with the Palestinian National Council. Shortly after that, the Palestinian National Council elected Yasser Arafat as chairman of the movement's "umbrella organization," called the Palestinian Liberation Organization.

Fatah opposed the Israeli invasion of Lebanon in 1982. After losing that conflict, the surviving members of Fatah were expelled from Lebanon and were reestablished in Tunisia.

In 1988 Fatah again changed strategy by announcing that it was abandoning the armed struggle against Israel in favor of a negotiated settlement. They called for the establishment of a Palestinian state in the West Bank and Gaza. For all intents, this was the Fatah recognition of a two-state policy in Old Palestine, one Israeli and one Palestinian.

The Fatah leadership mistakenly backed the Iraqi side in the Gulf War. When Iraq lost and Kuwait was liberated, a large portion of the Palestinian population working in that state was expelled.

Again reversing its stand, the mainline Fatah leadership, including Yasser Arafat, supported the peace talks with Israel. When these talks led to the establishment of the Palestinian Authority in the West Bank and Gaza, Fatah leaders moved from Tunisia to become prominent figures in the Authority's infrastructure. Yasser Arafat became the head of the Palestinian Authority.

Yasser Arafat and other Fatah members played prominent roles in the peace talks that have taken place between the Palestinians and Israelis. Probably the concessions offered to the Palestinians at the July 2000 Camp David Conference represented a high point for this Palestinian group. When the talks failed and they were later followed by the second Intifada, these old leaders may have let the situation get out of control.

As the struggle continues, no one really knows how much control the traditional Fatah leadership has over the situation. New younger, more radical leaders may emerge out of this latest confrontation with Israel to challenge Fatah for control over the hearts and minds of the Palestinian people. One thing is certain, the longer the violence of the second Intifada continues, the less likely the old Fatah leadership will go unchallenged.

Historical Memories

Deir Yassin   In 1948 the Irgun Zvai Leumi and other paramilitaries fighting for Israeli independence captured the Arab village of Deir Yassin. When the fighting ended, a massacre took place in which somewhere between 150 and 250 civilians, including women and children, were murdered. The massacre was widely publicized by both sides. This event was partly blamed for the spread of fear that caused many Palestinians to leave their homes to become refugees. Palestinians still bitterly point to the massacre as Israeli terrorism when outsiders raise the specter of Arab terrorism.

Intifada   In Arabic, "intifada" means shaking off. The intifada erupted in the occupied territories in 1987. The event caught people by surprise. Palestinians in the exile movements abroad were not involved. Local Palestinians opposed to the continued occupation of their territories opposed the Israeli army with rocks, bottles, and mass protests from 1987 until the resistance ended in 1993. What is important about this event is that it proved that the Palestinians in the occupied territories were prepared to resist Israeli occupation indefinitely. This resistance completely surprised observers who believed that it could not be sustained for a long period of time. It also convinced the Israelis that they could never assimilate the Palestinians of the West Bank and Gaza.

The 1972 Munich Olympic Massacre   On September 5, 1972, a Palestinian team of gunmen calling themselves Black September assaulted a housing unit being used by the members of the Israeli Olympic team. During the initial attack, two Israeli athletes were killed. What followed was a drawn-out hostage crisis that was viewed on television by millions of people all over the world.

The Black September organization issued a series of demands, which included the release of a number of prisoners being held in Germany and Israel. They also required aircraft to transport the team members and their hostages to a suitable airport. This would be the prelude to a flight to freedom abroad.

At Israeli insistence, the German authorities refused to negotiate on the basic demands. They did agree to provide passage out of the country in return for the release of the Israeli hostages.

Plans were made for a German attack on the Black September gunmen when they reached the airport prior to leaving the country. Unfortunately, this counterterrorist action failed. The surviving Black September members managed to kill the hostages before being subdued.

The Black September attack resulted in the deaths of eleven Israeli athletes. The Palestinians asserted that their action was designed to bring their cause to the center of world attention. In this effort they succeeded. However, over time, all but one known surviving member of the Black September team was eventually tracked down and killed by Israeli agents.

This attack made a lasting impression on Israelis in at least two ways. First, it clearly demonstrated to them that the Palestinians were prepared to attack Israeli targets anywhere in the world. Second, it showed that the Israeli response would also be global.

Since Munich, it has been established that Black September was a name used by Fatah for clandestine operations from 1971 to 1974. Fatah itself was the military arm of the Palestinian Liberation Organization.[13]

The Arab-Israeli War of 1973 This war was initiated by attacks on Israeli troops by Egypt and Syria. Because the war was fought in October and covered the Jewish holiday of Yom Kippur and the Muslim period of Ramadan, it has several names. Israelis called it the Yom Kippur War. To Israelis, this attack represents the kind of treachery that the Japanese Pearl Harbor attack does to Americans.

The Arabs call this conflict the Ramadan War. They see this as an effort to regain their territories occupied by Israel after their victory in 1967. They also point out that for more than a year, President Sadat had been warning that failing an Israeli withdrawal this attack would occur. The problem was that the leaders on the Israeli side did not believe him.

Outsiders either call this the October War or the 1973 War. They point out that with the exception of the Egyptian seizure of part of the Suez Canal, little change of territory occurred during the conflict. However, the war had major political implications for both sides. First, the Egyptians could make the claim that they won the war because they did not lose it. Their action eventually led to the peace with Israel and the Israeli return of the Sinai. Syria gained little except to remind Israelis of just how vulnerable their position on the Golan Heights was.

For Israelis, they realized that after the heady days of the 1967 victory, they could lose a war in the future. Thoughtful Israelis started to accept the fact that with enough time and money, the Arabs might at some time achieve a military parity with Israel. Then by using their superior numbers, they could inflict a decisive defeat on the Jewish State. The hard fact learned by Israelis in 1973 was that the Arabs could afford to lose many times, but Israel could never afford to suffer defeat even once. To Israelis, the fear of another surprise attack remains to this time.

The Political Impact of Petroleum on the Middle East and North Africa

WHAT ARE THE RULES OF THE PETROLEUM BUSINESS?

Petroleum is a Unique Energy Source for Several Reasons. First, it has reigned as the king of energy for only about 100 years. Prior to that time, most sources of oil were considered to be a nuisance, often interfering with the search for fresh water. It took the marriage of petroleum with the newly developed internal combustion engine to make oil the energy source of the 20th century. As the 21st century begins, oil has replaced wood and coal as a primary energy source. It has also withstood the challenge of atomic power, in its present form, to remain the cheapest, most versatile, and useful energy source in world history.

Second, unlike iron and coal when used to make steel, petroleum production does not require the producer to make great investments in human capital. Petroleum can be extracted in one place and easily transported to another for processing. In traditional societies like those found in the oil-producing areas of the Middle East and North Africa, this feature allows the oil to be extracted by a few specialists while most of the population maintains their culture. To be sure, the great amounts of wealth that have been injected into these areas have resulted in social change. However, the social disruptions resulting from petroleum production are minor when compared to those that occurred in Europe and America with the creation of the steel and coal industries during the Industrial Revolution. There the entire economy was changed from a rural agricultural one to the urban squalor of workers' districts in places like Newcastle, Birmingham, and Pittsburgh. It was in the slums of Europe, Russia, and America that the 20th century movements of socialism, fascism, and communism were born.

Third, although petroleum is a finite commodity and will theoretically run out some day, there are vast quantities of oil and gas available and more sources are being discovered every day. Certainly it no longer results in "burning bushes" or oozes on the ground as it once did. Still, there are deposits of oil and gas in the Middle East that are expected to last for more than 100 years. It is the author's opinion that just as was the case with both wood and coal, new, cheaper, more flexible sources of energy will be developed long before the oil reserves of the Middle East, North Africa, and elsewhere are exhausted.

Fourth, petroleum is a plentiful product. Ever since the early days of oil and gas, the big fear of the producers and the distributors was that overproduction could drop the price of petroleum to below that of water. Since the beginning, artificial controls on the supply of petroleum first by distributors and more recently by the producers have set the price of oil and gas. In one sense, oil can be compared to diamonds. Without limiting the distribution of diamonds and thus artificially controlling their price, diamonds would simply be rocks. Certainly, petroleum is a useful product and diamonds are a luxury "folly," so the comparison only involves the control of their prices.

The "oil people" of the Middle East and North Africa are good economists. They know that if the price goes too high for too long, consumers will seek alternative sources of energy. They also do not want the consumers in the West, and especially in the United States, to resume production of their higher-cost oil and gas. A reduction in the reliance on Middle Eastern and North African sources for oil and gas can occur when the price per barrel rises to above $25 (U.S. dollars) for an extended period of time. The trick for Middle Eastern and North African producers is to keep petroleum at a high enough price where profits can continue to fund development but not so high that it will encourage the establishment of new oil and gas production elsewhere. The cost of Middle Eastern oil is very low, some say as low as $2.00 a barrel for Saudi Arabian and Gulf oil. It is impossible for producers in the United States and Canada to compete at anything like that price. Under the best of conditions, North American producers need around $18.00 a barrel just to remain in business.

Since the bad old days of the Standard Oil monopoly at the beginning of the 20th century, the problem has been to control petroleum production in a way that will keep prices sufficiently high to ensure steady profits. Like everyone else, oil producers and distributors hate major supply disruptions because these are followed by price fluctuations in the market and calls for Western independence from foreign oil.

WHAT IS OPEC AND WHAT ARE THE POLITICS OF OIL?

In 1901, a Western adventurer, William D'Arcy, received a concession to explore for oil in Iran. At almost the same time, an Armenian, C. S. Gulbenkian, obtained a similar concession in the Ottoman Empire. Less than 50 years later, these concessions had grown into a vast oil cartel controlled by seven Western companies: Exxon, Mobil, Standard Oil of California, Texaco, Gulf, British Petroleum, and Shell. Called the Seven Sisters, these companies gained a virtual monopoly on the production, refinement, and distribution of Middle Eastern oil.

Designed to present a united front when negotiating prices with the oil companies, the Organization of Petroleum Exporting Countries (OPEC) was organized in 1960 by Iraq, Saudi Arabia, Iran, Kuwait, and Venezuela. Subsequently, OPEC membership grew to include Qatar, Libya, Indonesia, Algeria, Nigeria, Ecuador, Gabon, and the United Arab Emirates.

The OPEC cartel was only marginally effective until the October 1973 Middle East war. At that time, the sale of petroleum products became linked by the Arab members of OPEC to support for the war against Israel. The selective withholding of oil caused an energy crisis in the West. During the next decade, OPEC oil rose from a pre-1973 price of around $3.00 a barrel to over $30.00 a barrel. This oil shock was difficult for the developed world, but it destroyed the hopes of many developing states that were depending on low-cost energy to finance modernization. Ignoring 50 years of Western oil cartel exploitation,

Saudi Aramco
Located in Dhahran, the headquarters complex of Saudi Aramco administers the vast petroleum resources of Saudi Arabia.
Source: Joe Weatherby

newspapers of the time in Europe and the United States were filled with articles editorializing on the "evils" of OPEC. Today, more than 30 years after the first oil crisis in the 1970s, Western observers admit that although the economic impact of OPEC has been considerable, it is a political force in the developing world far out of proportion to its size.

In the mid-1980s, OPEC control of the petroleum market loosened. Some members failed to adhere to the cartel's price and production guidelines. This lack of discipline combined with non-OPEC production increases and Western conservation measures first began to stabilize and then to dramatically lower the world price of oil. As the price fell, states desperate to finance the high cost of development became suspicious of other states that exceeded their production quotas. The Iraqi charge that Kuwait was cheating on oil production was one of the main reasons for the August 1990 invasion.

By the late 1990s, the oil industry was in disarray. New discoveries in Central Asia, the threat of the removal of sanctions on Iraqi oil exports, and the dumping of oil products by OPEC members dropped the world price of oil by almost half. The problem for oil producers in the Middle East was to prevent the price of crude from falling further. At the present time OPEC supplies 40 percent of the world's daily petroleum needs.[14]

In an unexpected move, during the spring of 2000 the OPEC members limited production, causing a supply shortage in the West. The price of a barrel of crude rose from a low of around $10.00 a barrel only a year earlier to more than $30.00 a barrel. Although there were hardships in America and Europe, this action was not nearly as devastating as the price rises in the 1970s. Now there were other energy sources, and the West had become more fuel-efficient. This action also occurred during a period of great prosperity, and many people who consumed petroleum products could afford the price rise. Most observers expected the price of oil to eventually stabilize at around $25.00 a barrel. This price was not considered to be too high for consumers and was high enough to finance most development projects in the oil-producing states. The real uncertainty centered on the future plans of two very big players in the oil game: Iran and Iraq. Both had suffered under sanctions limiting their ability to freely sell their production. Both states were in need of capital to rebuild infrastructure and also to inject some wealth into their economies. The fear of most producers is simple. Once Iran and Iraq are free to produce, they will. They will have to go to full production in order to pay for the rebuilding of their economies. Since they have some of the world's largest petroleum reserves, their production would have a negative impact on the price worldwide. Most Middle Eastern states want to see Iran and Iraq resume production if for no other reason than that the lives of the Iranian and Iraqi people will improve. Still, the hope is that the resumption of production will stay within the guidelines set by OPEC. If not, their production could be a "fire sale" on OPEC oil that could have a negative effect on many economies in the Middle East and North Africa.

Finally, it should be remembered that the major market for oil is in the developed world. As in the days of colonialism, the developed countries will aggressively work to protect such essential resources. Political instability in the Middle East has forced the developed nations to seek alternative sources of energy. With the end of the Cold War, there are interesting possibilities for importing oil from Russia. In the short term, there may be more difficulties than advantages in utilizing Russian oil sources. But vast oil reserves exist in Siberia, and the Russians will have to sell a portion on the open market to finance their own economic development.

Little America
Looking like any neighborhood in the United States, this housing is provided for American oil workers who live in Dhahran Saudi Arabia.
Source: Joe Weatherby

The Political Conflicts Over Pipelines and Canals in the Middle East and North Africa

WHAT ARE THE CONFLICTS OVER PIPELINES IN THE NORTHERN TIER?

Since the beginning of the 1990s, the pipeline politics of the Northern Tier and Caspian regions have resembled the 19th century Great Game.[15] As early as 1889, the Russians built a 42-mile pipeline to carry petroleum over the mountains from Baku to Batum. This project was undertaken to compete for market control with the Standard Oil Company. Although only a footnote to history today, the Baku oil struggle was a part of the great power competition that spread across this region before World War I.

Since the collapse of communism, this area has again come into play as part of the United States effort to extend its influence in the areas formerly controlled by the Russians. American policy has been aimed at the dual containment and economic isolation of Iran and Iraq. At the same time, the United States has actively courted the newly independent Muslim states of the Caspian region.

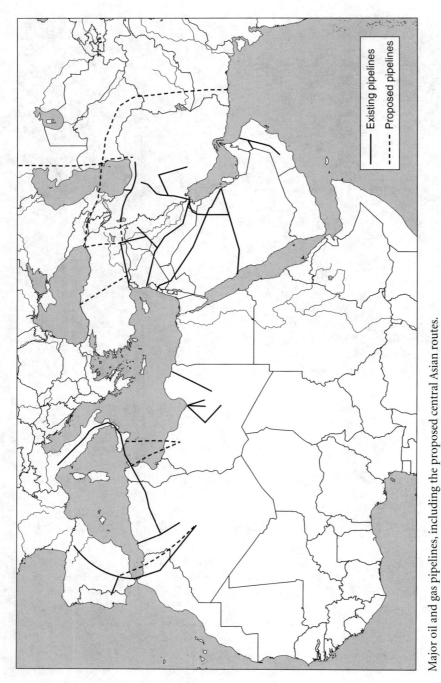

Major oil and gas pipelines, including the proposed central Asian routes.

Source: Adapted from *Middle East Patterns*, Westview Strategic Geography and the Changing Middle East, Brookings Institute *Atlas of World History*, Barnes & Noble. *Atlas of the Middle East*, Hammond. *The 21st Century World Atlas*, Millennium Edition. Trident Press International.

As part of American policy, the United States has encouraged Turkish involvement in the politics of the Caspian. The current conflict centers on the selection of a pipeline route to carry what is believed to be vast supplies of oil and gas from the Caspian to the markets in the West. The American objective has always been to further isolate Iran by supporting the building of oil and gas pipelines from the Caspian across the Caucasus region and Turkey to the Mediterranean Sea.

Most experts have opposed the American plan. They have charged that a pipeline running under the Caspian and then across the politically unstable Caucasus is both environmentally dangerous and too costly. Instead, they have advocated a shorter, less expensive route across Iran to the Persian Gulf. Much of the infrastructure for this route already exists.

The major opposition to the Iranian route is political and comes from the United States, who still prohibits American oil companies from trading with Iran. Unfortunately for American policymakers, the dual containment policy of Iran and Iraq is in the process of withering away. In the case of Iran, it is now virtually nonexistent outside the United States.

A major blow to the U.S.-Turkish pipeline plans occurred during the summer of 2000. Against the objections of Turkey and the United States, Russia and Turkmenistan signed a major gas agreement providing for Russia to buy a major portion of the region's gas production well into the future. By tying up a large portion of the Caspian's gas production, the Russians were able to threaten the plans for a Turkish pipeline. It looked like the U.S.-Turkish pipeline might be built and have no product to carry.

The Turks were also forced to reassess their relations with Russia. They would now have to get oil and gas from Russia or break the embargo and use the existing pipeline from Iraq. That move would effectively end the embargo of Iraq.

Russia's new president has engineered the formal Russian occupation of Chechnya. This move has reestablished some Russian influence in the Caspian region. They are in a position to challenge the United States from a geographic position much closer than that of the Americans. It now looks like the Russian gas deal may kill the U.S.-Turkish pipeline. There is still a good chance that a pipeline will be built from the eastern Caspian across Iran, regardless of American wishes. Finally, an energy-poor Turkey will likely have to eventually make accommodations with both Russia and Iraq.

For the United States these developments are another example of a policy that has failed to change with the times. Just as the U.S. policy for Cuban containment has been subject to worldwide criticism, so too does its containment policy in the Northern Tier lack support from the Western allies.

WHAT ARE THE PIPELINE CONFLICTS IN SAUDI ARABIA?

One of the major problems associated with Middle Eastern oil is getting this product to the consumer. Pipelines are an efficient alternative to ships for the movement of petroleum products from the Persian Gulf and Saudi Arabia to Europe. However, pipelines are vulnerable to sabotage during periods of political instability.

Saudi Arabia is located in a dangerous neighborhood. Until recently, Saudi pipelines went through third-party countries that could block oil flow in times of crisis. For example, the famous Trans Arabian Pipeline crossed from Dhahran, Saudi Arabia, skirting the border of Iraq, and passing through Jordan, Syria, and Lebanon before reaching the

Mediterranean Sea at Sidon. The vulnerability of this route should be obvious to anyone looking at a map.

On the other hand, transporting petroleum products by sea through the narrow and often hostile Straits of Hormuz at the southern end of the Persian Gulf has its own hazards. In order to reduce the danger of a downstream petroleum blockage either by land or sea, the Saudis built an alternate, totally Saudi Arabian pipeline. Completed in 1981, the Dhahran-Yanbu Pipeline allows petroleum products to be safely moved from the oil and gas fields of the east to the Red Sea.

The Kuwaitis constructed a spur that joins the Dhahran-Yanbu Pipeline. This addition was opened in 1989. These two lines have reduced some of the dangers of relying on pipelines to move oil out of Arabia. Until the political situation in the Middle East changes, the potential for moving most petroleum products by pipeline elsewhere will remain an unfulfilled dream.

WHAT ARE THE PIPELINE CONFLICTS IN ALGERIA?

In North Africa, political stability also remains the major threat to the success of pipelines. Thus far, the parties to local conflicts have failed to seriously disrupt oil production. Because no government can survive in Algeria without the income generated by petroleum, the oil sector has been generally free from serious attack by all parties. However, there have been a few hostile actions. In 1997 and 1998, the flow of gas through several pipelines was briefly disrupted by bombings. To protect these assets, the Algerian government created exclusion zones in the oil fields. These areas are now protected by Algerian forces backed up by foreign security agents hired by the oil companies. This combination has provided a stability not found in the more populated areas of the country.

At the present time, two large pipelines export petroleum products to Europe from Algeria. The Trans Med Line was Algeria's first pipeline to Europe. It runs from Algeria via Tunisia to Italy. Built to export gas, this line has been operational since early 1980. As previously stated, militants targeted it in 1998. As a protection against new disruptions by terrorists, enough gas to supply customers for several months has been stockpiled. The flow of gas was only briefly disrupted by the bombings. This line is in the process of having its capacity expanded. The Maghreb-Europe Gas Line has been in operation since 1997. This gas line runs across Morocco to Spain and then further into Europe through Spanish facilities.

British Petroleum Amoco, Algerian Sonatrach, and Spanish SEPSA agreed to a year 2000 feasibility study for the construction of an additional pipeline for Europe. This pipeline will also go from Algeria across Spain into the heart of Europe. If constructed, this project could send more natural gas to Spain and the European states further north. It is hoped that this pipeline will be a great boost to the Algerian economy.

WHAT ARE THE POLITICAL CONFLICTS OVER THE SUEZ CANAL?

The Suez Canal, including the Great Bitter Lake and Lake Timsah, is 101 miles long. It serves as the only direct sea passage from the Mediterranean to the Red Sea and the Indian Ocean. Much of the history of the modern Middle East has involved struggles for the control of this strategic waterway.

Although they initially opposed its construction, the British proved to be the main beneficiaries of the Suez Canal's existence. Authors Efraim and Inari Kirsh point out that the canal's new short route to Asia quickly became the major imperial lifeline to India.[16]

During World War I the Ottomans made several unsuccessful attempts to capture the Canal. It was only the British victory at El Alamein that prevented a German march on the Suez Canal during World War II. The Canal was fought over by Egyptians and Israelis in 1956, 1967, and 1973. Today, it still remains one of the most important chokepoints in the Middle East.

Although the Canal is at sea level and requires no complicated and easily sabotaged system of locks, its location near unstable, hostile neighbors makes access uncertain during times of trouble. Sinking ships in the channel closed the Canal during the Middle East wars of 1956, 1967, and 1973. In 1984 an unknown terrorist organization successfully mined parts of the Canal as well as the Red Sea, effectively preventing its use until the mines could be cleared. There is always a danger that the Canal could be blocked again during a time of international crisis.

Because the Suez Canal is almost 150 years old, its size is inadequate for the passage of large ships. Many supertankers can transit this passage when empty but must go around southern Africa when they are fully loaded. As it exists today, the Suez Canal can support shipping that draws no more than 56 feet.[17]

The Egyptian government is planning to widen and deepen the Canal. When this project is completed, the newly refurbished Suez Canal is expected to allow for the passage of more than 90 percent of the world's existing commercial ships. Since the Canal is one of Egypt's major foreign currency earners, the added versatility of the Canal should be of great economic value.

Religious Fundamentalism in the Middle East and North Africa

Author Michael Arditti takes a global fundamentalism approach by stating that,

> The rise of fundamentalism is the greatest danger facing the contemporary world, whether it is from Muslims in Tehran, Jews in the Occupied Territories, Siks in Amritsar, or Christians in America, such as Roman Catholics who firebomb abortion clinics or Protestants who pick the funeral of the gay murder victim, Matthew Shepherd.[18]

Before looking at Islamic fundamentalism, several questions What constitutes religious fundamentalism? Are there univ emergence of fundamentalist movements? Is there a m transcends specific religions?

It is probably more accurate to refer *lamists* rather than reusing the Christian *mentalist* is the term popularly used in the

WHAT IS THE MEANING OF *FUNDAME*

Fundamentalism is a word that was first used Christianity that developed during the early year the modernism and secularism that characterized ists sought to turn believers away from the secular l Bible both in matters of faith and as a literal historica

More recently, the term *fundamentalist* has also been applied to both Muslims and Jews who oppose the growth of Western secularism. Jewish and Muslim fundamentalists believe that the compromises that Western life forces on people have corrupted their respective religions.

WHAT ARE COMMON CONCERNS OF THE FUNDAMENTALISTS?

Although there is no monolithic world fundamentalist movement, there are some common fears that are manifested by most fundamentalists. First and foremost, they fear that the impact of modern science and secularism leads to dangerous marginalization of religion. This causes fundamentalists of all religions to be suspicious of many principles now accepted in modern societies. Sayyid Quth, a leading Islamic fundamentalist executed in Egypt in 1966, is quoted by the *Independent* newspaper as having stated the following:

> Humanity today is living in a huge brothel! One has only to glance at its press, films, fashion shows, beauty contests, ballrooms, wine bars, and broadcasting stations! Or observe its mad lust for naked flesh, provocative posters, and sick, suggestive statements in literature, the arts, and the mass media! And add to this, the system of usury which fuels men's voracity for money and endangers vile methods for its accumulation and investment.[20]

WHAT IS ISLAMIC FUNDAMENTALISM?

In the Middle East and North Africa, Islamic fundamentalist movements are politically significant because there is no separation of mosque and state. Here, Philip Hiro takes the broad position that a fundamentalist state is a Muslim-majority state that has its legislation based on Islamic law (Shariah). Using this standard, he believes that there may be as many as a dozen out of the 49 Muslim-majority states that could be described as fundamentalists.[21]

Foreign observers tend to call any Islamic group that opposes Western policy fundamentalist. The political reality of fundamentalism is much more complex than that. There have always been conservative Islamic movements that have exercised influence on Muslim society. Focus should be placed on the subgroup of politico-religious movements that have emerged within the past 25 years. Because of the Iranian Revolution's impact on the West, foreign observers see an Iranian behind every other movement so it is easy to simply treat them as part of a monolithic whole.

The politico-religious movements that have risen to challenge the discredited secular nationalist states of the region have been capitalizing on the social disruption and unhappiness of people caught up in the transition from traditional to new societies. Advocates of political Islam offer a purity and hope not found in the discredited political institutions that presently exist.

While similar conditions leading to this unrest may exist in many places, they are not the same. The politico-religious movements may have similar appearances, but they have emerged out of different situations. They are locally based and have not successfully expanded across borders to form a common movement. In fact, political Islam has successfully reversed only a handful of secular governments. Iran is the most notable, and even in the thrust of political Islam is being softened. It would seem that the impact of political Islam as a subgroup of Islamic fundamentalism is likely to be more of an "influence of Middle Eastern governments rather than an instrument to topple them in favor of a new system. Already, secular nationalist states like Egypt are moving to adopt some of the programs advocated by these groups. Could it be that, like so often happens with pressure groups in the West, political Islam's substance will eventually be absorbed into the Islamic political mainstream?

Certain myths concerning Islamic fundamentalism should be dispelled at this point. First, all Muslims are not fundamentalists. Second, all fundamentalists do not want to engage in violence. Finally, those fundamentalists who do engage in violence are a tiny percentage of the Muslims who live in the Middle East and North Africa. To repeat, it is a mistake to engage in the popular Western practice of labeling every Muslim who disagrees with Western policy as a fundamentalist. To use the word *fundamentalist* as a pejorative one is to prejudge the specific events occurring in the region without looking at the facts.

WHAT IS THE IMPACT OF ISLAMIC FUNDAMENTALISM?

The Muslim world is certainly more religious and conservative than it was 25 years ago. It may be that large parts of the Middle East and North Africa are coming of age politically. They are confident enough to accept the benefits of modernization without surrendering their own cultural traditions.

HOW DOES ISLAMIC FUNDAMENTALISM RELATE TO THE WEST?

How should the West deal with Islamic fundamentalist movements in the Middle East and North Africa? First, Western policymakers should deal with each situation on its own merits. It should be understood that an Islamic religious rebirth is taking place throughout large portions of the region. That does not necessarily mean, however, that the region will explode in chaos. Care should be taken to look at the situation with a view to the future. It may be wise to avoid the lure of a short-term policy victory, which will result in long-term hostility. This has most certainly happened with Iraq where most Muslims deeply resent the American blockade policy there. To them, this is just another form of Western imperialism. It is Muslim dissatisfaction and frustration over events like this that breed radical movements there and elsewhere in the region.

WHAT ARE SOME EXAMPLES OF POLITICO-ISLAMIC MOVEMENTS?

It cannot be denied that Islamic splinter groups exist in almost every state in the region and are actively engaged in activities that would be considered to be destabilizing forces. Many of these organizations believe that modern Islam has been corrupted. They work for a religion divorced from the compromises of Western secularism. They often see the United States and Israel as visible symbols of that corruption. Some of the best known of these include the following:

Hamas Born in Jerusalem, Gaza, and the West Bank, Hamas was established to drive Israel out of the occupied territories. Ironically, Hamas is believed to have received early support from Israel, whose leaders hoped to use it as a counterbalance to the secular-oriented Palestinian Liberation Organization. An example of an indigenous Islamic movement, Hamas gained a place of prominence in the West Bank because the PLO was largely an exile group. Furthermore, Hamas earned local support because it opposed the

Israeli occupation from a position in the West Bank and Gaza. Hamas was also active in the founding of Islamic charities, schools, and hospitals in the occupied territories.

Hizbollah Meaning "the party of Allah," Hizbollah is a political-religious movement that emerged from the Shiite resistance to the 1982 Israeli invasion of Lebanon. The long Israeli occupation of the Shiite territories in southern Lebanon caused the opposition to support Hizbollah. Over the years of occupation, Hizbollah became a very powerful opposition movement. Now that Israeli forces have been withdrawn, it remains to be seen if Hizbollah will retain its former influence in southern Lebanon.

Islamic Jihad Islamic Jihad is another Shiite movement that came to prominence because of the 1982 invasion of Lebanon. It has been accused of the April 1983 terrorist bombing of the American Embassy in west Beirut. In that attack, 63 people were killed. The Islamic Jihad also is credited with forcing the U.S. military to withdraw from Lebanon when it bombed the U.S. Marine barracks in October 1983, killing 241 troops. It is believed to be responsible for the kidnapping of a number of foreigners during the 1980s.

A splinter movement was active in the West Bank during the Palestinian "intifada" of the 1980s. It has opposed the peace agreements between Israel and the Palestinians by attacking targets in Israel. In recent years, the Palestinian Authority has taken steps to control the activities of the Palestinian Islamic Jihad.

Al Jihad al Islami The Egyptian Islamic organization was the fundamentalist group that was responsible for the assassination of President Anwar Sadat. This organization believed that the secular policies of the Egyptian leadership made them traitors to Islam. They hoped that the assassination of Sadat would lead to an Islamic revolution in Egypt. In this effort to provoke a revolt, they failed.

With the end of the war in Afghanistan, large numbers of veterans of that conflict have returned to Egypt. Some of these "fighters" have been attracted by this organization.

The Muslim Brotherhood in Egypt, Jordan, Palestine, Saudi Arabia, and Syria
By no means a monolithic organization, factions of the Muslim Brothers have been active in parts of the Middle East since their beginnings in the British-occupied Egypt of the 1920s. At times, the Muslim Brothers have had a great deal of power and influence in Egypt. However, the Brotherhood was suppressed there during most of the last half of the 20th century. The Muslim Brotherhoods throughout the Middle East are largely the result of that suppression in Egypt, which forced the Brothers to go into exile.

In Jordan, the Brotherhood has matured to the point that it has become an active participant in policies there. Because the Muslim Brothers were first suppressed by Egyptian President Nasser and because Nasser also opposed the Jordanian government, Jordanians welcomed the organization to their territory.

One Final Thought Islamic fundamentalism is not a nationalist movement. However, it does spring from some of the same frustrations that led to the growth of nationalist movements in the Middle East and North Africa. Unlike those movements and the Western imports of democracy, communism, and socialism, Islamic fundamentalism remains untainted by the impression of corruption and failure. As a movement to purify Islam, fundamentalism is a potent force in the region. Many people in the region have become frustrated with the failures of the past. They see fundamentalist movements with their social programs as filling a need not met by the corruption of the secular state. To them, fundamentalism is Islamic. It is an effective challenge to the discredited values from the West.

The Conflict Over Islamic Fundamentalism in Algeria

WHAT IS THE ALGERIAN DISPUTE?

The rise of Islamic fundamentalism and its accompanying violence have attracted the attention of the West. With the precedent of the Islamic Revolution in Iran in mind, Western observers have raised the specter of a fundamentalist victory in Algeria resulting in the creation of a militant anti-Western Maghreb. This in turn would cause southern Europe to be flooded by North African immigrants fleeing the region.

How did the conflict in Algeria develop? When Algeria won a hard-fought war for independence from France in 1962, a secular nationalist party called the Front de Liberation Nationale, or FLN, emerged to lead the newly independent Algeria. The first president was a French-educated revolutionary named Ahmed ben Bella. After holding office for only three years, he was overthrown by a military leader, Colonel Hovari Boumediede. Boumediede and his successor, Colonel Chadli Benjedid, held a tight grip on power until the early 1990s. During this period, European-trained military and security people ran Algeria as a largely secular but officially Muslim state. Like many other Arab states of the time, they developed a foreign policy that was tilted toward the Soviet Union. They were anti-Israeli and because of that they also usually opposed the United States.

In 1990, an opposition movement stressing fundamental Islamic values emerged to oppose the secularism of the past. The new party, Islamic Salvation Front, or FIS, defeated the FLN in local elections. Favored to win the 1992 parliamentary elections, the FIS saw "defeat snatched from victory" when the secular nationalist government cancelled the elections. Shortly afterward, the FIS was banned as a political party. This action provoked the beginning of violence that was to cause a virtual civil war that has gone on for almost a decade.

Although they had sought to take power democratically, the secularists charged the FIS with telling the Muslim voters that to vote against the religious parties was to vote against God. The secular nationalists used this as the excuse to cancel the elections and to ban the Islamic Salvation Front.

Since 1992, at least 75,000 Algerians have been killed in the conflict between religious and secular groups. In the West the leaders of the democracies have been placed in the uncomfortable position of supporting the secular authorities against the popular Islamic majority. Fearful of an Islamic "firestorm" in North Africa if the Muslim fundamentalists were to win, the West has allied with what was clearly a nondemocratic oligarchy made up of the military and security services desperately trying to hold on to power.

After years of fighting, the army drafted a former diplomat to serve as president. Abdelaziz Bouteflika, a respected Algerian, quickly moved to neutralize the conflict. He did this by offering a general amnesty to those Muslim fighters opposed to the government if they would lay down their arms and return to society. To the surprise of many, the largest opposition group accepted the offer. This action resulted in a dramatic reduction in violence. The question of what the amnesty has gained and lost for Algerians remains unanswered.

The problem is that the past is not forgotten by either side. The Islamic Salvation Front is still outlawed and the Secular Nationalists in the army and security forces are still in control. President Bouteflika is largely a figurehead. What is more important, thousands of "disappeared" on both sides are still unaccounted for. The major violence may have slackened, but the anger has not. Although the largest opposition group has ended the fight, other forces opposed to the secularists continue the violence on a small scale.

WHAT HAS BEEN THE WESTERN RESPONSE?

Why have the democratic powers, including the United States and the other members of NATO, remained passive in the face of decades of antidemocratic rule by the secular nationalists of Algeria? The answer is clear: Western leaders fear Islamic fundamentalism taking hold in North Africa in the same way that it expanded in Iran. In defense of their actions, Westerners often cite the prediction made by the political scientist, Samuel Huntington, who warned that future conflicts in the world would not be over economics or ideology but would be cultural disputes like the current one in Algeria.[22]

Western leaders believe that they must support the secular nationalists in Algeria. They fear that an Islamic fundamentalist victory in Algeria will destabilize friends of the West, not only in Algeria, but also in Morocco, Tunisia, and Egypt. They envision the horror of a militant threat emerging in North Africa and perhaps the Balkans that will be linked by the "spirit of the Iranian revolution."

Regardless of the final outcome of the civil struggle in Algeria, what lessons can the West learn from this sad event? First, to side with injustice to achieve an expedient end as the West did in Algeria only strengthens the opposition forces. Second, if situations like the one in Algeria are to be handled effectively, the West must recognize that Islam, even fundamentalist Islam, is no more monolithic than is Christianity. The Islamic fundamentalist movements in Iran, the West Bank, Egypt, Libya, and Algeria all spring from different root causes and grievances. They have little in common except broad general principles. They all support the idea of separate, special roles for men and women, oppose secular nationalism that they believe was imported from the West, reject Western cultural imperialism, and generally advocate a form of economic populism that aids the poor through Islamic institutions. There is little or no common political agenda that crosses state boundaries. To repeat, it is a mistake for the West to assume that every Muslim or even every fundamentalist Muslim is trying to start another Iranian revolution.

Western leaders should stick to the principles that they believe in regardless of who wins an election in the region. To do otherwise is to confirm the charge that "Western democracy was never for export when either money or politics was involved." To sacrifice support for the values of freedom and democracy to achieve a short-term political goal will ultimately work against Western interests. In the case of Algeria, the support of the anti-democratic secular nationalist government has resulted in an increased popular support for the Islamic militants. While the current rulers in Algeria stay in power with the support of the military, their legitimacy quietly slips away. Again, the West is in danger of being caught backing the wrong side in the long-term struggle for the support of the Algerian people.

The Changing Role of Women in the Middle East and North Africa

The role of women, like that of men, is rapidly changing throughout most of the developing world, including the Middle East and North Africa. Given the complexities of economic, political, and social role changes, however, these transformations occur in different ways and at different rates. That is certainly the case for women in the Middle East and North Africa. Furthermore, the changing roles for women here do not necessarily mean that women are becoming more Western. In some places, like in Turkey, that popular Western assumption may be true. Elsewhere women may seek to become "computer literate" while still retaining their traditional customs and values.

To understand the changing roles of women in this part of the world, it is important to approach this subject from a value-neutral position. This is difficult to do because since the 19th-century days of "colonialism," Westerners have been conditioned to believe that Western culture, including the status of women, is superior to cultures elsewhere. This cultural imperialism makes it difficult for Westerners to understand what is going on in the Middle East and North Africa. Because women in many parts of the region dress in exotic clothing, that alone is proof to many Western observers that little change has occurred in recent years.

In the first place, it should be remembered that Judaism, Christianity, and Islam were founded as patriarchal religions in what were patriarchal societies. Elements of those traditions still have a strong presence in both Judaism and Christianity. In Western society the practice of male dominance in both the family and the public world existed until the late 19th century. The following examples are offered to show typical Western views of the proper role for women at that time.

Concerning the idea that women could become physicians, the British Medical Journal, *Lancet,* is quoted by Christopher Hibbert as saying,

> The good sense of the sex will no more permanently tolerate the unseemly invasion of an unsuitable province of labor than women, as a class, will ultimately show themselves fitted for the discharge of the duties they have rashly and, as we believe, indecorously undertaken.[23]

Concerning voting and participation in politics, Hibbert quotes Queen Victoria as referring to the "mad, wicked folly of Women's Rights" and the "sense of womanly feeling and propriety."[24]

In the late 19th century, many women in the Middle East and North Africa probably had more legal and religious rights concerning divorce, marriage, and inheritance than their Western counterparts. In the West, divorce was almost impossible. The British required an act of parliament to divorce during the first half of the 19th century. In many places, Western women are still not guaranteed an inheritance from their husbands. Prenuptial agreements are still unusual in Western marriages. All of these traditions, plus dowries held separate from a husband's wealth, have been part of Muslim law and tradition since the founding of Islam.

IS THE WESTERN VIEW OF MUSLIM WOMEN DISTORTED?

The image that Westerners have of Middle Eastern women is stereotypical. It is based on centuries of misunderstanding compounded by distrust created through political conflicts that have placed Westerners in opposition to actions taken by the Arab world. The result is a constant barrage of misinformation that presents Muslim women in a negative way.

To be fair, women in both the developed and developing worlds have faced difficult struggles to gain a presence outside of the home. It can be said that World Wars I and II emancipated American women. For them, social change occurred only because the United States was locked in desperate struggles for survival. Women were needed for work outside of the home as an essential part of the war effort. Their arrival in the work force was due less to the generosity of men than to the necessities of war. This upward change in the economic status of women led to their expectation of participation in other areas as well, including education and politics.

It is impossible to generalize about the status of 100 million women living in the Middle East and North Africa. Each state and society has different customs and needs. The status of women is changing in Arab states as varied as Egypt and Qatar. In Egypt, schools are being built to meet the special needs of rural women who have been denied an education because of their sex. At the same time, the Emirate of Qatar has granted women the right to vote and to hold public office.

IS POLYGAMY COMMON?

Probably the most controversial aspect of Muslim marriage is polygamy. It is true that the Koran allows men to engage in plural marriage with up to four wives. What is often ignored by Western observers is that polygamy was common throughout the ancient world. In many of these early cultures, men may have had dozens of wives and concubines. The Muslim view was, at the time, considered to be a limit on plural marriage. First, it limited the number of wives that a man could have. Then, it required that a husband treat his wives equally. To many Muslims, that is impossible and therefore was a prohibition to most plural marriages. Although it is difficult to document, today most marriages in the Middle East and North Africa are not polygamous. Finally, Muslims point to the high divorce and remarriage rates in the West as simply polygamy in another form.

IS THERE GENDER EQUALITY?

What should be stressed concerning the gender roles in Islam is that God considers men and women to be equal. Men and women perform different primary functions to protect the family. Each is equally meritorious.

The Koran makes gender equality perfectly clear:

> For believing men and women,
> For devout men and women,
> For true men and women,
> For men and women who are
> Patient and constant, for men
> And women, who humble themselves,
> For men and women who give
> In charity, for men and women
> Who fast (and deny themselves),
> For men and women who
> Guard their chastity, and
> For men and women who
> Engage much in God's praise

For them has God prepared
Forgiveness and Great reward.[25]

It is certainly true that, as in all religions, the differences between theory and practice may vary greatly. Although Islam sought to replace the primacy of tribal custom with a more gender-equitable religious law, the rights that women exercise in practice will vary from place to place. This kind of patriarchal dominance is common in many parts of the world and is certainly not limited to the Muslims. The following short study is offered as an example of how the role of women is changing in one of the most traditional societies in the Muslim world.

WHAT IS THE CHANGING ROLE FOR SAUDI ARABIAN WOMEN?

The case of Saudi Arabia can be singled out as an interesting model for change within the intensely conservative context of the Arabian Peninsula. Saudi Arabia is a traditional Muslim state that is in the process of modernizing while at the same time attempting to avoid the negative pitfalls common in Western society. To maintain traditional cultural values while becoming an economically advanced society presents interesting questions as to the role that women should play in this effort. Saudi Arabia may offer an alternative for women caught up in the wrenching changes that are experienced when a traditional society attempts to become technologically advanced.

At the present time, Saudi Arabia has several problems resulting from the great amount of wealth being injected into the economy through the petroleum industry. First, it is a society accustomed to a nomadic life of hardship and need that is rapidly becoming urban and relatively wealthy. Second, wealth and expansion have created a shortage of skilled labor while at the same time allowing Saudi males to treat certain kinds of jobs with disdain. Third, improved medical care has indirectly caused a population explosion. Fourth, an improved educational system has raised expectations in the population. Fifth, the Saudi Kingdom's oil wealth has allowed the society to develop expensive duplicate educational, business, and social services for men and women. Finally, these changes have occurred in the most religiously conservative area of the Middle East.

Rapid change has upset many traditional ideas that could eventually threaten the social stability of the Kingdom. Many labor needs are being met by the importation of foreign workers. In 1998, almost one-third of the Saudi work force was foreign. Foreigners bring new ideas and traditions. Guest workers often become the source of the Kingdom's social problems. Although the Kingdom has actively encouraged the Saudization of labor, many Saudi males still refuse to take lower-level jobs traditionally done by guest workers.

The expenses of financing the Gulf War and post-war Saudi defense programs have combined with the volatility of oil prices to serve as an alert that the "oil party" will come to an end someday. There has been an increasing realization by many in the Kingdom that, like elsewhere in the developed world, both husband and wife may have to enter the work force if the family is to maintain a decent standard of living. Educated women may be needed to take jobs that have become vacant through Saudization.

This is not to say that Saudi women wish to become Western women; rather, they have a strong commitment to their responsibilities within the home and expect men to be the primary providers. Simply put, when women are needed to become a significant part of the employment pool in appropriate fields such as education, computer science, government service, and medicine, many may opt to bring additional income to the family. In

1998, Crown Prince Abdullah Ibn Abdul Aziz anticipated this future need when, laying the foundation stone of a new girls college, he said,

> Our daughters will learn useful subjects and develop their skills and abilities in line with the teachings and sayings of the Prophet Muhammad and our Islamic customs and traditions in an atmosphere of modesty and dignity.[26]

Since 1998, one-fourth of the Kingdom's budget has been allocated to education. There are 123,000 students presently studying in 68 women's colleges belonging to seven universities. In 1996, 13,700 young women graduated from Saudi universities. In 1998, over 5,000 female teachers held advanced degrees.

ARE THERE MOVEMENTS FOR CHANGE?

Everyone recognizes that Muslims and Westerners share very different cultural and family values. What might be misunderstood by Westerners is that Muslims within the Middle East and in North Africa also have different cultural traditions and values. There are places where women dress and work in much the same way as their Western sisters. There are other places where women are comfortable and fulfilled in their traditional roles as wife, mother, and homemaker. Finally, there are places where these traditional positions are beginning the painful process of change. Anyone familiar with the rise of the women's voting struggle, the women's political movement, and the controversies concerning the inclusion of women as part of the American Affirmative Action Program can surely empathize with the difficulties that change in gender roles brings to any society. Still, change will occur. Already in some Persian Gulf States the enrollment of women in schools and colleges rivals that of men. Even in states where women do not yet have the right to vote, like Kuwait, the Emirate has a female ambassador and women now outnumber men in their schools. Get ready, change is on the way. It will never mirror the way that the women's movement has developed in the West, but, within the cultural context of the region, change is inevitable.

The Impact of New Young Leaders on the Policies of the Middle East and North Africa

There is a British tradition that playing a game by the rules is more important than winning. Translated into political terms, this means that preserving the democratic system is more important than who is the winner of an election. In a democracy, citizens understand that even though their candidate may lose an election there will be another chance to win when the next election occurs. It is the expectation that there will be another election that deemphasizes the results of the current one. The fact that everyone knows that they will have another chance causes them to peacefully accept the results of a vote that they may not like. This is true for all true democracies including those with "rough and tumble" politics such as in Israel. Unfortunately, excepting Israel, the other states of the Middle East and North Africa are either weak democracies or no democracies at all. In the weak democracies, voters have no assurance that another election will occur. That makes the winning more important than preserving the system.

Most of the states of the region are not democratic. They are governed by traditional leaders who achieved powers outside the democratic process. Because they have failed to rely on the ballot box, they often maintain power through the creation of a "cult of personality." Because these rulers actually govern, their personal traits become extremely important when attempting to analyze policy.

During the past several years, young rulers have replaced their long-lived fathers in five of these traditionally ruled Middle Eastern and North African states: Morocco, Jordan, Syria, Bahrain, and Qatar. All but Qatar had a leadership change on the death of the father. In the case of Qatar, dissatisfaction with the slow pace of development caused Qatari elites to support the removal of the old Emir in 1995. He was replaced by his son, Hamad al-Thani. The other young leaders are Bashar Al-Asad in Syria, King Muhammad VI in Morocco, King Abdullah in Jordan, and Sheikh Hamad Ben Essa Al-Khalifa of Bahrain. All of these young leaders are sophisticated, well-traveled representatives of a new generation of Arab rulers.

There is no doubt that each of the five present different styles of leadership from that of their fathers. These young men are all products of the postcolonial world. They did not experience the humiliation of Israeli military victories, they were too young to take part in the Cold War, and in some cases they did not expect to take power at all.

In other parts of the region, there are the prospects of further changes. Yasser Arafat is in poor health. It is only a question of time before a new Palestinian leader will be selected. In Iraq, Saddam Hussein's son, Uday, is considered to be his likely successor. Even Libya's Mummar Qaddafi is grooming his son, Seial-Islam, for power. Leaders of long standing still remain in Egypt, Kuwait, and Saudi Arabia.

It may be that this new generation of leaders will not be tied to the old policies and positions of their fathers. The new battles may be over modernization and economics rather than the conflicts of the past. Most observers recognize that the states of the Middle East and North Africa must change structurally or be left as a political and economic backwater. The central problem remains that none of these new rulers has come to power by popular election as it is known in the West. All are the products of the authoritarian systems of the past. However, there appears to be widespread traditional support for most of these leaders. The question remains, can change occur without these new leaders repudiating the very oligarchies that elevated them to power?

Assuming that they wish to accomplish changes, these leaders will have to do it within the framework that currently exists. First, they are in power because of who their fathers were. They are there because the elites who profited from the past placed them there. The people had almost no role in their assumption of power. Except for their ages, these new leaders have very little in common. Each will have to deal with change in his own way.

On the positive side, all five leaders recognize the need to bring their states into the modern world economically. While they may move at different paces politically, they will support changes that their fathers could not. Their success or failure in overcoming the structural obstacles to reform will serve as models for other states soon to undergo changes of leadership.

Surprisingly, the leadership of Qatar has been the most flexible in moving to change the lack of inertia in the past. Even though the Qataris are some of the most conservative Muslims in the world, the new Emir has actively pushed Qatar in Gulf policies. Internally, women now participate in policies and actually outnumber men attending secondary schools and at the university. The Emir of Qatar has been able, through innovative approaches, to expand his state's influence far out of proportion to its size and power.

Although it is still much too early to evaluate the proclivity for change in the other leaderships, it is possible to assess their prospects. Jordan's new king would tend to be a reformer. His country's economic and military weaknesses may restrict his actions. He will need to be careful until he is believed capable of filling his father's shoes.

In Syria, the new leader was educated as an eye surgeon. He would not be in power were it not for his bigger-than-life father, Hafez al-Assad. On the other hand, Bashar al-Assad has not inherited the enmity of the majority Sunni Muslims that his Alawite Muslim father had. It is just possible that this new leader will be able to unify Syrian Muslim factions. A success like that will enable Syria to go a long way toward realizing its potential.

In Morocco, the new king has indicated that he would like to move the state into a real democracy. To do this he must solve Morocco's numerous border problems. Internally, he will have to overcome substantial conservative opposition to his reforms. Recently thousands demonstrated against his proposals to liberalize the social rights of Moroccan women.

The new Emir of Bahrain succeeded to power on the sudden death of his father on March 6, 1999. Ruler for 38 years, the late Emir left Bahrain an economically advanced but politically backward state. There were no elections or political parties. The National Assembly had not been permitted to meet for most of the old Emir's tenure in power.

Educated in the United Kingdom, the new Emir has had a great deal of experience living in the West. As a military man, he has completed officer-training programs in the United Kingdom and the United States. He is also an accomplished helicopter pilot. Will the new Emir follow the reformist course set by neighboring Qatar or will he continue the traditional personal rule of his father? It is too early to tell the Emir's intent on the issue of political reform. It is clear, however, that the Emir of Bahrain plans to continue along the path of economic modernization. Bahrain plans to continue with efforts to replace Lebanon as the banking and financial capital of the region.

All five young leaders are different. Although they have different goals, they represent the prospect for major changes in the politics of the Middle East and North Africa. Collectively, they are a far more important force for change than each is individually. They have an opportunity to make a real difference in resolving some of the problems that have troubled the Middle East and North Africa for more than 50 years.

The New "Great Game" in Central Asia

As previously mentioned, the great game of the 19th and early 20th centuries was played by Britain to keep the other great powers from developing positions of influence in Central Asia that could threaten British India.

The collapse of the Soviet Union resulted in the emergence of six Muslim states in the Caspian region. Now independent for ten years, the states of Azerbaijan, Turkmenistan, Kazakhstan, Uzbekistan, Kyrgyzstan, and Tajikistan have a combined population of 50 million Muslims. Unlike Slavic Russia, which has cultural connections with Europe, these states look to the Muslim south and west for cultural identity.

Initially, both Turkey and Iran vied for influence with these new states. Since most are Turkic speaking, Turkey had an advantage. Only in Iranian Azerbaijan were there ties to the north. In this area, former Soviet Azerbaijan and Iranian Azerbaijan were separated by an artificial boundary. Only in this region was Shiism practiced. Iran was clearly at a disadvantage elsewhere.

The situation has changed dramatically since vast reserves of oil and gas were discovered. If the experts are to be believed, the Caspian region could contain the world's third largest petroleum reserves, behind the Persian Gulf and Siberia.

The frenzy set off by oil's heady expectations threatened to turn the Caspian into a new "wild west." The competition for oil presented problems for the great powers not unlike those of the earlier 19th-century "great power game."

First there were the oil companies and then the United States, Russia, and Iran all vying for influence in their own ways. The United States sent the heads of its security agencies and state department to the region offering help against "Islamic fundamentalists." Russia offered help to fight terrorism. Even Israel expressed some interest in responding to Uzbekistan's request for aid in fighting Islamic terror. There was a great deal of suspicion that both Afghanistan and Iran were attempting to infiltrate Muslim militants into the region to destabilize the situation. In a predictable reaction, the United States quickly rushed to back any leader who cried out the dreaded words that Muslim fundamentalists were threatening his grip on power.

Before becoming too involved in another adventure to seek out and confront suspected Muslim militants, the United States should be careful to avoid making the matter worse. Just because the Soviet Union is gone, it does not follow that the successors are friends of democracy. Most of the leadership is from the same cadres of communists who ruled in brutal secular dictatorships. They exercise an oppressive rule over populations that are overwhelmingly Muslim. These leaders know that the easiest way to get Western support is to raise the specter of Iranian and Afghani Muslim fundamentalism. This is not to say that these revolutionary states do not present a threat. But the West should understand that the new "great game" is a very complicated one. If the West is to avoid the difficulties that were encountered in Iran, a long-term view of this region must be taken. The short-term goal of "making a deal with the devil" to get the oil will not work. If the West is to play the great game for the long term it should recognize by now that placing its hopes on the survival of a few "Third World" dictators is an unsustainable policy. In a dispatch about Azerbaijan, Marcel Theroux has raised fears that could echo through every state in the region. He writes that the future could be one of turmoil. He warns about what could happen when the current dictator of Azerbaijan goes. Speaking of this future, Theroux refers pessimistically to the foreign oilmen's hangout in Baku called Fisherman's Wharf. He states,

> What all of this will mean for the foreign oil interests is still unclear. But if I were at Fisherman's Wharf, I'd think about having that burger to go.[27]

If the United States is to avoid the forced fast exit similar to the one it experienced in Iran, it should be more sensitive to the cultural and religious realities of the region. Specifically, Americans should realize that to play the new "great game" will require sophistication. The dictators who are currently in power are not likely to last; history is against them. The Muslim population is there to stay. They are the ones who will determine their own future. If Americans truly believe in democracy, that is exactly how it should be. This does not mean that the United States and the other democracies should not encourage a positive integration of these states into a greater Muslim Middle East oriented toward the West. In 2000, the forward-thinking Emir of Qatar took steps to involve Turkmenistan,

Uzbekistan, Tajikistan, and Kyrgyzstan in the Ninth Summit of the Organization of the Islamic Conference. It is actions such as this that could go far in making the path from a Soviet system to an Islamic one, representing the views of the Muslim majority, peaceful.

By easing the transition of the six Muslim states of the Caspian region and Central Asia into a peaceful Muslim Middle East, the United States could participate in the new great game in a positive way. The prospect of the creation of a stable, prosperous region will make the current disputes unimportant.

The Muslim Rich Get Richer While the Muslim Poor Are Left in the Dust

There is a popular saying that where there are Muslims, there is oil. Perhaps a more accurate statement would be that Muslim oil is located away from the places where most Muslims live.

Clearly, petroleum products are the great natural resources of the region. The Persian Gulf States provide significant amounts of the oil needed by Europe, Japan, and the United States. What is perhaps more important is the realization that the oil states of the Middle East and North Africa control more than 60 percent of the world's proved oil reserves and 25 percent of the reserves of natural gas.

The problem of Muslim oil is geography. The population centers of the Muslim Middle East are far away from the sources of petroleum. The result of this is a Middle East with some of the richest states on earth. At the same time, the region as a whole has a per capita income that is probably less than $2,000 a year. Millions of people live in poverty without adequate water, shelter, or medical care. At the same time that upscale Western companies like Armani, Channel, and Calvin Klein are catering to the local rich in the Persian Gulf, people in the population centers of Cairo and Damascus have a hard time providing basics for their families.

The question asked by many is, if Muslims are truly "brothers," should not this wealth be used to benefit the many rather than the few? Is the wealth of the Gulf States a cause of shame to both Muslim and Arab society? During his 1990 invasion of Kuwait, Iraqi President Saddam Hussein used economic inequality as one justification for his actions:

> The malicious Westerners intentionally multiplied the number of countries with the result that the Arab Nation could not achieve the integration needed to realize its full capability. When fragmenting the Arab homeland, they intentionally distanced the majority of the population and areas of cultural depth from riches and their sources.[28]

This call certainly found willing responses in the poor sections of cities in Jordan and Egypt. Large numbers of guest workers living in Kuwait actively supported the invasion because they were promised economic, social, and political equality with Kuwaitis if Iraq's invasion was successful.

The rich are beginning to recognize that this disparity of income could prove to be their own undoing. In an effort to redress some of this economic inequity, Saudi Arabia has donated more than 120 billion dollars to aid developing states during the past half century. This aid has gone to 70 states, including 38 in Africa and 25 in Asia. The principal dollar recipients have been friendly, poor Arab states.[29]

Everyone knows that the scarcity of water is the most serious impediment to development in the Middle East and North Africa. In an experiment, the Gulf States and Saudi Arabia have made great strides, at high cost, in developing agriculture in the desert through the use of desalinized water. There have been calls for the rich to pay for the application of this technology to the poor parts of the region. Agriculture is labor intensive and, with adequate water, the industry could provide jobs for many. Could this approach using oil money succeed in making the non-oil-producing states the breadbaskets for the region? At the present, this Pan-Arab vision of agricultural regions established near areas of population remains a dream. Until jobs and opportunities can be offered in the areas of high population, the disparity of income between the oil rich and the poor will remain a source of tension.

Summary

This chapter discusses several major political issues in the Middle East and North Africa. First, the Palestinian-Israeli dispute is one of the most difficult problems in the world. Tales of abuse are cited by both sides. This chapter offers several possible solutions for resolving these disputes.

Second, the role of women is changing in parts of the region. Change may not follow the Western model, but it will occur. A case study on the changing role of women in Saudi Arabia is included.

Third, the impact of petroleum is discussed. This section includes the location of oil, the difficulty of transporting the product to the consumer, and the problem of rich and poor in the region.

Fourth, the issue of religious fundamentalism is detailed. The Algerian conflict is discussed. The point is made that all fundamentalists are not the same. Various fundamentalist groups are described.

Review Questions

1. List some of the issues that must be addressed in any settlement between Palestinians and Israelis.
2. What is the Clinton framework for peace?
3. What is the conflict over the route of oil pipelines in Central Asia?
4. What do religious fundamentalists in Christianity, Judaism, and Islam have in common?
5. How is the role of women changing in the Middle East and North Africa?

Suggested Readings

Nazih N. Ayubi, *Over-Stating the Arab State: Politics and Society in the Middle East,* L. B. Taurus and Co. Ltd., London, 1995.
Margot Badran, *Feminists, Islam, and Nation: Gender and the Making of Modern Egypt,* Princeton University Press, Princeton, New Jersey, 1995.
Robert D. Kaplan, *The Arabists: The Romance of an American Elite,* MacMillan, New York, 1993.

Robert Lacey, *The Kingdom, Arabia and the House of Saud,* Avon Books, New York, 1981.

Daniel Yergin, *The Prize: The Epic Quest for Oil, Money, and Power,* Simon and Schuster, New York, 1992.

Notes

1. Ron David, *Arabs and Israel for Beginners,* Airlift Books Co. (Enfield, England: 1993), p. 128.
2. John Lancaster, "Scholars Challenge U.S. Embassy Site: Israel Accused of Confiscating Plot," *International Herald Tribune* (August 28, 2000), p. 8.
3. William Orme, Jr., "In West Bank, Water Is as Touchy as Land," *The New York Times* (July 15, 2000), p. A6. Note: To Palestinians, water has a broader meaning than the way that it is commonly thought of in the West. It is an essential element in Islam where ritual cleansing is required before prayer. The lack of water is broader than the commonly referred to human consumption issue. There is a feeling that the Israelis are sullying the water by filling their swimming pools while members of the Muslim community are forced to go without.
4. "The Palestine Right of Return," *The Economist,* London, January 6–12, 2001.
5. Prime Minister Barak, "Upbeat on Peace Deal Prospects, U.S. Reaches Out to ICO J'lem Committee," *Mideast Mirror* (August 23, 2000), Vol. 14, No. 164.
6. President Mubarak, "Giving Up Jerusalem Would Invite 'Endless Violence,'" *Mideast Mirror,* (August 24, 2000), Vol.14, No. 163.
7. Isabel Kershner, "Bringing Jerusalem Down to Earth," *The Jerusalem Report* (August 28, 2000), p. 26.
8. Lee Hockstader, "Jerusalem, City of Faith, Defies Rational Solution: For Both Sides, Compromise Is Betrayal, *The International Herald Tribune* (July 21, 2000), News p. 1.
9. Editorial, "A Jerusalem Settlement Everyone Can Live With," Jimmy Carter, 39th President of the United States, *The New York Times* (August 6, 2000), Sec. 4, p. 15, Column 2.
10. Charles Krauthhammer, "Clinton Undermines U.S. and Israel," *Dallas Morning News* (January 15, 2001), p. 15A.
11. "Israel Refuses to Cooperate with U.N. Rights Mission; Panel Hat? Cited Abuse of Palestinians," *The Dallas Morning News* (February 11, 2001), p. 16A.
12. The Israeli foreign minister issued a report on February 1, 2001, clearing Ariel Sharon of the Palestinian charge that he was responsible for provoking the second Intifada. The report asserted that although the Sharon visit to the Temple Mount was insensitive, it was not the cause of the Intifada. The report stated that the visit was used by the Palestinians as an excuse to begin a campaign of violence that had been planned much earlier. "Israel Clears Sharon in Uprising," Associated Press Report, *The Dallas Morning News* (February 2, 2001), p. 15A.
13. Alexander B. Calahan, *Countering Terrorism: The Israeli Response to the 1972 Munich Olympic Massacre and the Development of Independent Covert Action Teams,* written in fulfillment of a requirement for the Marine Corps Command and Staff College, USA, April 1995, p. 9.
14. "OPEC May Cut Output: 1.5 Million Barrels Likely, Saudi Says," *The Dallas Morning News* (January 16, 2001), Section D, p. 1.
15. The "great game" was played out during the Victorian Period between Great Britain and the other European powers, especially Russia. The British idea was to limit other great power expansion into the Middle East and Central Asia by propping up the Muslim governments there. David Fromkin quotes the 19th-century British diplomat George Curzon as stating, "Turkestan, Afghanistan, Transcaspia, Persia . . . are the pieces on a chessboard which is being played out for the dominion of the world." David Fromkin, *A Peace to End All Peace: Creating the Modern Middle East 1914–1922,* Henry Holt and Co. (New York: 1989), p. 27.
16. Efraim and Inari Karsh, *Empires of the Sand: The Struggle for Mastery in the Middle East 1789–1923,* Harvard University Press (Cambridge, Mass.: 1999), p. 64.

17. Geoffrey Kemp and Robert Harkavy, *Strategic Geography and the Changing Middle East,* Brookings Institute Press (Washington, D.C.: 1997), p. 260.
18. Michael Arditti, "Rabid Dogmas," *The Times* (March 29, 2000), Features page.
19. *Webster's Encyclopedia Unabridged Dictionary of the English Language,* Gramercy Books (New York: 1989), p. 574.
20. Robert Irwin, "Do Fundamentalists Really Seek to Turn the Social Clock Back?" *The Independent* (April 22, 2000), Features, p. 10.
21. Philip Hiro, *Dictionary of the Middle East,* St. Martins Press (New York: 1996), p. 134.
22. Samuel P. Huntington, *The Clash of Civilization and the Remaking of World Order,* Simon and Schuster (New York: 1996), p. 21.
23. Christopher Hibbert, *The Horizon Book of Daily Life in Victorian England,* American Heritage Publishing (New York: 1975), p. 38.
24. Hibbert, *op. cit.,* p. 39.
25. Sura XXXIII, 35, *The Holy Qur'an, Translation and Commentary,* A. Yusuf Ali, American Trust Publications, USA, for the Muslim Students Association of the United States and Canada, 1977, p. 1116.
26. "New Girls College Being Built Near Riyad," *Saudi Arabia* (April 1998), Vol. 15, No. 4. Note: For an interesting article on Saudi women from official sources, see "The Growing Role of Professional Women in Saudi Society," *Saudi Arabia* (Spring 2000), Vol. 17, No. 1. Information Office of the Royal Embassy of Saudi Arabia, Washington, D.C.
27. Marcel Theroux, "The Oil Is Nothing to Do With Us: With an Oil Boom Worth Upwards of Dollars 80 Bn, Azerbaijan is Becoming the Texas of the Caspian Sea," *The Guardian* (September 7, 2000), p. 6.
28. Edward Mortimer and Michael Field, "Nationalism, the Steel of the Arab Soul," *Financial Times* (August 18/19, 1990), Section 11.
29. Alfred P. Prados, "Saudi Arabia: Post-War Issues and U.S. Relations," C.R.S., Issue Brief No. 1B9 3113, Congressional Research Service, Library of Congress, Washington, D.C., 1996.

Chapter 7

Some Final Thoughts for Americans About the Politics of the Middle East and North Africa

Eight Laws Shaping Politics

THE STATES OF THE MIDDLE EAST AND NORTH AFRICA ARE ARTIFICIAL

Look at a map of the region. If you see straight lines, these lines were most likely drawn in London, Paris, or Berlin. You can be sure that the local population was not consulted when these boundaries were established.

The Importance of Artificial Boundaries Since no natural boundaries follow the patterns just described, it may be useful to look at the impact that artificial boundaries have on current politics.

The often-stated aspiration of both Arabs and Muslims has been to create a single great state that would include most of the Middle East and North Africa. The reality is that there are at least 20 separate states located in the region. All of these states are in one way or another the products of either colonial rule or Western interventions. Even Iran and Saudi Arabia had the specifics of their borders shaped by the ambitions of the colonial powers. Prior to European intervention, Middle Eastern and North African entities had ill-defined borders. Maps used by Napoleon show only general locations for places like Syria and Palestine. Although not marked on a map, tribes and clans held the land. Everyone knew traditional boundaries, so no maps were needed. It is interesting to once more look at the dates of colonial occupation and their relationship to the establishment of specific borders in the region. These borders are Western in origin, and their creation had little to do with the needs or desires of the people living there. Beginning in the West along the Atlantic, the Spanish established Reo de Or during the 19th century. They expanded their territory, which became the Spanish Sahara in 1912. At the same time they established the Colony of Ifni, which was carved out of Morocco. France and Spain established the borders of Morocco when they divided it between themselves in 1912. Since the French had also controlled Algeria for almost 100 years, it was easy for them to mark the

Moroccan-Algerian border "without having local objections." Tunisia became a French possession in 1881. The Italian occupation of Tripolitania and Cyrenaica in 1912 led to their union as Libya. The British "temporarily" occupied Egypt in 1882 and the Sudan in 1898. They drew the border between these two territories.

In the Middle Eastern heartland, Turkey, Syria, Iraq, Lebanon, Palestine (Israel), and Jordan are the products of either the allied agreements during World War I or their political intrigues at the postwar peace conferences. British support for favored tribal chiefs led to the creation of Kuwait, Bahrain, Qatar, the States of the United Arab Emirates, and Oman. British agents and threats of intervention helped to establish the border between Yemen and Saudi Arabia. Although the British did not intervene in Arabia after World War I, their agents played significant roles in the tribal conflicts in both the Hejaz and the Nejd. The union of these territories by the Saud clan formed Saudi Arabia.

Iran is unique in that it has maintained a territorial integrity. Even here, however, Western interventions have been common. During the 20th century, the British intervened in Iran/Persia three times, the Russians two times, and the Americans once. There was almost constant turmoil along the northern border with Russia in Azerbaijan.

These decisions were made and the states created with one primary objective in mind: to further the colonial ambitions of the mother country! These states were established with the parameters created by the balance-of-power configuration that existed between the great powers at the time. The results of these actions are artificial states with borders that have little to do with the tribal, family, or religious boundaries that formerly existed. Many of the conflicts that exist in the Middle East and North Africa can be traced to this legacy of colonialism. Whether referring to the Western Sahara, the status of Lebanon, the existence of Israel, the problem of the Kurds, or the Shiites in southern Iraq, all have elements of a colonial past to thank for the present conflicts. The creation of unnaturally united groups by artificial state boundaries is one of the great evils perpetuated on the Middle East and North Africa.

THE PROBLEMS OF THE MIDDLE EAST CAN BE BLAMED ON GOD OR THE BRITISH

There is a saying that the problems of the Middle East are bones buried by the dogs of British imperialism. Why would the British have to shoulder so much of the blame for what is wrong with the Middle East? The answer is almost too simple. It is because they drew the maps!

At the end of World War I, the British and, to a lesser degree, the French were in a position to decide on the disposition of the Arab territories of the old Ottoman Empire. Had they chosen to do so, they could have encouraged the kind of evolution to the natural states that were created in Eastern Europe. Although some political regions were ill defined, there was little doubt as to who traditionally ruled each territory.

Instead, the British considered their holdings in the Middle East as simply part of a greater global empire. Arab nationalists were probably correct when they argued that it served British interest to pursue a policy of divide and rule. As long as the Arabs could be kept divided into a number of small states ruled by ambitious petty rulers, British colonial interest would remain safe.

Although the sun has set on the British Empire, these small states remain. The United States and Israel have continued to pursue similar divisive objectives. "Divide and rule" is still the watchword when dealing with the Arabs in a neocolonial environment. They have encouraged a division between the the rich and the poor by courting the rich Gulf States. The Arabs are in no position to effectively challenge either the United States or Israel. Since the decline of the Soviet Union into the Russian Republic, this situation has become acute. The destruction of Iraq during the Gulf War was a hard lesson for the Arabs. They must either deal with the realities of Western power or risk falling further and further behind.

It is interesting to speculate on what the Middle East would be like today if the early nationalist dreams of a single great Arab union had been realized. Would the wealth of the Gulf and Arabia have been used to uplift the millions of Middle Eastern people living in poverty at the present time? Would there have been a Middle Eastern counterpart to the American-supported European Community? No one will ever know. The reality is that the Middle East at the beginning of the 21st century is as weak and divided as it was after World War I. Probably some Western leaders who fear a resurgent Muslim Middle East would say that this is how it should be.

GOD HAS PROMISED THE SAME PROMISED LAND TO MORE THAN ONE CHOSEN PEOPLE

Judaism, Christianity, and Islam claim to share the same historic origins and to worship the same god, God. Each religion claims to have the correct unaltered truth given by God. Each religion views the other two as incorrect and therefore inferior. Each religion holds similar historic locations as sacred. Often each views the presence or even close proximity of the other two religions as profane. As previously stated, nowhere is the geographic conflict more explosive than in the Old City of Jerusalem. Here, within an area only approximately 1500 meters east to west and 1000 meters north to south, are some of the most sacred areas to Jews, Christians, and Muslims.[1] Within this walled city are located St. Anne's Church, the Chapel of the Flagellation, the Chapel of Judgment, the Church of Zion, the Church of the Savior, the Church of the Holy Sepulcher, the Dome of the Rock, the al-Aksa Mosque, the Wailing Wall, and Solomon's Stables. The Temple Mount is located in the southeastern part of the Old City. There on a flat esplanade only 250 meters by 175 meters is located the third holiest shrine in Islam, the Dome of the Rock. It is built over the spot where Jews believe Abraham planned to sacrifice his son, Isaac. Jews also believe that this spot is where the ancient Jewish Temple was located. Muslims believe that this site is where Muhammad was elevated to heaven. Literally below the Dome of the Rock is the Wailing Wall, a remnant of the ancient Jewish Temple. It is a place sacred to Jews. Only a short distance from the Dome of the Rock and the Wailing Wall is the Church of the Holy Sepulcher. European Christians engaged in the Crusades during the Middle Ages to recover this church from Islamic control. Today the competition for authority over this church is still fierce, even among Christians. Within the church itself, Latin Christians control the southern half of Mt. Calvary, the Altar of Mary Magdalene, and the Church of the Apparition. Greek Orthodox Christians claim the northern half of Mt. Cavalry, the Chapel of Adam, and the Prison of Christ. The Armenian Christians have jurisdiction over the Chapel of St. Helena and the Place of the Three Marys. Coptic Christians are limited to a small chapel at the rear of the Holy Sepulcher. Syrian Christians are given a presence across from the Coptic Chapel. The Abyssinians control the Tomb of Joseph of Arimethea. The Abyssinians have also built a small monastery on the roof of the Church of the Holy Sepulcher! This list of sacred places and their claimants is offered to illustrate the complexity of asserting religious claims in the Old City. Similarly, disputed religious sites exist in dozens of places throughout the Holy Land.

The obvious difficulty in reaching a peace settlement involving believers from opposing religions is their inability to separate the spiritual Holy Land from the political Holy Land.

Co-existence in the Old City of Jerusalem
The Wailing Wall, sacred to Jews, and a street sacred to Christians are only a few hundred meters apart. Above both is located the Dome of the Rock, a place sacred to both Muslims and Jews.
Source: Joe Weatherby

During recent decades, just the opposite has occurred on all sides. Nationalists have embraced what were once wholly religious ideas to strengthen their secular objectives. The result is a linkage of the secular with the religious Holy Land. People of good will may reach agreement on political issues. However, human beings may not presume to negotiate for God! Until the spiritual sites in Jerusalem and the rest of the Holy Land can be separated from the secular, there is little hope that some of these issues can ever be resolved. Many of the people of the three religions do not like, trust, or respect each other. That makes the resolution of these kinds of political religious disputes difficult, if not impossible.

THERE ARE PEOPLE IN ISRAEL AND AMONG THE ARABS WHO DO NOT WANT PEACE

Stated another way, there are people who are prepared to accept a peaceful solution to the Arab-Israeli dispute provided that they receive 100 percent of their demands accompanied by the total surrender of the other side. For Israeli maximalists, peace means that all of the land of Israel promised by God to the children of Israel will become part of Greater

Israel. If successful, this position would expand the borders of Israel to include the whole of the occupied territories and more. Although a minority even within the minority Israeli maximalist movement, some even call for the expulsion of the Arab population.

On the Arab side, maximalists call not only for the retaking of the Old City of Jerusalem, but they demand that all of the Palestinian exiles be allowed to return to their former homes in Israel. They also expect that the borders will be returned to those of the original United Nations Partition Plan. The most extreme Arab maximalists wish to see the State of Israel destroyed.

Simply stated the Arab and Israeli maximalists positions are a mirror of each other. The Arab maximalists do not want the Israeli Jewish state to exist, just as Israeli maximalists do not want a Palestinian Arab state to exist. The most extreme maximalists on both sides want to expell the other.

It should be made clear here that a large number of people on both sides might prefer the maximalists' positions. However, there is only a small minority of zealots who are willing to commit acts of violence to achieve their political and religious objectives. These small groups can and do commit acts that provoke the majority, making peace impossible. The most dangerous time for the cause of peace in the region occurs when movements for peace are closest to success. Provocative acts are often committed just before a peace conference is scheduled. The acts are designed to so inflame the situation that peace becomes impossible.

Stated simply, the issue is this: both Israeli and Palestinian maximalists oppose peace efforts because they know that peace means compromise! Compromise ensures that their objectives will not be realized. The reality is that although these militant minorities have goals that the majority of Arabs and Israelis may reject, their actions allow them to exercise a veto over any peace efforts involving a compromise with the other side.

Case Study: The Second Intifada

At the urging of the United States president, both Prime Minister Ehud Barak and Palestinian Chairman Yasser Arafat agreed to meet for peace talks at the Camp David retreat near Washington, D.C. These talks lasted from July 11 to July 25, 2000. As they continued, hopes for a comprehensive agreement were raised on both sides. Both sides came tantalizingly close to agreement. When the talks ultimately failed, there was a great deal of disappointment. Observers saw at the time that, given the frustrations on both sides, any incident could boil over into a major conflict. When an uneasy peace survived into the early fall, new hopes were raised that the peace talks could be resumed before President Clinton left office. In early September, President Clinton met separately with the leaders on both sides. As a show of good will the Palestinian Authority announced that they would postpone their unilateral declaration of a Palestinian state that had been set for September 13. It looked like the progress toward an agreement that had been made at Camp David might be built on at a new summit hosted by President Clinton. There was talk that this conference might take place in late September.

The spark that ignited the second Intifada and killed the September initiative was provided by Ariel Sharon, head of the opposition Likud party. In what was interpreted by the Palestinians as a provocative act, he led several hundred police, soldiers, and civilian followers to the Temple Mount to demonstrate Israeli authority over the area.

Since 1967 when the site sacred to Jews and Muslims was captured by Israel, sovereignty over the Temple Mount has been exercised by the Jewish state. In practice, Muslim authorities have maintained actual control over the area. To visit the site, one passes through a gate with Israeli security forces on one side and Muslim authorities on the other. While visiting the Noble Sanctuary, the visitor is subject to Muslim rules of conduct.

To the Palestinians, the Sharon visit was a challenge to their control at the very time when the final status of the Temple Mount was a subject for discussion at the yet to be scheduled peace talks.

The Palestinian response was immediate and violent, prompting an Israeli intervention. This incident was taken advantage of by maximalists on both sides. Militant Palestinian factions quickly increased actions against Israeli forces and settlers throughout the territories under Israeli control. In turn, armed settlers and elements of the military used great force against the Palestinian population. Within three months the battle had moved from rocks to guns, heavy weapons, and aircraft. Hundreds had been killed and thousands wounded. For the first time in years Israeli Palestinians had opposed Israeli authorities in Israel.

It is not the place here to detail the whole sad story of this conflict. It is simply to emphasize that maximalists on both sides successfully took advantage of what was initially a minor incident to influence the general population and undermine the efforts of those advocating a peace settlement.

In this case the incident was Sharon's visit to the Temple Mount, but it could have been anything. The result was exactly what the maximalists on both sides wanted, which was an end to the peace efforts that had appeared so promising in July.

What can be learned from this event? First, it is still possible for those minorities who refuse to compromise either to create or to take advantage of incidents that set in motion events that so inflame the masses that peace efforts become impossible. Second, the leadership on both sides will have to decide if peace is worth the price that must be paid in compromise if an agreement is to succeed.

When offered a form of independence from the British in 1922, the Irish were forced to choose between partition or continual low-intensity war and the impoverishment of the Irish people. They made the difficult compromise that eventually led to the establishment of the Republic of Ireland. Although not yet accepted by all, most observers would acknowledge that history has proved that the Irish made the right choice. The issues between Palestinians and Israelis may be more complicated than those that the Irish and British confronted. However, they are no less emotional.

Since neither Palestinians nor Israelis are willing to adopt the draconian genocide policies of Nazi Germany, both are going to have to deal with the reality that "the other side is going to remain." To prosper and perhaps even to survive, both sides are going to have to overcome the veto of the militant minorities to achieve a workable peace. The case of the second Intifada demonstrates that this task is not going to be an easy one.

MUSLIMS BELIEVE THAT GOD IS TESTING THEIR RESOLVE THROUGH ADVERSITY

Islam entered the world with one of the greatest conquests of territory in world history. Muslims have remained triumphant throughout most of the religion's existence. It has been only during the past 200 years that Muslims have been put on the defensive. During this period, attacks by imperialists from Christian Europe were followed by the humiliation of colonial rule. Muslims finally achieved their independence only to see defeat replace victory with Western support for the creation of Israel. To make matters worse, the Jewish State, relying on American help, became the dominant military power in the region.

Muslims know that they are the favored of God! They know that they are right in their beliefs. They know that God will never allow a permanent triumph of unbelievers over believers. Thus these defeats are for a purpose. Muslims rationalize that they must return to the true path of Islam before their enemies can be defeated.

THE UNITED STATES HAS INHERITED THE SEEDS OF COLONIALISM PLANTED BY THEIR EUROPEAN COUSINS

To people in the Middle East and North Africa who have experienced 200 years of European intervention, American actions in the region look disturbingly familiar. Not only do Americans look like European imperialists, they often appear to behave like them. Whether the Americans are bombing Libya or Iraq, people in the region believe that they are imitating the gunboat diplomacy of a European imperial past. The Arabs see the stationing of American troops in Saudi Arabia, where the two holiest places in Islam are located, not as a mutual defense arrangement but rather as a way to guarantee American control of their oil. To many Middle Easterners, the semipermanent presence of these foreign troops in Saudi Arabia is no different from the British use of their military in Egypt during the 19th and 20th centuries. Both states are viewed as using the military to protect their economic interests.

Perhaps the worst indictment of American policymakers is over the massive U.S. support for Israel. To Arabs, their defeats are excused because, to them, Israel is merely a surrogate for American imperialism. Following this logic, Israel would be no force in the region without American backing. To the Arabs, American support for Israel is just another example of neocolonialism.

Although most Americans would find these perceptions distorted, given the recent history of Western involvement in the region, it should not come as a surprise that these views are commonly held. The European imperialists have returned to Europe in defeat. The Americans remain the single visible power attempting to manipulate the politics and economies of the region. This is why the United States and its citizens are considered to be targets for militants throughout the Middle East and North Africa.

THE UNITED STATES FOREIGN POLICY DILEMMA IN THE MIDDLE EAST AND NORTH AFRICA

We are pro-Israeli and pro-oil! Unfortunately, God did not put the Israelis and the oil in the same place. Stated another way, American hearts are with Israel whereas American heads are with the Middle Easterners who have oil. The reality of this divided loyalty causes a foreign policy inconsistency that can never be resolved without peace between Israel and the Palestinians. In the present situation, the United States speaks with one voice to the Arabs and with another to Israel.

America and Israel The United States has been a strong supporter of Israel since the Jewish state's founding in 1948. Since the 1950s when American aid began, the United States has given far more aid to Israel than was sent to rebuild postwar Europe under the famous Marshall Plan.[2]

The reasons for American support for Israel are both simple and complex. Put simply, the overwhelming majority of Americans identify with Israel. They see Israel as a small state in a hostile world. They admire the "go it alone" spirit of the Israelis. They also identify with the Western attitudes and institutions in Israel.

The more complex reasons for American support for Israel are also interesting. Large numbers of Protestants in the United States consider themselves to be evangelicals. As evangelicals, most believe that the establishment of Israel is fulfillment of a prophecy. Two passages from Jeremiah express their viewpoint:

> For thus saith the Lord, the God of Israel, concerning the houses of this city, and concerning the houses of the Kings of Judah, which are thrown down by the mounts and by the sword.[3]
>
> And I will cause the captivity of Judah and the captivity of Israel to return and will build them, as at the First.[4]

To these American Christians, the establishment of Israel is a sign that God's promises are coming to pass.

Jewish Americans represent the largest community of believers in Judaism in the world. Since the end of World War II, most American Jews have actively supported efforts to aid Israel. The American-Israeli Public Affairs Committee (AIPAC) with over 100 national and state affiliates has become one of the most effective political action committees advocating American support for Israeli. Like other Americans, members of this organization believe that America and Israel have common interest in the region. Therefore, it is patriotic to urge American policymakers to maintain a policy supportive of Israel.

America and Oil   At this time, America and the West cannot survive without an uninterrupted supply of low-cost oil! The survival of American democracy and the American way of life depends on imported oil. To the public, petroleum products delivered at an affordable price have become an essential political necessity resembling that of low-cost bread for the peasants at the time of the French Revolution. No Western government can afford to let the price or availability of oil get out of control without risking survival. In a continental-sized country like the United States, nothing can move without oil. At the present time, the best high-quality, easily recovered, reasonably priced petroleum products come from the Middle East and North Africa.

Current U.S. efforts to secure energy from the region are hampered by several constraints. First, the political events and policy choices of the past several decades have eliminated Iran, Iraq, and Libya as suppliers. This means that the primary regional sources for petroleum products destined for the United States and the West come from the Persian Gulf States and Saudi Arabia.

U.S. strategy has been to cultivate friendship with these oil states while continuing support for Israel. Although the oil kingdoms are not as involved in the Arab-Palestinian-Israeli dispute as are others, they do support Palestinian aspirations for statehood. As conservative Muslim states, they also take seriously the concerns about the status of Jerusalem and the control of the holy sites.

All this means that U.S. policy in the region is inevitably inconsistent. To overcome the obvious policy differences, U.S. strategists have tried to isolate the Palestinian-Israeli dispute, while at the same time conducting normal relations with the Arab oil states. The Americans can justify their position by asserting that they are the only peace brokers that both sides are willing to deal with. The fact remains that until a peace between Palestinians and Israelis is achieved, Americans will be forced to pursue the contradictory policies of being pro-Israeli and pro-oil.

THE MOST IMPORTANT BATTLE BEING FOUGHT FOR THE MIDDLE EAST DOES NOT TAKE PLACE IN THE REGION, BUT IN WASHINGTON

Almost 40 years ago the Middle East specialist Maurice Harari wrote the following recommendation:

> Obviously, U.S. policy should vigorously pursue a settlement of the Arab-Israeli problem. But, in the meantime, U.S. policy should be based on aid programs designed to bolster the flagging Middle East economy. Also a firmer U.S. identification against the vestiges of European colonialism—especially Britain and France—would enhance U.S. prestige in the entire Afro-Asian world and make Western denunciations of Soviet colonialism in East Europe ring more true.[5]

At the beginning of the 21st century, the Soviet Union is no more and Eastern Europe is free. The rest of Harari's recommendation is as true today as it was when written in 1962. The key to peace and prosperity in the Middle East is finding a solution to the dispute between Israelis, Arabs, and Palestinians. Solving that issue will lead to a resolution to most of the other problems that plague the region.

With the fall of the Soviet Union, the United States is the only great nation still standing whose money, power, and prestige can have a major influence on the outcome of the conflict between the Israelis and the Palestinians. Both sides know that they cannot hope to achieve their objectives without American support. Both sides know that without American support their long-term survival is problematical. It is because of these realities that the actual battle is not in the streets of Gaza or Jerusalem; it is, by way of television, in American homes. Washington may not be able to force the sides to ever agree to a settlement, but the failure to support one side or the other will certainly doom that side's aspirations in the struggle.

For years American leaders have postured themselves as "honest peace brokers" while assuring Israel that their interests in the dispute will be protected. This policy has often won Americans the distrust of Israel and the enmity of the Arabs. Few people in the Middle East and North Africa seriously consider the United States to be an honest broker in the region. They see the United States as tilting toward Israel with money and weapons while steadfastly asserting that they are completely neutral.

However, all parties know that sooner or later it is only the United States that can bring some order to the chaos that currently exists between Israelis and Palestinians. It is because of this reality that contending parties are actively engaged in campaigns to win over the hearts and minds of the American people. The Israelis and Palestinians both believe that influencing the American government will largely determine the final outcome of this dispute.

The United States has a unique opportunity to exercise a positive influence on both sides. To do this, the United States must win back the trust of the Palestinians while at the same time not alienating the Israelis. Walking this fine line will be difficult for Americans. On occasion our leaders may find themselves in opposition to Israeli policies. However, only by pursuing genuinely even-handed policies can Washington hope to move the parties involved to a peaceful solution. A failure to make this effort will cause the United States to be, in part, responsible for a future war.

What Are the Future Prospects for the Middle East and North Africa?

DOES THE FATE OF THE REGION REQUIRE IT TO BE WESTERN TO BE MODERN?

To most people in the West, being modern is to be Western. Is secular Westernization the enviable consequence of modernization? This is one of the great questions confronting those who live in an area stretching from the Atlantic to Pakistan.

The Middle East and North Africa stand on the verge of a new revolution. Will it be like the one in Baghdad during the Middle Ages? Will the region undergo a new religious crusade, which will again place a Muslim stamp on the rest of the world? Or will the Middle East slip back into religious bigotry and petty conflict? The latter approach will surely doom the region to further decline.

Perhaps there is a middle ground, a ground that can serve as a model for others in the developing world. To do this the people of the Middle East and North Africa will have to make use of the technologies of modernization while resisting the seduction of Western secular culture.

On a small scale, there are places in the region where the transition to the modern technological world is taking place while keeping the values of Muslim society. There are halting attempts to encourage the evolution of tribal Bedeau-democracy into a system where truly democratic practices may emerge. The newly granted right of women to vote and hold office in Qatar is offered as an example of this process.

In spite of some positive signs, Bernard Lewis is absolutely correct when he states that, "As long as conflict and repression prevail, there is little hope of the Middle East achieving a real equality with more advanced countries and, therefore, of preserving independence from them."[6]

Lewis's comments can also be applied to North Africa. The Middle East and North Africa must adapt their institutions to the reality of modernization or they will have the stark choice of either becoming Western or drifting into a new dark age. For those who admire and respect the people who live in this part of the world, they can only hope that their choice is a wise one.

There are no guarantees of a peaceful and prosperous future for the inhabitants of the Middle East and North Africa. One thing is certain, it is impossible for them to return to the past. Their future may be unclear, but by exercising tolerance and wisdom in the present, determined people can create a better future for themselves and their children. We can only hope that Isaiah was right when he prophesized the following:

> The people that walked in darkness have seen a great light; they that dwell in the land of the shadow of death, upon them hath the light shined.[7]

Summary

The Middle Eastern and North African states are the products of Western colonialism or neocolonialism. Their present borders are largely the product of previous colonial divisions. Because the borders often have little relation to tribal and family boundaries, there is an inherent instability built into the present system.

The United States is the last remaining superpower. All of the parties involved in the dispute between Israelis and Palestinians must deal with the United States. The American people are overwhelmingly supportive of Israel. Because of America's reliance on Arab oil, there is an incentive to help in the resolution of the dispute.

Review Questions

1. Why are the states of the Middle East and North Africa called artificial countries?
2. Why do Judaism, Christianity, and Islam all lay claim to the Old City of Jerusalem?
3. Why does the United States have an inconsistent policy in the Middle East?
4. Why does the United States play a pivotal role in the dispute between Palestinians and Israelis?
5. Why are the British blamed for many problems in the Middle East?

Suggested Readings

Michell G. Bard, *The Complete Idiot's Guide to the Middle East Conflict,* MacMillan, New York, 1999.

James Donnigan and Austin Bay, *A Quick and Dirty Guide to War: Briefings on Present and Potential Wars,* William Morrow, New York, 1996.

Andrew Duncan and Michel Opatowski, *War in the Holy Land: From Meggido to the West Bank,* Sutton Publishing Ltd., Thrupp-Stroud, Gloucstershire, U.K., 1998.

David Fromkin, *A Peace to End All Peace: Creating the Modern Middle East 1914–1922,* Henry Holt & Co., New York, 1989.

Efraim Karsh and Inari Karsh, *Empires of the Sand: The Struggle for Mastery of the Middle East 1789–1923,* Harvard University Press, Cambridge, Mass., 1999.

Notes

1. For a map showing the Christian, Armenian, Muslims, and Jewish Quarters of the Old City in Jerusalem refer to page 16 of the Holy Land by Fabio Bourbon and Enrico Lavagno, White Star Pub., (Vercelli, Italy, 2001).
2. Note: According to Bailey, the Marshall Plan provided over 12 billion dollars in aid to Europe during a four-year period. Thomas A. Bailey, *A Diplomatic History of the American People,* 10th Ed., Prentice Hall (Englewood Cliffs, N.J.: 1980), pp. 799–802.
3. Bible, Jeremiah 33: 4.
4. Bible, Jeremiah 33: 7.
5. Maurice Harari, *Government and Politics of the Middle East,* Prentice Hall (Englewood Cliffs, N.J.: 1962), p. 170.
6. Bernard Lewis, *The Future of the Middle East,* Phoenix Paperback (London: 1997), p. 52.
7. Bible, Isaiah 9:2.

Chapter 8

Country Profiles

Algeria

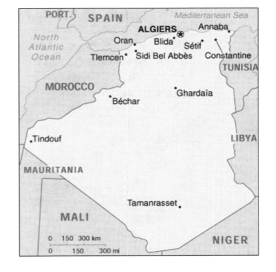

Official Name: Democratic and Popular Republic of Algeria
Area: 919,600 square miles
Capital: Algiers
Infant Mortality (per 1000 Live Births): 43
Life Expectancy (Years/Males): 68
Urban Population: 56 percent
Literacy Rate: 61.6 percent
Arable Lands: 3 percent
Per Capita GDP: $4600
Religion: Muslim 99 percent, Christian/Jewish 1 percent
Language: Arabic, French, Berber
Population: 31,193,917
Population Growth: 2.1 percent
Website: http://www.arab.net/algeria/algeria_contents.html
Economics: Through the 1980s, Algeria was considered to have the most centrally planned state economy in the region. Since that time, the Algerians, with International Monetary Fund help, have done more to loosen governmental controls on the economy. Foreign investment has been encouraged. The major hindrance to normal economic development has been the continuing internal conflict between Islamic traditionalists and reformists.
Government: Structurally, Algeria has an elected president, prime minister, and appointed council of ministers. The legislation is bicameral, with a directly elected

National People's Assembly, and an indirectly elected Council of Nations. The Algerian legal system is a combination of French and Islamic law.

Political Snapshot: Algeria entered into the political "dark ages" in 1992 when the authorities cancelled what was apparently victory in the elections that year. Here was a case where the Western-backed secularists invalidated a democratic election because they opposed the outcome. A low-intensity civil war began that continues today. The government of the current president has offered amnesty to the Islamic parties as an inducement to cease the violence. This policy has defused a good part of the conflict. It will take time to see if current authorities are serious about reintegrating all of the elements of Algerian society into the political life of the state. Before a true democracy can exist in Algeria, the violence on all sides must be reduced. The army's political power must be reduced. Finally, the Western-oriented leaders currently in power must be willing to allow the opposition to have a place in Algerian life.

Azerbaijan

Official Name: Azerbaijani Republic
Area: 33,400 square miles
Capital: Baku
Infant Mortality (per 1000 Live Births): 83
Life Expectancy (Years/Males): 58
Urban Population: 57 percent
Literacy Rate: 100 percent
Arable Land: 18 percent
Per Capita GDP: $1640
Religion: Muslim
Language: Azeri
Population: 7,748,163
Population Growth: 0.27 percent
Web site: http://www.azerbaijannews.net

Economics: Early in the 20th century, Azerbaijan was the top petroleum producer in the world. Oil production is still the major part of the economy. One hundred years after oil was discovered, the area around Baku is considered by many to be the most polluted spot on the planet. There is limited agriculture in other parts of the state.

The possibility of a major system of pipelines being constructed to carry petroleum from Turkmenistan to Turkey may improve the economic situation in Azerbaijan.

Government: Although Azerbaijan held democratic elections in 1992, the president was overthrown in 1993. Since that time the old communist apparatus has run the state as "new capitalists." Haydar Alliyev has held on to power since 1993. There is a unicameral parliament, but the president holds effective power.

Political Snapshot: Azerbaijan has been involved in an on-again, off-again war with Armenia over the Christian-dominated territory of Nagorno-Karabakh since 1992. They also have a border dispute with Turkmenistan over oil rights in the Caspian. In the past there were also border tensions with Iran. At the present time, both Iran and Turkey are seeking to gain influence in Azerbaijan.

Bahrain

Official Name: State of Bahrain
Area: 240 square miles
Capital: Manama
Infant Mortality (per 1000 Live Births): 16.4
Life Expectancy (Years/Males): 73
Urban Population: 91 percent
Literacy Rate: 85 percent
Arable Land: 2 percent
Per Capita GDP: $13,100
Religion: Muslim
Language: Arabic, English, Persian, Urdu
Population: 634,137
Population Growth: 2.6 percent
Website: http://www.strategic-road.com/pays/morient/bahrain.html

Economics: Bahrain has one of the oldest and most developed petroleum industries in the Persian Gulf. Today more than half of the economy is tied to the oil and gas industry. The government is attempting to develop other sources of income. There are some long-term concerns that the standard of living cannot be sustained when the oil supply runs out. Bahrain remains both a banking center and a home for many multinational corporations doing business in the Gulf.

Government: Bahrain is a monarchy. It is considered to be one of the Gulf states that is resisting political modernization. The Emir is the head of state. The prime minister is head of government. The national assembly has not met since 1975. There are no political parties allowed. There are no elective offices.

Political Snapshot: Bahrain is a paradox. The government is not responsible to any elected body. The economy and the social life of the island are fairly open. The large Shiite population on the island dictates that the Bahrainis maintain reasonable relations with Iran. Bahrain still has a territorial dispute with Qatar over the Hawar Islands.

A new Emir, Sheikh Hamad Essa Al-Khalifa, became the leader of Bahrain in March 2000. He spent a large portion of his youth studying in the United Kingdom and the United States. There is great hope that he will modernize the government of the Emirate to bring it into harmony with the economic system.

Cyprus

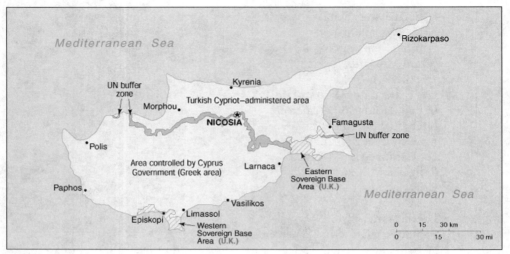

Official Name: Republic of Cyprus (Greek); Turkish Republic of Northern Cyprus (Turkish)
Area: 3,600 square miles
Capital: Nicosia (Greek), Lefkosa (Turkish Nicosia)
Infant Mortality (per 1000 Live Births): 7.39
Life Expectancy (Years/Males): 75
Urban Population: 56 percent
Literacy Rate: 94 percent
Arable Land: 12 percent
Per Capita GDP: $13,000 (for Greek population), there are no figures for Turkish population.
Religion: Greek Orthodox 78 percent, Muslim 18 percent
Language: Greek, Turkish, English
Population: 758,363
Population Growth: 0.67 percent
Website: http://kypros.com
Economics: The economy is primarily based on tourism. Because of the continuing conflict between Greeks and Turks that has divided the island, this industry depends on the political situation of the moment. The Turkish-controlled part of the island remains without diplomatic recognition, which makes loans for development difficult to arrange. Greek Cyprus has a small oil refinery.
Government: The Greek portion of Cyprus is governed under the system that existed prior to the island being divided. The president is elected by the Greek majority. The office of vice president is vacant because it is reserved for a Turk. There is an elected unicameral parliament.

The Turkish portions of the island mirror the Greek area in that there is an elected president and parliament.

Political Snapshot: The division of Cyprus dominates the policies of the island. This issue is discussed in Chapter 2. The issue of membership in the European Community provides an impetus to the peaceful resolution of this dispute.

Cyprus is also considered to be a transshipment point for illegal drugs being moved to Europe from the Middle East.

Egypt

Official Name: Arab Republic of Egypt
Area: 386,700 square miles
Capital: Cairo
Infant Mortality (per 1000 Live Births): 67
Life Expectancy (Years/Males): 62
Urban Population: 55 percent
Literacy Rate: 51 percent
Arable Land: 2 percent
Per Capita GDP: $2850
Religion: Muslim 94 percent, Christian/Jewish 6 percent
Language: Arabic, English, French
Population: 68,359,979
Population Growth: 1.6 percent
Website: http://www.idsc.gov.eg

Economics: The Egyptian economy has been plagued by problems of inefficiency and state corruption. These problems have been compounded by an exploding growth in population. Since the early 1990s the International Monetary Fund has offered advice to Egyptian planners. The State has continued to move away from the "Arab socialism" of the past toward a free market system. Thus far, this effort has met with only limited success. Some new foreign investment has occurred, indicating increasing confidence that, over the long term, the economy is moving in the right direction. There were setbacks in 2000 when the stock market declined and property values dropped. It is hoped that the higher prices for oil will improve the economic picture for 2001.

Government: Structurally, there is an elected president with an appointed prime minister and cabinet. The legislative branch is bicameral. The People's Assembly is elected by popular vote. The Advisory Council is also popularly elected but has only advisory powers. There is a Supreme Constitutional Court.

Although there are opposition parties, the Egyptian government functions as a one-party dominated state. The party of President Mubarak is called the National Democratic Party. As in the past under Nasser and Sadat, the President's party under any name wins the elections! However, the constitutional court has on occasion stepped into the political process when the ruling party domination became too excessive. It nullified general elections in 1984 and 1987. More recently, it ruled that the 1990 and 1995 elections were also tainted.

There is also some concern that women are not playing a more active role in the political process. Although free to stand for office, women hold only a handful of seats in the parliament. This is in sharp contrast to the significant part that Egyptian women play in diplomacy, governmental administration, health care, and education.

Political Snapshot: The Egyptian government has attempted to position itself between Israel and the United States on the one side and the Arab hardliners on the other. Egyptians no longer pursue the Arab Nationalist lines of Nasser, but they do take an active part in Arab affairs. Most recently, President Mubarak has called for a summit of Arab leaders to develop a common position on the Palestinian question. This action is indicative of the leadership position that Egypt still exerts in the region.

Iran

Official Name: Islamic Republic of Iran
Area: 636,000 square miles
Capital: Tehran
Infant Mortality (per 1000 Live Births): 29
Life Expectancy (Years/Males): 68
Urban Population: 60 percent
Literacy Rate: 72 percent
Arable Land: 8 percent
Per Capita GDP: $5000
Religion: Muslim 99 percent, Zoroastrian, Jewish, Christian, Bahai 1 percent
Language: Persian, Turkic, Kurdish
Population: 65,619,636
Population Growth: 1.7 percent
Website: http://www.eia.doe.gov/emeu/cabs/iran.html

Economics: Iran's economy continues to have high inflation and unemployment. After suffering under decades of a Western embargo of Iranian products, however, it seems that this period is drawing to a close. Most European states have already resumed trade with the Islamic Republic. For its part, the United States has relaxed some trade restrictions and more relaxations are expected in 2001. Two issues have forced the United States into a policy change. First, the Caspian Sea oil discoveries have set off a battle over pipelines to transport the oil to the West. The U.S. opposition to using the cheaper, more practical Iranian route has become increasingly unrealistic. It looks like the Iranian pipeline will become a reality with or without U.S. support. The second issue involves the recent Iranian purchase of a new generation of aircraft for its airline from the European consortium, Airbus. Finally, it looks like the United States will be forced by economic reality to recognize that Iran is simply too large and important to be permanently boycotted.

Iranian economics have also received a boost from the rise in the price of oil. This additional revenue has allowed the state to buy time until the normalization of relations with the West takes hold.

Government: Since the Islamic Revolution of 1979, the Iranian government has been run as an Islamic state. The chief of state is appointed for life and exercises power. There is also a president who is head of the government. The president selects a council of ministers with the approval of the legislature. The legislature is elected by popular vote. The head of state has great power over the elected portions of the government.

Political Snapshot: In the year 2000 elections for the legislative assembly, moderates won a landslide victory. It would appear that this victory signaled the beginning of the end for the clerics who have held a tight grip on Iranian politics since the revolution. The conservatives lashed back with assassinations, arrests, and silencing of the press that had supported the moderate forces who had won the election. Still, most knowledgeable observers believe that it is only a question of time until there is a relaxation of control in the Islamic Republic. An acknowledged expert on Iranian affairs, Robin Wright, puts it this way:

> But the days of a single leader, Ayatollah Ruhollah Khomeini, during the revolution's first decade, and President Hashemi Rafsanjani, during the second, are over. Public determination and brazen grit of a growing number of reformers are ending a tradition of autocratic rule that dates back more than 2,500 years.[1]

Iraq

Official Name: Republic of Iraq
Area: 168,754 square miles
Capital: Baghdad
Infant Mortality (per 1000 Live Births): 62
Life Expectancy (Years/Males): 66
Urban Population: 75 percent
Literacy Rate: 58 percent
Arable Land: 12 percent
Per Capita GDP: $2400
Religion: Muslim 97 percent, Christian 3 percent
Language: Arabic, Kurdish, Assyrian, Armenian
Population: 22,675,617
Population Growth: 3.0 percent
Website: http://www.Iraqi-mission.org

Economics: After losing two wars, Iraq has fallen from one of the most prosperous Middle Eastern states to one of its most economically devastated. Economic sanctions placed by the United Nations on Iraq have now been in effect for 10 years. This period has exceeded the sanction periods for both Germany and Japan after World War II! According to the United Nations, the oil for food program has allowed Iraq to earn about 20 billion dollars during a three-year period. All of this money has been used either for war reparations, food, or health care. In spite of this program, the United Nations has estimated that one in seven Iraqi children under the age of 5 still dies because of the sanctions.[2] Until the sanctions are lifted, the Iraqis cannot hope to restore their economy. The United States and the United Kingdom are being left in an increasingly isolated position regarding their insistence on the maintenance of the sanctions against Iraq.

Government: Iraq is a Republic controlled by the military and the Ba'ath Party. Its president, Saddam Hussayn, rules a tribal system that has placed his relatives and tribal associates in positions to control the military and the security services. The formal apparatus of government does not necessarily reflect the real positions of power. The authorities have used minorities including Christians to maintain power for a number of years. The most important minorities who remain outside the government include the Shiite Muslims, who make up almost half of the population, and the always-troublesome Kurds.

Political Snapshot: Saddam Hussayn's personal rule has eliminated most political opposition. He uses the apparatus of state terror to keep firm control of almost all aspects of society. The inability of the United States to remove him, coupled with the diminished support for sanctions, has actually strengthened Saddam's power. He has been adept at "turning the tables" to paint the United States as the villain. Increasingly, Iraq's neighbors have begun to conclude that the sanctions policy of the United States is counterproductive. It would seem that the days of the U.S. containment policy in Iraq are numbered.

Israel

Official Name: State of Israel
Area: 8000 square miles
Capital: Jerusalem
Infant Mortality (per 1000 Live Births): 7.55
Life Expectancy (Years/Males): 76
Urban Population: 91 percent
Literacy Rate: 95 percent
Arable Land: 17 percent
Per Capita GDP: $18,100
Religion: Jewish 82 percent, Muslim 14 percent, Christian 2 percent
Language: Hebrew, Arabic, English
Population: 842,454
Population Growth: 1.4 percent
Website: http://www.israel.org
Economics: Originally, Israel's founders envisioned a system based on the principles of "humane socialism." In the years since independence this idea has been downgraded. Still there is a great deal of government participation in the economy. The economic system is arguably the most highly developed in the Middle East and North Africa. Israel specializes in diamond cutting, sophisticated manufacturing, and high technology. There is also a developed export market for high-value agricultural products. On the debit side, much of Israel's success has been gained through loans and grants from abroad. About half of Israel's debt is owed to the United States. As outside aid diminishes, Israel will have to rely more and more on domestic resources to maintain the current standard of living.
Government: Israel is a parliamentary democracy. Although there is no constitution as such, there are understandings that act in similar ways to a constitution. The office of president is a symbolic one. The president is chosen by the parliament. The prime minister holds the real political power because of control over the majority coalition in parliament and in the cabinet. In recent years the prime minister has been elected by the people. The unicameral parliament, called the Knesset, has 120 members who are chosen indirectly from a party list system of voting. The party system maximizes small single-issue parties, which change constantly. All must join the majority coalition if they expect to participate in ruling the state. There is religious freedom in Israel, but Orthodox Judaism is recognized by the government.

Political Snapshot: The founders of Israel faced the difficult challenge of creating a single people out of many. To do this, they devised a political system that maximized the influence of small groups. In practice, this has meant that small groups could often frustrate the aims of the majority in parliament. Since 1948, no single political party has gained a majority in the parliament. All have had to rule by uniting the small splinter parties into a coalition to achieve a majority. This fact of political life has proved to be particularly frustrating in the peace talks with the Arabs. If a political leader attempts to make a dramatic move, that action can be stopped by a breakup of the alliances required to gain the parliamentary majority necessary to rule. In the summer of 2000, the Prime Minister met with the Palestinian leadership at a site in the United States. After a great deal of negotiation, the peace talks failed. When the Prime Minister returned to Israel, he faced the degeneration of his coalition over the concessions that he had offered. The leader of the opposition charged that the Prime Minister's actions would destroy Israel. Israeli dissatisfaction with the labor coalition led to new elections and the election of the liked leader Ariel Sharon as Prime Minister.

Jordan

Official Name: Hashemite Kingdom of Jordan
Area: 34,445 square miles
Capital: Amman
Infant Mortality (per 1000 Live Births): 31
Life Expectancy (Years/Males): 71
Urban Population: 72 percent
Literacy Rate: 87 percent
Arable Land: 4 percent
Per Capita GDP: $3500
Religion: Muslim 92 percent, Christian 8 percent
Language: Arabic, English
Population: 4,998,564
Population Growth: 3 percent
Website: http://www.nic.gov.jo
Economics: Jordan is resource poor. There is little water for agriculture, which makes up less than 7 percent of the GDP. Since the Gulf War, Jordan has been hard pressed to absorb the Jordanians returning from the Gulf. Little economic growth, high international debts, and a low standard of living make short-term, positive economic gains for the Kingdom doubtful.
Government: The government of Jordan is a constitutional monarchy. King Abdullah II is one of the new generation of Arab leaders coming to power. The monarch appoints the prime minister, who then selects the cabinet. There is a bicameral national assembly. The senate is appointed by the king. The house of representatives is elected by popular vote. The Kingdom is the last remaining Hashemite rule. The current king is a descendant of the Sherif of Mecca. It was the Hashemites who led the famous Arab revolt against the Ottoman Empire.

Political Snapshot: King Abdullah II came to the throne by surprise. It was often assumed that his father, King Hussein, would nominate his brother as his successor. Shortly before his death, King Hussein surprised everyone by picking his oldest son. Although trained as a military man, the new king has been portrayed as one of the new generation of Arab leaders arriving on the scene. He has pledged to continue his father's policy of moderation. Jordan is a poor, small state in a very tough region. It will take great skill for the new monarch to chart a safe course for the Kingdom.

Kazakhstan

Official Name: Republic of Kazakhstan
Area: 1,049,200 square miles
Capital: Astana
Infant Mortality (per 1000 Live Births): 59.39
Life Expectancy (Years/Males): 57.7 years
Urban Population: 56 percent
Literacy Rate: 98 percent
Arable Land: 12 percent
Per Capita GDP: $3100
Religion: Muslim 47 percent, Russian Orthodox 44 percent
Language: Kazakh, Russian
Population: 16,733,227
Population Growth: 0.05 percent
Website: http://www.kazakhstan.news.net
Economics: Kazakhstan is the second largest former Soviet Republic and is rich in natural resources. With the break up of the Soviet Union, however, the market for resources used in heavy industry largely dried up. After 1991 there was a decline in Kazakhstan's economy.

In recent years the development of a petroleum industry has caused the economy to improve. It is hoped that the proposed pipelines to move product to markets in the West will cause an economic boom.

There is still a large non-Kazakh population left over from the old Soviet days. For years Kazakhstan was home to a large Russian military industrial complex. The waste dumps left over from this period offer substantial clean-up problems.

Agriculture has a potential for expansion. This is especially true in the areas of livestock and grain production.

Kazakhstan is not usually considered part of the Middle East. However, the issues of pipelines and petroleum have drawn Kazakhstan into the policies of the Middle East, which is why this former Soviet Republic is listed here.

Government: Kazakhstan is technically a republic. The president, Nursultan Nazarbayer, has held on to power since 1990. Under the post-Soviet constitution adopted in 1995, the prime minister is head of government. He is appointed by the elected president. The president has the power to issue decrees, appoint the members of the government, dismiss parliament, and call for referenda. He also appoints the heads of administrative regions and cities.

The parliament is bicameral. There is a supreme court and a constitutional council that makes legal rulings.

The government is considered to be democratic only because there are elections and opposition parties. Clearly the president has political dominance.

Political Snapshot: The issue of pipelines is discussed in Chapter 7. Internally, the most serious problem involves balancing the interests of the native population with that of the Russian immigrants. The Russian population has declined since Kazakhstan's independence from the former Soviet Union.

There are boundary problems with Azerbaijan, Iran, Russia, and Turkmenistan. Russia still leases the Baykonur Cosmodrome for their space program.

In recent years, Kazakhstan has become a transshipment point for illicit drugs destined for Russia, Europe, and the United States. In spite of government efforts to curtail cultivation of opium poppies, they are still grown in isolated parts of the state.

Kuwait

Official Name: State of Kuwait
Area: 6900 square miles
Capital: Kuwait City
Infant Mortality (per 1000 Live Births): 10
Life Expectancy (Years/Males): 75
Urban Population: 79 percent
Literacy Rate: 79 percent
Arable Lands: 0 percent
Per Capita GDP: $22,700
Religion: Muslim 85 percent, Christian and Hindu 15 percent
Language: Arabic, English
Population: 1,991,115 (includes 1,220,935 non-nationals)
Population Growth: 3.8 percent
Website: http://www.moc.kw/

Economics: Ten years after the Gulf War the economy of Kuwait still has problems. Most of the economy rises or falls on the price of oil. Petroleum provides almost 90 percent of the Kingdom's export revenues. Recently, a fire at the major al-Ahmadi Refinery forced Kuwait to import oil for a time! A state with 10 percent of the world's petroleum reserves that is forced to import that product attracts attention. The second pillar of the economy, the stock market, has also fallen in value during the past year. Many say that Kuwaites are still suffering from the Iraqi invasion, which has caused business insecurities.

There are some signs of possible improvement on the horizon. Some political leaders are talking about establishing a free trade zone and making Kuwait a road and rail hub linking Saudi Arabia to Iraq and Iran. At the present time this scheme seems to be well in the future. For the present, Kuwaites will have to rely on the price of oil continuing to remain high to keep the economy on track.

Government: On the surface, government in the Kingdom is personal. Only 10 percent of the population, all male, is allowed to vote for parliament. The head of state is the emir. He is there by heredity. The emir appoints the prime minister and the cabinet.

The parliament has been more active since the Gulf War. However, it is supposed to serve only as a "watchdog" on government action. It is more conservative than the emir. It has vigorously opposed the emir's plan to give women the vote.

There are informal family associations called Diwaniyas. These meetings often discuss and implement their decisions by using traditional "informal" means. In Kuwait, they have earned the title of "second parliaments."

Political Snapshot: During the Gulf War, the emir promised that the political system would be opened up after the war was over. Since that time, some progress toward liberalization has occurred. Non-native Kuwaites who have been naturalized have been given the right to vote in parliamentary elections. Although supported by the emir, the efforts to secure voting rights for women have not been successful.

Halting efforts aimed at opening some ties with Iraq have been made, but these have not yet been reciproacted. Parts of the disputed border with Saudi Arabia have been resolved. Kuwait remains a staunch supporter of the United States policy of containment of Iraq. There are still 605 Kuwaites that are missing from the Gulf War.

Kyrgyzstan

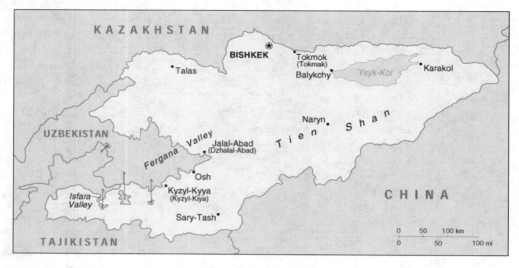

Official Name: Kyrgyz Republic
Area: 76,600 square miles
Capital: Bishkek
Infant Mortality (per 1000 Live Births): 77
Life Expectancy (Years/Males): 59
Urban Population: 33 percent
Literacy Rate: 97 percent
Arable Land: 7 percent
Per Capita GDP: $2200
Religion: Muslim
Language: Kyrgyz, Russian
Population: 4,685,230
Population Growth: 1.4 percent
Website: http://www.kyrgyzstannews.net

Economics: Kyrgyzstan is still primarily an agricultural country. Much of the agricultural products formerly went to the Soviet Union. After 1991 the state suffered a severe economic downturn as these exports were halted. With outside help, Kyrgyzstan initiated a series of reforms that have resulted in some economic growth. In addition to agriculture, the state exports gold, mercury, uranium, and electricity.

Government: Like other former Soviet Republics, Kyrgyzstan still retains elements of the old system. In a 1996 referendum the powers of the president were expanded at the expense of the legislature. The prime minister and cabinet of ministers are appointed by an elected president. The current president is Askar Akyev, who has held power since 1990. The weak bicameral parliament is elected for 5-year terms.

Political Snapshot: Like the other Muslim states that were members of the Soviet Union, Kyrgyzstan is not part of the Middle East. It is included here only because religion ties it to some of the politics of the region.

There is an unsettled boundary dispute with Tajikistan. The isolation of the state also has made it a transshipment point for drugs to Russia.

Lebanon

Official Name: Republic of Lebanon
Area: 4,000 square miles
Capital: Beirut
Infant Mortality (per 1000 Live Births): 29
Life Expectancy (Years/Males): 68
Urban Population: 88 percent
Literacy Rate: 92 percent
Arable Land: 21 percent
Per Capita GDP: $4400
Religion: Muslim 75 percent, Christian 25 percent, a small number of Druse
Language: Arabic, French, English, Armenian
Population: 3,578,036
Population Growth: 1.3 percent
Website: http://www.erols.com/Lebanon/stat.html

Economics: Once called "the Switzerland of the Middle East," Lebanon's economy was virtually destroyed by repeated Israeli and Syrian interventions, and a devastating civil war. In the aftermath of the 16-year civil war, large parts of Lebanon suffered both Syrian and Israeli occupation. In the late 1990s, the Lebanese started a concerted campaign to restore the economy. It will be difficult to recapture the banking business lost to the Persian Gulf States during the troubled times. A great deal of capital will need to be raised to rebuild the destroyed infrastructure. Agriculture still suffers from the importation of low-priced Syrian farm products. The hope for improvements in the economy depends on continued peace in Lebanon. The Lebanese have been business leaders in the region for centuries. It is hard to imagine that, given peace, the Lebanese will not be able to restore their economic prosperity.

Government: Lebanon is a republic. The constitution traditionally allocated positions in the government to the recognized sectarian groups. In the aftermath of years of political turmoil, a new governmental organization has yet to be finalized. Syrian political control colors almost all governmental activities.

Political Snapshot: Lebanon was created by the French as a tool of the French Empire. Since that time, Lebanon has functioned as a buffer state located between powerful, hostile neighbors. After years of occupation, Israel withdrew from the territory that it held in southern Lebanon. At the time this unilateral decision caused concerns from both Lebanon and Syria. Their response was surprising because both states had protested the Israeli occupation for years. The reason for the Israeli change in position seems clear: the withdrawal of Israeli troops deprived Syria of one of the main reasons for keeping its own troops stationed in Lebanon. For their part, many Syrians still believe that Lebanon was "stolen" from Greater Syria by the French in the first place. Although not reincorporated into Syria, it is easy to see how Lebanon is doomed by geography to remain a pawn in a much bigger game being played by powerful regional neighbors.

Libya

Official Name: Socialist People's Libyan Arab Jamahiriya
Area: 679,000 square miles
Capital: Tripoli
Infant Mortality (per 1000 Live Births): 28
Life Expectancy (Years/Males): 73
Urban Population: 86 percent
Literacy Rate: 76 percent
Arable Land: 2 percent
Per Capita GDP: $6700
Religion: Muslim
Language: Arabic, Berber, Italian, English
Population: 5,115,450
Population Growth: 3.2 percent
Website: http://www.undp.org/missions/libya

Economics: Libya has a socialist economy. The revenue from oil finances state programs. There has been an effort to shift the non-oil economy away from agriculture to production of oil-derived products and manufacturing. Still oil is the machine that generates the per capita GDP in North Africa.

Government: Technically Libya is a state of the masses, or Jamahiriya. This means that the people govern indirectly at all levels through councils. In practice, it is a military state under the leadership of Colonel Muammar al Qaddafi. Formally, Libya has a premier, a people's committee or cabinet, and a unicameral people's congress or legislature. The courts use Italian and Islamic law.

Political Snapshot: Libya has made moves that are bringing the state back into the mainstream of international political and economic affairs. After years of negotiations, the Libyans finally surrendered the people charged with the 1988 Pan American Airline bombing for trial in the Netherlands. In 2000, Libya played a major role in gaining freedom for Westerners kidnapped and held in the Philippines. The result of these moves has been that European leaders have become frequent visitors to Colonel Qaddafi's "tent." Only the United States continues to embargo trade and travel with Libya. As the boycott barriers come down in Iran, there is little doubt that American opposition to Colonel Qaddafi's government will come to an end shortly.

Morocco

Official Name: Kingdom of Morocco
Area: 172,000 square miles
Capital: Rabat
Infant Mortality (per 1000 Live Births): 50
Life Expectancy (Years/Males): 68
Urban Population: 53 percent
Literacy Rate: 44 percent
Arable Land: 21 percent
Per Capita GDP: $3200
Religion: Muslim 98 percent, Christian 1.1 percent, Jewish 0.2 percent
Language: Arabic, Berber, French
Population: 30,391,000
Population Growth: 1.6 percent
Website: http://www.mincom.gov.ma/

Economics: The Moroccan economy has been in difficult straits in recent years. Gains that have been made with the advice of the World Bank have been offset by population growth. Unemployment continues to rise. A two-year drought has devastated the agricultural section. On the positive side, the government is moving to shift the economy away from agriculture to industry. Steps are being taken to encourage foreign investment. There are also efforts to privatize more of the economy. To date, this last policy has largely remained in the planning stage.

Government: Morocco has been returned to a monarchy since gaining independence from France and Spain in 1956. The king takes an active role in policymaking. The executive branch, including the prime minister and the cabinet, serves at the pleasure of the monarch. The bicameral legislature has an upper house chamber of councilors, who are indirectly elected by local councils, professional organizations, and labor. The lower house, called the Chamber of Representatives, is elected by popular vote. Regardless of the structure, the king rules Morocco. Now that Morocco has a young reformist leader, there is hope that positive changes will occur in the not too distant future.

Political Snapshot: King Muhammad VI is one of the younger rulers who has recently arrived on the Arab political scene. He inherited a government that was considered to be a major violator of human rights. He quickly moved to replace some of his father's most repressive advisors. He freed a number of political prisoners. He has also made changes in foreign policy. He has moved Morocco closer to the United States and away from France and Spain, the traditional allies of Morocco. Morocco still needs to resolve a number of border disputes. Domestic problems include rising Islamic fundamentalism and the resistance of conservatives to expand the political rights of women.

Oman

Official Name: Sultanate of Oman
Area: 82,000 square miles
Capital: Muscat
Infant Mortality (per 1000 Live Births): 26
Life Expectancy (Years/Males): 71
Urban Population: 78 percent
Literacy Rate: 59 percent
Arable Land: None
Per Capita GDP: $7900
Religion: Muslim
Language: Arabic
Population: 2,533,389
Population Growth: 3.8 percent
Website:
http://www.legend.net/oman/gov.htm

Economics: Oman has been one of the world's most isolated places. Without oil, it probably would still be largely unknown in the West. There is little economic industry outside of oil. Agriculture is at a subsistence level. It is believed that Oman has enough oil reserves to last for 20 years at current levels. Within that time frame, Omani leaders must diversify before "the good times" end.

Government: Oman is a monarchy, with the sultan also holding the position of prime minister. In power since 1970, Sultan Qaboos bin Said Al Said is the primary decision-maker. There is a cabinet whose members are appointed, and an upper house is appointed by the sultan. The lower house is elected, but membership can be vetoed by the Sultan. The houses propose and offer advice to the sultan.

Political Snapshot: Oman has generally been at peace since a rebellion was suppressed with the help of Iran during the 1970s. There are still problems defining borders in isolated areas with the United Arab Emirates.

Qatar

Official Name: State of Qatar
Area: 4416 square miles
Capital: Doha
Infant Mortality (per 1000 Live Births): 16
Life Expectancy (Years/Males): 72
Urban Population: 92 percent
Literacy Rate: Women 80 percent, Men 79 percent
Arable Land: 10 percent
Per Capita GDP: $17,100
Religion: Muslim
Language: Arabic
Population: 744,483
Population Growth: 2.3 percent
Website: http://www.mofa.gov.qa
Economics: Qatar has a petroleum-based economy. Oil and gas have carried the people of Qatar from one of the world's poorest to one of the world's richest economies in less than half a century. Qatar is believed to have enough oil to produce at current levels for another 20 years. Qatar has the world's third largest gas reserves and can maintain production for another hundred years. The challenge for Qatar is to diversify the economy. Qatar must also walk a fine line between modernization and the destruction of the traditional culture.

Government: The government of Qatar is a traditional emirate. The Emir is the head of state. Qatar has a unicameral state advisory council. For the first time, the recent municipal election allowed full participation of women. There are plans to establish an elected parliament in the near future.

Political Snapshot: Although Qatar is considered to be a traditional monarchy, great changes seem to be on the horizon. The young Emir, Hamad ben Khalifa Al Thani, assumed power in 1995. He moved to place Qatar in the forefront of Gulf modernization efforts. Using what some critics call "shock therapy," he put Qatar on the map by making contacts with Israel and by giving women the right to vote, and to run for elective office. He also established the Al Jazeera satellite channel, which airs a variety of political opinions on both Gulf and world issues. This television channel has attracted the notice of other Gulf states where information is tightly controlled. Qatar's most important foreign policy problem involves a dispute with Bahrain over the status of the Hawar Islands.

Saudi Arabia

Official Name: Kingdom of Saudi Arabia
Area: 756,983 square miles
Capital: Riyadh
Infant Mortality (per 1000 Live Births): 36
Life Expectancy (Years/Males): 69
Urban Population: 84 percent
Literacy Rate: 63 percent
Arable Land: 1 percent
Per Capita GDP: $9000
Religion: Muslim
Language: Arabic
Population: 22,023,506
Population Growth: 3.3 percent
Website: http://www.saudiembassy.net

Economics: Saudi Arabia has the world's largest reserves of petroleum. It is the world's largest explorer of oil. Of particular interest is the low cost of production and the high quality of Saudi crude. Because oil production does not require the kind of massive infrastructure that is found in the production of other sources of wealth such as steel, the Saudis have been able to amass a great deal of wealth without surrendering their culture to the modern world. Still the presence of almost 5 million foreign workers associated with the petroleum industry is a source of concern for Saudi cultural purists. Since the Gulf War, foreign troops have been stationed in the Kingdom. The cost for their upkeep has stretched the budget and forced some program cutbacks.

Government: The Kingdom is a state in which the king exercises ruling powers. It is also an informal system where the ruling family is linked by marriage to the major families there. Family members hold the most important posts in the government. At each level of government there is a council of elders who give advice to the government. There are no formal political parties. The constitution is the Koran. There are "understandings" that guarantee most normal civil rights for the people.

Political Snapshot: The Saudi state follows the Wahhabi tradition. Wahhabism is a conservative approach to Islam. The Saudis are strict in their interpretation of the social customs surrounding everyday life for both men and women.

The Saudi government has recently resolved its long-standing border disputes with Kuwait and Yemen. In the case of Yemen, this dispute had at times been bitter. The agreement between the Kingdom and Yemen was signed by Saudi Prince Saud Al-Faisal and Yemeni Abdul Qader Bajamal on June 12, 2000.[3]

Syria

Official Name: Syrian Arab Republic
Area: 71,500 square miles
Capital: Damascus
Infant Mortality (per 1000 Live Births): 35.24
Life Expectancy (Years/Males): 67
Urban Population: 54 percent
Literacy Rate: 79 percent
Arable Land: 28 percent
Per Capita GDP: $2500
Religion: Muslim 90 percent, Christian 10 percent
Language: Arabic
Population: 17,213,871
Population Growth: 2.7 percent
Website: http://www.syrianembassy.org/

Economics: Syria has a state-run economy. Symbolically socialist, the Syrian economy has been stagnant for a number of years. Most Syrian agriculture is totally dependant on rainfall. The industrial base is out of date and inefficient. Syrian export products are of poor quality and not very competitive in the global marketplace. This is ironic because out of all of the states in the region, Syria is one that has the potential to develop a normal, broad-based economy. Unfortunately, the problem of Syria has not been geographic but political.

Government: Syria is a republic controlled by the military. The new president is a 34-year-old physician, Bashar Al-Assad. He is considered to be part of the revolution of young leaders emerging on the scene in the Middle East and North Africa. Syria has a prime minister and a people's council. Just as in Iraq, a branch of the Arab Socialist Renaissance, or Ba'ath Party, rules Syria. Although ideologically similar, the Syrian and Iraqi parties are bitter enemies.

Political Snapshot: Syria in its present geographic form is the product of French Imperialism. To rule, the French played the game of "divide and conquer." The French carved out the Christian part of Greater Syria and named it Lebanon. They created autonomous regions for the Druse and the Alowites. The majority Sunni Muslims were controlled by uniting the minorities of Syria against them. After the Assads came to power, they followed the same strategy. The Alowite rule of the Assads was reinforced with Christian and Druse support to control the Sunnis. As Bashar al-Assad assumes power, his sect, the Alowites, control the armed forces, the security service, and the Ba'ath Party. The politics of tribe and clan are alive and well in Syria.[4]

Tajikistan

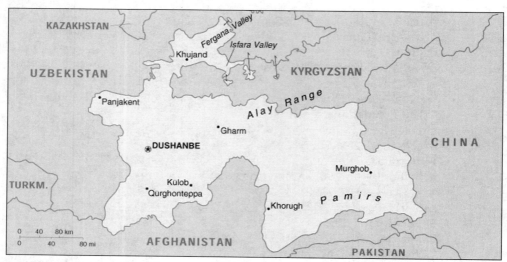

Official Name: Republic of Tajikistan
Area: 55,300 square miles
Capital: Dushanbe
Infant Mortality (per 1000 Live Births): 117
Life Expectancy (Years/Males): 60
Urban Population: 32 percent
Literacy Rate: 100 percent
Arable Land: 6 percent
Per Capita GDP: $990
Religion: Sunni Muslim
Language: Tajik
Population: 6,440,732
Population Growth: 2.12 percent
Website: http://www.tajikistan.news.net

Economics: There is a great deal of pollution due to poor sanitation, excessive use of pesticides, and over-utilization of water for irrigation. The pollution problem has had a negative impact on the economy.

The breakup of the Soviet Union almost ruined the economy that existed prior to 1991. Most skilled people left for Russia. The surviving elements of the economy were reduced to barter to survive. Today Tajikistan has the lowest per capita GDP of the former Soviet Republics.

At the present time there is some light industry. Carpet making is still practiced. Some agricultural products are sold locally. Tajikistan receives international humanitarion aid plus economic assistance from Russia and Uzbekistan.

Government: Like the other Central Asian republics, Tajikistan has a strong president. Emomali Rahmonov has held power since 1994. In 1999 he was reelected to a 7-year term. The president appoints the cabinet and prime minister. There is an elected bicameral parliament. In recent years legal opposition parties have begun to participate in the political process. There is hope that after years of turmoil Tajikistan may develop a stable political system.

Political Snapshot: Since independence in 1991, Tajikistan has survived three changes in government and a civil war. Russia has deployed peacekeeping forces throughout the country. Thousands of refugees from fighting in neighboring states have been received, complicating an already difficult situation. Because of its isolated location and its proximity to Afghanistan, Tajikistan is a major transshipment point for illicit drugs. There are outstanding border disputes with China and Kyrgyzstan.

As a central Asian republic, Tajikistan is not part of the Middle East. It is listed here because religion and location may involve Tajikistan in some aspects of Middle Eastern politics.

Tunisia

Official Name: Republic of Tunisia
Area: 63,200 square miles
Capital: Tunis
Infant Mortality (per 1000 Live Births): 31
Life Expectancy (Years/Males): 72
Urban Population: 63 percent
Literacy Rate: 67 percent
Arable Land: 20 percent
Per Capita GDP: $5200
Religion: Muslim 98 percent, Christian 1 percent, Jewish 1 percent
Language: Arabic, French
Population: 9,593,402
Population Growth: 1.5 percent
Website: http://www.tunisiaonline.com/
Economics: Tunisia is one of the major tourist spots in North Africa. It has beautiful beaches, historic sites, and the attractions of the great city of Tunis to tempt the visitors. At the present time, about 5 million tourists visit Tunisia each year. Tourist volume now has reached a level that is equal to more than half the population of Tunisia! The state also has a diversified economy of agriculture, industry, and mining.
Government: The chief of state, President Zine El Abidine Ben Ali, has been in power since 1987. In 1999, he was elected to a third term with more than 99 percent of the vote. His party, the Constitutional Democratic Rally Party, has held power since Tunisia's independence from France. Tunisia has a prime minister and a cabinet. The legislature

(Chamber of Deputies), is elected by popular vote. Tunisia is governed by a combination of French and Islamic law.

Political Snapshot: Although located near dangerous neighbors, Tunisia pursues a policy of moderation in foreign affairs. The Tunisians have an agreement with the European Community to reduce tariffs. They support the efforts of the United States to resolve the Arab-Israeli dispute. Domestically the government has supported the emancipation of women. Recently 20 percent of the governmental positions and two cabinet positions were held by women. The veil is banned from governmental offices. Eighty percent of Tunisians own homes. All religions are accorded equal respect.

Turkey

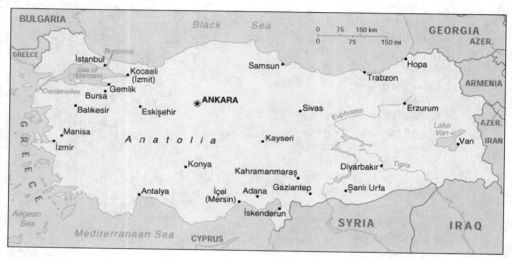

Official Name: Republic of Turkey
Area: 301,400 square miles
Capital: Ankara
Infant Mortality (per 1000 Live Births): 35
Life Expectancy (Years/Males): 70
Urban Population: 71 percent
Literacy Rate: 82 percent
Arable Land: 30 percent
Per Capita GDP: $6600
Religion: Muslim
Language: Turkish, Kurdish, Arabic
Population: 65,666,677
Population Growth: 1.4 percent
Website: http://www.turkey.org
Economics: Turkey has a diverse economy that ranges from heavy industry in the urban areas to agriculture and crafts in the countryside. One of the most serious problems that the Republic has is high inflation. Turkey also suffers from a lack of foreign investment. It is expected that the situation will improve if Turkey is admitted to the European Community (EC).

Government: Structurally Turkey is a republic. The governmental organization is similar to systems in the West. There is a president, a prime minister, and a cabinet called the Council of Ministers. The legislature, called the Grand National Assembly, is popularly elected. There are dozens of political parties presenting candidates in elections. The negatives in the system center around the propensity of the military to intervene or threaten to intervene if the elected officials cause displeasure.

Political Snapshot: Three issues dominate Turkish politics: Cyprus, the Kurds, and the desire to join the EC. Both Cyprus and the Kurds are tied to the issue of membership in the EC. In the summer of 2000, the EC delivered a series of conditions that had to be met by the Turks before they could be considered for EC membership. Among these conditions was a resolution of the Kurdish problem. The threat of military interventions also must be permanently removed from Turkish politics.

The Turks have also been warned to resolve the issue of Cyprus satisfactorily or Greece will oppose admission to the EC. These EC conditions present the Turks with the difficult task of resolving issues that have been "swept under the carpet" for years. Still they must be met head on if the Turks are to realize Ataturk's dream of Turkey becoming a modern European state.

Turkmenistan

Official Name: Republic of Turkmenistan
Area: 188,500 square miles
Capital: Ashgabat
Infant Mortality (per 1000 Live Births): 73
Life Expectancy (Years/Males): 57
Urban Population: 45 percent
Literacy Rate: 100 percent
Arable Land: 3 percent
Per Capita GDP: $1630
Religion: Muslim
Language: Turkmen

Population: 4,518,268
Population Growth: 1.87 percent
Website: http://www.turkmenistan.com

Economics: Turkmenistan is the least industrialized of the former Soviet Muslim Republics. The economy is based on cotton production. Since 1991, cotton has been traded for hard currency. Other products from agriculture include livestock and grain. Turkmenistan also produces coal, petroleum products, and sulfur. There are hopes that what are believed to be extensive petroleum reserves will be exploited in the future.

Government: Although Turkmenistan has a formal governmental structure with a bicameral parliament, the state is ruled by a strong president. The president, Saparmurat Niyazov, has maintained absolute control over the country since 1990. No opposition parties or movements are tolerated.

Political Snapshot: Turkmenistan is not considered part of the Middle East. However, because of religion and the fact that it borders Iran mean that the state is involved in issues involving the Middle East. This is especially true because the potential oil and gas production means that pipelines will have to be constructed to get these products to markets in the developed world. The issue of pipeline routes is discussed in Chapter 6. The primary problems that remain before the oil boom begins are political, not technical.

United Arab Emirates

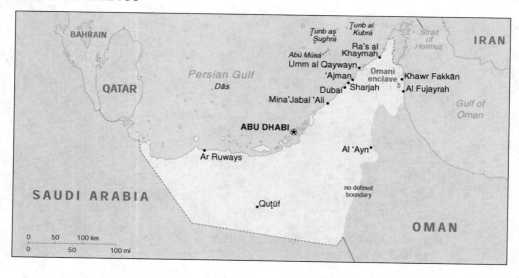

Official Name: United Arab Emirates
Area: 32,000 square miles
Capital: Abu Dhabi
Infant Mortality (per 1000 Live Births): 16
Life Expectancy (Years/Males): 73
Urban Population: 84 percent
Literacy Rate: Male 78 percent, Female 79 percent

Arable Land: None
Per Capita GDP: $17,400
Religion: Muslim 96 percent, Other 4 percent
Language: Arabic, Persian, English, Hindi, Urdu
Population: 2,369,153
Population Growth: 2.2 percent
Website: http://www.ecssr.ac.ae/

Economics: The members of the United Arab Emirates (UAE) have been transformed from among the world's poorest areas to the richest in only 25 years. The primary sources of wealth derive from the production of oil and gas. Both of these resources are in abundant supply. It has been estimated that, if explored at current levels, the UAE has enough oil and gas reserves to last for over 100 years.

Government: The UAE is made up of seven small principalities, called Emirates. They include Abu Dhabi, Ajman, Dubai, Al Fujayrah, Sharjah, Ra's al Khaymah, and Umm al Qaywayn. All of the Emirates are governed by both secular and Islamic law. The UAE has an umbrella governing body that includes a president who is elected from and by the Emirate leaders. They also appoint members of an advisory council. There are no political parties or pressure groups. Tribal traditions still govern most activities.

Political Snapshot: When oil was discovered, land in the UAE began to have value. What had once been loosely administered tribal lands became the subjects of bitter disputes. There are still long-standing boundary disagreements with both Saudi Arabia and Iran.

As their wealth has increased, the Emirates have been exposed to new ideas. There are tensions between those principalities calling for modernization leading to political reform and those who are opposed to change. The reformers argue that change will occur! Only by moving for change, including holding democratic elections, can this change be controlled. Thus far, political reforms have remained rhetorical rather than real.

In foreign policy, the UAE is often torn between exercising decisions on the basis of being a wealthy Gulf power and identifying with Greater Arab politics. These issues have been particularly controversial as the UAE has moved to normalize relations with Iraq. On the other hand, UAE members have watched with concern as other Gulf states increased their contacts with Iran. The issue of establishing some relations with Israel is also a new source of tension. Qatar has already established ties with the Jewish state. Whether the UAE continues to hold to the Arab policy of isolating Israel is an open question at this time.

Uzbekistan

Official Name: Republic of Uzbekistan
Area: 172,700 square miles
Capital: Tashkent
Infant Mortality (per 1000 Live Births): 72
Life Expectancy (Years/Males): 60
Urban Population: 37 percent
Literacy Rate: 97 percent
Arable Land: 9 percent
Per Capita GDP: $2500
Religion: Sunni Muslim
Language: Uzbek
Population: 24,755,519
Population Growth: 1.6 percent
Website: http://www.gov.uz

Economics: Uzbekistan has a well-established cotton industry. Textile production is found in Tashkent, Bukhara, and Samarkand. Gold and natural gas are important natural resources currently being exploited. There has been little economic reform since the end of Soviet rule. The structure still reflects the old command economy with a largely closed system. Foreign investors have been reluctant to enter this area until the system becomes more open.

Government: The political system still reflects the former Soviet system. Structurally, Uzbekistan is an authoritarian republic. Almost all power is concentrated in the presidency. As in the Soviet days, the subunits of government all report through a chain of command to the president. The legal system is an evolution of Soviet law.

Political Snapshot: Like the other former Soviet Muslim republics, Uzbekistan is not considered part of the Middle East. History and religion, however, draw Uzbekistan into the politics of the Middle East on issues such as religion, oil, Afghanistan, and Iran.

The government has been able to stop the domestic consumption of illicit drugs. In spite of this success, Uzbekistan remains an important transshipment point for drugs from Afghanistan to the rest of the world.

Yemen

Official Name: Republic of Yemen
Area: 203,800 square miles
Capital: Sanaa
Infant Mortality (per 1,000 Live Births) 68
Life Expectancy (Years/Males): 59
Urban Population: 34 percent
Literacy Rate: 43 percent
Arable Land: 6 percent
Per Capita GDP: $2300
Religion: Muslim
Language: Arabic
Population: 17,479,206
Population Growth: 3.3 percent
Website:
   http://www.al_bab.com/yemen/gov/gov.htm

Economics: Yemen is one of the poorest states in the Arab world. In ancient times this land was a source of spices. Today Yemen produces small amounts of textiles, leather goods, and handicrafts. In recent years there has been some oil production. The port of Aden operates a petroleum refinery, but it is not as important as it once was under the British. The government of Yemen has allowed the International Monetary Fund to offer economic advice. This has improved the economic situation and made the state more attractive for foreign investment. The major economic problem for Yemeni leaders is to create jobs to match the population increase caused by the high birthrate.

Government: Yemen is a republic. Officials are elected. Both men and women have the right to vote and to hold office. The government includes a president who appoints the prime minister. The Council of Ministers is also appointed by the president. The unicameral legislature, called the House of Representatives, is popularly elected.

At the present time, there is much talk about law replacing tribalism at the local level. However, the tribes and family leaders still exercise great influence.

Political Snapshot: Many of Yemen's political problems can be traced to the state's colonial past. Northern Yemen gained independence from the Ottoman Empire in 1918. The southern half remained under British control until 1967. It should not be surprising that the two Yemens remained hostile to each other.

After independence, Southern Yemen became a Marxist state. Northern Yemen remained one of the most conservative Arab states. The two were finally united in 1990. The uneasy alliance almost came apart in the late 1990s when factions in the south unsuccessfully attempted to break away. Internal unity remains a serious problem. In 2000 the long-standing border dispute with Saudi Arabia was resolved. It is hoped that better relations with Saudi Arabia will attract increased Saudi investment in Yemen's economy. The Port of Aden was the site of a terrorist bombing of a United States Naval vessel in October 2000. This attack caused the loss of life of 17 American service personnel.

Sources Adapted From

The World Fact Book 2000, prepared by the Central Intelligence Agency, Brassey's Publishing, Washington DC, 1999.

Audrey Shabbas, *The Arab World Studies Notebook,* AWIR: Arab World and Islamic Resources and School Services and Middle East Policy Council, Berkeley, CA, 1998.

The 21st Century World Atlas Millennium Edition, Trident Press International, Naples, FL, 2000.

2001 World Almanac and Book of Facts, World Almanac Books, Mahwah, NJ, 2001.

Web Sources

When available, official websites are listed.

Other websites taken from *The 2001 World Almanac,* and *Book of Facts* with general sites selected by the author.

Maps

The World Fact Book 1999, prepared by the Central Intelligence Agency, Brassey's Publishing, Washington DC, 2000.

Notes

1. Robin Wright, "Rumblings of Democracy: Iran Has a Way to Go but the Days of a Single, Powerful Leader Are Over," *The Gazette,* Montreal, Canada, Editorial page, B5, June 23, 2000.
2. Denis J. Halliday, former United Nations Assistant Secretary General, Humanitarian Coordinator in Iraq, Letter to the Editor, Re "U.N. Chief Assesses Benefits to Iraq of Oil-for-Food Program," *The New York Times,* section 4, column 6, March 19, 2000.
3. "Saudi Arabia and Yemen Finalize Their Common Land and Marine Borders," *The Monthly Newsletter of the Royal Embassy of Saudi Arabia,* Washington D.C., vol. 17, number 7, July 2000.
4. Susan Sachs, "New Patronage Puts Small Sect on Top in Syria," *The New York Times,* New York, section A, p. 3, column 1, June 22, 2000.

Index

Abbassid Dynasty, 122–127
Abu Bakr, 83–84
Abyssinians, 196
Adversity as test, 199–200
Agadir Incident, 152
Agreement
 Camp David, 147–148
Agreement, Sykes-Picot, 139
Al Jihad al Islami, 180
al-Sadat, Anwar, 147
Algeria
 border with Morocco, 54–56
 Islamic fundamentalism in, 181–182
 in Maghreb Union, 6–7
 pipeline conflicts in, 176
 profile of, 205–206
Ali, 84–85, 124
 nationalism and, 141
Ali, Hussein ibn, martyrdom of, 25
Almsgiving, in Islam, 77–78
Alphabet, Arabic, 106
American framework for Israeli-Palestinian peace, 162
Amir, 65
Anatolian mountain range, 17
Anatolian Plateau, 17–18
Anglo-Iranian Oil Company, 146
Ankara, importance of, 18
Anti-Semitism, European, 97
Arab culture, 103–116
 architecture of, 108
 art of, 107–108
 Bedouin, 109–111
 in cities, 112–116
 domination of, 104–106
 dress of, 102–103
 oral, 108
 in village, 111
Arab Emirates, profile of, 230–231
Arab Gulf, 60. *See also* Persian Gulf
Arab-Israeli War, 169

Arab League, Egypt and, 147–148
Arab Maghreb Union, 6–7
Arab nationalism, 149–150
 development of, 142
 Young Turk movement and, 153
Arab-Palestinian-Israeli dispute, 157–169
 American framework for resolving, 162–165
 blaming victims in, 157–158
 historical memories of, 168–169
 issues in, 158–161
 Jerusalem and, 161–162
 nonacceptance of peace in, 197–199
 organizations in, 167–168
 personalities in, 165–167
Arab Socialist Renaissance Party, 153
Arab world, 4
Arabian Peninsula, deserts of, 12
Arafat, Yasser, 166–167
 Fatah and, 167–168
 second Intifada and, 198
Architecture, Arab, 108
Armenian culture, 117
Armenian Orthodox Church, 92
Army of Ottoman Empire, 129
Art, Arab, 107–108
Ascension, of Muhammad, 5
Asian Turkey, 17
Assassins, 153
Assyrian Church, 93
Aswan High Dam, 19–20
Ataturk
 Ankara as capital and, 18
 nationalism and, 144–145
Atlas Mountains, 12
Ayatollah Khomeini, 146
Azerbaijan, 188–190, 206
Aziz, Abdul, 8

Baalbeck, 29–30
Ba'ath, 153
Bab, 65–66

Baghdad, history of, 17
Baghdad Mecca Railway, 8
Baghdad Pact, 45–46
Bahai, 89
Bahrain
　　boundary disputes and, 62–63
　　new leadership in, 187, 188
　　profile of, 207
Balfour Declaration, 139
Baptismal site, Jordan River as, 23
Barak, Ehud, 151, 165–166
　　second Intifada and, 198
Battle
　　of Karbala, 24–25
　　of Kosovo, 127
Bazaar, 33
Bedo-nationalism, 148–149
Bedouin culture, 109–111
Belief, in Islam, 74
Benjedid, Colonel Chadli, 181
Berber culture, 117
Bethlehem, significance of, 24
Black Sea, 38
Black September massacre, 168–169
Bosporus, 58–60
Boumediede, Colonel Hovari, 181
Boundary, hejaz, 33
Bouteflika, abdelaziz, 181–182
British
　　Anglo-Iranian Oil Company and, 146
　　Arab nationalism and, 142
　　blamed for problems, 195–196
　　Dardanelles and Bosporus and, 58–59
　　duplicity of, 139–140
　　Gibraltar and, 52
　　Hussein-McMahon correspondence and, 139
　　imperialism of, 41–42
　　Sykes-Picot agreement and, 139
　　19th Century politics of, 132–133
　　Trucial Coast, 7
Bureaucracy in Arab culture, 114
Burton, Richard, 12
Bush, President George W., 164
Business, petroleum, 169–171

Caillié, René, 10
Cairo
　　importance of, 14
　　settlement patterns in, 112–114
Caliph, rightly guided, 83–85
Caliph Ali, 124
Camp David peace plan, 161
　　Barak's concessions in, 166
　　Egypt and, 147–148
　　peace plans of, 162
　　second Intifada and, 198

Capitulation to colonialism, 131–132
Carter, President Jimmy, 161, 162
Carthage
　　modern, 27–28
　　ruins of, 13
Casbah, 32
Caspian region, new states in, 188–190
Caspian Sea, 38
CENTCOM, 2
Central Asia, 188–190
Ceuta, argument over, 52
Chalcedon, 91
Chosen people, 196–197
Christianity
　　Bethlehem significant to, 24
　　history of, 89–94
　　Holy Land important to, 4–5
　　Jordan River and, 23
　　Muslim beliefs shared by, 94
　　as patriarchal society, 183
　　promised land of, 196–197
Church of the Nativity, 24
Circassian culture, 117–118
Citadel of Cairo, 14
City
　　Arab, 112–116
　　of Fertile Crescent, 16–17
　　North African, 14–15
　　sand, 27–32
Climate, of Iran, 18
Clinton, President Bill, 162
Cold War
　　communist containment at end of, 47–48
　　global theories and, 43
Colonialism, 131–140
　　blamed for problems, 195–196
　　capitulations and, 131–132
　　French invasion of Egypt and, 132
　　Islamic dynasties and, 131
　　rise of nationalism and, 140–153. See also
　　　　Nationalism
　　in 19th century, 132–133
　　in 20th century, 133, 136, 138
Colony, European loss of, 2, 4
Communism, containment of, 44–49
Community, Muslim, principles guiding, 81–87
Compensation of Palestinians, 158–159
Condominium, 66
Conquest in Ottoman Empire, 130
Constantine, 90
Containment of communism, 44–49
Convention, definition of, 66
Coptic Church, 91–92
Crimean War, 24
Crude oil, price of, 170–172
Crusade to Holy Land, 5

Culture
    Arab, 103–116
        architecture of, 108
        art of, 107–108
        Bedouin, 109–111
        in cities, 112–116
        domination of, 104–106
        oral, 108
        in village, 111
    minority, 117–119
    Persian, 116–117
    politics of, 101–119
    Semite, 104
    Turkish, 116
Cyprus
    dispute over, 56–58
    profile of, 208–209

Dam, in Nile River, 19–20
Damascus, history of, 16–17
Dar al-Harb, 87
Dar al-Islam, 87
Dardanelles, control over, 58–60
Dasht, definition of, 33
Dasht-e Kavir, 18
Dasht-e Lut, 18
de Seversky, Major Alexander, 40–41
Declaration, Balfour, 139
Deir Yassin, 168
Democracy. *See also* Western *entries*
    Islamic fundamentalism and, 182
    tradition and, 186
Desert
    Bedouin culture of, 109–111
    definition of, 33
    of Iran, 18
    of North Africa, 10–12
Doctrine, Truman, 45
Dome of the Rock, 5
Druze, 89
Dynasty
    Abbassid, 122–127
    Ottoman Empire and, 127–130
    Safavid, 152
    Umayyad, 121–122
Dynasty, Islamic, 121–130

Eban, Abba, 165
Economics
    Algeria, 205–206
    Azerbaijan, 206
    Bahrain, 207
    Cyprus, 208
    Egypt, 209
    Iran, 210
    Iraq, 211–212

    Israel, 213
    Jordan, 214
    Kuwait, 217
    Kyrgyzstan, 218
    Lebanon, 219
    Libya, 220
    Morocco, 221
    Oman, 222
    Qatar, 223
    Saudi Arabia, 224
    Syria, 225
    Tajikistan, 226
    Tunisia, 227
    Turkey, 228–229
    Turkmenistan, 230
    United Arab Emirates, 231
    Uzbekistan, 232
    Yemen, 233
Egypt
    British military command moved to, 4
    Copts of, 91–92
    French invasion of, 132
    Islamic fundamentalism in, 182
    Islamic Jihad in, 180
    Muslim Brothers of, 180
    nationalism in, 141, 146–148
    profile of, 209–210
    Protestant churches in, 93
    Qattra Depression of, 10
Embargo, on Iraq, 48
Emir, 65
Empire
    Ottoman, 127–130
    Sassanian, 152
Episcopalians, in Egypt, 93
Esfahan, significance of, 25
Euphrates River, characteristics of, 21
Europe
    anti-Semitism in, 97
    capitulation of Ottoman Empire to, 131–132
    embargo on Iraq by, 48
    Turkey and, 144–145

Faith, in Islam, 75
Far East, definition of, 2
Farming in Iran, 18
Fasting in Islam, 78
Fatah, 167
Fear of Islam, 72–73
Fertile Crescent, significance of, 15–17
FIS, 181
Five pillars of Islam, 75–81
Flashpoint, geopolitical, 49–66
    Bosporus, 58–60
    Ceuta, 51–54
    Cyprus dispute, 56–58

Flashpoint, geopolitical (*continued*)
    Dardanelles, 58–60
    Gibraltar, 51
    Gulf region, 60–64
    Melilla, 51–54
    Morocco-Algeria border, 54–56
    Saudi Arabia–Yemen border, 64–65
    Western Sahara dispute, 49–51
FLN, 181
Foreign workers, threat of, 115
France
    duplicity of, 139–140
    imperialism and, 41–42
    in Levant, 5–6
    Morocco and, 55–56
    Ottoman Empire and, 131
    Sykes-Picot agreement and, 139
Frente Popular para la Liberacion de Saguia y Rio de Oro, 51
Front de Liberation Nationale, 181
Fundamentalism, religious, 177–182

Gaza, Hamas and, 180–181
Gender equality, 184–185
Gentile society, Jews assimilating into, 97–98
Geographic theorist, 39–41
Geography
    importance of, 37–38
    names associated with
        Hejaz, 9
        Holy Land, 4–5
        Levant, 5–6
        Maghreb, 6–7
        Trucial Coast, 8–9
    overview of, 1–4
    politics of, 39
    special features of, 9–19
        Fertile Crescent, 15–17
        Northern Tier, 17–19
        plains of North Africa and Arabia, 10–15
        rivers in, 19–23
Geopolitical flashpoint, 49–66. *See also* Flashpoint, geopolitical
Geostrategy
    Cold War and, 43
    containment and, 47–49
    flashpoints in, 49–66
    geopolitical flashpoints in, 49–66. *See also* Flashpoint, geopolitical
    overview of, 37–38
    Russian Communism strategy and, 44–47
    terminology used in, 65–66
    theorists on, 39–41
    Western imperialism and, 41–43
Germany, imperialism and, 42–43
Gibraltar, argument over, 52
Glubb, Sir John Bagot, 165

God
    blamed for problems, 195–196
    in Islam, 73, 74–75
    promise of land, 196–197
    testing through adversity, 199–200
Golan Heights, 23
Golden Age of Islam, 125–127
Gospels, 90
Government
    Algeria, 205–206
    Azerbaijan, 206
    Bahrain, 207
    Egypt, 209–210
    Iran, 211
    Iraq, 212
    Israel, 213
    Jordan, 214
    Kuwait, 217
    Kyrgyzstan, 218
    Lebanon, 219
    Libya, 220
    Morocco, 221
    Oman, 222
    Qatar, 223
    Saudi Arabia, 224
    Syria, 225
    Tajikistan, 226
    Tunisia, 227–228
    Turkey, 229
    Turkmenistan, 230
    United Arab Emirates, 231
    Uzbekistan, 232
    Yemen, 233
Great Mosque of Mecca, 78, 88
Greece, Cyprus and, 56–58
Gulf, Arabia and Iran conflict about, 60
Gulf Cooperation Council, definition of, 7–8
Gulf states, definition of, 66
Gulf War
    Fatah and, 167–168
    Shatt al Arab and, 21

Haganah, 167
Hajj, 78–79
Hamas, 179–180
Hashimite Sharif of Mecca, 8
Hejaz, 8, 33
Hejaz mountain chain, 12
High Atlas, 12
High Dam, Aswan, 19–20
History, political. *See also* Islam, political history of
Hizbollah, 180
Holy book, Koran, 80–81
Holy Land, definition of, 4–5
Holy Struggle in Islam, 79–80
Hussein-McMahon correspondence, 138–139

Ibn Saud, 8, 149
Imam, 85–86
Independence
    Israeli, 158–159
    as issue in Arab-Palestinian-Israeli dispute, 160–161
Intifada, 168
Iran
    containment of, 48–49
    geography of, 18–19
    nationalism in, 145–146
    new Central Asia states and, 188–190
    Persian culture and, 116–117
    profile of, 210–211
    Russian threat to, 44
Iraq
    boundary disputes and, 63–64
    containment of, 48–49
    Fatah's backing of, 167
    Karbala of, 24–25
    new leadership in, 187
    profile of, 211–212
Irgun Zavi Leumi, 167
Islam, 71–89
    Arabic language and, 105–106
    beliefs of, 74
    Christian beliefs shared by, 94
    five pillars of, 75–81
    fundamentalist, 178–181
        in Algeria, 181–182
        definition of, 178–179
        impact of, 179
        movements in, 179–181
        relations with West, 179
    Golden Age of, 125–127
    influence on politics, 71–72
    living faith of, 75
    monotheology of, 74–75
    new religions from, 89
    political history of, 121–154
        Abbassid Dynasty and, 122–127
        nationalism and, 140–154. *See also* Nationalism
        Ottoman Empire and, 127–130
        Umayyads and, 121–122
        Western colonialism and imperialism in, 130–133, 136–140
    popularity of, 73–74
    principles of, 81–87
    promised land of, 196–197
    rise of cities and, 14
    terminology of, 87–89
    Western ignorance about, 72–73
    women's role in, 183–186
Islamic Jihad, 180
Islamic Republic of Iran, 146
Islamic Salvation Front, 181, 182
Island in Persian Gulf dispute, 60–61

Israel
    Jerusalem as capital of, 24
    Jordan River and, 23
    in Levant, 6
    Munich Olympic massacre and, 168–169
    nationalism in, 150–151
    Palestinian prisoners in, 160
    profile of, 213–214
    United States and, 200–201
Israeli-Palestinian-Arab dispute, 157–169. *See also* Arab-Palestininan-Israeli dispute
Israeli War for Independence, 158
Issues, politics of
    Arab-Palestinian-Israeli dispute, 157–169. *See also* Arab-Palestinian-Israeli dispute
    Central Asia, 188–190
    petroleum, 169–177. *See also* Petroleum
    religious fundamentalism, 177–182
    women's role, 183–186
    young leaders, 186–188
Istanbul, importance of, 18

Jabal, 34
Jail, Palestinian prisoners in, 160
Jebel, 34
Jebel Sharr, 12
Jericho, history of, 22–23
Jerusalem
    Hamas and, 180–181
    Holy Land centered around, 5
    as issue in Arab-Palestinian-Israeli dispute, 160–161
    Peace plan for, 161–162
    significance of, 24
Jewish refugees, potential, 160
Jewish religion. *See* Judaism
Jidda, rise of, 14
Jihad, 79–80, 180
Jordan
    Muslim Brothers of, 180
    new leadership in, 187, 188
    profile of, 214–215
Jordan River
    significance of, 21–23
    water disputes about, 159
Jubail, 15
Judaism
    Gentile society and, 97–98
    history of in Middle East, 94–98
    Holy Land important to, 4–5
    as patriarchal society, 183
    promised land of, 196–197

Kaaba, 78, 88
Kairouan, significance of, 25–26
Karbala, significance of, 24–25
Kasbah, 32

Kavir, 33
Kazakhstan
    as new state, 188–190
    profile of, 215–216
Koran, 80–81
Kosovo, Battle of, 127
Krauthhammer, Charles, 162
Kurdish culture, 118–119
Kuwait
    boundary disputes and, 63
    profile of, 216–217
Kyrgyzstan, 188–190
    profile of, 218

Lake Nasser, 20
Lake Tiberius, 21, 23
Land, as issue in Arab-Palestinian-Israeli dispute, 158–159
Language
    Arabic, 105–106
    Semitic, 104
Lawrence, T. E., 8
Lawrence of Arabia, 8
    nationalism and, 142
Laws shaping politics, 194–204
    adversity as test, 199–200
    artificial boundaries and, 194–195
    blame for problems, 195–196
    colonialism and, 200
    foreign policy dilemma, 200–202
    peace and, 197–199
    promised land, 196–197
    Washington and, 202
Leader, young, 186–188
Lebanon
    in Levant, 6
    profile of, 219
Leptis Magna, ruins of, 13
Levant, definition of, 5–6
Liberation of Palestine, 167–168
Libya
    Islamic fundamentalism in, 182
    in Maghreb Union, 6–7
    profile of, 220

Mackinder, Sir Halford, 40
Maghreb, 6–7
Mahan, Admiral Alfred Thayer, 39–40
Mamluks, 152
Marrakech, significance of, 26–27
Marshall Plan, 45
Martyrdom, of Hussein ibn Ali, 25
Massacre, Munich Olympic, 168–169
Mauritania, in Maghreb Union, 6–7
McMahon correspondence, 138–139
    Arab nationalism and, 142

Mecca
    pilgrimage to, 78–79
        illegal immigrants and, 116
    praying in direction of, 76
    significance of, 25
Medina, 25
Mediterranean Sea, 38
Melilla, 52–54
Memorization, Arab tradition of, 108
Mercenary, 141
Middle Atlas, 12
Middle East
    cities of the sand of, 27–32
    geographical features of, 9–19
        Fertile Crescent, 15–17
        Northern Tier, 17–19
        plains of North Africa and Arabia, 10–15
        rivers in, 19–23
    location of, 2–4
    names associated with, 4–9
    smaller cities of, 23–27
    terminology in, 32–34
Millet System, 89, 129
Misrule in Ottoman Empire, 130
Missionary activity, nationalism and, 141–142
Monophysites, 91
Monotheistic religion, 70–98
    Christianity, 89–94
    Islam, 71–89
    Judaism, 94–98
Monotheletists, 92
Montreaux Convention, 59
Morocco
    Ceuta and Melilla and, 52–54
    in Maghreb Union, 6–7
    new leadership in, 187, 188
    profile of, 221
    in Western Sahara, 49, 51
Morocco-Algeria border, 54–56
Mosque
    architecture of, 88
    pointer toward Mecca, 76
Mountain
    in Levant, 6
    of North Africa, 12–13
    in Northern Tier, 17–18
Movement
    for Palestine liberation, 167–168
    politico-Islamic, 179–181
    Young Turk, 142–143, 153
Mubarak, Hosni, 147–148
Muezzin, 76
Muhammad
    ascension of, 5
    life of, 81–83

Muhammad Ali
    modernization of Egypt by, 154
    nationalism and, 141
Muhammad Reza, 145–146
Munich Olympic Massacre, 168
Muslim. *See also* Islam
    Holy Land important to, 4–5
    rich vs poor, 190–191
Muslim Brothers, 180
Muslim quarter of Jerusalem, 24
Muslim women, role of, 183–186
Muslim world, 4
Mustafa Kemal, nationalism and, 144–145

Najd, 8
Napoleon I, as geographic theorist, 39
Nasser, Abdul, 146–147, 148
Nationalism, 140–153
    examples of, 143–151
        Arab, 149–150
        in Egypt, 146–148
        in Iran, 145–146
        in Israel, 150–151
        in Saudi Arabia, 148–149
        in Turkey, 144–145
    factors contributing to, 141–142
    uniqueness of, 140–141
    Young Turk movement and, 142–143
NATO
    creation of, 45
    Islamic fundamentalism and, 182
Near East, definition of, 2
Nile, damming of, 19–20
Nineteenth century
    nationalism and, 141–142
    Western colonialism in, 132–133, 136
    women's roles in, 183
Nixon Doctrine, 46
Nizaris, 153
Nomadic culture, 109–111
North Africa
    coast of, 13
    deserts of, 10–12
    human geography of, 14–15
    imperialism in, 41–43
    mountains of, 12–13
    names associated with, 4–9
North Anatolian mountain range, 17
North Atlantic Treaty Organization
    creation of, 45
    Islamic fundamentalism and, 182
Northern Tier, 17–18

Obligation in Islam, 75–81
Oil. *See* Petroleum

Old Walled City, 24
    dispute about, 160–161
Oman
    boundary disputes and, 61–62
    profile of, 222
    Trucial, 7–8
OPEC cartel, 171–172
Oral tradition, Arab, 108
Organization of Petroleum Exporting Countries, 171–172
Orthodox Eastern Church, 91
Ottoman Empire, 127–130
    capitulation of, 130–131
    Dardanelles and Bosporus and, 58, 59
    decline of, 141
    revolt against, 142
    Young Turk movement in, 142–143

Palestinian
    desire for independence, 161
    Israeli nationalism and, 150–151
    Munich Olympic massacre by, 168–169
    Muslim Brothers of, 180
    new leadership in, 187
    as refugee, 159–160
    water disputes and, 159
Palestinian-Israeli-Arab dispute, 157–169. *See also* Arab-Palestininan-Israeli dispute
Palestinian National Council, 167
Palmyra, 31
Passage, Middle East as, 1–2
Patriarchal society, 183
Peace effort, Israeli-Palestinian, 150–151, 161–162
    nonacceptance of, 197–199
    United States and, 202
Peninsula, Anatolian, 17
People
    chosen, 196–197
    culture and, 103–104
People of the Book, Muslims as, 88–89
Persecution, of Copts, 91
Persepolis, 31–32
Persian culture, 116–117
Persian Gulf
    disputes about, 60–64
    geostrategic importance of, 38
    Trucial Coast of, 7–8
Persian Gulf War, 48–49
Petra, discovery of, 29
Petrochemical complex in Saudi Arabia, 15
Petroleum
    new Central Asia states, 189
    OPEC cartel and, 171–172
    pipeline conflicts and
        in Algeria, 176
        in Northern Tier, 172–175

Petroleum, pipeline conflicts and (*continued*)
    in Saudi Arabia, 175
    politcal impact of, 169–177
    rules concerning, 169–171
    Suez Canal and, 176–177
    United States and, 201–202
    wealth and, 190
Philby, Harry St. John, 12
Pilgrimage to Mecca, 78–79
Pipeline conflict
    in Algeria, 176
    in Northern Tier, 172–175
    in Saudi Arabia, 175
Plain of North Africa, 10–13
Plateau, Anatolian, 17–18
Polisario, 51
Politics
    of Algeria, 206
    of Azerbaijan, 206
    of Bahrain, 207
    of culture, 101–119. *See also* Culture
    of Cyprus, 209
    of Egypt, 210
    of geography, 39
    of Iran, 211
    of Iraq, 212
    Islamic, 121–154. *See also* Islam, political history of
    of Israel, 214
    of issues, 157–191
        Arab-Palestinian-Israeli dispute, 157–169
        Central Asia, 188–190
        petroleum, 169–177
        religion, 69–98, 177–182. *See also* Religion; Religious fundamentalism
        religious fundamentalism, 177–182
        women's role, 183–186
        young leaders, 186–188
    of Jordan, 215
    of Kuwait, 217
    of Kyrgyzstan, 218
    laws shaping, 194–204
        adversity as test, 199–200
        artificial boundaries and, 194–195
        blame for problems, 195–196
        colonialism and, 200
        foreign policy dilemma, 200–202
        peace and, 197–199
        promised land, 196–197
        Washington and, 202
    of Lebanon, 219
    of Libya, 220
    of Morocco, 221
    of Oman, 222
    of Qatar, 223
    of Saudi Arabia, 224
    of Syria, 225
    of Tajikistan, profile of, 227
    of Tunisia, 228
    of Turkey, 229
    of Turkmenistan, 230
    of United Arab Emirates, 231
    of Uzbekistan, 232
    of Yemen, 233
Polygamy, 184
Pontic mountain range, 17
Prayer beads, 87–88
Presbyterians, 93–94
Price of oil, 170–172
Prisoners, as issue in Arab-Palestinian-Israeli dispute, 160
Protestantism, 93

Qatar
    boundary disputes and, 62–63
    new leadership in, 187
    profile of, 223
Qattara Depression, 10
Qur'an, 80–81

Race, culture vs, 103–104
Racism, in Islam, 74
Railway, Baghdad Mecca, 8
Red Sea, 38
Refugees in Arab-Palestinian-Israeli dispute, 159–160
Religion, 69–98
    Christianity, 89–94
    importance of, 70–71
    Islam, 71–89. *See also* Islam
    Judaism, 94–98
    Zoroastrianism, 98
Religious fundamentalism, 177–182
    common concerns of, 178
    definition of, 177–178
    Islamic, 178–181
        in Algeria, 181–182
Repatriation, Palestinian, 159–160
Republic of Iran, 146
Revolt, against Ottoman rule, 142
Revolution
    Judaism and, 95–96
    Young Turk, 142–143
Reza Shah, 145
Riff Mountains, 12
Rightly guided caliphs, 83–85
Ritual prayer, in Islam, 75–76
River
    Euphrates, 21
    Jordan, 21–23
    Nile, 19–20
    Shat al Arab, 21
    Tigris, 20
Riyadh, as capital, 11
Rize, climate of, 17–18
Roles of women, 183–186

Roman Catholic Church, 93
Rub al Khali, 11–12
Ruins, of Carthage, 13
Russia
    communist threat by, 44–49
    Sykes-Picot agreement and, 139

Safavid Dynasty, 152
Sahara
    Spanish, 66
    Western, dispute over, 49–51
Sahara Atlas, 12
Sahara Desert, geography of, 10
Saint Mark the Evangelist, 91
Salat, 75–76
Sand city, 27–32
Sassanian Empire, 152
Saudi Arabia
    border dispute with Yemen, 64–65
    desert of, 10–11
    Hejaz of, 8
    Muslim Brothers of, 180
    nationalism in, 148–149
    petrochemical complex in, 15
    profile of, 224
    women's roles in, 185–186
Sawm, 78
Sbeitla, 28–29
Script, Arabic, 106
Second Intifada, 198–199
Semitic language, 104
Shahadah, 75
Sharif of Mecca, 8
Sharon, Ariel, 166
Sharon peace plan, 164
Shatt, 34
Shatt ab Aran, 21
Shaykhdom, 65
Sheik, 87
Sheikdom, 65
Shiite
    Hizbollah and, 180
    Karbala significant to, 24–25
Shiite Muslim, 85–86
Sipahis, 129
Slavery in Ottoman Empire, 129
Slum, of Cairo, 112–113
Souk, 32
Soviet Union
    communist threat by, 44–49
    Dardanelles and Bosporus and, 59
    in latter 20th century, 43
Spain
    Ceuta and, 52–54
    Gibraltar and, 52
    in Western Sahara, 49
Spanish Sahara, 66

Spykman, Nicholas, 40
State Department, definition of Middle East, 2
Stereotype of Muslim women, 183–184
Storytelling, Arab tradition of, 108
Strait of Tiran, 66
Straits, 58–59
Subha, 87–88
Suez Canal
    European interest in, 42–44
    petroleum and, 176–177
Sufis, 86–87
Suleyman the Magnificent, 127
Sultan, 65, 127, 129
Sunni Muslim, 85–86
Suoq, 32–33
Suq, 32
Sykes-Picot agreement, 139
Syria
    Jordan River and, 23
    in Levant, 6
    Muslim Brothers of, 180
    nationalism of, 153
    new leadership in, 187, 188
    profile of, 225
Syrian Orthodox Church, 92

Tajikistan, 188–190
    profile of, 226–227
Taurus, 17
Tehran, population of, 18
Tell Atlas, 12
Terrorism, 73
Theorists, geographic, 39–41
Thomas, Bertram, 12
Tigris River, significance of, 20
Trade in Ottoman Empire, 130
Trade route, 1
Treaty
    Jordan River associated with, 23
    of Sevres, 152–153
Trucial Coast, 7–8
Trucial Oman states, 61–62
Truman Doctrine, 45
Tunisia
    cities of, 28–29
    in Maghreb Union, 6–7
    profile of, 227–228
Turkey
    culture of, 116
    Cyprus and, 56–58
    Dardanelles and Bosporus and, 59–60
    geography of, 17–18
    nationalism in, 144–145
    new Central Asia states and, 188–190
    profile of, 228–229
    Russian Communist threat to, 44–45
    Young Turk movement in, 142–143

Turkmenistan, 188–190
    profile of, 229–230
Twentieth century colonialism, 133, 136, 138

Umayyad Dynasty, 121–122
United Arab Emirates
    boundary disputes and, 61–62
    profile of, 230–231
United Nations embargo on Iraq, 48
United States
    colonialism and, 200
    containment of Iraq and, 48
    Cyprus and, 57–58
    Department of Defense of, 2
    foreign policy dilemma of, 200–202
    framework for Israeli-Palestinian peace, 162
    Israel and, 200–201
    new Central Asia states and, 189–190
    petroleum and, 201–202
Urban settlement, in Arab culture, 114
Uthman, 84
    successor of, 124
Uzbekistan, 188–190
    profile of, 232

Village, Arab, 111

Wadi, 34
Wafd, 153
War
    Battle of Karbala, 24–25
    Battle of Kosovo, 127
    Israeli, for Independence, 158
    World War I, 20
    World War II
        changes after, 2
        Qattra Depression and, 10
Water
    as issue in Arab-Palestinian-Israeli dispute, 159
    wealth and, 191
Wealth, 190–191
Weizmann, Chaim, 165
West Bank
    Hamas and, 180–181
    Islamic fundamentalism in, 182
Western colonialism, 130–140. *See also* Colonialism
Western culture
    Islamic fundamentalism and, 179
    in Algeria, 182
    nationalism and, 141
Western ignorance of Islam, 72–73
Western imperialism, strategic geography during, 41–43
Western Sahara, dispute over, 49–51
Women's roles, 183–186
World War I, Tigris River and, 20
World War II
    changes after, 2
    Qattra Depression and, 10

Yemen
    border dispute of, 64–65
    mountains of, 12
    profile of, 233
Young leaders, political impact of, 186–188
Young Turk movement, 142–143
    Syrian nationalism and, 153

Zionism, 95–96
    as nationalism, 150
Zoroastrianism, 98